T0390346

ANCIENT
GREECE

ANCIENT
GREECE

DK ✸ Smithsonian

PRODUCED FOR DK BY COBALT ID
Senior Editors Kay Celtel, Marek Walisiewicz
Editor Diana Loxley
Senior Art Editors Paul Reid, Darren Bland

DK LONDON
Senior Editor Laura Sandford
Senior Art Editor Jane Ewart
Senior US Editor Megan Douglass
CGI Author and Researcher Justine Willis
CGI Coordinator Phil Gamble
CGI Artworks Peter Bull Art Studio
Cartographer Ed Merritt

Senior Managing Art Editor Lee Griffiths
Managing Art Editor Luke Griffin
Managing Editor Gareth Jones
Senior Production Editor Andy Hilliard
Senior Production Controller Rachel Ng
Picture Researcher Sarah Smithies
Project Jacket Designer Juhi Sheth
Senior DTP Designer Harish Aggarwal
Senior Jackets Coordinator Priyanka Sharma Saddi
Jacket Design Development Manager Sophia MTT
Publishing Directors Georgina Dee, Liz Wheeler
Art Director Maxine Pedliham
Managing Director, DK Living Liz Gough

Smithsonian

EXPERT
For National Air and Space Museum;
Dr. F. Robert van der Linden, Curator.

FOR SMITHSONIAN ENTERPRISES
Avery Naughton Licensing Coordinator
Paige Towler Editorial Lead
Jill Corcoran Senior Director, Licensed Publishing
Brigid Ferraro Vice President of New Business
and Licensing
Carol LeBlanc President

SMITHSONIAN
Established in 1846, the Smithsonian is the world's
largest museum and research complex, dedicated
to public education, national service, and scholarship
in the arts, sciences, and history. It includes 21 museums
and galleries and the National Zoological Park.
The total number of artifacts, works of art, and
specimens in the Smithsonian's collection is
estimated at 155.5 million.

First American Edition, 2025
Published in the United States by DK Publishing,
a division of Penguin Random House LLC
1745 Broadway, 20th Floor, New York, NY 10019

Copyright © 2025 Dorling Kindersley Limited
25 26 27 28 29 10 9 8 7 6 5 4 3 2 1
001-340515-Apr/2025

A catalog record for this book
is available from the Library of Congress.
ISBN: 978-0-5939-6159-9

Printed in UAE

www.dk.com

Front cover image: Sectional reconstruction of the east end of
the Parthenon, Athens

Back cover image: Detail from the Brygos Cup, a red-figure kylix
depicting the Sack of Troy, c. 490 BCE

Image p. 1 Cycladic marble harp player from 2800–2700 BCE

Image p. 2 View of the tholos at the sanctuary
of Athena Pronaia, Delphi, Phocis, Greece

MIX
Paper | Supporting
responsible forestry
FSC™ C018179

This book was made with Forest
Stewardship Council™ certified
paper—one small step in DK's
commitment to a sustainable future.
Learn more at
www.dk.com/uk/information/sustainability

contents

1 Beginnings
Prehistory–900 BCE

2 Rise of the City-State
900–600 BCE

3 The Late Archaic Age
600–500 BCE

4 Classical Athens and Sparta
500–400 BCE

5 Disunity and Order
400–323 BCE

6 Hellenistic Greece
323–31 BCE

7 The Afterlife of a Culture

31 BCE–

Contributors

CONSULTANT

Professor Emma Stafford

Emma Stafford is Professor of Greek Culture at the University of Leeds. Her research and teaching focuses on Greek cultural history, especially religion and art. Her publications include books on Heracles and his reception by later cultures, and on the worship of personified abstract ideas, especially Nemesis.

WRITERS AND SPECIALIZED CONSULTANTS

Tony Allan
After studying History at Corpus Christi College, Oxford, Tony Allan served as series editor on the 24-volume Time-Life *History of the World*. As a freelance author, he has written books on mythology and history including *Ancient Rome: Life, Myth & Art*; *Prophecies*; and *Vikings: The Battle at the End of Time*.

Dr. Abigail Baker
Abigail Baker is Research Associate on the Being an Islander project at the Fitzwilliam Museum, Cambridge. Her research explores the history of museum archaeology, from the first exhibition of the finds from Troy to exhibitions of Greek art in World War II.

Dr. Kay Celtel
A writer, editor, and historian, Kay Celtel has written and contributed to a number of books on subjects ranging from history to architecture, culture, and literature, including DK's *History of the World Map by Map* and *Imperial China: The Definitive Visual Guide*.

Professor Susan Deacy
Susan Deacy is Professor Emerita of Roehampton University, Honorary Professor of Classics at Bristol University, and Honorary Associate of the Institute of Classical Studies in London. Her recent publications include a book of lessons for autistic young people based on classical myths.

Michael Kerrigan
Michael Kerrigan was born in Liverpool, and now lives in Edinburgh. He is the author of *Greece and the Mediterranean*; *The Ancients In Their Own Words*; and *Ancient Rome*, among other books, and articles on art, culture, and history. He also provides regular reviews for *The Times Literary Supplement*.

Philip Parker
Philip Parker is a historian specializing in the classical and medieval world. He is the author of *World History* (*DK Eyewitness Companions*) and *The Empire Stops Here: A Journey Around the Frontiers of the Roman Empire*. His work also focuses on the use of maps to tell history, including *The History of Cities in Maps*.

Dr. Anna Reeve
Anna Reeve completed a PhD in Classics at the University of Leeds, and now teaches Classical Studies for the Open University. Her research interests focus on material culture from the ancient world, especially from Cyprus, and its reception in the United Kingdom from the 19th century onward.

Dr. David Smith
David Smith is an Associate Researcher at the University of Liverpool. His current work is focused on social organization and material culture in the prehistoric Cycladic islands, and the study of material from the ancient city of Olynthus, northern Greece. Most recently, he has published an analysis of prehistoric pottery and other objects from the Cycladic site of Phylakopi.

Marcus Weeks
Marcus Weeks studied Music and Philosophy at Sheffield University and worked as a teacher, musician, and piano technician before deciding to embark on a career as a full-time nonfiction writer. He has written and contributed to numerous books on philosophy, psychology, and the history of ideas, science, and the arts.

Introduction

In this book we tell the story of Greece, from the appearance of early humans in Greece around 400,000 years ago to the end of the Byzantine Empire in the 15th century CE. By "Greece" we mean not only the territory that bears this name today, but the lands where Greek culture flourished. At its farthest extent, in the Hellenistic period, Greece stretched from its colonies in southern Italy and Sicily in the west as far as the borders of India in the east, and to the south it encompassed Egypt. Under the Early Byzantine Empire, while the easterly regions were no longer Greek, parts of North Africa and southern Spain would be added to this picture.

Greece's story is one of conflict. At a local level, strife between the individual city-states that made up the Greek world was endemic, the Peloponnesian War between Athens and Sparta being just the most extensive example of a well-established pattern of competition for resources and preeminence. And yet in the early 5th century BCE, the city-states came together to drive back the threat of Persia in a clash of epic proportions. Conflict also characterized the 4th century BCE, with Alexander the Great's demolition of the Achaemenid Empire and conquest of its territories, and continued into the 3rd–1st centuries BCE, as Alexander's successors fought to establish and preserve their divisions of his empire, until the rising power of Rome swept all away.

A colorful world

From its earliest beginnings, the ancient Greek world was highly visual. The Cycladic, Minoan, and Mycenaean cultures of the Bronze Age produced a wealth of sculpture, painted pottery, wall paintings, and small-scale artifacts in precious metals. The culture that then emerged in the Early Iron Age applied geometric patterns to its early artwork, but quickly developed techniques in both sculpture and painting,

◁ **Painted myth**
This red-figure painting on the inside of a cup from around 420 BCE depicts Athena, the goddess of war, and the hero Theseus, who is shown dragging the defeated Minotaur behind him.

borrowed from Egypt and the Eastern Mediterranean, to facilitate the representation of the human form. Impetus for this was provided by the Greeks' love of storytelling, as first evidenced in the Homeric epics, with their tales of the Trojan War, and in stories of gods and goddesses, heroines and heroes, and men and women that were retold again and again in later poetry, drama, and prose. Storytelling in visual form often required the use of name labels to help identify specific characters in vase and wall paintings, alongside the development of an iconographic language of costume and attributes, so we can recognize, for example, the god Poseidon by his trident, and the hero Heracles by his lion skin and club.

As time went on, over the Archaic and Classical periods, architectural techniques developed too, so stone temples, gymnasia, theaters, civic buildings, and colonnaded stoas began to provide a monumental backdrop to daily life. These structures formalized the space for religious worship, dramatic and athletic contests, political debate, commerce, and social exchange. In the Hellenistic and early Roman periods, stylistic influences from all over the Mediterranean were taken up by Greek artists, with an increasing interest in landscape and realism in sculpture and wall painting, while new art forms such as mosaic were developed.

The wealth of the surviving material culture, alongside literature and inscriptions, allows us to reconstruct a great deal of the story of ancient Greece. And new discoveries and new interpretations are adding to our knowledge, particularly of groups poorly represented in the world of Greek literature, such as women, children, and disabled people.

An enduring gift

The legacy of ancient Greece can be traced in modern political thought, especially the ideal of democracy, in the modern sciences that descended from Greek philosophy, in literature and drama, in the visual arts, and in the stories that continue to be told in myriad forms in modern popular culture. An understanding of ancient Greece is fundamental to an understanding of the world we live in today.

Griffin facing the throne

Unearthed in 1900, the Throne Room was at the heart of the palace complex at Knossos, Crete, and was constructed in the 15th century BCE. The room's walls revealed fragments of frescoes depicting gray palm trees on a hilly red ground and two griffins painted on the walls on either side of one of the room's entrances. Subsequently, the frescoes in the room were re-created by Swiss artist Emile Gilliéron and his son (also called Emile), who combined elements of the fragments in a plan that included two griffins facing the stone chair (or throne) in the center of the north wall.

Greek and World History

A timeline of dynasties, empires, and global events

Ancient Greece was home to the earliest advanced civilization in Europe and one of the earliest in the world. Below is a chart comparing Greece with some of the world's other great civilizations, offering a selection of key events and innovations that put its history in a wider context.

- **c. 12th century** BCE Homeric date of the Trojan War if it was a real event

- **c. 1200/1190** BCE Mycenaean civilization collapses at the start of a period once characterized as a "Dark Age"

- **c. 1700** BCE Start of the Early Mycenaean period on mainland Greece

- **c. 3100** BCE Early Cycladic culture emerges in the Aegean islands

- **c. 2000** BCE First Minoan palaces constructed on Crete

- **c. 1450** BCE Minoan civilization declines, possibly owing to natural disasters and Mycenaean invasions

ANCIENT GREECE	c. 3200–1100 BCE Bronze Age	1200-800 BCE Greek "Dark Age"

3500 BCE	3000 BCE	2500 BCE	2000 BCE	1500 BCE	1000 BCE

WORLD EMPIRES AND KINGDOMS

- Ancient Egypt
- Indus Valley civilization
- Vedic civilization
- Dynastic China
- Sumerian civilization
- Assyria
- Early Dynastic Period Mesopotamia
- Akkadian Empire
- Ancient Andean civilization

- **c. 3100** BCE Narmer unifies Egypt

- **2667** BCE Djoser Step Pyramid constructed in Egypt

- **c. 1790** BCE Hammurabi establishes a legal code for his Babylonian Empire

- **c. 1003** BCE Jewish king David unites Israel and Judah

- **c. 3000** BCE Sumerians in Mesopotamia develop the first known writing system

- **c. 2300** BCE Sargon the Great founds the Akkadian Empire in Mesopotamia

- **c. 1550** BCE The New Kingdom period begins in Egypt, marked by powerful pharaohs such as Ramses

- **c. 2600** BCE Planned cities in the Indus Valley

- **c. 1500** BCE Development of the Rigveda, one of the oldest sacred texts of Hinduism, in the Indian subcontinent

- **c. 2600** BCE Stone circle erected at Stonehenge in England

- **c. 1046** BCE Zhou Dynasty takes power in China; it is China's longest-lasting dynasty

- **c. 900–700** BCE Geometric period in art, characterized by pottery painted with geometric patterns

- **c. 650** BCE Introduction of the hoplite phalanx military formation revolutionizes Greek warfare

- **336–323** BCE Reign of Alexander the Great of Macedonia

- **293** CE Emperor Diocletian divides the Roman Empire into two administrative halves

- **c. 730–710** BCE Rise of the city-state (*polis*), with Sparta and Athens gaining prominence

- **431–404** BCE Peloponnesian War between Athens and Sparta

- **c. 50** CE The Apostle Paul travels to Greece, spreading Christianity

- **c. 750–700** BCE The epic poems the *Iliad* and the *Odyssey* are composed

- **480** BCE Battle of Thermopylae and Battle of Salamis, key Greek victories in the Persian Wars

- **31** BCE The Battle of Actium ends the Hellenistic period

- **c. 594** BCE Solon lays the foundations for democracy in Athens

- **146** BCE Greece falls under Roman control after the Roman victory at the Battle of Corinth

- **776** BCE First Olympic Games held in Olympia

- **490** BCE Greece defeats the first Persian invasion at the Battle of Marathon

- **330** CE Constantine the Great makes Constantinople capital of the Byzantine Empire

- **c. 900–800** BCE The Greek alphabet is developed from the Phoenician alphabet

- **c. 507** BCE Cleisthenes further reforms the Athenian political system, establishing a more democratic structure

- **323–281** BCE Rise of Hellenistic kingdoms following the breakup of Alexander's empire

c. 1100–750 BCE
Early Iron Age

750–500 BCE **Archaic Age**	500–323 BCE **Classical Greece**	323–31 BCE **Hellenistic Greece**	31 BCE–330 CE **Roman Greece**	330–1453 CE **Byzantine Empire**

800 BCE	**500** BCE	**300** BCE	**30** BCE	**300** CE	**500** CE

Ancient Rome

Indian kingdoms

Achaemenid Empire

Ancient Carthage, North Africa

- **753** BCE Rome is founded and Romulus becomes the city's first king

- **c. 50** BCE The Maya introduce a calendar that has a cycle of 52 years, known as the Calendar Round

- **c. 814** BCE The Phoenicians found Carthage on the coast of North Africa

- **550** BCE Cyrus the Great establishes the Achaemenid Empire

- **c. 221** BCE Qin Dynasty unifies China and becomes its first imperial dynasty

- **79** CE Mount Vesuvius erupts, destroying Pompeii, Herculaneum, and several other Roman towns

- **650** BCE The earliest known coins are minted in Ephesus

- **146** BCE Romans destroy Carthage

- **c. 27** BCE Octavian becomes Rome's first emperor, as Augustus

- **c. 563** BCE Suggested date for the birth of Siddhartha Gautama (Buddha) in India

- **c. 322** BCE Chandragupta Maurya founds the Maurya Empire in South Asia

- **c. 33** CE Jesus Christ is crucified

◁ **Mask of Agamemnon**
Made from a sheet of gold,
this funerary mask was once
thought to show the face of
Agamemnon, legendary king
of Mycenae during the Trojan
War. Modern research dates
it to the 16th century BCE,
around 300 years before
the war's supposed date.

1
Beginnings
Prehistory–900 BCE

Greece's Earliest Cultures

The prehistory of Greece stretches back hundreds of thousands of years. It saw the arrival of archaic human species more than 400,000 years ago (YA), and their subsequent replacement by anatomically modern humans, *Homo sapiens*, around 50,000 YA. The era also witnessed the critical shift from mobile hunting and gathering to Neolithic settlement and agriculture around 9,000 YA. At its apex, two of the most significant cultures of the Bronze Age in Europe (c. 3200–1100 BCE) emerged: the Minoan, centered on the Aegean island of Crete, and the Mycenaean, on the Greek mainland.

Early civilizations

Neolithic technology had reached Crete by around 7030 BCE. Alongside the exploitation of domestic animals and plants, pottery emerged as a vital tool for negotiating identity, as people adapted to the challenges and opportunities of communal life. The wide circulation of pottery and other craft products demonstrates the extensive reach of shared ideologies and beliefs and of social and economic networks during the period. From around 5500 BCE, these networks had begun to carry the first metal objects across the Aegean.

By the start of the Early Bronze Age (c. 3200–2050 BCE), distinct regional and cultural identities had emerged on Crete, on the Greek mainland, and in the Cyclades. On Crete, the Minoan palaces—the centers of consumption, storage, production, administration, and ritual that emerged around 2050 BCE at places such as Knossos, Phaistos, and Malia—became key to the expansion of Minoan cultural influence across the Aegean. Minoan networks reached as far as Mesopotamia, the Levant, and Egypt. The Minoans also developed several written scripts, including Linear A, and surviving frescoes, pottery, and seal carvings demonstrate a sophisticated aesthetic sensibility.

Competition and collapse

The aftermath of the eruption of the volcano on Thera around 1627 BCE left the Minoan palace system vulnerable to exploitation by the Mycenaean groups that had risen to power on the Greek mainland. Mycenaean culture was indebted to the Minoan model and to the weaponization of Minoan culture by competing mainland elites pursuing power and status. Organized societies emerged around 1420 BCE, as competition abated with the consolidation of authority among a successful few groups, such as those occupying Mycenae, Tiryns, and Pylos. The palace centers that developed at these sites and elsewhere housed an administrative hierarchy with a ruler, or *wanax*, at its head. The system endured for around 200 years before implicit vulnerability and external pressure—likely from natural disasters, problems with long-distance trade, and opponents of the palace system—brought about its downfall.

Mycenaean culture would survive the palatial collapse for another century before fading to memory, but the period once called the "Dark Age" had begun, and Greece likely became a much more violent and insular place. Literacy disappeared. Long-distance trade and population declined. Yet, as communities adapted, they prepared the ground for developments that would help shape later Greek history.

◁ **Female figurine from the Minoan sanctuary at Piskokefalo, Crete, 1800 BCE**

c. 8200 BCE Greece's earliest open-air "village," Maroulas, is established on the Cycladic island of Kythnos.

c. 5500 BCE Earliest metal objects begin to circulate in Greece

c. 3000 BCE First communal tholos tombs are built on Crete

c. 2200 BCE The first sailing ships appear in the Aegean, opening up trade

c. 2200 BCE First use in Greece of the potter's wheel, which speeds up pottery production

❶ Huge Minoan jars from Phaistos, Crete

❷ Antelope fresco from Akrotiri, on Thera

❸ The Lion Gate guarded the entrance to Mycenae

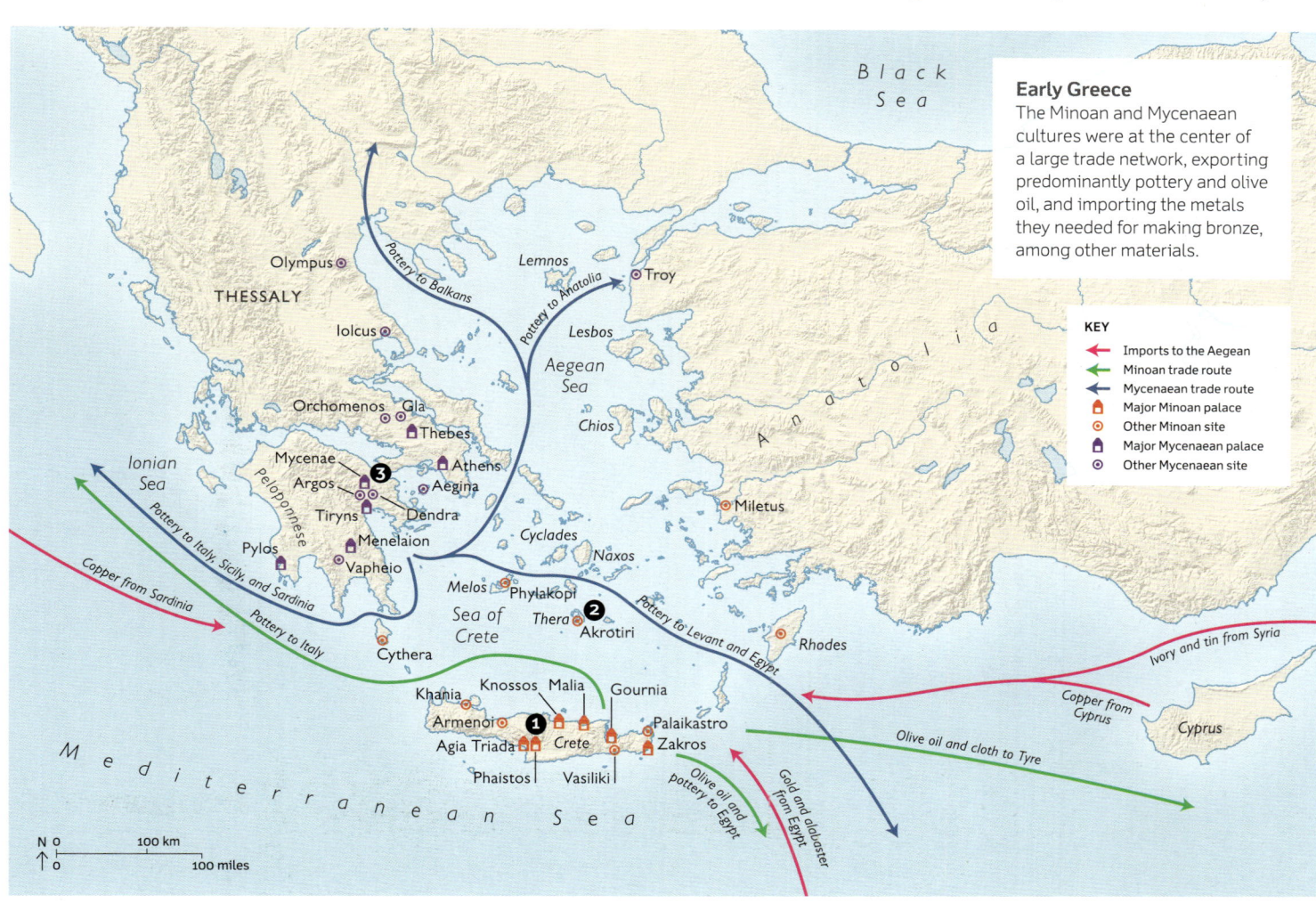

Early Greece
The Minoan and Mycenaean cultures were at the center of a large trade network, exporting predominantly pottery and olive oil, and importing the metals they needed for making bronze, among other materials.

KEY
- Imports to the Aegean
- Minoan trade route
- Mycenaean trade route
- Major Minoan palace
- Other Minoan site
- Major Mycenaean palace
- Other Mycenaean site

c. **2000** BCE First palaces built in Crete, at Malia, Knossos, and Phaistos

c. **1800** BCE The script known as Linear A develops in Crete

c. **1700** BCE Crete's palaces are damaged by earthquakes or violence

c. **1700** BCE Beginnings of Mycenaean civilization in mainland Greece

c. **1627** BCE Thera's volcano erupts, triggering a tsunami and spreading ash across the Aegean

c. **1470** BCE Construction of the Mycenaean palace centers

c. **1300** BCE The Minoan palace of Knossos is destroyed, and the site is abandoned

c. **1200/1190** BCE The collapse of the Mycenaean palace system creates a power vacuum

▷ **Dwarf deer form**
The first certain example of Paleolithic art in Greece comes from Asphendou Cave in the Sphakia region of Crete. It includes depictions of a type of Cretan dwarf deer that went extinct more than 11,000 years ago.

Prehistoric Greece

Out of the Stone Age

Greek history is a story 400,000 years in the making. Its earliest chapters are sparse and difficult to read, their prehistoric protagonists barely identified, yet their importance is immeasurable.

△ **Neanderthal skull**
This skull is among the earliest hominin fossils known from Greece. Found in the Petralona Cave, on the Chalkidiki peninsula, it may be up to 350,000 years old.

Around 400,000 years ago (YA), a small group of archaic humans stopped by a seasonal lake in what is now southern Greece to butcher the carcass of a straight-tusked elephant. The site, Marathousa-1, represents the earliest elephant butchering site in southeastern Europe and one of the first known events of human history in Greece. This period, the Early, or Lower, Paleolithic, saw itinerant hunter-gatherers moving through the Greek landscape in search of foraging opportunities, fresh water, migratory prey species, and shelter from often harsh climatic and environmental conditions.

Although a handful of archaic hominin fossils are known from Greece, stone tools provide our best evidence for how and where these early populations lived. The discovery of such tools on Crete suggests that some hominins may have been capable of undertaking sea voyages across the Mediterranean at least 130,000 YA.

With time, other technically superior, and increasingly specialized, tool-making traditions emerged. One, the so-called Mousterian, is linked to the arrival into Greece of *Homo neanderthalensis* during the Middle Palaeolithic. *Homo sapiens*, anatomically modern humans, followed toward the end of the phase, coexisting and interbreeding with Neanderthal groups until the latter's extinction sometime around 39,000 YA.

Emerging culture

Theses groups developed new ideas of life and death, place, and self. They began to modify their surroundings with hearths, walls, and art, to change their appearance with jewelery and pigments, and to bury their dead in accordance with emerging beliefs around spirituality and the afterlife. Red ocher (used to dye hides, textiles, and the bodies of living and dead alike) was being systematically extracted using hammerstones, antler wedges, and aurochs-bone tools from the first underground mine in Europe, at Tzines on the island of Thasos, by around 20,000 YA.

At the same time, as the climate changed at the end of the last ice age (c. 23,000–19,000 YA), so too did diet and lifestyle. The sea became a key resource, for both food and the development of extensive maritime exchange networks. Groups began to spend increasing amounts of time in one place. Caves like that at Franchthi near the village of Kiladha in the eastern Peloponnese were still preferred for habitation, but open-air settlements like those at Maroulas and Kerame I, on the islands of Kythnos and Ikaria respectively, point to emergent ideas of community and preface prehistory's most important technological development—agriculture.

Settlement and status

The Early Neolithic period (c. 7000–5800 BCE) was marked by a shift toward permanent settlement and the development of agriculture based on domesticated crops, including wheat, and animal species, such as goats, sheep, and pigs. Neolithic technology had already reached Knossos on Crete by c. 7030 BCE and was likely transmitted by settlers or trading contacts

△ **Stone hand-ax**
Hand-axes such as this Mousterian example were made from a piece of flint, sharpened and shaped to sit comfortably in the palm with stone and wood hammers.

△ **Neolithic settlement**
Located near Volos in Thessaly are these archaeological remains from the prehistoric site of Sesklo, which had a monumental circuit wall and a megaron (great hall) building.

from Anatolia. It would take a further 500 years to reach northern Greece, as some groups failed to adapt to it and others rejected it altogether. In Thessaly, the availability of light, well-watered soils gave rise to an extraordinary number of farming settlements, marked by artificial mounds known as "tells," housing up to 300 people. Typically less than 2 miles (3 km) apart, these formed a dense network of communities across which ideas and resources were easily exchanged.

As life became more predictable, populations grew. New types of material culture developed to structure emerging social norms and ways of being. Early in the period, fine painted pottery served to signal status and affiliation at public events. By the Late Neolithic (from c. 5800 BCE), the first metal objects, made in copper, silver, and gold, would play a similar role. Early metalsmiths favored small items of jewelry. Some were made of Anatolian ore; others echoed Balkan designs. Knowledge of metallurgy gradually spread throughout the Aegean, influencing settlement choices and social and economic strategies, and paving the way for the cultural changes of the Bronze Age.

EARLY POTTERY

The fertile Thessalian Plain in eastern Greece offered a perfect environment for Neolithic farmers and, during the later part of the period, the region was filled with settlements. Among their populations, highly decorated pottery, now known as Dimini ware, assumed new importance. Jars such as this example (right) from c. 5300–4800 BCE would have been used during communal feasts to publicly communicate the identity of individual households and reinforce or reframe relationships between other groups within the settlement, and beyond it. Dimini ware was also widely traded, and examples have been found as far away as Albania.

Cycladic Culture

Bronze Age island life

The Cycladic archipelago was home to a network of complex, interconnected communities that were able to survive, adapt, and thrive against a backdrop of shifting political and economic power in the Aegean.

The first successful permanent settlement of the Cycladic archipelago, located between mainland Greece and Crete, took place in the Late Neolithic period. Life on the islands was made viable by the exploitation of sheep, goats, and their secondary products and the cultivation of drought-resistant crops, possibly including the olive. Fish, such as tuna, and foodstuffs foraged at the shore were a valuable additional resource. Most of these "Saliagos culture" communities (named for the site of the first excavated Late Neolithic settlement) were small, but a few, like Ftelia on Mykonos, grew larger and more complex. Collectively, they heralded the arrival of a way of life that lasted 5,000 years.

Trade and networks

Occupying a strategic position in the Aegean, the Cycladic islands offered a range of natural resources, including metal ores and obsidian. The obsidian outcrops at Sta Nychia and Demenegaki on Melos had long attracted visitors, who used the volcanic glass for tools. The development of permanent settlements dramatically improved access to Cycladic raw materials, and new maritime networks developed, linking the Cyclades with sites such as Nerokourou and Petras-Kephala on Crete, and others on the Greek mainland. Seafaring was fundamental in maintaining these connections and the deep local interdependencies through which Cycladic communities thrived.

The appearance of ships and other marine themes in rock art of the Final Neolithic period (c. 4500–3200 BCE attests to an emerging maritime ideology.

The Early Bronze Age (c. 3200–2050 BCE) was a period of prosperity and development. Occupation spread to smaller islands, as local know-how made all but the harshest corners of the archipelago livable. Larger, fortified sites, such as Chalandriani on Syros and Skarkos on Ios, served as nodes in networks of smaller settlements. Specialized craftspeople made objects in metal, ceramic, and marble that joined the islands' exports of raw materials, and perhaps food,

◁ **Cycladic figure**
Stone-carved female figurines with crossed arms and a defined nose on a smooth face, as seen on this example from c. 2500 BCE, are typical of Cycladic sculpture.

▽ **Early settlement**
Skarkos, a settlement on Ios, is one of the best-preserved Early Bronze Age sites in the Cycladic archipelago. Excavations have revealed the remains of multistory buildings and a variety of everyday objects.

THE LADY OF **SALIAGOS**

The Lady of Saliagos is, currently, the oldest marble figurine known from the Cycladic Islands. She dates to c. 5300–4500 BCE and was found in the 1960s at a now partially submerged settlement on the islet of Saliagos (between Paros and Antiparos) by British archaeologists John Davies Evans and Colin Renfrew. Heavily worn and missing her head and right shoulder, the figure exhibits steatopygia, fat accumulation around her thighs and buttocks. The motif may symbolize fecundity and fertility, which were no doubt key concerns for the early Cycladic farmers of Saliagos.

Incised spiral and geometric patterns that may have had symbolic meaning

◁ **A Cycladic curiosity**
Covered with geometric and other motifs including female genitalia, boats, birds, and fish, terra-cotta "frying pans" are a type of Early Bronze Age object. Their function is unknown.

in the hulls of the first Aegean sailing ships as well as of oared craft like the longboat. A major pan-Cycladic sanctuary developed at Kavos on Keros, most likely supported by a sophisticated settlement on the nearby islet of Dhaskalio, attracting people from across the region who carried with them fragments of marble figurines and other objects intended for ritual burial on its hillsides.

Shifting influences

During the Middle Bronze Age (c. 2050–1700 BCE), larger populations occupied nucleated settlements like Phylakopi on Melos and Ayia Irini on Ceos (now Kea). The Aegean became increasingly connected, and Cycladic communities began to adopt innovations, ideas, and fashions from Minoan Crete, some transmitted through trade networks; others, no doubt, carried with settlers who made the islands their home.

On Thera (also known as Santorini), the settlement of Akrotiri was preserved beneath a layer of pumice and ash from the eruption of the island's volcano around 1627 BCE. It provides a model for Cycladic life at the start of the Late Bronze Age (c. 1700–1100 BCE). There, paved streets and public spaces flanked by buildings up to three stories high offered a distinctly urban feel. Buildings incorporated Cretan architectural features; walls bore vibrant frescoes illustrating scenes and themes of ritual and daily life. Wooden furniture filled rooms; pantries held jars of snails, figs, nuts, flour, and fish paste, while beehives delivered honey. Luxury items flowed into the settlement from around the Mediterranean.

Following the eruption on Thera, Crete's influence on the Cyclades was replaced by that of the mainland. The Mycenaeans brought new ideas to the islands. Rich tholos tombs were built on Mykonos and Tenos, and some sites, including Phylakopi, appear to have engaged with mainland administrative practices. Mycenaean influence declined after c. 1200 BCE (see p.46), and from c. 1100 BCE, there is evidence of the Cycladic settlements being destroyed or abandoned.

△ **Saffron gatherer**
This detail from a fresco found in one of the buildings excavated at Akrotiri depicts a young woman harvesting saffron, a valuable commodity used for dye and perfume.

> "In the midst of **dark earth** mixed with ash, coals, and ceramic fragments, a **terracotta disk** was found."
>
> LUIGI PERNIER

This wavy band symbol resembles sign A076 in Linear A texts

This sign may be a conch shell, an example of which was found at Phaistos

The plumed head appears most frequently on the disk at 19 times

This helmet symbol appears 15 times on Side B, but only 3 times on Side A

The Phaistos Disk

A mystery from Minoa

In 1908, Italian archaeologist Luigi Pernier was conducting excavations at Phaistos, a Minoan palace site in southern Crete said to have been founded by the legendary King Minos or his brother Rhadamanthys. Digging down into a basement identified as a temple depository by the presence of burned cattle bones, he made an intriguing discovery.

The object he uncovered was a disk of fired clay, just 6 in (15 cm) across, inscribed on both sides with symbols set in a spiral pattern. The characters had apparently been stamped into the soft clay with the aid of metal matrices, which left impressions that remain clearly defined more than three millennia later. Creating these metal stamps must have been an intricate and time-consuming task, suggesting that they were made for reuse.

Deciphering the disk

Scholars quickly began trying to decipher the symbols on the Phaistos Disk. They turned first to comparing the symbols with those of the earliest writing system known from Minoan Crete: Linear A. Identified by British archaeologist Arthur Evans, Linear A has still never been deciphered. Yet, mysteriously, the markings on the Phaistos Disk do not correspond to the signs used for Linear A, which was also inscribed in a different way, by using a stylus to cut images into wet clay. Nor did initial investigations find any correspondence between the disk's symbols and the Cretan hieroglyphs—other markings thought to have preceded Linear A—that were known by the early 20th century.

An enduring enigma

The 242 signs printed on the disk's two sides consist of 45 separate characters, most of which can be identified as depictions of physical objects. These range from human heads through shields, hides, and helmets to tuna fish, doves, and eagles. Most scholars assume that the text should be read from the outside of the spiral inward. Yet repeated attempts to find some coherent explanation of the significance of the symbols and their placement have all failed. The disk's purpose remains a subject of speculation: proposals have ranged from a religious invocation to a calendar or board game.

Recently, some commentators have suggested that the Phaistos Disk might be a modern forgery. However, most scholars discount this notion, partly because the details of its discovery are so well known but also because of apparent links between its symbols and some of the more recently discovered Cretan hieroglyphs. Many more of these hieroglyphs would have to be identified before any serious attempt at decipherment could be successfully undertaken. For now, the Phaistos Disk remains an enigma.

▷ **Side A**
Arthur Evans called this side of the disk Side A, although scholars still disagree over which is the front and which the back. Side A is slightly concave and is inscribed with 123 characters.

◁ **Side B**
Designated Side B, this side of the disk is slightly convex and has 119 symbols. The spiral appears to sit inside an outer ring of characters.

This shield sign occurs with the plumed head 13 times

These lines may mark off different words

This group of four symbols (plumed head, shield, eagle, and horn) appears more than any other group

The eagle symbol features only on Side A

Akrotiri's Ship Procession fresco
This wall painting is one of several found during excavations in the 1960s/'70s at Akrotiri, a Bronze Age settlement on the island of Thera (now Santorini). The frescoes' scenes have provided invaluable information on Minoan culture. The ship fresco is 20 ft (6 m) long and shows a fleet of 11 oared vessels traveling from one port to another, possibly as part of a maritime or religious festival. Shown here is a detail from the left of the fresco, where people in the port can be seen watching the ship procession (shown in the center of the fresco). A volcanic eruption destroyed Akrotiri around 1627 BCE, but the ash helped preserve the frescoes.

Minoan Crete

A cultural powerhouse

Named for Minos, the legendary king of Knossos, Minoan Crete was one of Europe's oldest civilizations. Its political and economic influence was felt across the Bronze Age Aegean and beyond.

In 1900, British archaeologist Arthur Evans took up the task of excavating the Minoan palace at Knossos. He uncovered a vast, labyrinthine complex that was clearly the site of a substantial power. His findings suggested there was some historical truth in both the mythical and the literary stories about Crete's early history. According to myth, Crete had

◁ **King Minos**
French artist Honoré Daumier's 19th-century sculpture shows Minos as one of the judges of the dead in the Underworld.

a labyrinth that imprisoned the Minotaur—the monstrous half-man, half-bull son of Pasiphaë, wife of King Minos, and a beautiful bull (known as the Cretan Bull). Meanwhile, other ancient sources, including the Athenian historian Thucydides, offered an alternative image of Minos, positioning him as the head of a maritime empire, or thalassocracy, which brought the central Aegean under Cretan dominion.

Minoan Crete is known for its court-centered complexes. The processes by which these "palaces" emerged was already underway at the end of the Neolithic period. Monumental tombs secured

communal claims to land and resources, and feasts became arenas for social and political negotiation. By the Early Bronze Age, a major reorganization of space at some sites served to accommodate these and other ceremonial activities, and soon the first "palatial" architecture appeared.

By the Middle Bronze Age, maritime networks linked Crete with sites across the Aegean, Egypt, and the Eastern Mediterranean. A Cretan presence was established on the island of Cythera, off the coast of the Peloponnese, with important implications for mainland political development into the Late Bronze Age. Cuneiform records identify Cretan merchants at the Levantine port of Ugarit (now in Syria).

Centers of power

Settlements were established across Crete and some became very large. Knossos, for example, had a population of up to 15,000 and represented one of the largest communities in the Mediterranean. These early palatial centers, such as Knossos, Phaistos, and Malia, were once considered "royal" sites with state-level political and economic authority. However, their function was more nuanced, their layouts varied, and their relationships with each other, and with the communities in their hinterland, more complex. Collectively, they were major centers of consumption, incorporating administrative, performance, and sanctuary spaces, along with residential rooms, storerooms, and workshops. They accommodated ceremonial activities, connecting them to the wider ritual landscape of peak and cave sanctuaries across the Cretan uplands. Administrative record-keeping prompted the development of perhaps the earliest writing systems in Europe: Cretan hieroglyphs and Linear A (see p.58).

Destruction and decline

Around 1700 BCE, the palaces were damaged by fire. Subsequently, they were rebuilt, some larger than before. The complex at Knossos was expanded (see pp.28–29). At some sites, smaller "palaces," such as the monumental buildings at Petras and Zominthos, also appeared, alongside architecturally elaborate and lavishly decorated "villas." In the wake of the eruption at Thera

△ **Minoan coffin**
The Hagia Triada (or Agia Triada) sarcophagus is a Minoan limestone coffin (c. 1400 BCE) found near the site of the palace of Phaistos. It was probably used for the burial of an elite Minoan and is decorated with funerary scenes in fresco.

▷ **Knossos**
The reconstructed north portico (shown to the right) in Knossos, with its colorful bull fresco, gives some sense of how the complex might have looked in Minoan times.

THE **CULT OF THE BULL**

The bull featured prominently in the political propaganda of Knossos, and held a wider importance in Minoan cultural and religious life. The Minoans' fascination with the bull perhaps reflected humankind's tenuous mastery of nature but may have expressed cosmological beliefs that are now lost. Events involving bulls, such as the bull-leaping shown below in a fresco from the Palace of Knossos, may have taken place inside the palaces and had religious significance. Depictions of bulls in other art forms probably reflect further rituals.

(c. 1627 BCE), the palace system became increasingly unstable, culminating in major upheaval around 1490 BCE. During this period, Knossos may have assumed political and economic authority over central, eastern, and western Crete.

However, a shift toward mainland practices and material culture suggests that Knossos had fallen under Mycenaean control, or perhaps that a Knossian elite had reoriented itself toward the mainland. For example, Mycenaean Greek became the administrative language. Knossos dominated for a time, but other former palatial centers began to show signs of resurgence. Around 1300 BCE, the final palatial period came to a close with the destruction or abandonment of those sites whose influence had once been felt across the Mediterranean.

Knossos Palace

A ceremonial and political center

Located around 3 miles (5 km) from the north Cretan coast, the Palace of Knossos reached its final form around 1450 BCE. Palace centers such as Knossos fulfilled a variety of economic and social functions. These dictated the layout of its public and private spaces, resulting in a complex multistory plan organized around the Central Court, which very probably served as an arena for bull sports, along with other forms of public ritual.

Around 1,400 rooms across an expansive complex of up to five stories housed administrative, ritual, craft, kitchen, storage, and residential activity. At strategic points, vibrant frescoes covered walls and floors and fine masonry adorned façades. Rooms incorporated advanced architectural features, including light wells and pier-and-door partitions to increase natural light and ventilation, and a sophisticated drainage system carried away rainwater and plumbed one of the earliest "flush" toilets in Europe.

The West Court was a public area outside the palace

The Theatral Area may have hosted performances or ceremonies

Raised walkways crossed the West Court

The West Magazines held tens of thousands of liters of olive oil

Important religious and ceremonial spaces were located in the West Wing

A monumental bridge crossed the Vlychia stream

▽ **Stepped Portico**
Built early on in the development of the palace, perhaps at the same time as the so-called "viaduct" across the Vlychia stream, the Stepped Portico was a towering colonnaded stairway leading to the Southwest Entrance of the palace.

◁ **Throne Room**
Accessible only from the Central Court, the Throne Room takes its name from its gypsum "throne," which, framed by a fresco depicting altars and a heraldic griffin, perhaps served as the seat of a priestess.

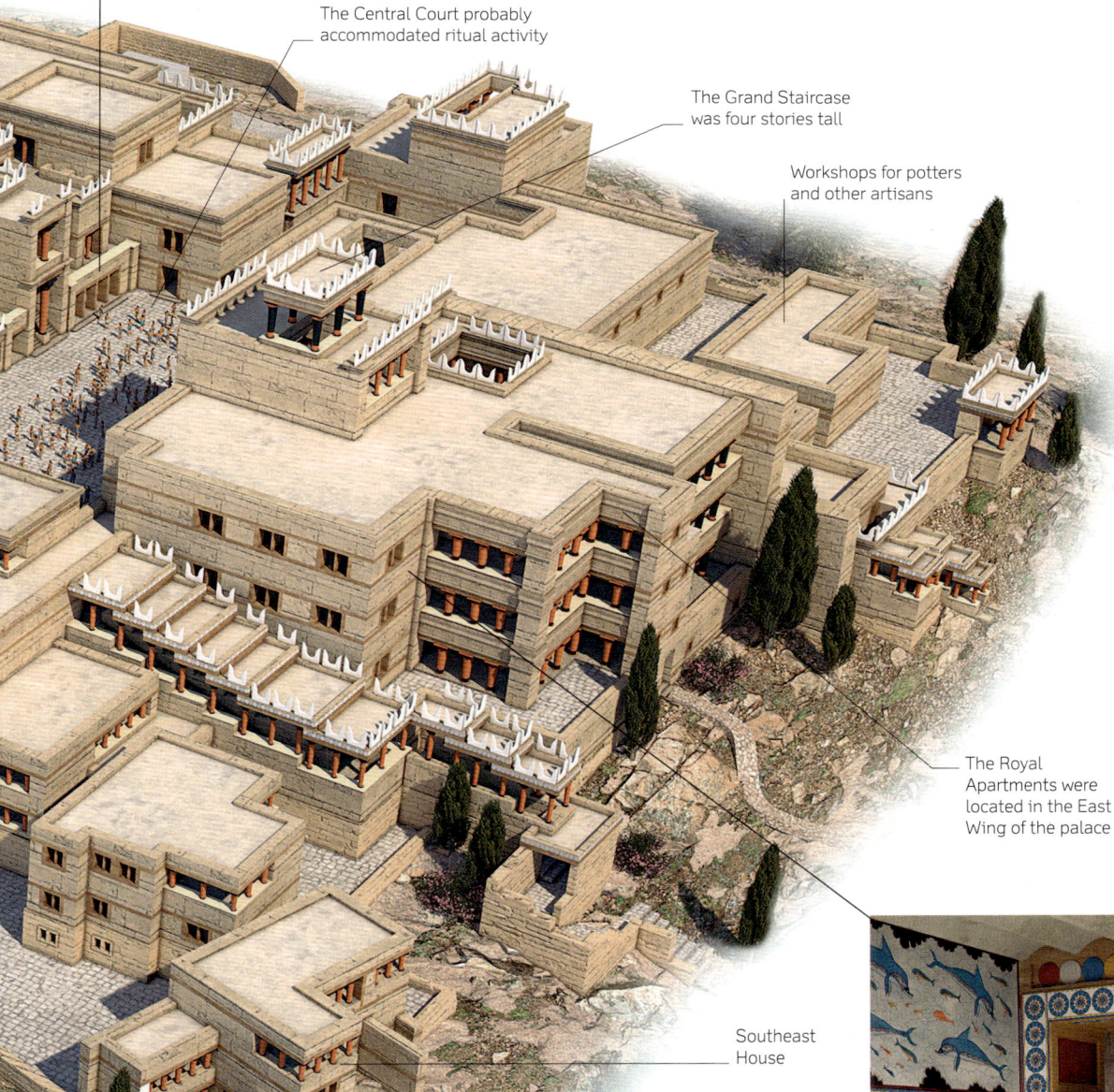

The Central Court probably accommodated ritual activity

The Grand Staircase was four stories tall

Workshops for potters and other artisans

The Royal Apartments were located in the East Wing of the palace

Southeast House

△ **Blue Bird fresco**
This bird belongs to a larger naturalistic frieze known as the Monkey and Bird fresco painted across three walls of a room within the House of the Frescoes to the northwest of the palace.

▽ **The Queen's Megaron**
Located in the Domestic Quarter, the Queen's Megaron was a private suite, perhaps staterooms, though there is no evidence that the suite ever housed a "queen." Including a toilet and a terracotta bathtub, the rooms were lavishly decorated with frescoes.

◁ **Palace layout**
Knossos, like other Minoan palaces, was built around its Central Court. Its builders worked from this central point outward, and expanded the palace's footprint as necessary.

Minoan Arts

Signifiers of wealth, status, and devotion

The Minoans left an abundance of material that reflects the vibrancy of their culture. From stone carving to pottery production, sculpting to jewelery, Minoan craftspeople were highly skilled, and their work has provided valuable insights into the religious and daily lives of the Minoan elite.

A lion, guardian of the dead

Chrysalises, symbols of renewed life

△ **Signet ring**
This carved gold ring from c. 1600–1450 BCE has a central "world tree" whose branches divide the face into four scenes believed to relate to the Minoan underworld.

◁ **Snake goddess**
This figure is made of faïence, a material made from crushed quartz and fired to give luster to the color. Found in the Temple Repository at Knossos, it dates from c. 1460 BCE.

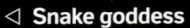

One of the "snakes" that give the figure its name

Bull's tail swinging in motion

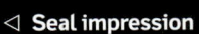

◁ **Seal impression**
The Minoans were master stoneworkers, as shown by the intricate details on the bulls in this clay impression from a seal carved from agate around 1450–1375 BCE.

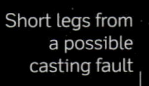

Short legs from a possible casting fault

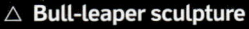

△ **Bull-leaper sculpture**
This bronze sculpture of an acrobat somersaulting over a bull's horns from 1600–1450 BCE was cast in one piece, an impressive feat in spite of some possible mistakes.

▽ **Terra-cotta larnax**
This painted chest from c. 1400–1300 BCE is decorated with papyrus plants. These were not native to Crete but frequently appeared as a motif in Minoan art.

△ **The Minoan Lady**
This figure from the Camp Stool fresco at Knossos wears a sacral knot at the back of her neck and provides clues about the beauty regimes of palace women.

Kohl-rimmed eyes and reddened lips

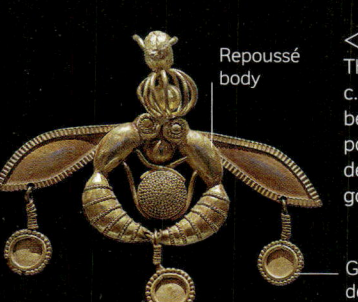

◁ Bee pendant

This elegant pendant from c. 1700–1600 BCE shows two bees with a ball of honey or pollen. Found at Malia, it demonstrates some expert gold-working techniques.

Repoussé body

Granulated decoration

▽ Stone bull's head rhyton

This original (left) portion of this reconstructed ritual libation vessel from Knossos was carved from steatite around 1550–1500 BCE and given jasper and painted rock-crystal eyes.

Incised details combining zigzags with leaf pattern

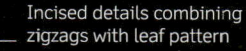

◁ Gold double-headed ax

The double-headed ax was an important symbol associated with female deities. Small examples were often used as votive offerings; this one was found in central Crete, in the Archalokori Cave.

▷ Terra-cotta pyxis

The quality of pottery painting declined in post-palatial Crete, but pottery production and firing reached a high point, as seen in the thinness of the clay used in this terra-cotta box from 1400–1100 BCE.

▷ Polychrome pot

This storage jar (a pithos) from 1800–1700 BCE is Kamares ware, elite Minoan tableware with red, white, and blue decoration on a black field and stylized plant and marine motifs.

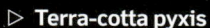

Stylized octopus design

Bird crown identifies the goddess as a protector of nature

Inlaid shell representing hair around the bull's snout

Octopus arm with clearly visible suckers

▷ Octopus pot

Hand-painted with an octopus, a symbol of the Minoans' connection to the sea, this stirrup jar dates to c. 1450 BCE and was designed to hold expensive goods such as oil.

▷ Nature goddess

Found a the Karphi sanctuary in east Crete, this large terra-cotta figurine dates to c. 1200–1100 BCE. Several such stylized cult figures with raised arms have been found.

Skirt represented by a simple cylinder

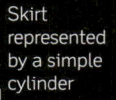

Rise of the Mycenaeans

A Peloponnesian powerhouse

Mainland Greece in the 2nd millennium BCE was a crucible of elite competition, influence, and opportunity, from which emerged the Mycenaeans—one of the most important cultures of the prehistoric Mediterranean.

Mycenaean culture emerged around 1700 BCE from the relatively simple and somewhat insular Middle Helladic culture (c. 2100–1700 BCE) of mainland Greece and in the shadow of the palatial culture of Middle Minoan Crete (c. 2100–1700 BCE). Against this backdrop, competing elites sought to define and reinforce their identity through displays of wealth and the adaptation of foreign ideas and practices.

Cretan traditions and material culture seem to have reached the Peloponnesian coastal regions of Argolis and Laconia via the nearby island of Cythera. This was probably first visited by Minoan groups in the Early Bronze Age (c. 3200–2050 BCE) and, during the Middle Helladic period, saw the foundation of at least two Minoan-type peak sanctuaries. The later part of the

◁ **Status symbol**
This gold diadem accompanied an important woman, perhaps a priestess, buried in Shaft Grave III, Grave Circle A, at Mycenae. It dates to the 17th century BCE.

Middle Bronze Age (c. 2050–1700 BCE) witnessed a dramatic increase in trade and exchange in these regions, particularly with the Cyclades and Crete. At the same time, a large number of new settlements were founded. This development probably coincided with a period of population growth and innovation in agricultural technology that enabled cultivation over a larger area, and likely contributed to conflicts over territory.

Mycenaean culture and influence

During the Early Bronze Age, there were important changes in the treatment of the dead that point to an emerging warrior elite. This is seen most clearly in the appearance of the shaft grave (see p.206). The earliest example of a shaft grave in Greece belongs to a probable military or political leader buried at Kolonna on Aegina with weapons and a boar's tusk helmet. Late in the period, the first shaft graves were dug in Grave Circle B at Mycenae, and the tholos tomb also appeared in Messenia.

An extraordinary selection of high-status objects was buried with the dead in Grave Circles A and B at Mycenae, including weapons, tools, jewelery, and other precious and semiprecious objects from Egypt, the Eastern Mediterranean, Afghanistan, and the Balkans. More than 33 lb (15 kg) of gold was recovered from Grave Circle A, alongside some of the most important known examples of Mycenaean art: the so-called Mask of Agamemnon (see p.14–15) and the Lion Hunt Dagger. Reflecting a trend toward "conspicuous consumption," at least some of this

▽ **Royal cemetery**
Built beyond Mycenae c. 1700 BCE, Grave Circle A was enclosed within the citadel's fortifications around 1250 BCE. The circle measures 90 ft (27.5 m) across and contains six shaft graves.

wealth most likely derived from business or political transactions. At that time, Mycenae's elite probably controlled a sizable territory, including most of the Argive Plain on which it was located.

Other parts of the Early Mycenaean period (c. 1700–1420 BCE) mainland witnessed different developments at different times. Distinctly "Mycenaean" pottery that reflected influences from the Cycladic and Saronic islands and Minoan Crete appeared in southern and central Greece. During the same period, monumental buildings appeared at those mainland sites that would later become palatial centers: the Maison de Chef at Tiryns, Palace II on the acropolis at Mycenae, and probably Mansion I near Sparta. The first large-scale

architecture at Pylos was constructed a little later, around the time of the burial there of a wealthy leader known as the "Griffin Warrior," c. 1450 BCE. These developments reflected a change in the political dynamic, as the earlier power struggles between minor chiefdoms gave way to the consolidation of power in the hands of a successful few. With the collapse of the Minoan palace system on Crete around 1420/1410 BCE, the mainland polities rose to prominence and the Mycenaean palatial period began.

△ **The Mycenaean Lady**
A fragment of a larger 13th-century BCE wall painting found in the Cult Center of the citadel at Mycenae, this fresco shows a woman, perhaps a goddess, holding a necklace.

▷ **Lion Hunt Dagger**
This bronze dagger, inlaid with niello (a mixture of copper, lead, and silver sulfides), depicts a lion hunt on one side and a lion attacking a group of deer on the other.

Minoan Sea Traders

Forging new routes in the Mediterranean

The Minoans created one of the world's first overseas trading empires. Their mariners turned the waters of the Aegean Sea into a hub of maritime commerce that served the far shores of the Eastern Mediterranean.

Ancient Greece was a land of hills and valleys where communities were often cut off from their neighbors and the sea provided the easiest means of communication and trade between settlements. The Egyptians had pioneered coastal trade up the eastern Mediterranean shoreline, but the Minoans were the first to make themselves masters of the Aegean. They created a trading network that stretched from Egypt to the Greek mainland, taking in the Syrian coast, the Cyclades, and possibly even Sicily.

One spur for exploration was the Minoans' need for imported metals: among other essentials, they lacked the tin and copper to make bronze. Archaeological finds indicate that other merchandise also reached them from abroad: gold and silver from Egypt and Anatolia; ivory perhaps from Syria; volcanic obsidian from the island of Melos, 90 miles (150 km) to the north of Crete. Frescoes show that wealthy Minoans kept primates, now identified as Hanuman langurs from the Indian subcontinent.

▽ **Setting sail**
The largest ship depicted in this fresco from Akrotiri shows the oarsmen sitting beneath a furled sail. At the rear, a standing figure steers the ship with a long oar.

△ **Dolphin fresco**
This colorful seascape fresco shows the importance of the sea in Minoan culture, and was found at the Palace of Knossos. Painted behind the dolphins and fish is a blue net pattern thought to represent the sea.

> "**Minos** is the **earliest** of all those known to us by **tradition** who acquired a **navy**."

In return, the Minoans exported luxury goods. Cretan pottery, jewelery, bronzes, and woven fabrics have been found across the Eastern Mediterranean region. There was also strong demand for more day-to-day commodities, including lumber from the island's wooded hills and olive oil, which was produced in vast quantities. Excavations at Knossos revealed a storage area with room for as many as 400 giant jars that between them had an estimated capacity of 62,000 gallons (23,400 liters).

Akrotiri's Ship Procession fresco (see opposite) indicates that the boats in which the traders carried their goods differed significantly from those of their Egyptian predecessors. The presence of tall trees on Crete meant that they could be constructed with a long, strong keel. From this starting point, the ships were then built outward, the shipwrights equipping them with rounded hulls and high bows and sterns.

New connections

Although Knossos itself lay inland, most of the other Minoan palaces so far discovered were located on or close to the coast, and probably served as entrepôts for foreign trade. Across the sea, trading stations set up and at least partly inhabited by Cretans waited to receive the goods. Archaeologists have found houses decorated with Minoan artwork on islands from Rhodes and Cyprus in the east to Cythera, off the Peloponnesian coast. Some of these settlements were of considerable size. Akrotiri, for example, was estimated to have been home to 30,000 people. Relations with Egypt seem to have been particularly strong: papyrus documents record the Egyptians' frequent

▽ **Minoan seal**
This stone and plaster seal (c. 2100–1900 BCE) shows a typical Minoan ship, with a blunt bow, a high trefoil stern, and one mast, stabilized by six stays.

dealings with the Keftiu (the Egyptian name for the Cretans), and a school slate has even been found that lists Cretan place names and was apparently used as a writing exercise for students.

For centuries, Minoan seafaring skills guaranteed the island's control of the shipping lanes, but the Theran eruption (see p.27) changed that. Until then, the Mycenaeans on the Greek mainland had been primarily a land-based power. However, by around 1450 BCE, they apparently had sufficient mastery of the seas to mount a conquest of Crete, whose ports and harbors were unfortified and easily overcome.

As Minoan power declined, the Mycenaeans inherited access to the sea routes earlier opened up by the islanders. However, the era of free navigation that the Minoans had exploited was passing. By the end of the 13th century BCE, Mycenae too would go the way of Minoan Crete as lawlessness spread over both the land and the sea.

▽ **Gifts from the Cretans**
This painting from the tomb of the Egyptian vizier Rekhmire (c. 1479–1425 BCE) at the Theban necropolis on the Nile shows tribute or gifts from the Keftiu being presented to him.

◁ **The violent cup**
The vigorous scenes of the later cup found at Vapheio show a bull tossing one hunter in the air while trying to trample a second underfoot. To the right of this are scenes in which a bull is caught in a net while another leaps away through the trees. The repoussé work is noticeably rougher than on the quiet cup.

A bull trying to gore one of the hunters

Figure with two left hands being trampled by a bull

Fine details hammered, or chased, into the surface

Anatomically accurate bull

> ## "The men are insignificant compared to the stupendous bulls."
>
> ART HISTORIAN KENNETH CLARKE, 1956

The Vapheio Cups

Masterpieces of Bronze-Age metalwork

◁ ▽ **The quiet cup**
The Minoan-manufactured quiet cup shows a bull approaching a cow (left) to mate, while (below) the man lassos the bull by its hind leg. The gold work's quality is visible in the smooth flanks of the bulls and in the intricate details of the foliage in the tree and at the base of the cup.

In 1889, Greek archaeologist Christos Tsountas discovered two gold cups in a Bronze-Age tholos (tomb) he was excavating at Vapheio, south of Sparta. Both cups—found held by the deceased, one in each hand—were richly decorated with elaborate sequences of pictures, hammered out in relief. Dating from 1675–1410 BCE, the cups show groups of men using two very different methods to hunt wild bulls.

The first cup (known as the "quiet" cup) shows a man using a cow to entice a bull. The bull and cow then mate, in a somewhat coy scene. Finally, the man is able to loop a rope around the bull's hind leg. The second cup (known as the "violent" cup) shows one bull caught in a net, while a second escapes, and a third attacks two hunters. The scenes bring to mind Plato's description of the imaginary city of Atlantis, where the city's princes hunted the bulls roaming free in the precincts of Poseidon's temple "with staves and nooses but with no weapon of iron."

Makers' marks
Differences in the style and quality of work point to the cups having been made by different hands. Appropriately, the quiet cup has a smoother finish; the violent cup is more roughly made. The quiet cup's pictorial scheme has clearly been

conceived with the handle's positioning in mind; on the violent cup, the handle cuts across the picture as though just stuck on with little thought.

The freedom with which the figures on the quiet cup are formed, and the ease with which they flow, contrast with the sense of stress and energy we get from the violent one. The figures on the violent cup are more roughly represented and less anatomically convincing than the figures on the quiet cup. More gestural and impressionistic, the violent cup's figures help us appreciate the power of the bull as it attempts to trample the men.

Minoan or Mycenaean?
Some of these stylistic differences, along with compositional and constructional variations, have led some scholars to believe that the quiet cup is Minoan and the violent cup is Mycenaean. For example, the L-shaped strip used to attach the handle to the quiet cup is found on other Minoan cups; the shorter, curved strip seen on the violent cup is seen on cups produced on the mainland. And the man beneath the body of the bull on the violent cup has two left hands, an Egyptian convention imported into Mycenaean art and not known in Minoan art. Though their full meaning remains unclear, the cups' hunting scenes perhaps hint at the survival of the bull cult from Minoan into Mycenaean times.

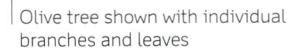
Olive tree shown with individual branches and leaves

Dawn of the Gods

Ancient tales of the world's beginnings

The Greeks created a genealogy of their gods, providing a comprehensive narrative of the different stages of creation, into which they also integrated five ages of humankind.

Greek attempts to explain how the world began found early expression in Hesiod's *Theogony* (literally, "the birth of the gods"), composed in the 8th/7th century BCE. In it, the poet drew on oral traditions that may have been influenced by Babylonian and Hittite myth to provide a detailed account of the world's creation.

In Hesiod's narrative, life evolved out of the immense void of Chaos, from which first emerged Gaia (Earth), Tartarus (the Underworld), and Eros (desire). Erebus (darkness) and Nyx (night) soon

followed, and they joined to produce two offspring: Aether (the upper atmosphere) and Hemera (day). In turn, Gaia alone produced Uranus (sky), Pontus (sea), and Ourea (mountains).

Thereafter, the process of creation became strife-torn. Uranus and Gaia produced 18 children, among them 12 Titans and 3 Cyclopes. Finding these children "terrible to behold," Uranus buried them deep within Earth—their own mother's body. Outraged, she gave the youngest of the Titans, Cronus, a sickle, which he

"**Chaos** came first of all, but next appeared **broad-bosomed Gaia**."

HESIOD, *THEOGONY*

used to castrate his father. From drops of Uranus's blood that fell on the earth sprang the race of Giants, who were fearsome, aggressive creatures.

Cronus assumed supreme power. Warned that one of his own children would overthrow him, Cronus swallowed the first five of his offspring birthed by the Titan Rhea. Desperate to save her next child, Rhea fled to Crete, where she hid the newborn Zeus deep in a cave. She then gave Cronus a disguised rock to gulp down in the baby's place.

Zeus duly grew up to challenge Cronus. He called on the Cyclopes and other divine beings to aid him in a ten-year war against his father and his allies, the Titans. The defeated Titans were thrown into Tartarus, and Zeus was proclaimed king of the gods.

Hesiod's cosmogony was accepted across ancient Greece, but it was not the only creation story known. Other tales told of a primordial egg from which the universe and everything in it hatched. And although they accepted Zeus as the supreme deity, Hesiod, Homer, and subsequent writers also gave a special place to the three Moirai, or Fates—goddesses with the power to shape human destinies.

The ages of humankind

Hesiod narrated his account of the history of humankind in his poem *Works and Days*. Like the gods, humans had passed through several different ages. In the Golden Age, which ended when Zeus overcame the Titans, people lived in primordial bliss. In the succeeding Silver Age, the year was divided into seasons and people had to work, until Zeus destroyed them for not honoring the gods. A warlike race of people was created anew from ash trees in the Bronze Age, but was later destroyed. Next came the Age of Heroes (see p.42), the time of the semidivine humans who also had a significant place in Greek myth. Then came Hesiod's own Iron Age, a time of toil and trouble whose inhabitants were themselves fated ultimately with extinction.

Hesiod's cosmogony gave order to the many conflicting origin myths that had been transmitted orally through Greece and the adjoining lands in preliterate days. In time, its very comprehensiveness gave it strength.

The mythological history Hesiod laid out, taking in entire ages of gods and men, proved so compelling that it passed down through the ensuing centuries as an accepted explanation of the mysteries of how the universe had begun. It subsequently moved on into Roman myth and influenced the way in which Western peoples viewed creation for more than a millennium.

△ **The Fates**
Seen here in a 19th-century Danish sculpture Clotho (left) spins the thread of a person's life, while Lachesis (right) decides how much time to allow them, and Atropos (middle) waits to cut the thread

△ **Creation myth**
This 16th-century painting depicts the story of Phanes, the deity of goodness and light. According to some Greek creation myths, Phanes was born from a silver egg created by Cronus and warmed by a snake.

◁ **Cronus carrying off two infants**
The winged figure of Cronus drags away two of his children, intent on destroying them before they can destroy him, in this 18th-century statue by Czech artist Lazar Widemann.

The Olympians

Greece's principal family of gods

Ancient Greeks looked to superhuman beings to explain the forces of nature and the vicissitudes of life. But for all their divine majesty and potency, the separate deities who made up the pantheon had distinctly human failings.

Having gained supreme power on the defeat of his father, Cronus, and the Titans, Zeus ruled the world in the manner of a successful warlord. According to Homer, his chosen place of residence was Olympus, an acropolis located just below the summit of Mount Olympus, Greece's highest mountain. There he assembled a court of other immortals, each one linked with a specific part of the natural world or area of human activity.

Origins and responsibilities

Including Zeus, there were 12 principal Olympians—often, but not always, seven male and five female. All were related: Zeus's wife Hera (goddess of marriage) was also his sibling, having been born like him to Cronus and Rhea, as were Poseidon (who presided over the sea) and Demeter (goddess of agricultural fertility and the seasons). The other Olympians were usually Aphrodite (goddess of love) and Ares (god of war), along with Athena, Dionysus, Artemis, Apollo, Hermes, and Hephaestus—all of them children of Zeus. However, in some traditions, Hestia (goddess of the hearth and home), Leto (mother of Apollo and Artemis), or Heracles replaced other deities—most frequently Dionysus.

For most Greek citizens, the origins of the gods were considerably less important than the roles they played in daily life. Different deities had special roles as patrons of individual city-states. Athens, for example, looked to Athena, the goddess of wisdom to whom the Parthenon temple was dedicated (see pp.176–177). Yet Zeus, Ares, and Hephaestus were also worshipped in Athens. Citizens would frequently turn to individual deities for assistance with the challenges of everyday life: women looked for help in childbirth to Artemis (the goddess of hunting, and protector of women in childbirth), just as those setting out on sea journeys sought Poseidon's protection.

◁ **Aphrodite, goddess of love**
This 2nd-century BCE bronze statuette shows Aphrodite, an icon of female beauty. She was married to Hephaestus, the blacksmith god, but bore children to Ares, god of war.

Some of the Olympians attracted special devotion because of the myths that were associated with their names. One such was Demeter. Her daughter Persephone was abducted by Hades, god of the Underworld. Demeter gave up everything to find her daughter, and as she searched, crops ceased to grow. With humankind under threat of starvation, Zeus persuaded Hades to give up his bride for six months each year—in spring and summer, when the earth once more bore fruit. This saga explained the yearly cycle, but it also inspired a mystical interpretation turning on themes of death and rebirth that was celebrated in the Eleusinian Mysteries, the best known of all ancient Greek cults.

Another Greek deity who inspired intense devotion was Dionysus, god of drunkenness, wine, and religious ecstasy. His followers practiced uninhibited dancing in a cult that served as a release from the rational norms of everyday life. In their frenzy, they were seen as released and empowered by the god himself.

Transgressing moral codes

Being immortal, the Olympians followed their own moral code. While acknowledging the importance of order and justice in the human world, they were nonetheless only too capable of transgressing the bounds of accepted morality in pursuit of their own interests and desires. No one unleashed their passions more prominently than Zeus himself, who had the power to take on multiple disguises—including a bull, a swan, a cuckoo, and a shower of gold—in his lustful pursuit of mortal women.

△ **Council of the gods**
To the right of this detail from a 16th-century fresco painted by Raphael's workshop, Zeus (his foot on a globe) agrees to Eros's marriage to his human lover, Psyche, while the other gods listen to the debate. At the far left, Hermes, god of trade, wealth, and travel, hands the gift of immortality to Psyche.

Heracles, Zeus's son, who was sometimes included among the Olympians

Dionysus converses with Apollo, god of music and arts

Ares, god of war, is shown wearing armor and holding a spear

Eros pleads his case before Zeus; to his left is his mother, Aphrodite

Zeus sits with his wife, Hera, to his left and daughter Athena (with spear) behind

> **Divine majesty**
Found by fishermen off the coast of the island of Euboea in 1928, this 5th-century BCE bronze figure is thought to represent either Poseidon, god of the sea, or Zeus, king of the gods. Poseidon would have held a trident (now lost) in his right hand; in the case of Zeus, it would have been a thunderbolt.

"It is **not possible** to **deceive** or **thwart** the **will of Zeus**."

HESIOD, *THEOGONY*

HADES AND **THE GODS BELOW**

In contrast to the Olympians, another group of Greek deities was linked to the Underworld, where souls went after death. Foremost among these chthonic (Underworld) gods was Hades, ruler of Tartarus (shown here with his wife, Persephone). Others included the Furies, vengeful divine beings. Some gods could take on chthonic aspects if they had dealings with the world of the dead; Demeter was sometimes known as Demeter Chthonia when her quest to rescue Persephone was cited.

HADES AND PERSEPHONE

Greek Heroes

Mortals with superhuman powers

Working in the late 8th century BCE, the poet Hesiod attempted to outline the history of humankind in his poem *Works and Days*. He told a story of decline, from the harmonious Golden Age to the toil-wearied Iron Age, in which he situated himself. Before this age, he inserted an Age of Heroes, which provided a way to explain the tales of heroic mortals that filtered down orally through the years of illiteracy that followed the fall of the Mycenaean civilization (see pp.46–47) around 1200/1190 BCE.

Many of the heroes appeared in the *Iliad* and the *Odyssey*, the two great epic poems of Hesiod's near-contemporary Homer—foremost among them Achilles and Odysseus. Others were remembered as founders of cities, whose residents sought to embellish their past by linking it to individuals with extraordinary powers. Emerging from a Bronze Age era of aristocratic warriors, most of the heroes were male and distinguished by their fighting prowess, be it against humans or monsters such as dragons, huge boars, and flesh-eating horses.

Origins and survival

Much about the origin of the stories remains murky, but the growing knowledge of Greece's early history over the past 150 years or so has uncovered some clues. Memories of the labyrinthine palace of Knossos in Minoan Crete may lie behind tales of Theseus and his struggle with the Minotaur. Early exploration of the Black Sea in the centuries after 1000 BCE

△ **Cadmus**
Famed for slaying the dragon that guarded a spring sacred to Ares, Cadmus was one of the earliest Greek heroes and the founder of Thebes. Herodotus (see p.149) claimed he came from the Eastern Mediterranean and brought with him knowledge of writing.

△ **Heracles**
Claimed by Herodotus to have been born a couple centuries after Cadmus, Heracles (left) is shown here killing the Giant Alcyoneus. Heracles, the son of Zeus and a mortal woman, was the greatest of Greek heroes. A demigod, he was worshipped in cult rituals, and his death was commemorated at the Heracleia festival.

△ **Theseus**
One of the youths sent to be fed to the Minotaur as part of Athens' annual tribute to King Minos, Theseus succeeded in slaying the monster in the Labyrinth with the help of Ariadne, Minos's daughter. He later abandoned Ariadne on Naxos.

"That dauntless, **furious spirit**, that **lionheart**."

TLEPOLEMUS ON HIS FATHER, HERACLES, IN THE *ILIAD*

presumably informed the tale of Jason's epic journey with the Argonauts and Atalanta to Colchis, on what is now the coast of Georgia, to steal the Golden Fleece that would secure Jason's claim to the throne of Iolcus. Homer's *Odyssey* may reflect even earlier memories of the wanderings of ancient mariners around the shores and islands of the Mediterranean, opened up to trade by the Mycenaeans and Minoans.

Not much is known about how the stories passed down through the centuries. The most likely theory is that bards known as *aoidoi* performed accounts orally, perhaps accompanied by musical instruments, such as lyres. Other legends no doubt survived as bedtime stories, passed down from generation to generation in the same way as folk tales around the world.

Whatever the origin of the stories, they are marked by an unrivaled narrative zest that ensured their survival over the centuries that followed. The expansion of Hellenistic civilization in the wake of Alexander the Great's conquests carried them across western Asia as far as the borders of India. This, together with the stories' constant refinement in the hands of talented poets and narrators, ensured that the tales of the Greek heroes were inherited by Rome, which spread its grip over formerly Greek-ruled lands in the 2nd and 1st centuries BCE. Greece's political defeat did not mean the end of its legends—instead they were appropriated, sometimes in Romanized form (Heracles became Hercules, Odysseus became Ulysses), becoming a part of the new imperial culture.

△ **Achilles**
Central to Homer's *Iliad* (c. 750–700 BCE), Achilles was revered as the consummate warrior, although he had one weak point: his heel. He famously faced the choice between a long life and an untimely but glorious death.

△ **Orpheus**
Hailing from Thrace, north of Greece, and venerated as the greatest of poets and musicians, famed for his skill with the lyre, Orpheus earned his place in the roll-call of heroes through his journey to the Underworld to rescue his wife, Eurydice. The story inspired the later cult of Orphism, promising followers life after death.

△ **Atalanta**
One of the few women among the Greek heroes, Atalanta joined the hunt for the boar sent by Artemis to ravage Calydon, in Aetolia. She won its skin for drawing first blood. Famed for her speed, she refused to marry any man who could not beat her in a running race.

The Trojan War

Finding facts among the legends

Long accepted as historical fact but later decried as the stuff of legend, the Trojan War as described by Homer may reflect memories of a real-life siege passed down orally by generations of storytellers.

Greeks of the Classical era who knew of the Trojan War from Homer's *Iliad* largely accepted the author's account as historical truth. The work spoke of a ten-year siege of Troy, a city on the Asian mainland in what is now Türkiye, by the Achaeans, a group of forces gathered from many separate realms of the Greek lands across the Aegean Sea. Homer dated the war to 400 years before his own time, so sometime in the 12th century BCE. Although the *Iliad* itself concentrated on a short period toward the end of the war, other sources fleshed out details of the boat-borne invasion. According to these stories, Paris, younger son of Troy's ruler, Priam, abducted Helen, wife of the Mycenaean king, Menelaus. In revenge, Menelaus's brother, Agamemnon, led the assault on Troy, devoting himself to destroying the city.

Tales of Troy

The names of the heroes of both sides—the Achaean Greeks Achilles and Patroclus, and the Trojan Hector, Priam's older son—resounded through the centuries. Generations knew the stories told of the war, particularly that of the enormous wooden horse used to sneak the Greek warriors into Troy.

However, doubts emerged about the *Iliad* and the story of the Trojan War. These doubts blossomed into fully-fledged skepticism in the 19th century, as

△ **Mortal enemies**
Achilles, standing in his chariot, is shown dragging Hector's body around the walls of Troy in this marble relief from a 2nd-century CE Roman sarcophagus from Tyre, Lebanon.

▽ **The Trojan horse**
A detail from the Mykonos Vase, made around 675 BCE, this is the earliest-known depiction of the story of the Trojan horse. Soldiers can be seen looking out from inside the horse.

△ **Achaean soldiers**
This detail from a relief on the modern Monument of Alexander in Thessaloniki's Nea Paralia district shows Achaean soldiers in fighting formation with spears and shields.

"On the **armies** came as if the **whole earth** were **devoured** by **wildfire**."

HOMER'S *ILIAD*

scholars began to take a greater interest in folk stories and poems. The idea of an individual poet named Homer authoring the *Iliad* and its companion work the *Odyssey* came under attack. So too did the veracity of his tale of a siege that must have taken place sometime in the Mycenaean period, several hundred years before the poems were composed in the 8th century BCE. Instead, it was suggested, the tales of the Trojan War were the stuff of legend, passed down orally by bards for their audiences' entertainment.

The search for Troy
Undeterred by such skepticism, Heinrich Schliemann, a German businessman with a passion for ancient history and archaeology, set out in the 1870s to find hard evidence for the siege of Troy. He began digging at a site now known as Hisarlik, on the Turkish mainland about 4 miles (7 km) from the mouth of the Dardanelles Strait. He found evidence of a fortified settlement inhabited over many centuries, but his brutal methods damaged the levels of the site that held the ruins of Homer's Troy. Among the levels subsequently explored by others at the site, one—labeled variously VIh or VIIa—shows evidence of destruction that has been dated to the early 12th century BCE, consistent with the time assigned to the Mycenaean collapse.

At Mycenae, Schliemann unearthed several objects from shaft graves that he chose to identify with Agamemnon and the forces that had sailed against Troy. But he also discarded items that did not fit his hypothesis. His interpretation has since been proved wrong: the gold found dates from as many as 400 years earlier than the date assigned to the Trojan War.

Archaeologists and scholars continue to probe Hisarlik's secrets. In recent years, their attention has focused on Hisarlik's position at the head of the Dardanelles Strait, which probably lay around a mile (a couple of kilometers) away at the time that the siege is said to have taken place. On its high mound overlooking the coastal plain, the fortified town controlled access to the main trade route linking the Aegean to the Black Sea. As such, it was a prize worth conquering. As German archaeologist Manfred Korfmann notes, it is true that the area was a geographically important location over which wars were fought, but "the question of whether there ever was a Paris, or a Helen, must take a back seat."

▽ **Menelaus and Hector**
The Achaean leader Menelaus (left) and Trojan Hector (right) fight in single combat over the body of the fallen Trojan hero Euphorbos on this plate made in Cos in the late 7th century BCE.

Geometric and volute patterns

Inscription identifying Menelaus

End of the Mycenaeans

Destruction and adaptation

The collapse of the Mycenaean palace centers of mainland Greece sent ripples across the Aegean, their impact varying from community to community. Change was unavoidable, but ruin for some spelled opportunity for others.

△ **Funerary stele**
Including registers of horses and armed warriors, the Painted Stele from Mycenae dates to the post-palatial period and represents the last example of Mycenaean fresco painting.

Around 1200/1190 BCE, just over two centuries after the advent of the palatial period, the palaces and palatial structures of the Greek mainland—at Pylos, Mycenae, Tiryns, Thebes, and Orchomenos—were destroyed. The center at Gla, in Boeotia, had collapsed a generation earlier. The palaces had suffered episodes of destruction or serious damage throughout the Late Bronze Age (1700–1100 BCE), but these were usually followed by reconstruction and renewed building on the same scale. This time, for the most part, there would be no rebuilding of the Mycenaean centers, and key elements of the culture, such as writing and administration, were lost or rejected.

The final disappearance of the palace system at the beginning of the 12th century BCE does not seem to have been caused by one single event. Rather, it was likely the result of a cumulative process of collapse that had begun some time before. The preceding period was probably one of major internal unrest. At several sites, fortifications were strengthened, and at Mycenae, Tiryns, and Athens, efforts were made to secure the water supply—a clear sign of competition, strategic planning in anticipation of violence, or both. Indeed, the so-called o-ka series of Linear B tablets from the palace at Pylos refers to units of men "guarding the coast," indicating some unspecified

▷ **Mycenaean warriors**
The 12th-century BCE Warrior Vase depicts two units (one on each side) along with a woman (far left) raising her hand in farewell. The artist may also have painted the grave stele shown above.

"**Deprived** of the **protection** that the **palaces** had **provided**, many left their **homes**."

PROFESSOR CHRISTOPHER MEE

threat. There are hints too of disruption in palatial trade and trade networks, perhaps as independent merchants subverted the market, undermining the palaces' economic power. There is also some evidence that a drier climate in the years preceding collapse may have put pressure on the agricultural economy.

Ultimately, no one theory is sufficient to explain why the palace system failed. Collectively, however, the conditions indicated by the evidence may have contributed to a loss of palatial control, or a reduction in resilience that left the palace centers vulnerable to natural disaster or external and internal pressure.

After the palaces

Mycenaean culture persisted into a "post-palatial" period for a further 100 years or so, until around 1090–1050 BCE, though not in the same form. The incipient literacy evident in the Linear B script vanished for several hundred years; fresco painting disappeared; and the minor arts, with the exception of bronzework and ceramics, were also diminished. Many sites that had thrived during the palatial period were abandoned; others saw their populations shrink.

However, some formerly palatial sites were able to endure. Tiryns, for example, was reorganized and expanded in the post-palatial period, and may have accommodated refugees from nearby settlements. A new building was erected in the ruins of the former throne room, in what may have been an attempt by Tiryns' rulers to establish legitimacy. Any site that offered security and opportunity would have seemed an attractive prospect, and some previously relatively minor sites, such as Lefkandi (see pp.48–49) on Euboea and Perati near Athens, increased in size and importance.

Some refugees from the palatial system escaped eastward, founding cities such as Smyrna and Ephesus in Asia Minor, and establishing themselves on Cyprus. Others took refuge in the Peloponnesian mountains, where they clung to their independence.

Politically, mainland Greece was fragmented, with local rulers or groups taking advantage of the power vacuum to establish control over smaller territories with much reduced access to resources. Some of the first of these rulers may have been former low-ranked regional administrators, known as *basileis*, under

the palatial system. Warrior burials, which had been common during the Early Mycenaean period, reappeared in some regions, and scenes of warfare on painted pottery suggest that there was a renewed focus on the use of violence as a means of establishing and maintaining power. Raiding and banditry may also have played a role in acquiring resources.

Some communities that had been peripheral to the palatial system were perhaps able to subsist in much the same way as they always had done. Others may have been forced to adapt, accepting new homes and new livelihoods, and pledging allegiance to new rulers with new demands and facing new threats. This uncertainty would persist, perhaps for generations, before giving way to order in the Early Iron Age.

◁ **Mycenaean tablet**
Linear B was the script used for administration under the palatial system. Clay tablets such as this example, recovered from the so-called Palace of Nestor at Pylos, survived only because they were fired like pottery in a kiln during fires that destroyed the palaces. After the collapse of the palace system, writing disappeared from the mainland for several centuries.

△ **A great hall**
Excavations have uncovered this large rectangular building known as the "Megaron" at Xeropolis, the settlement at Lefkandi. Xeropolis is about 1,640 ft (500 m) from the cemetery at Toumba.

Despite the large ears, the face has an unmistakably human look

The body and head were discovered in separate graves and subsequently reattached

The body is a hollow cylinder, shaped on a potter's wheel

Zigzag and lattice painted decorations are typical of the Geometric pottery of the time

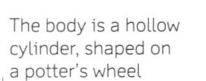

▷ **The Lefkandi centaur**
Found in one of the tombs at Toumba and dated to the late 10th or 9th centuries BCE, this terra-cotta figure, standing just 14 in (36 cm) tall, is the earliest-known three-dimensional representation of a centaur, a mythical half-man, half-horse creature. Scholars suggest that the intended subject was the centaur Chiron, the teacher of Achilles.

"One of the **most important** Late Bronze Age sites in the **Aegean**."

ARCHAEOLOGIST PROFESSOR IRENE LEMOS

Lefkandi

A light in Greece's "Dark Age"

A remarkable coastal settlement on the island of Euboea, Lefkandi managed to survive and prosper through the centuries following the Mycenaean collapse, maintaining trading relations across the Eastern Mediterranean world.

Since the 1960s, archaeological excavations around Lefkandi, a small village on the island of Euboea, have been turning up extraordinary finds. Located between the ancient cities of Chalcis and Eretria, the site has provided evidence of unbroken occupation from around 2100 BCE to 700 BCE. However, perhaps the most exciting discovery was the building found at Toumba, a hillock near Lefkandi.

Cultural treasures

The mound at Toumba sat in the middle of a site that had already been explored by archaeologists for more than a decade when in 1980 an overeager property developer sent bulldozers to begin digging at its summit. Archaeologists hurried in to prevent further damage after the workers hit a building, destroying part of it. They found that the structure dated to the 10th century BCE and was part of a cemetery. As such, it was to cast invaluable light on Greece during the centuries between the collapse of the Mycenaean palace system around 1200/1190 BCE and the start of the Archaic period, which was heralded by the reappearance of written records toward the end of the 8th century BCE.

Even before the Toumba finds, Lefkandi had provided important evidence of cultural continuity in the form of decorated pottery and clay molds for casting sophisticated bronze objects. Several burial grounds had already been located, suggesting the existence of a large settlement, and the grave goods found in them, including weapons, jewelery, and ceramics, indicated trade contact with the eastern shores of the Mediterranean and Egypt. One grave turned up bronze wheels from Cyprus and a ring bearing the image of the Egyptian god Ammon; another, two Egyptian bronze vases.

The graves found at Toumba were, however, by far the most impressive site. The site's centerpiece was a building 164 ft (50 m) long, dated to around 950 BCE. Flanked by a colonnade that prefigured Classical architecture, it housed three rooms whose focal point was two burial shafts in the central room. One contained the remains of four horses, which had apparently been offered up as sacrifices. The other housed the cremated remains of a warrior, who was laid to rest with his weapons. Lying alongside him was the body of a woman adorned with a precious electrum (an alloy of gold and silver) ring and an antique Babylonian throat protector. She was found with an ivory-handled knife by her shoulder that may have been used to sacrifice her, although conclusive evidence is lacking. Outside the building were other wealthy graves, presumably of family members or other representatives of Lefkandi's ruling caste.

Scholars argue over whether the building was a heroon (see below) or simply the final resting place of a locally important couple. Whatever the case, the sophistication of the goods found buried there suggests that life in that part of Euboea was far from primitive. As for the settlement at Lefkandi, it survived for a couple centuries after its 10th-century BCE heyday but was then abandoned, possibly as the result of a war. Thereafter, it remained mute for more than two and a half millennia until excavations revealed its secrets.

PRECIOUS FINDS

Jewelery found at Lefkandi provides a useful insight into its people's lives. The Ammon ring (see left) offers evidence of international trade, as do finds of necklaces from Southwest Asia. Lefkandi's wealth is reflected in the burial of one woman with a gold pendant (shown here), earrings, and sheet-gold disks covering her breasts.

▽ **The heroon**
The size and elaboration of the largest tomb excavated at Lefkandi indicate that it might have been a heroon, a shrine for the veneration or cult worship of heroes.

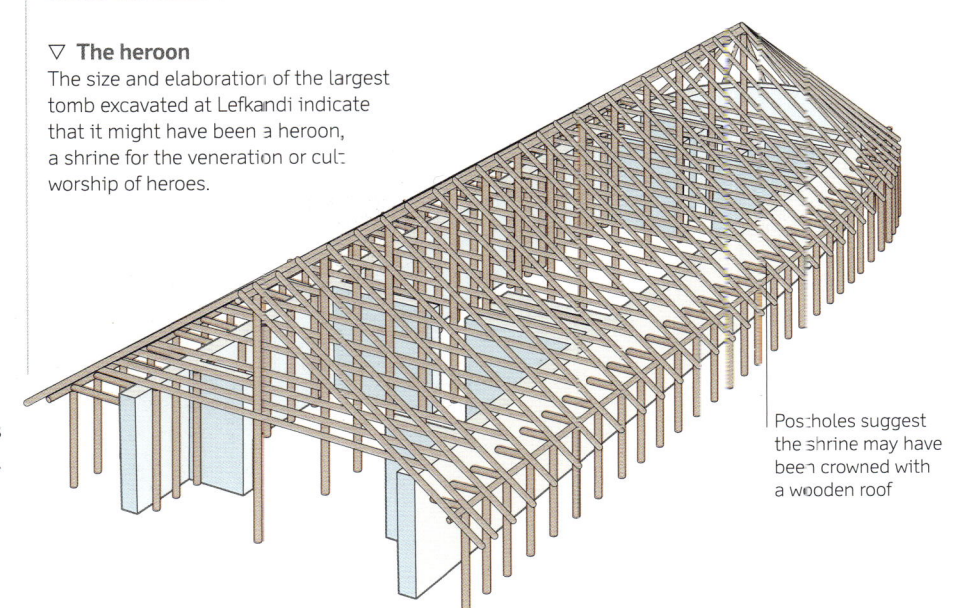

Postholes suggest the shrine may have been crowned with a wooden roof

2

Rise of the City-State

900–600 BCE

Out of the "Dark Age"

The period from 900 to 600 BCE, encompassing the latter part of the Early Iron Age (c.1100–750 BCE) and the early part of the Archaic period (c.750–500 BCE) witnessed major sociocultural and political change, including the formalization of ideas and institutions that would define Greece for centuries to come. However, the reasons for these changes, and how and where they emerged, are unclear.

The city-state

Foremost among these developments was the rise of the city-state, or *polis*. Although alternative political systems persisted long after its appearance, the *polis*—comprising the *asty* (city), *chora* (countryside), and *demos* (people)—had a transformational impact on Greek identity. Formed through the agglomeration (*synoikismos*) of existing communities, the *polis* required constitutional and legal reform to preserve social and political stability. These reforms were often attributed to a single lawgiver: at Sparta, this was Lycurgus; at Athens it was Draco, a man renowned for the "draconian" severity of his sentences. Some of these men were probably real, others probably not, and there is no evidence that makes their true contribution entirely clear.

Surviving legislation from these early *poleis* illustrates a clear civic identity and concerns about the abuse of power. The earliest surviving inscribed law from ancient Greece comes from Dreros on Crete and dates to c.650 BCE. It was passed by groups known as the *demoi* and the "twenty of the *polis*" and limited the time any man could serve as *kosmas* (principal magistrate). A similar hint of democracy marks early legislation from Tiryns and Olympia in the Peloponnese, and from Tholopotami on Chios, although early *poleis* remained vulnerable to aristocratic tyranny. In ancient Greece tyrants were not necessarily cruel or oppressive rulers; some were good, some were bad, and although tyranny was undemocratic, it was often fueled by popular support.

Cultural shifts

In art and culture, the period saw the composition of the *Odyssey* and *Iliad*, among the most famous works of ancient Greek literature. There was a shift toward figurative ceramic art, driven by the development at Corinth of the black-figure technique around 720 BCE and its subsequent refinement at Athens. Increased contact with Asia Minor as Greeks moved eastward, establishing the trading center of Al-Mina in Anatolia around 800 BCE and the Ionian cities later, influenced the development of monumental sculpture, typically depicting *korai* (young women) and *kouroi* (young men), and monumental public buildings. These developments reflect a growing civic identity keenly felt in another important innovation: the creation of the first Greek coinage.

As the *poleis* developed, conflict between them became commonplace, and the transition to the Archaic period was accompanied by changes in the way war was waged. At its core was a new type of heavy foot soldier called the hoplite, a self-funded citizen soldier named for the equipment he carried (*ta hopla*), and a ranked fighting formation known as the phalanx. War was dictated by the agricultural calendar; food supply, after all, determined a city's survival as much as the skill of its warriors.

◁ **Bronze cauldron from Olympia, 8th century** BCE

776 BCE Traditional date for the foundation of the Olympic Games

C. 750 BCE Pithecusae, in Ischia, Italy, is the first Greek colony overseas

720–680 BCE Traditional date of the Lelantine War—the first conflict between multiple allied cities.

C. 750–700 BCE The epic poems the *Odyssey* and the *Iliad* are composed

C. 720 BCE Black-figure pottery painting is developed at Corinth

C. 700 BCE The poet Hesiod composes his history of the gods, the *Theogony*

① Relief from Cyzicus, a Greek city in Anatolia

② The Greek theater at Metapontum in Italy

③ Ruins of Pontic Olbia on the Black Sea coast

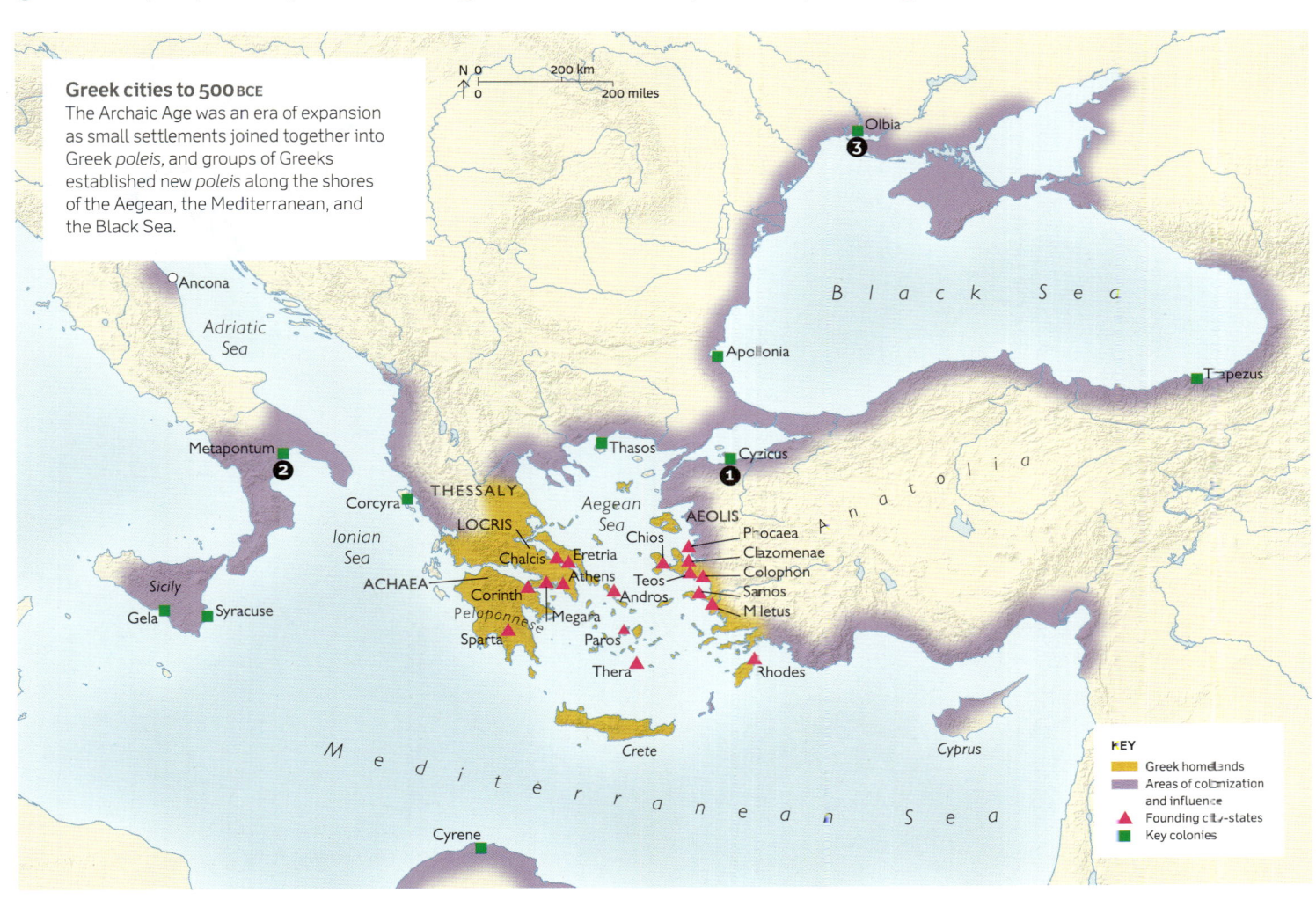

Greek cities to 500 BCE

The Archaic Age was an era of expansion as small settlements joined together into Greek *poleis*, and groups of Greeks established new *poleis* along the shores of the Aegean, the Mediterranean, and the Black Sea.

N
0   200 km
0   200 miles

Black Sea

Olbia ③

Adriatic Sea

Ancona

Apollonia

Trapezus

Metapontum ②

Thasos

Cyzicus ①

Anatolia

Corcyra

THESSALY

Aegean Sea

AEOLIS

LOCRIS

Chios

Phocaea

Ionian Sea

Chalcis

Eretria

Clazomenae

Colophon

ACHAEA

Athens

Teos

Samos

Sicily

Corinth

Andros

Miletus

Gela

Syracuse

Megara

Peloponnese

Sparta

Paros

Thera

Rhodes

Crete

Cyprus

Mediterranean Sea

Cyrene

KEY
- Greek homelands
- Areas of colonization and influence
- ▲ Founding city-states
- ■ Key colonies

690–650 BCE Temple of Poseidon constructed, Corinthian Isthmus

c. 657 BCE The tyrant Cypselus takes power in Corinth

c. 650 BCE The Dreros Law Code is installed at Dreros on Crete

c. 632 BCE Athenian aristocrat Cylon's attempted coup triggers political reforms

c. 670 BCE The Messenians revolt against Sparta

c. 650 BCE One of the earliest surviving *korai*, the Nikandre *kore*, is set up at Delos

c. 640 BCE The Chigi vase provides the first depiction in art of the hoplite phalanx

c. 600 BCE The first Greek coinage is issued by the city-state of Aegina

Greece in the Iron Age

An era of change

The ruins of the Bronze Age collapse were the crucible from which emerged a series of social, cultural, and political innovations—including the *poleis* and Panhellenic sanctuaries—that changed Greece forever.

Much of the Early Iron Age (c. 1100–750 BCE) in Greece was once poorly understood and considered part of a "Dark Age" that followed the collapse of Mycenaean civilization and lasted until around 800 BCE. This was, perhaps, partly because the writer Hesiod described the Iron Age in bleak terms. Today, excavation and research have helped to lift the darkness and reveal a period of innovation and adaptation. It is true, though, that the artistry and grandiose monumentality of the Bronze Age were conspicuously absent, for a time at least.

The period is characterized by the widespread adoption of iron technology, probably from Cyprus. In reality, iron had arrived in Greece by the later Bronze Age, but its use was typically reserved for small, high-value objects. As people became familiar with the technology and its

◁ **The Dipylon Oinochoe**
Marked with one of the earliest known inscriptions using the Greek alphabet, this Geometric wine jug is from the 8th century BCE.

potential, and as the copper and tin required to make bronze became hard to source, they embraced iron. This shift was accompanied by an increase in production and technological innovation; with this, and the status that came with ownership, a wider range of iron objects began to be manufactured. One such object, the large *oboloi* (iron spits), served as currency in Greece before the advent of coinage in the 7th century BCE.

Iron Age life

The 8th century BCE saw the start of a colonizing movement that spread Greek influence across the Mediterranean (see pp.76–77). Closer to home, the period witnessed the foundation and development of some of Greece's most important religious centers, including the sanctuaries of Zeus at Olympia and Apollo at Delphi. These new sanctuaries were highly political. Cults became a focus for the display of wealth and power, and a way for groups to define and distinguish themselves, not least through participation in the Olympiad (said to have begun around 776 BCE). This was one of several different processes from which the city-states, or *poleis*, emerged.

The works attributed to Homer (see pp.60–61) and Hesiod provide early references to communal assemblies, known as *agorai*, which served as public forums for communal governance by the first half of the Early Iron Age. The term "agora" was later used to describe the physical location of these gatherings. By the end of the period, agoras had been formalized in stone at Dreros on Crete and at Megara Hyblaea in eastern Sicily, where we also find the first evidence

△ **Bronze horse**
Horse figurines, such as this example, were a common votive offering in the sanctuaries of mainland Greece in the 8th century BCE.

for urban planning on a "Hippodamian," that is rectangular, grid pattern. For many, home was a relatively simple timber building, consisting often of a single room housing a variety of domestic activities. The *oikos*, which comprised the building and the household, was the primary social and economic unit. A few buildings stand out as having belonged to elites, or as serving special functions, for example as cult buildings. Over the course of the period, as the population increased, settlements also grew, and buildings became more complex.

Writing revival

The Early Iron Age also saw the return of literacy to Greece—lost in the aftermath of the Bronze Age collapse (see pp.46–47)—following the adaptation of the Phoenician alphabet, and with it the composition of some of Europe's first literary works. The earliest form of this new Greek alphabet survives on a group of copper plaques from Egypt from c. 800 BCE, and other important inscriptions point to its use during the later 8th century BCE. These include the Dipylon Oinochoe from Athens, and a drinking cup inscribed with a skolion (drinking song) that identifies it as "Nestor's Cup." The mention of Nestor's cup is the earliest independent reference to Homer's *Iliad*, where the legendary cup of the hero Nestor is described.

△ **Urban planning**
The orthogonal grid pattern of the streets in Megara Hyblaea, a colony founded near Syracuse on Sicily around 728 BCE, is still clearly visible today.

> "For now **truly** is a **race of iron**, and men **never rest** from **labor** and **sorrow** by day, and from **perishing** by night."

HESIOD, *WORKS AND DAYS*

Agriculture

Farming in a stony land

Greece's city-states looked to their agricultural workers to feed their peoples. Sometimes the produce harvested from the country's stony, mountainous terrain was insufficient, encouraging resourceful groups to seek fresh lands overseas.

Agriculture was vital to life and the economy in ancient Greece. Even though the Greek culture most familiar to us is largely urban, scholars believe that as much as 80 percent of the population may have been involved in food production, whether working in the fields or at sea.

Land and resources

Much of Greece is split up by mountain ranges that make the landscape unfavorable to agriculture. Now, as in ancient times, cultivable land is limited to narrow valleys, small plains opening out near river mouths, and a mostly thin coastal strip. Today, barely a fifth of the land is suitable for arable farming and a third cannot be put to agricultural use at all. The rest typically consists of rough pasture suitable for olive-growing or raising sheep and goats.

The broken nature of the countryside limited the extent of large estates in ancient Greece, but they did exist. Most of the big landholdings were worked by enslaved people, but some were worked by peasant landowners forced into serfdom through a form of debt bondage. Outdoor labor was mostly done by men, while women worked inside.

The Greeks' main crops were grains, grapevines, and olives. Wheat and barley were staples, but many city-states struggled to produce enough to feed their populations. From at least the late 7th century BCE, Athens in particular relied on imported food; data analysis from a couple of centuries later suggests that it imported well over half of its wheat. Legumes, including beans and chickpeas, were widely eaten; fish from rivers and coasts was more highly regarded than meat as a protein source. Farmers kept oxen, mainly for plowing. Besides sheep and goats, a typical smallholder kept chickens, and bees for honey.

◁ **Grinding wheat**
From the mid-5th-century BCE, this terra-cotta model found at Kamiros, Rhodes, is just under 5 in (13 cm) tall and depicts a woman grinding wheat.

Every farmer had to cope with the vagaries of the climate. Long, dry summers favored the cultivation of vines and olives. The winter months provided crucial rainfall, but the supply of rain was unpredictable and could vary across the country, with some regions well watered while others suffered drought. Good storage facilities were an essential precaution against hard times, when people could otherwise be forced to forage for nuts and berries.

Over the centuries, the challenges of feeding a growing population, exacerbated by the harshness of the Greek landscape and the uncertainty of its climate, drove people to explore new, sometimes more fertile lands; the shores of the Black Sea were especially productive (see p.76–77). In a way, it was the limitations of the Greek environment as much as the enterprise of its people that helped spread Greek culture around the Mediterranean basin.

THE FARMER'S YEAR

In his *Works and Days*, the poet Hesiod (fl. c. 700 BCE), himself a farmer, offered advice on how to make the best use of the land. November, he said, was for plowing—and the first essential was an ox. During winter there was little to do but keep warm, but by early May farmers should be preparing to bring in the harvest. The main thing, though, was to always work hard, "for a sluggish worker will not fill his barn," and "a man who puts off work is always wrestling with ruin."

▽ **Bronze billy goat**
This 5th-century BCE bronze billy goat was discovered in the Kephisia area of Athens. Goats and sheep were usually kept by smallholders for wool, dairy products, and meat—the latter was mainly consumed at religious festivals.

△ **Farming landscape**
Landholding was a huge status symbol in ancient Greece. This typical Greek farming landscape near Olympos on Karpathos has stone-built retaining walls that form terraces.

Twin handles made pouring easy (most amphorae held wine)

Clusters of olive leaves decorate the neck of the vase

A young man sits at the top of the tree shaking the branches with a stick

Twisted, gnarled trunks are characteristic of the hardy olive tree, which thrives in full sun and is well suited to Greece's Mediterranean climate

A long stick is used to beat the olive branches

Fallen olives are collected in a basket

Individual leaves form a pattern around the base

▷ **Harvesting olives**
Farm workers bring in the olive crop on this Attic amphora (vase) dating from about 520 BCE. Besides their value as food, olives served to make oil for cooking and fuel for lamps as well as an unguent that athletes rubbed onto their bodies.

"**First of all**, get yourself an **ox** for **plowing**."

HESIOD, *WORKS AND DAYS*

Language and Writing

How Greek evolved

The people of ancient Greece were not a unified nation, but a collection of kinship groups that developed into separate city-states, spread across the Balkan peninsula and the Eastern Mediterranean. Similarly, the language of ancient Greece was a family of dialects, with distinct pronunciations, idioms, and local vocabulary. As these were mutually intelligible, it is thought they developed from a common ancestor, Proto-Greek, which appeared in 2200–1900 BCE.

The linguistic differences within Greece arose from the geographical separation of its regions. Broadly speaking, there were three groups of related dialects: the western Doric, northwest Greek, and Achaean Doric; the central Aeolic and Arcado-Cypriot; and the eastern Attic and Ionic.

Writing first appeared in ancient Greece in the 18th century BCE, when the Minoans used a syllabic writing system known as Linear A and a hieroglyphic system. In syllabic systems, each symbol represents a syllable or other unit of speech rather than a letter that works with others to spell a word. Linear A has yet to be deciphered but probably represents an attempt to record the Minoan language.

Around 1400 BCE, Linear A and the Cretan hieroglyphs were joined by another syllabic script known as Linear B, which has been deciphered. Both Linear A and Linear B were used in administrative contexts. Sometime before c. 800 BCE, however, a writing system was adopted that was better suited to the Greek language than Linear B. Instead of the

△ **Mycenaean Greek**
Linear B—shown here on a tablet from c. 1400 BCE written in Mycenaean Greek—was derived from the Minoan Linear A script and was, in turn, adopted by the Minoans when Crete fell under Mycenaean influence sometime after c. 1600 BCE.

△ **Greek alphabet from Phoenician**
This stele shows examples of the Phoenician (top) and Greek (bottom) alphabets. The Greeks developed their alphabet from the Phoenician alphabet, creating the first script to have distinct letters for vowels and consonants. Over time, the letter shapes were refined, and local variants of the alphabet emerged.

△ **Nestor's cup**
The earliest-known writing using the Greek alphabet is an 8th-century BCE inscription on a ceramic cup, shown here. It reads: "I am Nestor's cup … Whoever drinks this cup empty, straightaway desire for fair-crowned Aphrodite will seize him."

"From **Homer** to **modern Demotic**, the **Greek language** has enjoyed a **slow, organic,** and uninterrupted **growth**."

PHILOLOGIST WILLIAM HAAS, 1982

syllabic script, the new system used an alphabet derived from the letters of the alphabet used by the Phoenicians. The Greeks expanded the Phoenician alphabet by adding vowels and changing some consonant sounds to match the needs of the Greek language. There were at first local variations, and some letters went through shape alterations, but in the 5th century BCE a 24-letter version of the Ionic alphabet became the standard, after it was adopted by the people of Athens.

A common tongue

Similar things happened to the language itself during the Classical period (500–323 BCE). Classical culture was generally centered on Ionia and Attica, and Athens in particular. Unsurprisingly, a fusion of the Attic and Ionic dialects predominated, paving the way for a common Greek dialect. What emerged was called Koine Greek, which quickly became the lingua franca of Greece, the Eastern Mediterranean, and beyond, as Alexander the Great's conquests in the 4th century BCE helped spread it to parts of Asia and Africa.

Even after Rome's conquest of Greece in 146 BCE, Koine Greek retained its importance as the second language of the Roman Empire, and as the language of the Christian apostles and New Testament. Although superseded by Latin and the Romance languages in western Europe, Koine Greek remained an official language of the Byzantine Empire (see pp.296–297) and evolved into modern Demotic Greek.

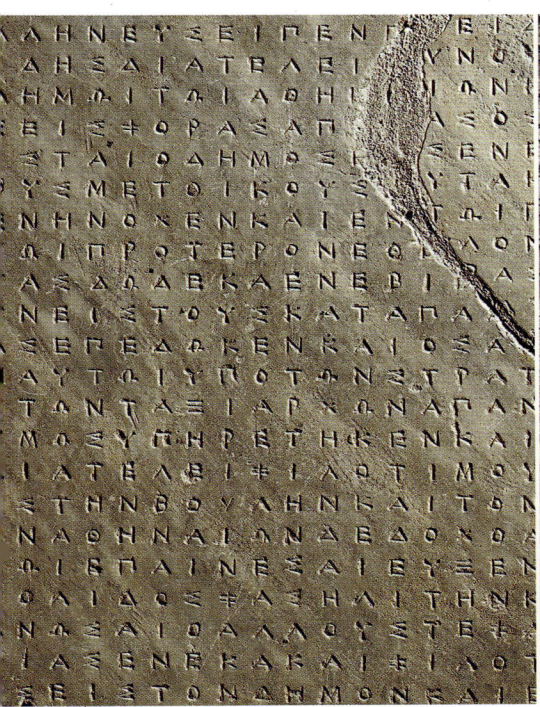

△ **Stoichedon style**
Early Greek writing was often confined to inscriptions in stone, in capital letters that were evenly spaced, with no spaces or punctuation between words, and sometimes, as here, in stoichedon style, aligned vertically as well as horizontally.

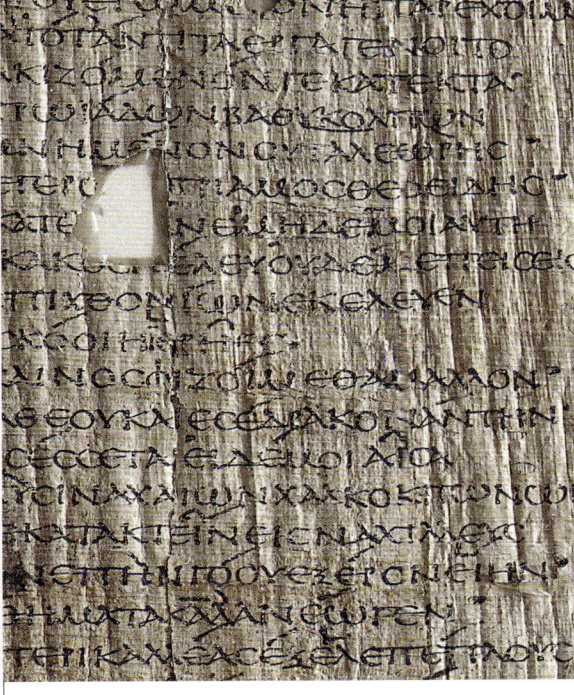

△ **The "Bankes Homer" manuscript**
This 2nd-century CE manuscript on papyrus, known as the "Bankes Homer," is a transcription of part of the *Iliad* (see p.60–61). Originating in the 8th century BCE, the epic poem was passed down orally and was first committed to writing only centuries later. It was then copied and recopied by scribes multiple times.

△ **Codex Sinaiticus**
The earliest surviving manuscripts of the New Testament of the Bible, from the 4th century CE, are written in Koine Greek. This example from the Codex Sinaiticus is in the stylized early Christian calligraphic style of Greek capital-letter script known as uncial script.

The Iliad and Odyssey

Epic tales of heroism, gods, and war

The *Iliad* and the *Odyssey* combine history and mythology to recount the heroic and tragic events at the end of the Trojan War. The two works were revered as masterpieces in ancient Greece and remain popular today.

△ **A legendary poet**
The *Iliad* and *Odyssey* are traditionally ascribed to the poet Homer, but as well as speculation concerning his authorship of the texts (see right), there is also considerable debate as to whether he even existed.

Tales of the heroes of bygone ages were told by storytellers long before Homer's time; these were passed orally from one generation to the next, and revised at each retelling. A popular subject was the legendary Trojan War, stories of which likely reflected memories of a real-life conflict in the 13th or 12th centuries BCE.

Somewhere around the middle–late 8th century, some of these stories were collated into two extended narratives, the *Iliad* and the *Odyssey*, which firmly established the form and style of the epic poem. Scholars are divided on the question of whether both poems were the work of the same man, Homer, or that of multiple people. Either way, they continued to be part of an oral tradition and were not committed to writing until much later.

Epics are lengthy (the *Iliad* stretches to almost 16,000 lines, the *Odyssey* to more than 12,000), and were originally intended to be recited from memory. To aid recitation, they were composed in a regular meter, dactylic hexameter, and certain phrases and ideas were repeated, making the work easier to memorize. Both epics were in what is now known as Homeric Greek—a blend of Ionic Greek and

Penelope weaves as she waits for Odysseus to return

Odysseus, disguised as a beggar, arrives back in Ithaca after his arduous journey

Odysseus and Penelope are finally reunited

elements from several regional dialects and periods, indicating the influence of the different sources of the work. Both this hybrid dialect and the meter became recognized features of Greek literature. The stories themselves would have been well known throughout Greece when the epics were composed, as would the legendary heroes and mythological gods.

Enduring tales

Rather than giving a simple historical account of the Trojan War, the *Iliad* describes a 51-day period in the final year of the decade-long conflict. Themes of rage, pride, glory, and fate are explored against a backdrop of war between Greece and Troy, each side aided by different gods, who are shown to have their own conflicts. The *Odyssey* tells of Odysseus's tortuous return to Ithaca after the fall of Troy. On the way, he faces temptations and threats from the gods, in the form of Poseidon, Calypso, the Sirens, and the one-eyed Cyclops Polyphemus. Details of the Trojan War are told in flashbacks, but running through the tale is the theme of *nostos*—the hero's longing to return home to be with his wife, Penelope.

The *Iliad* and *Odyssey* were not the only examples of epic literature to have been composed in the Greek "Dark Age." A collection of poems known as the Epic Cycle has also survived, as well as other works that were at one time ascribed to Homer. Whatever the truth of their composition, the *Iliad* and *Odyssey* ascribed to Homer, transcribed and copied multiple times since their composition, have consistently been regarded as classics of storytelling and cornerstones of Western literature.

△ **A lasting legacy**
Long after the 8th century BCE, the epics were preserved for posterity in manuscripts on papyrus, such as this 1st-century BCE fragment from a copy of the *Odyssey*.

THE JOURNEY OF ODYSSEUS

Throughout the ages, scholars have tried to identify the places mentioned in the *Odyssey*, and to trace Odysseus's journey around the Mediterranean, from Troy to Ithaca via North Africa, Iberia, Sicily, and Italy. The map shown here was created by Flemish cartographer Abraham Ortelius in 1597, and is the first known attempt to show the route he might have taken.

The Polis

The characteristic Greek city-state

After the fall of the Mycenaean civilization, Greece emerged not as a single unified nation, but rather as a collection of independent urban settlements, known as *poleis*, scattered around the Eastern Mediterranean.

Urbanization began in Greece during the Early Iron Age (c. 1100–750 BCE), when numerous settlements began forming around fortified strongholds across the Greek-speaking world. Because of the difficult terrain of the region, these were isolated towns and villages, often in remote areas, or on islands, and were populated by a particular kinship group.

Over the centuries, more than 1,000 of these settlements emerged, varying in size and importance from small towns to major cities such as Corinth and

Thebes. By the beginning of the Archaic period at the end of the 8th century BCE, such settlements, known as *poleis* (sing. *polis*) had become the model for Greek urban development. Some, notably Athens and Sparta, grew into major political powers, with jurisdiction over large populations and areas.

The different *poleis* shared many similarities. At the center of the *polis* was often a walled citadel, the acropolis, built on top of a hill. Around this were both residential areas and public spaces, such as the

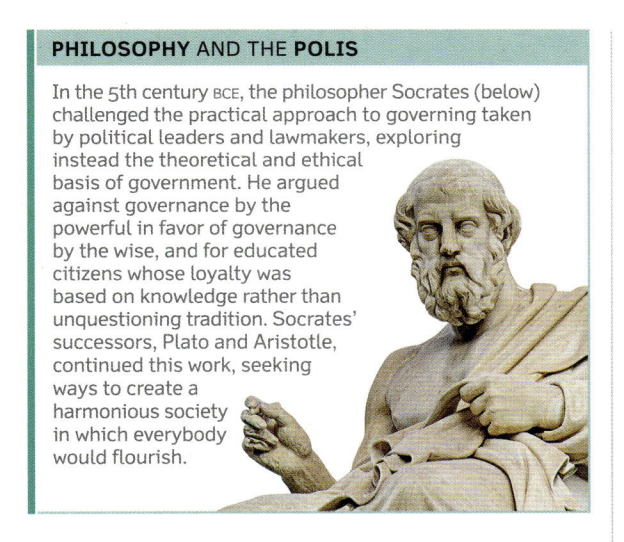

PHILOSOPHY AND THE POLIS

In the 5th century BCE, the philosopher Socrates (below) challenged the practical approach to governing taken by political leaders and lawmakers, exploring instead the theoretical and ethical basis of government. He argued against governance by the powerful in favor of governance by the wise, and for educated citizens whose loyalty was based on knowledge rather than unquestioning tradition. Socrates' successors, Plato and Aristotle, continued this work, seeking ways to create a harmonious society in which everybody would flourish.

agora (the marketplace and central city square), the gymnasia, temples, and theaters. Beyond lay the surrounding countryside, the *chora*, with agricultural land to provide food for the *polis*. Taken as a whole, the *polis* functioned as an autonomous state (the word *polis* is widely translated as "city-state"). Its political, judicial, and legal institutions were its own and it could act as an independent state in international trade and affairs.

Identity in the city-state

Whether the *polis* was governed by a king, a tyrant, oligarchs, or democratically elected leaders, the majority of its inhabitants did not enjoy citizenship: this was reserved for men, and sometimes restricted to those with a certain level of wealth. However, citizens and noncitizens—women, enslaved people, the poorest of men, and resident foreigners—alike would have mingled in the agora, which served as a marketplace and a communal meeting space. The city center also played host to festivals throughout the year that were dedicated to the city's patron gods or celebrated significant dates in the city's calendar. These, along with sporting events and even wars with neighboring *poleis*, helped cement the distinct identity of each city-state.

Ancient powerhouses

Inevitably, certain cities emerged from the rivalry between *poleis* as more powerful than others. Sparta and Athens were already developing as major powers in the Archaic period, and secured their status in the Classical period. Even more powerful, however, was the Macedonian monarchy. Its acquisition of territory across Greece in the 4th century BCE precipitated a decline in the independence of individual *poleis*, while ensuring that the institution of the *polis* as a model for urban society, if not its autonomous status, was adopted throughout West Asia and beyond in the Hellenistic period.

"Man is by **nature** an **animal** of the **polis**."

ARISTOTLE, *POLITICS*

△ **Athenian owl**
Silver tetradrachms like the one shown above were known as Athenian owls and minted for 400 years from the 6th century BCE. The owl was a symbol of Athena, patron goddess of Athens, and of the city-state.

◁ **Key city-states**
This map shows the important city-states founded from before 800 BCE to the end of the 7th century BCE.

Argos

A thriving Peloponnesian city

The coastal plain of Argolis has been inhabited since prehistoric times, and is home to one of the first and most enduring urban settlements in Greece—its historic capital city, Argos.

△ **Devoted sons**
These *kouroi*, or statues of young male figures, were found at Delphi and made around 580 BCE by the Greek sculptor Polymedes of Argos. They represent Cleobis and Biton, the sons of a priestess of Hera (see right).

Today, Argos is a medium-size agricultural center sheltering in the shadow of the castle-topped Larissa, the site of ancient Argos's acropolis. There is evidence that the Argolis region in which Argos is situated, in the northeastern corner of Greece's Peloponnese peninsula, may be the oldest settled urban area of Greece, possibly of all of Europe. Excavations show it was continuously occupied from Neolithic times, around 7,000 years ago.

Argolis rose to prominence in the 2nd millennium BCE as the site of the city of Mycenae, just north of present-day Argos, which was to give its name to the Bronze Age realm of Homer's legendary king Agamemnon in the *Iliad* (see pp.60–61). Yet Argos itself was also an important part of that realm, accorded its own king, Diomedes, in Homer's list

of the allies that accompanied Agamemnon to Troy. In legend, the city's origins hark back to the "all-seeing" Giant Argos Panoptes, who was given multiple eyes by the goddess Hera, wife of Zeus, which enabled him to be constantly on guard for potential intruders. As a result, Hera was always sacred to the city. The shrine raised in her honor, the Heraion, stood on the slopes of a hill some 5 miles (8 km) outside Argos's walls and served other cities of the Argolis region, such as Mycenae and Tiryns. Work on the site is thought to have started as early as the 8th century BCE. The early 7th-century temple burned down in 423 BCE, reportedly when a priestess fell asleep after leaving an oil-fueled lamp too close to inflammable wreaths, but a new temple was built soon after. It remained in use until the spread of Christianity caused all pagan places of worship to be shut down.

In its heyday, the temple was the destination for an annual procession from the city of Argos in honor of Hera. Herodotus tells the story of a priestess of Hera whose sons, Cleobis and Biton, agreed to pull the cart in which she was taking offerings all the way from the city when the oxen that would normally have drawn it could not be found. The mother asked Hera to reward them for their efforts, and the goddess did so by casting them into a peaceful sleep from which they never awoke—for that, the moral had it, was the greatest blessing that could befall humankind.

Changing fortunes

Meanwhile, the town itself was thriving. It rose to prominence under a 7th-century BCE ruler named Pheidon, who used hoplite phalanxes (see p.68)—possibly his own invention—to defeat the armies of Sparta and establish Argos's predominance in the Peloponnese. According to Herodotus, he also brought in a uniform system of weights and measures.

Over the ensuing centuries, the city's fortunes waxed and waned. Its military importance diminished as Sparta regained supremacy, decisively defeating its

▽ **The citadel at Argos**
The ruins of the Byzantine castle at Larissa, the Acropolis of Argos, command a spectacular position, overlooking lush valleys, imposing mountains, and the modern town of Argos.

"Argos, in those days the most important place in the land called Hellas."

HERODOTUS, *HISTORIES*

△ **Hera's sanctuary**
This early 20th-century watercolor by American architect Edward Lippincott Tilton imagines how Argos's Heraion may have looked in antiquity.

former conqueror at Sepeia in 494 BCE in what was said to be the bloodiest battle of the Classical era. Thereafter, Argos's people embraced a democratic system of government, and so many citizens had been lost in the battle that marriage to citizen-class women and tenure of important administrative functions was opened up to men previously not of citizen status.

Endurance and decline

The city played a relatively passive role in subsequent military campaigns, including the Persian and Peloponnesian wars (c. 499–449 BCE and 431–404 BCE). Argos escaped occupation by Macedonia under Philip II and Alexander the Great, who chose to trace their lineage back to Temenos, a legendary early king of Argos, and called their line the Argead Dynasty.

Through it all, the city continued to flourish both economically and culturally—according to Herodotus, 5th-century BCE Argives were Greece's finest musicians. In later centuries, Argos suffered the fate of the rest of Greece, falling first to the Romans, before becoming part of the Byzantine Empire. In the 12th century CE, the Byzantines built a castle at Larissa. Today, the ruins of the castle dominate the conurbation below, bearing witness to the myth-strewn centuries that continue to cast their shadow over the Argolis region.

PHORONEUS: PRIMORDIAL KING OF ARGOS

Another version of the Argos foundation story (see opposite) traces the city's history back to a legendary culture hero called Phoroneus, shown here (center) in a 14th-century CE relief made for Florence Cathedral. Phoroneus was born of the union of a nymph and a river god. In his *Description of Greece*, the 2nd-century CE geographer Pausanias gave Phoroneus a pivotal role as the pioneer who first brought people together to live in cities. His importance for Argos lay in the belief that he put the city under the protection of the goddess Hera, and that he introduced the use of fire and the blacksmith's forge, which was claimed to have first been used in the city.

"With **horses** and **chariots** let us draw near and **mourn** Patroclus."

HOMER'S *ILIAD*

Geometric Grave Marker

A monumental funerary vase

Standing more than 3 ft (1 m) tall, this huge vessel was found in Attica and served as a grave marker. It dates to the late Geometric period, around 750–735 BCE, when monumental grave markers were first introduced. Such vases were used until carved stone markers were introduced in the Archaic period. The vase shape is that of a krater. Men's graves were marked with kraters; women's graves were marked with amphorae, long-necked vessels with handles on the belly. Kraters were designed to be mixing bowls for water and wine, but this one is far too large for practical use. The potter also made a hole in the base before it was fired. Perhaps this allowed people to make libations that would sink into the ground as an offering to the dead.

Technique and style

Throwing such a large vase on a pottery wheel would have been a great technical achievement. Only the richest clients would have been able to afford to pay for both its manufacture and its elaborate decoration.

In the early Geometric period, Greek vases were decorated with abstract patterns and repeated motifs. This vase's decoration reflects the late Geometric interest in figural representation and increasingly varied non-figural motifs. The vase's decoration is divided into horizontal strips of different heights. Some are filled with solid paint, some with abstract decoration, and those around the belly of the vase with scenes. These scenes are flat and do not use perspective. The painter shows everything at once, including all 12 legs and three heads of each team of horses pulling the chariots. The treatment of faces is interesting too—each one is depicted side on with a single dot for an eye.

A story of grief and glory

In the center of the upper scene, the deceased lies on a funeral bier. Above him, the checkered panel represents his shroud. The seated figure to the left is probably a close relative, perhaps his wife. She has a child on her lap and her feet on a footstool. The smaller figures at the foot of the bier might also be children. The people standing on either side hold their hands to their heads in a gesture of mourning.

The lower scene shows a procession of chariots and men carrying shields from a much earlier period, perhaps indicating the deceased was a warrior. It may be a reference to the heroic age of Greek myth, as it brings to mind Homer's description of the funeral games held for Patroclus (see p.207). Whoever the deceased was, he was clearly a man of wealth and distinction.

▽ **Terra-cotta krater back**
On the krater's reverse, the scene of mourning in the upper panel is replaced with a band of geometrical patterns, including swastikas and concentric circles, which fill all the space.

A running meander decorates the rim of the pot

The dead man is laid out on a funerary bier

Deer are among several creatures in the decoration

All the space around figures is filled with small patterns, adding a sense of energy

▽ **Terra-cotta krater side**
The chariot procession continues in an unbroken ring around the pot while the funeral procession comes to an abrupt halt at the handles.

hourglass shields evoke an earlier, heroic age

Two-wheeled chariots are shown with the wheels side by side

▷ **Terra-cotta krater front**
The deceased's bier takes center stage on the front of the vase, and all the figures in the upper scene point toward it. The figures in the lower scene move in procession to the right.

A tall stand adds to the impressive height

Greek Warfare

From phratries to the hoplite phalanx

Over the centuries, the Homeric tradition of aristocratic champions leading their followers gave way to a more democratic style of fighting, with citizen-soldiers confronting the enemy in tightly organized phalanx formations.

Warfare was endemic in the Greek world. City-states vied for land and enslaved people, or at least subject populations. They were so conflict-prone that Sparta, one of the most successful of all contenders, based its constitution and lifestyle on breeding and training soldiers.

At some point between Mycenaean and Classical times, probably in the 8th or 7th centuries BCE, the nature of war changed. The *Iliad* (see pp.60–61) depicts the Trojan War as a conflict in which individual heroes could alter the course of a battle by their courage and fighting skills. The epic enshrined folk memories of a Bronze Age world in which only wealthy aristocrats could afford the full panoply of available armor and weaponry. These warriors were supported in the field by phratries, groups of followers made up of family relations and dependents.

The hoplite revolution

By the Classical Age (500–323 BCE), Greece's armies were made up of hoplites—citizen-soldiers drawn from the ranks of small landowners and artisans, who used their own military equipment. The name came from *ta hopla*, a general term for their gear, which was based around a circular shield with an elbow grip in the center of the inner face and a hand grip on one side. Hoplites also wore body armor covering the chest and legs, and a helmet, sometimes with a plume. The principal weapon was a long, metal-tipped thrusting spear; most hoplites also bore a short sword for hand-to-hand fighting. The full hoplite gear could

◁ **Archaic helmet**
This 8th-century BCE crested bronze helmet, found in a grave in Argos, has a backpiece and cheekpieces to protect the head from lethal sword strokes.

weigh up to 78 lb (35 kg). But mobility was not an issue because their chosen battle formation was the phalanx, an unbroken line of soldiers who fought shoulder to shoulder, often eight or ten ranks deep. This mode of combat proved its worth in 490 BCE at the Battle of Marathon (see pp.144–145), when Athens's hoplites defeated the less organized but larger Persian army, killing 6,000 of the invaders. However, the need to remain war-ready put a strain on citizens, who were at times expected to remain in reserve up to the age of 60. By the late 5th century BCE, the homegrown volunteer forces were increasingly supplemented with mercenaries. Lighter-armed fighters, who were known as peltasts and typically wore no armor and bore lighter shields and spears, also had a growing role as skirmishers and in protecting the flanks of the phalanxes. Sieges also became a feature of military campaigns, thanks to the development of powerful catapults and siege towers.

In its heyday, though, the hoplite revolution did much to transform Greek society. The organization and social commitment it demanded of ordinary, middle-class citizens helped stimulate a sense of community and civic responsibility. And that, in turn, increased the demand for a political say in the affairs of the city-state, encouraging the spread of democracy.

An aulos player accompanies the hoplites into battle

Inscription reads: "Theodoros dedicated (me) to (Zeus) the king"

◁ **Olympia spear**
Unearthed in Olympia, in the Peloponnese, this spearhead, inscribed on both sides, dates from around 500 BCE.

A plumed helmet made warriors look tall and more intimidating

The thrusting spear with a metal tip is held overhead

Shield designs varied greatly, ranging from animals (as here) and faces to more abstract patterns

The shield is attached to the left forearm, leaving the right arm free for combat

A dense wall of shields affords maximum protection

△ **Hoplites at war**

Hoplite phalanxes face each other in this detail from the so-called Chigi vase from the 7th century BCE. It is thought to be the first ever depiction of the new Greek form of armed combat and organization.

Creatures of Myth

Fable and folklore in ancient Greece

The thought-world of the Greeks was inhabited by a myriad of fantastical, and often fearsome, creatures that roamed the woods, mountains, seas, and rivers of Greece and beyond. These beings appeared in the writings of Homer and Herodotus, among many other authors, entering the canon of Greek myth.

△ **Nereid**
Dating from the 3rd century BCE, this gilded silver jewelery box shows a Nereid riding a sea monster. The Nereids were the 50 sea-nymph daughters of Nereus, known by Homer as the "Old Man of the Sea."

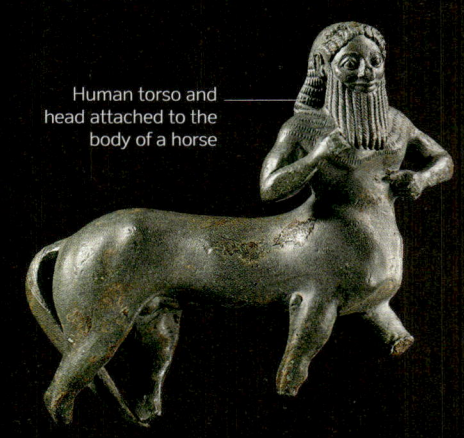

Human torso and head attached to the body of a horse

△ **Centaur**
This cast-bronze statue of a centaur was made c. 530 BCE. The *kentauroi* (centaurs) lived in Thessaly and were the wild children of the cloud nymph Nephele.

Medusa's grimace, complete with boars' tusks

△ **Medusa**
Dating from c. 480 BCE, this sculpture shows Medusa, one of the three Gorgons, with serpentine hair and lolling tongue.

Eagle's wings attached to the body of a lion

A single eye, the identifying feature of a Cyclops

△ **Scylla**
The sea monster Scylla, who terrorized seafarers, is shown in this 3rd-century BCE flask from Canosa, Italy.

◁ **Polyphemus**
This marble head from c. 150 BCE is of the Cyclops Polyphemus, the one-eyed shepherd who captures Odysseus in Homer's *Odyssey*.

△ **Sphinx**
This gold earring from around the 4th century BCE depicts the Sphinx, a monster that plagued Thebes, killing those who failed to solve the riddles she set.

◁ **Satyr**
Carrying a torch and a full wineskin, the satyr in this bronze statue from the 3rd–2nd centuries BCE is depicted on his way to take part in a Dionysian revel.

Bull's head atop
a man's body

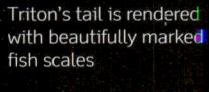

Triton's tail is rendered
with beautifully marked
fish scales

The Siren has the body
of a bird here possibly
a waterfowl

△ Minotaur

Born to the Minoan king Minos's wife, Pasiphaë,
and the Cretan Bull, the Minotaur—shown here
in a statue from 450 BCE—was imprisoned in
Minos's Labyrinth until Theseus killed it.

△ Triton

In the center of this 6th-century BCE Attic
black-figure kylix, the hero Heracles is shown
fighting Triton, the merman son of Poseidon
and the sea nymph Amphitrite.

△ Siren

The lustrous color in this 6th-century BCE
faience alabastron (oil flask) in the shape of
a Siren, a sea nymph whose song lured sailors
to their deaths, comes from crushed quartz.

Descriptions vary, but the hind parts of
the Chimera were said to be those
of a snake or a dragon

A goat's head
rises from the
Chimera's back

▷ Griffin

This cast-bronze ornament from
625–575 BCE shows a griffin, a half-eagle,
half-lion creature—a group of which was
said by Herodotus to guard the gold in
Scythia, north of the Black Sea.

◁ Chimera

A bizarre multi-part creature known as
the Chimera, shown here in an Etruscan
bronze from 400–350 BCE, terrorized Lycia
(in Anatolia) until the Greek hero
Bellerophon defeated it.

The Chimera's stance suggests it
is contorted in pain; a hole in the
beast's left flank may show where
a spear once pierced the statue

Governing Greece

Kings, oligarchs, tyrants, and democrats

The Greek city-states experimented with an array of different constitutional systems, from rule by a supreme king or a tyrant to participatory democracy involving thousands of citizens.

△ **Birth of democracy**
This marble stele, c. 337 BCE, shows a standing figure, representing democracy, placing a crown on the head of a seated man embodying the people of Athens.

In Mycenaean times, Greece was ruled by local dynasties of kings ensconced in heavily guarded fortress-palaces. These power centers broke up in the "Dark Age" (c. 1200–800 BCE) that followed, and much of the country seemingly reverted to life at the village level.

Gradually, though, the villages coalesced into larger units. When stability returned in the 9th century BCE, a world of competing city-states emerged, divided politically but linked by culture, religion, and language. Within these entities, different political systems developed. Looking back on this period, later sources spoke of individual kings initially exercising power in the manner, if not on the scale, of the Mycenaean rulers.

As time passed, their authority was challenged, and in many places kingship gave way to oligarchic rule exercised by the heads of aristocratic clans. Birth became a key factor in other respects as well, because the original kin groups cemented their position by establishing a hereditary right of citizenship that excluded later arrivals—only those born in the *polis* qualified for full civil rights—all women, foreign-born residents, and the vast enslaved underclass.

◁ **Corinthian coin**
Pegasus, tamed by Corinth's legendary founder Bellerophon, is shown on this coin from 700–300 BCE from the city-state, which was among the first to overthrow its hereditary king.

Sparta in the Peloponnese came to represent an extreme form of this exclusivity. The Lycurgan reforms (see pp.74–75) created a military oligarchy of soldier-citizens. From the age of 7 up to 60, their lives were tightly controlled by the state, which held uneasy sway over a vast, potentially rebellious underclass of enslaved subjects drawn from nearby city-states that had been defeated in battle.

Tyranny and democracy

In other city-states, conflicts among the ruling elite or popular unrest enabled ambitious individuals to seize power. These were the "tyrants," a term used at that time to denote absolute rulers with no hereditary claim to power. During their heyday in the early 6th century BCE, some proved to be successful rulers. For example, Cleisthenes of Sicyon led his city-state to victory in wars against its neighbors, while the historian Herodotus described how Polycrates, tyrant of the island of Samos, created a naval force that for a time enabled him to build a small Aegean empire.

Yet ancient Greece's greatest contribution to future constitutional history lay in forging a path to participatory democracy—and here Athens led the way. It too had experienced hereditary kingship and oligarchic rule, followed in the 6th century BCE by four decades of tyranny under the autocrat Pisistratus and his sons. But in the late 5th century BCE, the city-state opted for a radically different system based on consulting the popular will. Although participation was still limited to free male citizens, the reforms (see pp.116–117) served in later ages as a beacon for lawmakers eager to pass power to the people.

DEATH OF **A TYRANT**

After ruling the island of Samos for two decades, the tyrant Polycrates (shown dressed in red) came to a grisly end. Legend has it that his ally, the Egyptian pharaoh Amasis, cautioned him to counterbalance excessive good fortune by throwing away his most treasured possession. However, the ring Polycrates duly tossed into the sea came back to him in the belly of a fish, although the artist in this 15th-century French manuscript confused the French word *annel* (ring) for *agnel* (lamb). Despite this omen, Polycrates accepted an invitation from the Persian satrap of nearby Sardis, who offered large sums of money in return for any protection he might need. It proved a fatal mistake. Polycrates was murdered on arrival in Sardis and his body hung up (shown right).

△ **Supreme ruler**
This painting on a Greek vase depicts a scene from
the *Iliad* and shows a petitioner, Chryses, kneeling
before King Agamemnon, who had the ultimate
power to deny or grant the favors asked of him.

Chryses falls on his knees
to beg for the release of his
daughter, taken as a war prize

Agamemnon, representing
monarchical authority, will
turn down Chryses' request

Lycurgus

Sparta's legendary lawmaker

Ancient writers credited the peculiarities of Sparta's constitution to the work of Lycurgus, a figure said to have lived any time between the 10th and 6th centuries BCE and whose existence scholars still argue over today.

The first mention of Lycurgus is from Herodotus's *Histories*, written in the 5th century BCE. Herodotus tells how Sparta's people were once the worst-governed in Greece, and how it only became an authoritarian and tightly regulated state thanks to the intervention of Lycurgus, "a distinguished Spartan," who had sought advice from Delphi's oracle (see p.154). Whether from the advice he received there or by following the example of Minoan Crete, Lycurgus is said to have transformed the situation while serving as regent and guardian for Sparta's infant king, his nephew Charilaus. Herodotus maintained that "as soon as he received this appointment he made fundamental changes in the laws, and took good care that the new ones should not be broken."

Sparta's reformation

According to the historian Plutarch, among Lycurgus's greatest reforms was the establishment of the *gerousia*, a council of 28 elders aged 60 or over set up to assist Sparta's rulers and to decide when public votes should be taken on matters of importance. Lycurgus was also said to have divided the nation's land into 30,000 equal-size plots, each assigned to full citizens and to be worked by helots enslaved at Messenia. Finally, he

◁ **Lycurgus mirror**
This Etruscan bronze mirror featuring Lycurgus (*right*) demonstrates the lawmaker's influence beyond Greece.

banned gold and silver coins, instituted communal eating and a simple diet, and outlawed unnecessary art. With these changes, Plutarch says, Lycurgus hoped to "expel from the state arrogance and envy, luxury and crime." Lycurgus refused to let his laws be written down, instead believing the Spartans should embody the discipline that underlay his constitution.

Whether or not Lycurgus ever actually existed, his name became indissolubly associated with the Spartan regime of strict equality among full citizens, rigid separation of the sexes, and continuous military training (see p.108). The constitution attributed to him, known as the Great Rhetra, remained influential throughout Greece's heyday and into Roman times.

△ **Head of Lycurgus**
Dating from the 2nd–1st centuries BCE, this bronze coin from Laconia with a portrait of Lycurgus illustrates his continuing importance in Spartan society.

> "**Training** is more **effective** than **nature** for **good**."

ATTRIBUTED TO LYCURGUS BY PLUTARCH, *SPARTAN SAYINGS*

c. **1000–900** BCE Date of Lycurgus's reforms according to Xenophon

743–724 BCE Sparta enslaves the helots in the First Messenian War

c. **440** BCE First written record of Lycurgus's life, in Herodotus's *Histories*

c. **100** CE Plutarch includes a biography of Lycurgus in *Parallel Lives*

c. **900–800** BCE Date of reforms preferred by later Classical historians

c. **675** BCE Lycurgus's reforms according to modern historians

c. **380** BCE Xenophon records Lycurgus's reforms in *Polity of the Lacedaemonians*

1949 Lycurgus is honored as one of 23 forefathers of the US Constitution

△ **The city of Cyrene**
Shown here are the remains of the Temple of Zeus in the Greek colony of Cyrene, in Libya. Herodotus relates that a group from Thera founded the colony in 631 BCE, with Battus I as king.

Greek Colonization

Expanding Greece's influence

Driven by political strife, overpopulation, and trade, the Greeks established settlements across the Mediterranean and around the Black Sea that brought both cooperation and conflict with the local populations.

Already part of a large trading network created by Minoa and Mycenae, the Greeks began establishing hundreds of settlements around the Mediterranean in the 8th century BCE. By the 6th century BCE, the coastline from Iberia to Asia Minor and North Africa was dotted with emporia (manufacturing and trading settlements) and *poleis*. Settlers had also established themselves around the Black Sea, including at Olbia, in what is now Ukraine.

The Greeks were impelled by many different motives, from political upheavals to the search for valuable commodities that could not be found at home. But a key driver was undoubtedly the limited resources available in many of the coastal and island city-states, which struggled to feed their people as their populations grew. As a result, some Greeks were forced out of their homeland. Famine, for example, caused the rulers of Chalcis to send one tenth of its population in search of a new home; they found it at Rhegium in southern Italy in around 743 BCE. Yet these Greek outposts were also founded for more positive reasons, with a view to expanding economic opportunities and trading links. In such cases, city fathers would choose an *oikistes*—an individual to lead the planned enterprise. If the settlement prospered, the *oikistes* would be venerated as the colony's founder.

The first settlements were implanted close to Greece, on the Aegean islands and the coast of Asia Minor, where Greek-speaking communities had already flourished in Minoan and Mycenaean times. The Ionian city-states (see pp.80–81) of Asia Minor, notably Miletus, themselves became active founders of colonies. Greek enclaves spread south down the eastern Mediterranean coastline and to Egypt. There, according to Herodotus, Greeks driven onto the coast by storms at sea were taken into service by the pharaoh and given land in the Nile Valley. They subsequently provided mercenaries for Egypt's armies and were rewarded with the trading port of Naucratis.

Local relations

We have only snippets of written evidence from the early centuries of settlement for the relations between the Greeks and the local populations in the places they settled in. For example, a fragment composed in the 7th century BCE by the poet Callinus suggests that there was conflict between the citizens of the Greek colony of Ephesus and the Cimmerians—a nomadic people in Asia Minor. Archaeology has provided a

◁ **Iberian bust**
This 1st-century CE bronze was made in Emporion, a Greek colony founded c.575 BCE (now in Catalonia, Spain).

little more evidence, with pottery shards found at the sites of the Greek colonies giving some indication of whether the Greeks settled in an uninhabited or inhabited place. Finds from Larissa in Asia Minor, for example, show that the site was occupied from the early Iron Age by the Anatolian, who had contact with the Greeks in the 8th century BCE. The Greeks drove them out around 700 BCE.

In some places, it seems relations between Greeks and local peoples were close; indeed, the Ionians and Carians—the ancient inhabitants of southwest Anatolia—intermarried. Colonies that relied on trade could succeed only if Greeks and locals cooperated. The evidence of cultural exchange suggests too that the Greeks and the local populations were mutually interested in each other. The Lydian king Gyges sent offerings to the Sanctuary of Apollo at Delphi, while the Greeks seem to have adopted the Anatolian mother-goddess, Cybele, associated with nature and fertility. The concept of the city-state became embedded in Asia Minor, while coinage made its way from there to Greece.

OLBIA

One of the main emporia on the Black Sea coast, Olbia was founded in the 7th century BCE at the mouth of the Bug River in modern-day Ukraine. From its docks, fish and locally grown grains were sent back to Miletus, the mother city on the eastern shores of the Aegean. The settlement was protected from its potentially hostile Scythian neighbors by a defensive wall. By the 5th century BCE, the colony was producing its own coinage, which included distinctive dolphin-shaped coins, and was established enough to be visited by Herodotus.

"Some **traders** became **founders** of **great cities.**"

PLUTARCH, *LIFE OF SOLON*

◁ **North African cat**
Made from marble, this sculpture was found in the Greek colony of Naucratis in Egypt, and dates from 332–30 BCE.

Health and Leisure

The gymnasium and the symposium

With the increase in prosperity that came with the rise of *poleis* (see pp.62–63), Greek society became more settled, and there was greater opportunity for leisure activities, at least for wealthier citizens. The gymnasium and the symposium emerged as focal points for the social lives of men, and soon became major cultural institutions of ancient Greece.

The gymnasium

Originally a facility for young men preparing for military service in the Archaic Age (c. 750–500 BCE), the gymnasium was simply a training ground, with a water supply for bathing, and often groves of trees to provide shade. Physical training was a key part of the education of wealthy Greek males, and the gymnasium was considered an educational institution. Later, it became a center for athletes preparing to compete in games, with facilities such as running tracks and covered areas for wrestling and boxing.

Reverence for the beauty of the healthy young male body had been a feature of Greek culture since the Archaic Age. The athletes trained naked (the word "gymnasium" derives from the Greek *gymnos*, naked) to demonstrate their dedication to this ideal—and to show off their physical superiority to the lower classes.

As well as its educational and cultural importance, the gymnasium became a central feature of the *polis*. It was often built as a courtyard enclosed by colonnades, and included purpose-built baths, and porticoes that served as classrooms.

△ **Naked wrestlers**
During the Archaic Age, the fitness of military trainees was admired for aesthetic reasons as well for the strength it gave them in battle, and sporting activities often featured in Greek art, as in this marble relief of two young men wrestling from c. 610 BCE.

△ **Greek warrior**
This painting of a warrior inside a kylix harks back to the origins of the symposium in the celebratory feasts of fighting men in the Greek "Dark Age". The camaraderie and high spirits of these feasts were ritualized in the symposium, which developed into an essential element of the culture of the city-state.

△ **Mixing wine and water**
Classical Greeks considered that drinking undiluted wine led to unruliness and loss of self-control, hence their custom of watering down their wine in kraters such as this example from 550 BCE, depicting satyrs and maenads.

"So far as **drinking** is concerned, you have my **hearty approval**."

XENOPHON, *SYMPOSIUM*, LINES SPOKEN BY SOCRATES

The symposium

Another social institution that emerged from military roots was the symposium. The warrior banquets of the "Dark Age" (c. 1200–800 BCE) became formalized into civic feasts in the *poleis* and developed into smaller private gatherings. These took the form of a banquet followed by a social gathering (*symposion*) and became a feature of aristocratic male Greek life.

Symposia were held in private homes, in a room known as the andron, which was furnished with low tables and couches on which the participants reclined while drinking wine from a cup called a kylix, enjoying entertainment, and conversing. Proceedings followed a more or less formal ritual: the wine was diluted with water in a mixing jug, the krater, and a libation offered to the gods; the guests then enjoyed an evening of games, music, poetry, and socializing. The gathering was also an opportunity to conduct business or discuss serious topics. By the Classical period (500–323 BCE), it had as much a reputation for intellectual debate as for entertainment: philosophers such as Socrates and Plato often participated.

Both the gymnasium and the symposium evolved far beyond their original functions; their educational and cultural significance grew with the progress of the *poleis* in which they thrived, and they became distinctively Classical Greek institutions. Their legacy persists to the present day in the centers of physical activity known today as gymnasiums, and in the use of the word "symposium" for an academic conference.

△ **Kottabos stand**
A popular game at symposia was *kottabos*, which involved flicking wine lees, or residue, at a target, such as the 3rd-century BCE Etruscan *kottabos* stand shown here.

△ **Female entertainment**
Guests at a symposium were high-born men. Female company (shown above) was provided by *hetairai*, female sex workers, usually enslaved and trained as musicians and entertainers. As such, they were able to join in cultural debates.

△ **The andron**
The andron, a room reserved for the symposium in Greek houses, was designed to promote social interaction. There were cushioned couches around the room that each accommodated a symposiast, with room for a younger man to sit beside him (as above). The number of participants was limited to facilitate group discussion.

△ **The Academy**
Plato established his school of philosophy around 387 BCE at the Academy gymnasium in Athens. This 1st-century BCE Roman mosaic from Pompeii is thought to show Plato (center) holding a class in the colonnade; the students shown may include his protégé Aristotle.

The Ionian League

Greek outposts in Asia

With a history stretching back into Bronze Age times, a dozen Greek communities on Anatolia's Aegean coast planted far-flung colonies across the seas and provided the foundations of Classical philosophy.

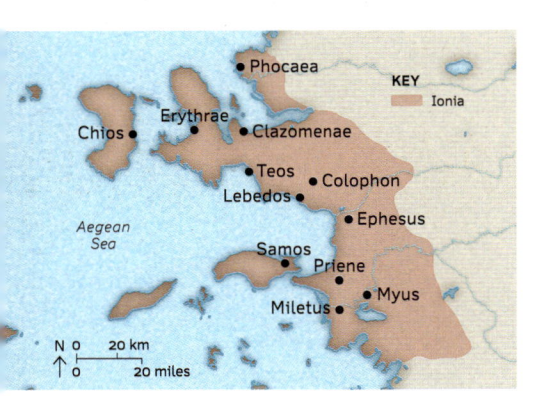

△ **The Ionian League**
This map shows the ten cities and two island city-states that were part of the Ionian League from the 8th century BCE.

The region called Ionia occupied the central part of the Aegean Sea's eastern coastline, in present-day Türkiye. Its fragmented topography, consisting of three main river valleys separated by highlands, favored the growth of independent communities. Around the 8th century BCE, ten Ionian cities—Miletus, Myus, Priene, Ephesus, Colophon, Lebedos, Teos, Erythrae, Clazomenae, and Phocaea—and the island city-states of Samos and Chios joined together to form the Ionian League.

Scholars argue over the prehistory of the region. A growing body of opinion holds that the term "*Ahhiyawa*" gave rise to the term "Ionian." It was used in Hittite texts from what is now central Türkiye as the name of a powerful state to the west, and may have referred to the Achaeans, as the Mycenaean Greeks were known at the time. It seems too that there were Mycenaean outposts on the Asian coast at Miletus and Ephesus as well as on the Ionian islands. If so, settlement must have been disrupted in the lawless years following the fall of Mycenae, when Dorian invaders from northern Greece moved south and the so-called "Sea Peoples," a seafaring confederation, began raiding the coastal towns and cities of the Mediterranean region c. 1276–1178 BCE. Miletus gets only one passing mention in the *Iliad*, when Homer ascribes its foundation to the Carians, the indigenous people of southwest Anatolia, who formed an alliance with Troy.

In the decades of the 11th and 10th centuries BCE, the settlements that would eventually form the Ionian League started to take shape. Migrants may have crossed the sea from Athens, with which Ionia always retained close ties, especially because the Athenians and Ionians shared the same Ionic dialect (see pp.58–59).

The League members were also linked by a festival, the Panionia, dedicated to the sea god Poseidon and held annually on the slopes of Mount Mycale, which is on a peninsula stretching out toward Samos. The festivities included religious ceremonies, athletic competitions, and a general assembly.

By the 7th century BCE, the region—blessed with a fine climate and rich lands in the river valleys—had established widespread trading links with other areas of Greece and the Phoenician ports to the south. Ionian colonies were set up around the Black Sea, and on the Mediterranean coasts of Spain and France,

> "The **Ionians** ... have built their **cities** under the **finest sky** and **climate** of **the world**."
>
> HERODOTUS, *HISTORIES*

ANCIENT **ANATOLIA**

Encompassing modern-day Türkiye, ancient Anatolia was occupied by a rich tapestry of peoples, including the Hittites, the Phrygians, the Lydians, and the Greeks. It served as a crossroads between Europe, Asia, and Africa that fostered trade and cultural exchange but also left it exposed to the depredations of expansionist powers, such as the Persian Achaemenid Empire, the Macedonian ruler Alexander the Great, and the Romans.

ELECTRUM LYDIAN COIN

where Marseille was founded by people from Phocaea around 600 BCE. In the 6th century BCE, Miletus became the birthplace of Greek philosophy and scientific inquiry (see p.96) as Anaximander, Thales, and Anaximenes began developing an empirical approach, using observation to explain the world around them. The tradition continued with Xenophanes of Colophon and Pythagoras of Samos.

Changing fortunes

By the mid-6th century BCE, Ionia's political situation was changing. The mainland cities fell under the control of the inland kingdom of Lydia and its ruler, the legendarily wealthy King Croesus, in 560 BCE. When Lydia in turn fell to the Persian king Cyrus the Great in 547 BCE, the Ionian lands became part of the huge Achaemenid Empire. In 499 BCE, Ionia rose up against its Persian rulers and the Greek tyrants they had installed in its cities. The uprising was put down, but it had huge consequences: to punish Athens for the support it had given the rebels, the Persians invaded Greece (see pp.144–145).

△ **Ancient Samos**
Famed for its sanctuary (shown here) dedicated to its patron goddess Hera, Samos was also renowned for its wine and olive oil, the profits from which made the island wealthy.

Ionia never regained the independent power it had at its height. But in its heyday in the 7th and 6th centuries BCE, Ionia's contribution demonstrated that Greek civilization was never just the product of the land we now call Greece. Later history may have separated the two sides of the Aegean Sea, but in the Archaic and Classical periods, they were intertwined.

▽ **Artemis's temple**
This model of what Ephesus's second Temple of Artemis may have looked like shows the prestige of the Ionian city. Built around 560 BCE, it was one of the largest Greek temples ever constructed.

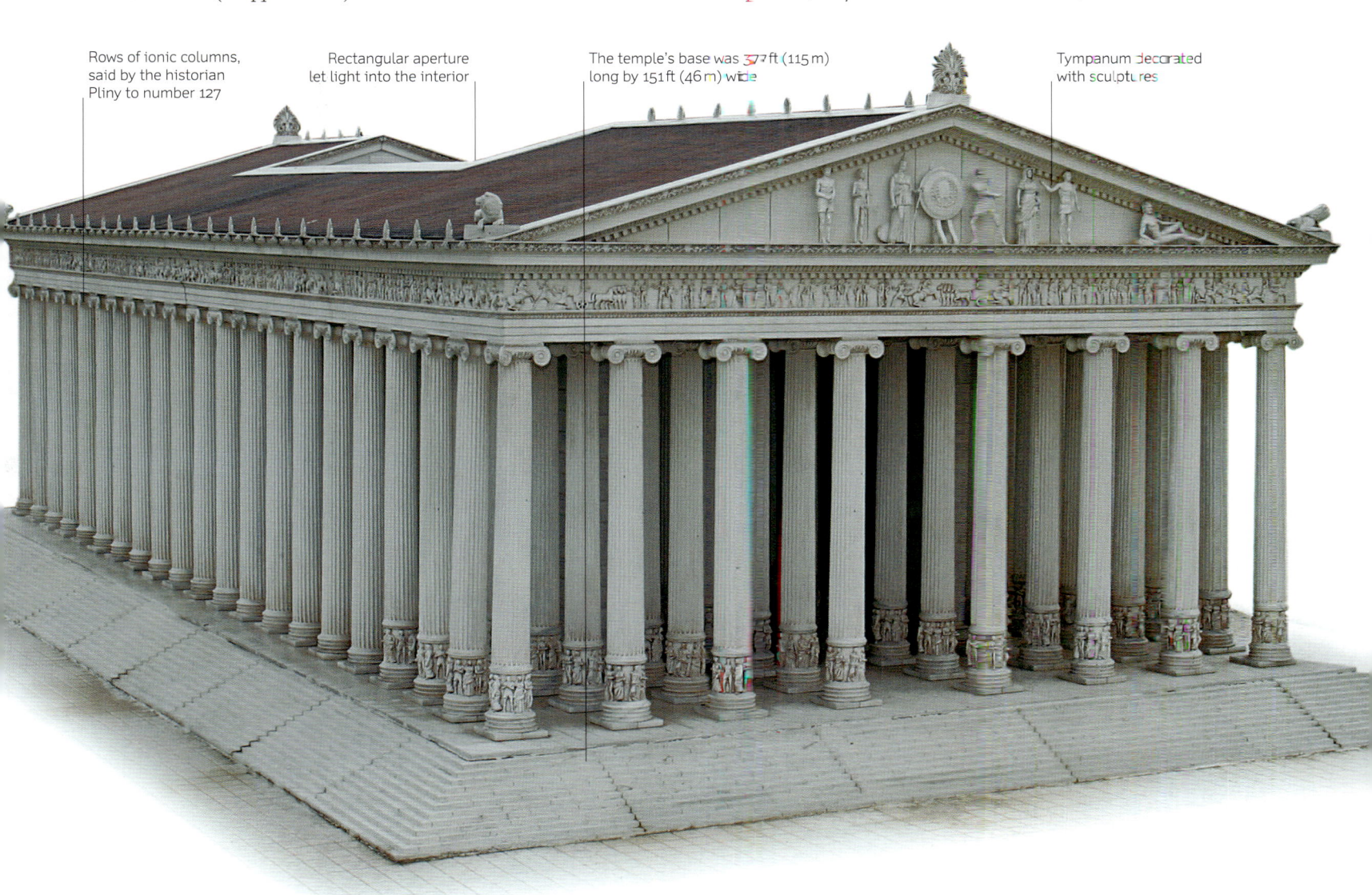

Rows of ionic columns, said by the historian Pliny to number 127

Rectangular aperture let light into the interior

The temple's base was 377 ft (115 m) long by 151 ft (46 m) wide

Tympanum decorated with sculptures

Ancient Miletus

The principal port of ancient Ionia

Situated on the coast of present-day Anatolia, Miletus was the major trading city of Greek Asia Minor during the Archaic period, and became famous as the birthplace of the Greek philosophical tradition.

△ **Ionian pottery**
Decorated with black-figure paintings of sphinxes, waterbirds, dogs, and herds of deer and wild goats, this pitcher was made in Miletus in c. 625 BCE in the "Wild Goat" style popular at the time in Asia Minor.

According to myth, the city of Miletus, in what is now southwest Türkiye, was founded by Miletus, son of Apollo and the nymph Aria, who was exiled from Crete by King Minos. Indeed, Minoans seem to have settled there in about 2000 BCE. Some 500 years later, it became an important outpost of the Mycenaean civilization. The Mycenaeans successfully held the city against the forces of the Hittite Empire, but sometime in the 12th century BCE it was destroyed when it fell to the so-called Sea Peoples (see pp.80–81). Miletus was abandoned until Ionian Greeks began to colonize the region in the period from 1200 to 800 BCE, building a city that became a great intellectual center.

Changing fortunes
Miletus once more became a busy and wealthy trading port, and was one of the 12 Ionian city-states that formed the Ionian League in the 8th century BCE, maintaining the Greek presence on the coast of Asia Minor. Ionia's neighbor, the Lydian Empire, was a particular threat to the city, especially during the reigns of Sadyattes (died c. 610 BCE) and Alyattes (r. c. 610–560 BCE), his son. Their forces raided Miletus for 12 years, until the Milesian tyrant Thrasybulus negotiated an alliance with the Lydians, restoring peace and prosperity to the city. Culture and trade flourished and during the 6th century BCE, the city was home to the thinkers Thales (see pp.96–97), Anaximander, and Anaximenes, fathers of the Greek philosophical and scientific tradition.

Toward the end of the 6th century BCE, however, the city faced a new threat. Lydia had been defeated by the Persians, and Miletus soon came under Persian rule. Aristagoras, who was tyrant of Miletus, led the uprising against the Persians in 499 BCE that escalated into the Ionian Revolt (see pp.142–143), which in turn sparked the wider Greco-Persian Wars. Darius I ("the Great") of Persia retaliated, storming Miletus and violently putting down the rebellion, but was eventually forced to relinquish control when Greek

> "Miletus, son of **Apollo** by **Aria** … landed in Caria and there **founded** a city which he called **Miletus**."

PSEUDO-APOLLODORUS, *LIBRARY*

◁ **Greco-Roman amphitheater**
The theater at Miletus was built by the Roman emperor Trajan (98–117 CE) on top of an earlier Hellenistic theater; it could hold 15,000 people.

forces claimed a decisive victory over the Persian Empire (see p.145). Freed from Persian control, Miletus sought new allies, joining Athens and others in the Delian League (see pp.158–159).

Miletus rises again

Weakened by conflict, Miletus struggled to return to its former glory, but in the latter part of the 5th century BCE it began a process of restoration, rebuilding the city on an innovative grid plan devised by the architect Hippodamus, and establishing colonies across Anatolia and around the Black Sea. Ionia was for a time ceded to the Persian Achaemenid Empire in the following century, but was retaken by Alexander the Great when Macedonian forces laid siege to Miletus in 334 BCE, marking the beginning of his conquest of Asia Minor (see pp.226–227).

Under Macedonian rule, Miletus grew in size and stature, becoming a major port of the Eastern Mediterranean once again. After

Alexander's death in 323 BCE, Miletus was granted autonomy by his successors, but it then came under the aegis of the Seleucids (see pp.246–247) followed by the Ptolemaic dynasty (see pp.238–239), and finally became part of the Roman province of Asia.

Because of its strategic position on the Aegean Sea, and at the European end of the trade routes into Asia, Miletus was especially valued by the Romans. The emperors Augustus and Trajan in particular invested in maintaining the city's status, building on the already well-established infrastructure. Many of its finest structures, such as the magnificent Greco-Roman theater, date from this Roman period of its history.

△ **The Sacred Way**
The Ionic stoa (a roofed colonnade) on the eastern side of the Sacred Way, which led from Miletus to the sanctuary of Didyma, was built around 50 CE.

▷ **Lion guardian**
This 6th-century BCE marble lion, one of a pair that guarded the entrance to Miletus's necropolis at Kazartepe, reflects Egyptian influence on Ionian art.

Ancient Delphi
Nineteenth-century French architect Albert Tournaire's interpretation of how the sanctuary at Delphi may have looked in antiquity captures the scale and beauty of the place, which was the religious center of the ancient Greek world—the omphalos. The site was dominated by the Temple of Apollo, home to the Pythia (Delphi's oracle), and by the theater built into the hillside behind. Lining the sanctuary walls in the foreground are the treasuries of the Siphnians, Thebans, and Boeotians, among other buildings. To the right is a colossal statue of Apollo.

ECHELLE

Greek Sanctuaries

A world full of gods

Created wherever the ancient Greeks settled and formed communities across the Mediterranean world, and ranging from simple rural shrines to large complexes, sanctuaries became focal points for Greek life.

△ **Bronze hydria**
An inscription on the mouth of this 5th-century BCE water vessel reveals that it was given as a prize in games in honor of the goddess Hera at her sanctuary in Argos, in the Peloponnese.

The ancient Greeks believed, in the words of the philosopher Thales, that "everything is full of gods," and the landscape and cities of Greece were full of sanctuaries dedicated to these gods. An ancient Greek proverb, "Sing as you sail into Delos," conveys the sense of wonder, anticipation, and excitement that people may have felt as they approached somewhere thought to be infused with the divine. In the case of Delos, this was the island believed to have been the birthplace of the god Apollo (see p.159).

Sanctuaries were often established in distinctive locations. These included caves (typically associated with nymphs and Pan, god of the wild, shepherds, and flocks), springs, and valleys. Sanctuaries on high places, such as hills and promontories, were often home to temples dedicated to maritime gods such as Poseidon, or to Athena or Aphrodite, who were also associated with the sea. The summit and slopes of the Acropolis in Athens, for example, were packed with sanctuaries, notably of Athena in guises including Polias (of the city) and Ergane (worker), along with those of other divine entities such as Artemis, Poseidon, Aphrodite, Pan, Demeter and her daughter Kore (another name for Persephone), and Hephaestus.

Such sanctuaries were readily accessible to visitors, many of whom left votives (offerings) to the god or gods in question. These could vary from small gifts from individuals, such as a spindle offered to the weaver deity Athena, to colossal statues bestowed by wealthy individuals or cities. Sanctuaries were also places where people in desperate need, from escaped enslaved people to exiled leaders, could seek asylum, that is, "sanctuary."

◁ **The owl goddess**
Dating from c.460 BCE, this small bronze statue of Athena flying her owl was perhaps a votive offering left at one of her sanctuaries in Athens.

△ **Monument to Zeus**
Commissioned by Philip II of Macedonia after his victory at Chaeronea in 338 BCE, this circular monument in Olympia, in the Peloponnese, was dedicated to Zeus.

Public sanctuaries were set apart from day-to-day existence, but there was also a sacred dimension to everyday life. Indeed, every ancient Greek *oikos* (household) had its own small shrines dedicated to Apollo Agyieus (of the streets, who protected the entrance), Zeus Ktesios (of the household), and Zeus Herkeios (of the surrounding wall).

Festivals and games

Groups of people, drawn from the local community and sometimes farther afield, would visit sanctuaries at designated dates for festivals (see pp.156–157) in honor of the divine entities associated with the site in question. At some of these festivals, competitors (usually adult men, but sometimes boys) would gather to take part in games. The best known of these games were held at the Panhellenic sanctuaries of Zeus at Olympia, Poseidon at Nemea and Isthmia, and Apollo at Delphi. Of course, Delphi was also one of the Greek world's many oracular shrines.

Canopy held up by four *thyrsoi*—staffs sacred to Dionysus and associated with prosperity and fertility

The horse has a simple halter, held by the youth, and a harness attaching it to the cart's shaft

A youth wearing a conical-shaped cap and a short tunic leads the horses pulling the cart

"As you go **down** from the **marketplace** you see on the right of the street called Straight **a sanctuary** of **Apollo Prostaterios** (Protecting)."

PAUSANIAS ON THE CITY OF MEGARA, *DESCRIPTION OF GREECE*

△ A god on tour

Carved around 50 BCE, this relief depicts a statue of Dionysus, the god of wine, being transported by cart to a sanctuary or festival, where it would form part of the celebrations. The carving shows the statue sitting on a folding stool beneath a canopy. The statue depicts the god with his long hair tied at the back, wearing a long robe and holding a libation bowl.

Sanctuary at Olympia

Seat of the Olympic Games

The sanctuary of Zeus at Olympia, in the western Peloponnese, was among the most important in the Greek world. It was here, every four years, that the Festival of Zeus took place, combining sacred rites with athletic contests held in the god's honor. At the beginning, around the 8th century BCE, there was only one sporting event: a footrace over 600 Olympic feet (631 ft). Three centuries later, the festival had developed into a five-day program of running, jumping, and throwing competitions; combat sports; and horse and chariot races, interspersed with ceremonial processions, sacrificial offerings, and feasting. The Games, in which only male Greeks who were free citizens could compete, became closely associated with Greek culture and pride, and victory at an Olympiad, requiring such prized attributes as speed, strength, skill, focus, and discipline, was the ultimate honor.

▷ **The Olympic site**
This reconstruction depicts the sanctuary around 330 BCE. Temples, altars, and dedications (to gods, athletes, and military victories) filled the sacred enclosure, with administrative buildings and athletic facilities arranged around the outside.

▽ **Olympia through time**
Olympia's first monumental stone temple was dedicated to Hera around 600 BCE. As the festival evolved, so did the site, continuing to acquire temples, monuments, and athletic facilities into the Roman era.

△ **Altar of ashes**
The festival's religious climax was the hecatombe, a sacrifice of 100 oxen at the Altar of Zeus, culminating in a meat feast for all. The ever-growing altar, consisting of ashes from centuries of cumulative sacrifices, stood several meters tall.

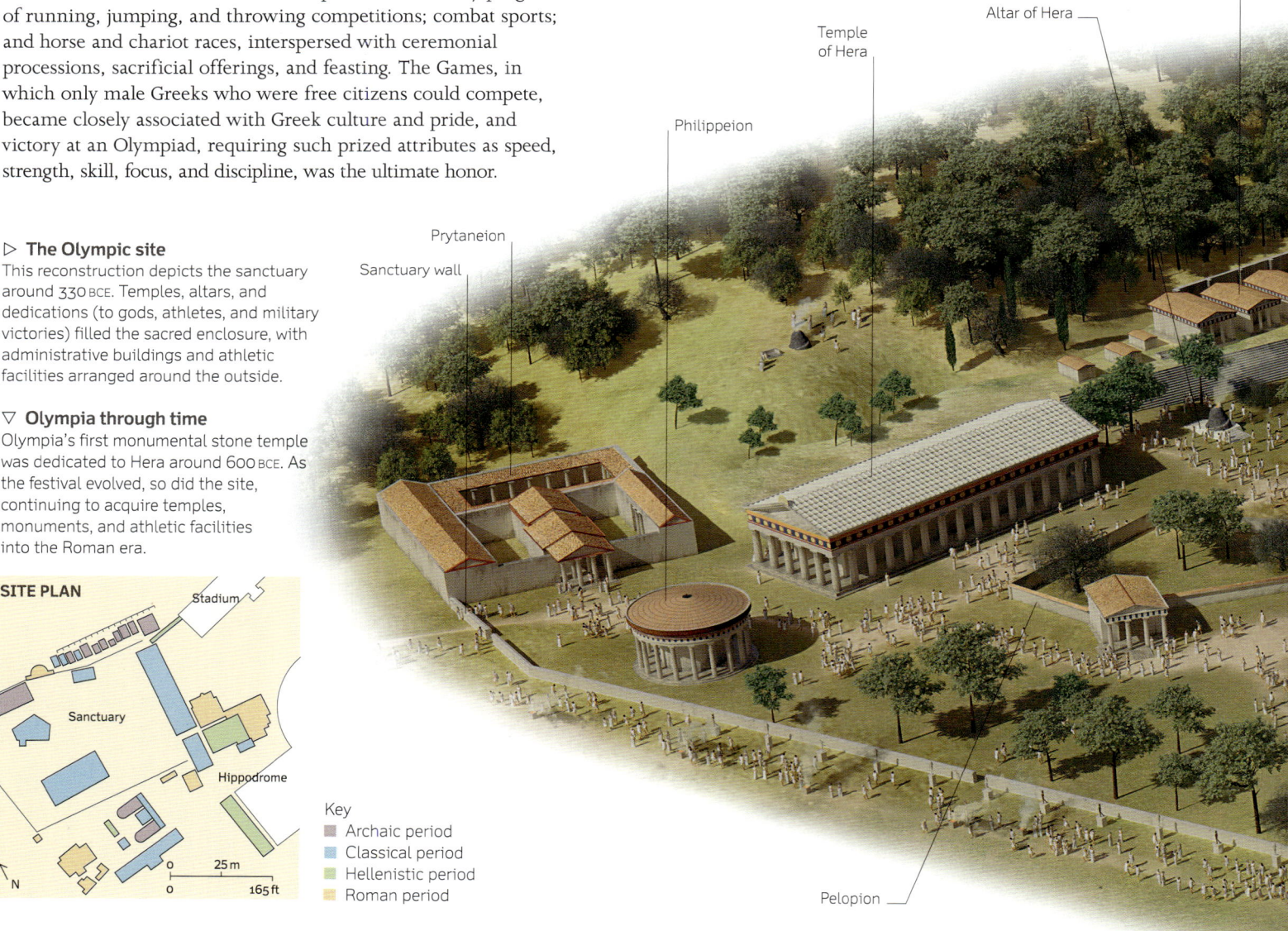

Treasuries

Altar of Hera

Temple of Hera

Philippeion

Prytaneion

Sanctuary wall

Pelopion

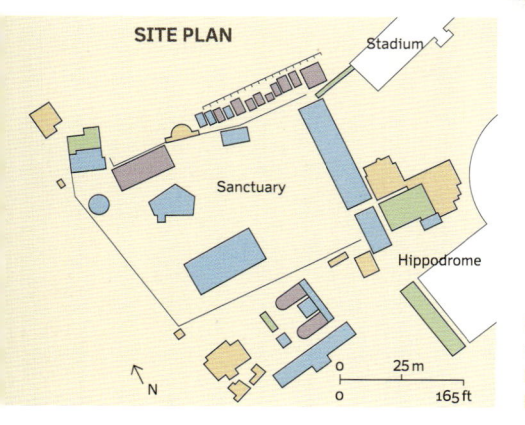

SITE PLAN

Stadium

Sanctuary

Hippodrome

N

0 — 25 m

0 — 165 ft

Key
- Archaic period
- Classical period
- Hellenistic period
- Roman period

△ Pankration

Of the combat sports, pankration—a cross between boxing and wrestling—was the most popular. Contestants wore no protection, and the only things against the rules were biting, gouging, and attacking the genitals.

△ At the Hippodrome

In the prestigious chariot races, it was the winning chariot's owner, not the driver, who won the race. This rule saw Spartan princess Cynisca become the first female Olympic victor in 396 BCE.

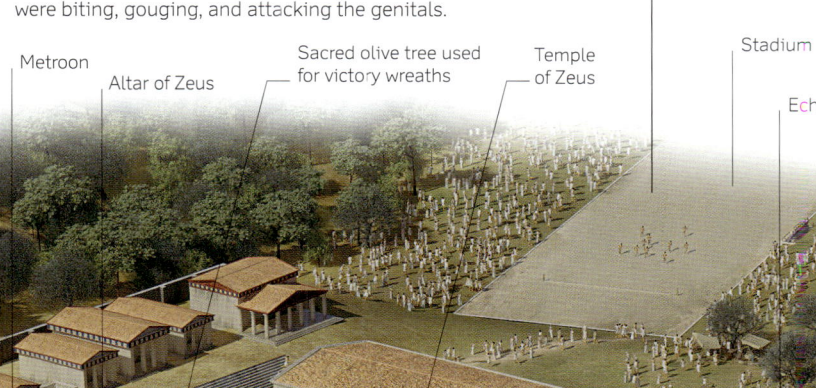

Metroon
Altar of Zeus
Sacred olive tree used for victory wreaths
Temple of Zeus
Stadium
Bouleuterion
Echo Stoa
Southeast building
South Stoa

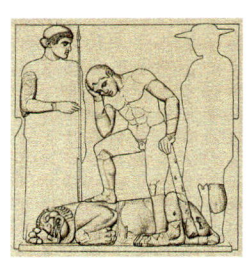

NEMEAN LION

HYDRA

STYMPHALIAN BIRDS

CRETAN BULL

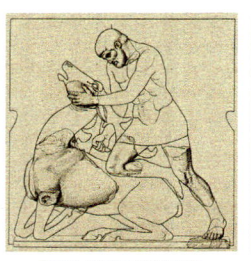

CERYNEIAN HIND

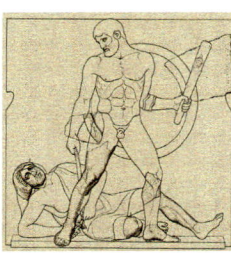

HIPPOLYTE'S BELT

△ **Labors of Heracles—west porch**
Each of the 12 metopes depicts Heracles, son of Zeus and mythical founder of the Olympic Games, using his formidable strength and skill to complete a seemingly impossible task.

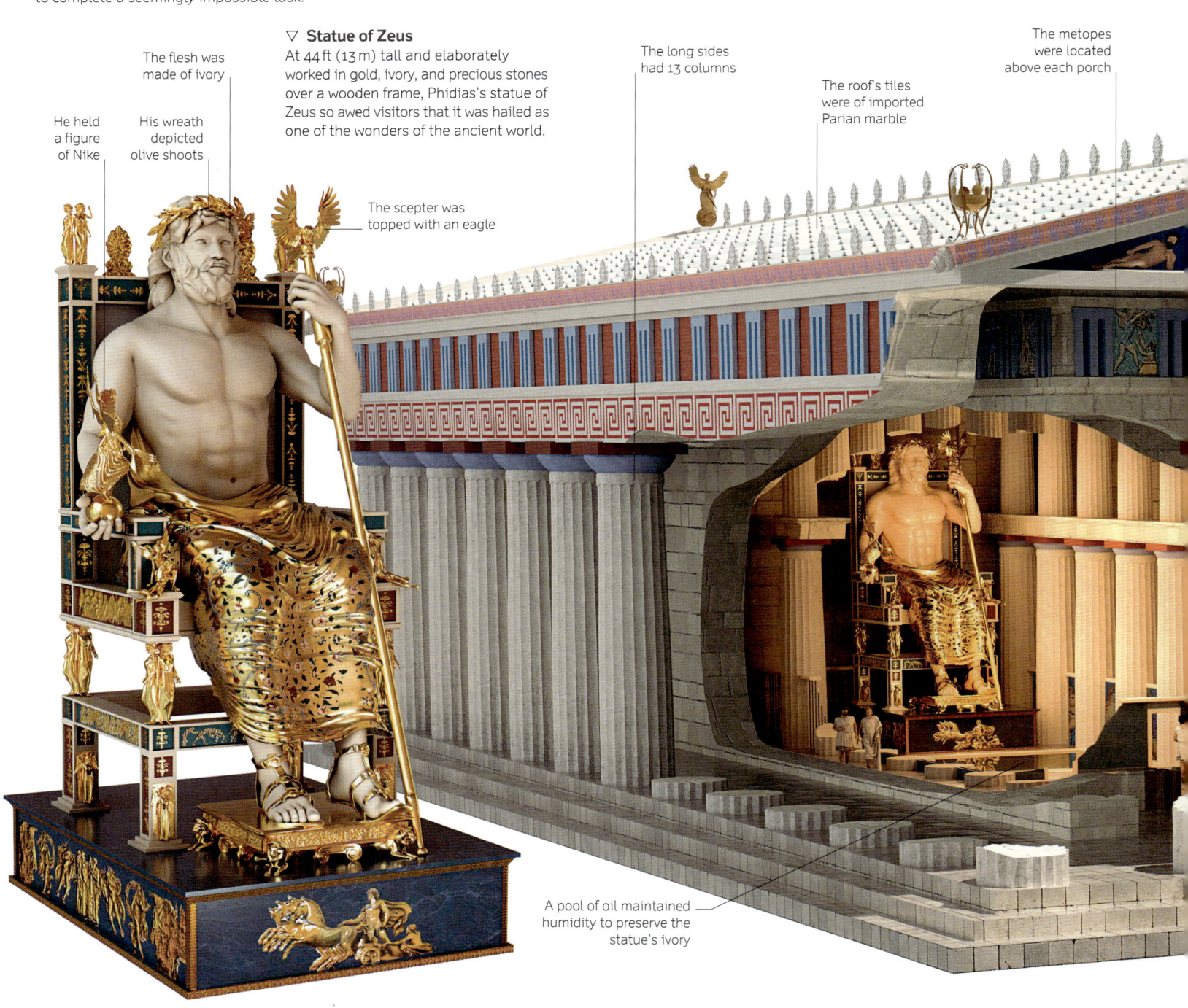

▽ **Statue of Zeus**
At 44 ft (13 m) tall and elaborately worked in gold, ivory, and precious stones over a wooden frame, Phidias's statue of Zeus so awed visitors that it was hailed as one of the wonders of the ancient world.

He held a figure of Nike

His wreath depicted olive shoots

The flesh was made of ivory

The scepter was topped with an eagle

The long sides had 13 columns

The roof's tiles were of imported Parian marble

The metopes were located above each porch

A pool of oil maintained humidity to preserve the statue's ivory

ERYMANTHIAN BOAR

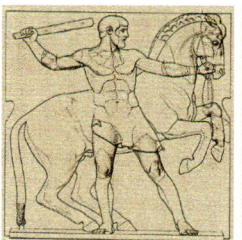

HORSES OF DIOMEDES

CATTLE OF GERYON

APPLES OF THE HESPERIDES

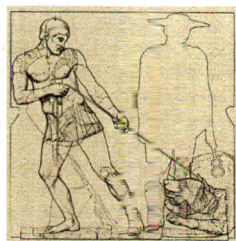

CERBERUS

AUGEAN STABLES

△ **Labors of Heracles – east porch**
The scene order differs from that in which Heracles is usually said to have performed his feats, but follows artistic logic, interspersing calmer compositions between those showing the hero in dynamic action.

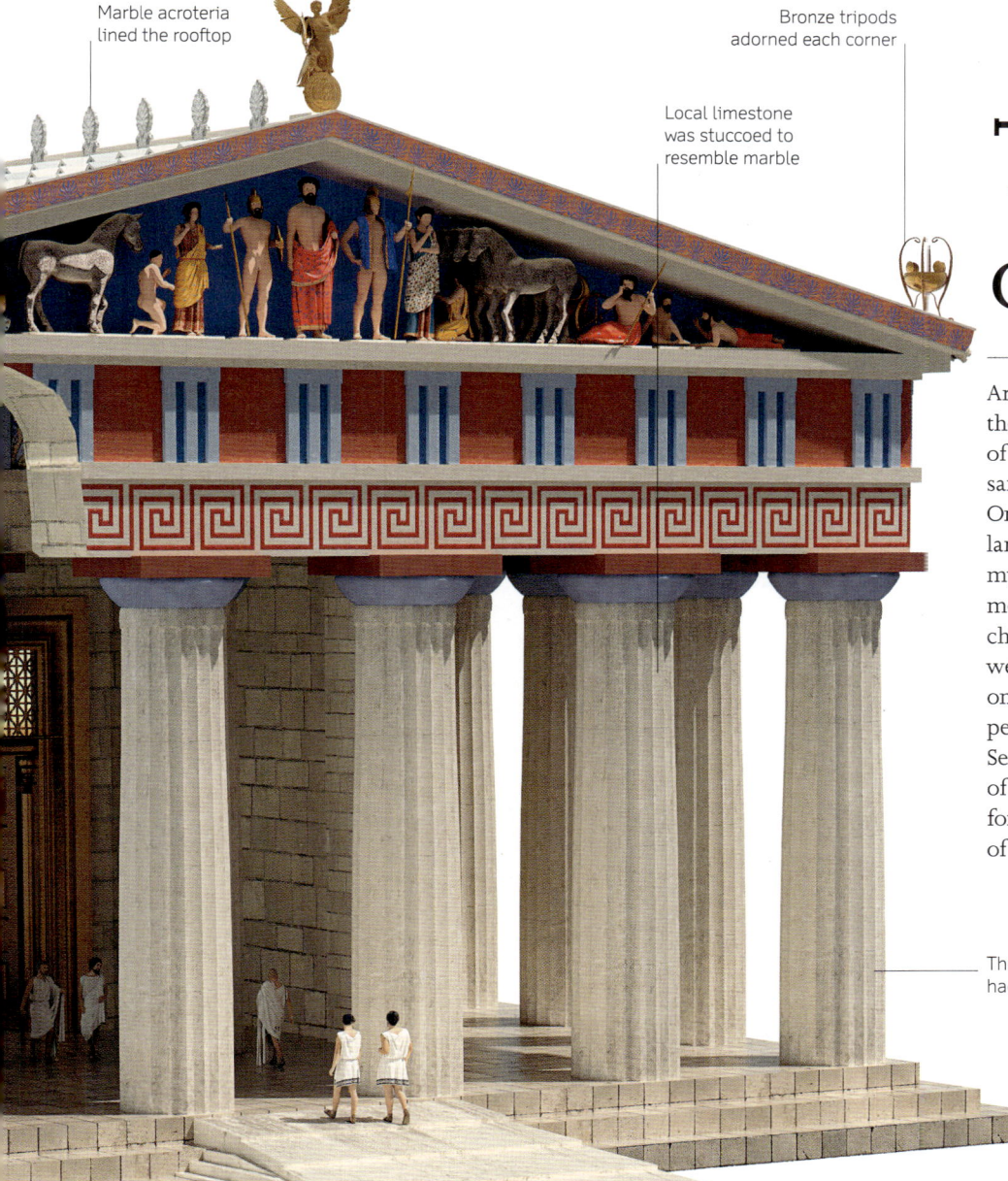

Marble acroteria lined the rooftop

Bronze tripods adorned each corner

Local limestone was stuccoed to resemble marble

The short sides had six columns

The Temple of Zeus

Around 470 BCE, the city-state of Elis commissioned the architect Libon to design a fine temple at the heart of the sanctuary of Olympia—one befitting the sanctuary's patron deity and religious importance. On completion in 457 BCE, the Temple of Zeus was the largest temple in mainland Greece, with grand-scale mythological scenes decorating its pediments and metopes. Depicting Lapith men battling centaurs, a chariot race, and the Labors of Heracles—all subjects well known to Panhellenic visitors—their emphasis on heroic strength and victory over adversity was perfectly suited to the arena of the Olympic Games. Seeking a worthy cult statue for the temple, sanctuary officials turned to the sculptor Phidias, renowned for creating his monumental gold and ivory statue of Athena for the Parthenon in Athens.

◁ **Temple of Zeus**
The temple is an example of Early Classical (Severe) style, with elegant Doric columns. The sculpted figures are characterized by naturalistic bodies combined with expressionless faces and weighty-looking drapery.

◁ **Spartan workmanship**
This Laconian kylix (drinking cup) was created in Sparta around 575–550 BCE. It is typical of the black-figure style common in the Late Archaic period and shows the myth of Bellerophon and Pegasus, the winged horse, battling the Chimera.

3

The Late Archaic Age

600–500 BCE

A Cultural Awakening

The 6th century BCE, like the previous two centuries, was a time of great cultural, political, religious, and intellectual change across the now-expansive and scattered cities and regions that made up the Greek world. During the century, a sense of a distinctive local identity came to be further solidified in the cities, in part marked by the construction of impressive new temples. Conversely, the period also saw a renewed sense of shared Greek identity, exemplified by the establishment or reorganization of competitive games at the Panhellenic (all Greek) sanctuaries at Delphi, Nemea in the Peloponnese, and Isthmia on the Isthmus of Corinth.

Philosophy, poetry, and power

The key intellectual center of the 6th century BCE was the city of Miletus, the home of such foundational "pre-Socratic" thinkers as Thales and Anaximander, and the crucible of philosophy and a new approach to scientific inquiry, both of which rapidly spread across the Greek world.

Epic poetry remained popular throughout the century, with the Homeric poems the *Iliad* and the *Odyssey* reaching their final form. However, the century also saw the growing popularity of lyric poetry. Intense and more intimate than epic poetry, as well as far shorter, this poetry regularly drew from Homeric subject material, sometimes subversively.

In the middle of the century, the Persian Achaemenid Empire exerted its power over the *poleis* of Ionia, where tyrants were installed in cities including Ephesus and Miletus. As other cities of Asia Minor came under Persian control, many of their inhabitants headed west to the Greek cities in France, Italy, and Iberia. The Etruscans of Italy and Carthaginians of North Africa stopped Greek expansion west of Italy around 535 BCE. But by then the Greeks controlled many places in southern Italy and Sicily, and cities such as Syracuse were consolidating their already considerable control.

Athens and Sparta

On the Greek mainland, Athens and Sparta emerged as dominant powers in the 6th century BCE. These two cities differed from one another in terms of their political systems and way of life. Sparta thrived with a dual monarchy, a powerful warrior elite, and a focus on austerity and self-discipline; in Athens, Solon's reforms at the beginning of the century had started reducing the authority of the aristocracy, widening participation in government. Athens and Sparta also differed from other Greek cities in growing their power within Greece, rather than expanding overseas. In Athens' case, this was via the unification of Attica; in Sparta's case, it was through the conquest of the southern Peloponnese and the creation of the Peloponnesian League. Consequently, both cities had access to huge territories (by ancient Greek standards) and resources.

The two powers clashed in 510 BCE, when Sparta interfered in Athenian politics, driving out the tyrant Hippias and installing an oligarchy. The Athenians rebelled in 508 BCE, and the reforms of Cleisthenes shifted the city further toward democracy. However, the increasing ideological division between Athens and Sparta set them more at odds, laying the scene for much greater conflict between them.

◁ **Statue of the philosopher Xenophanes**

c. 600 BCE The lyric poet Sappho is active on the island of Lesbos

582 BCE First Isthmian Games, and the Pythian Games are reorganized

566 BCE Establishment of the Panathenaea festival in Attica

c. 561 BCE Pisistratus comes to power as Athens' first tyrant

594 BCE Solon's reforms in Athens begin the move toward democracy

575 BCE Miletus emerges as Greece's main intellectual center

❶ Temple of Apollo in ancient Corinth

❷ Temple of Aphaea on the island of Aegina

❸ Ancient Greek ruins at Miletus, now in Türkiye

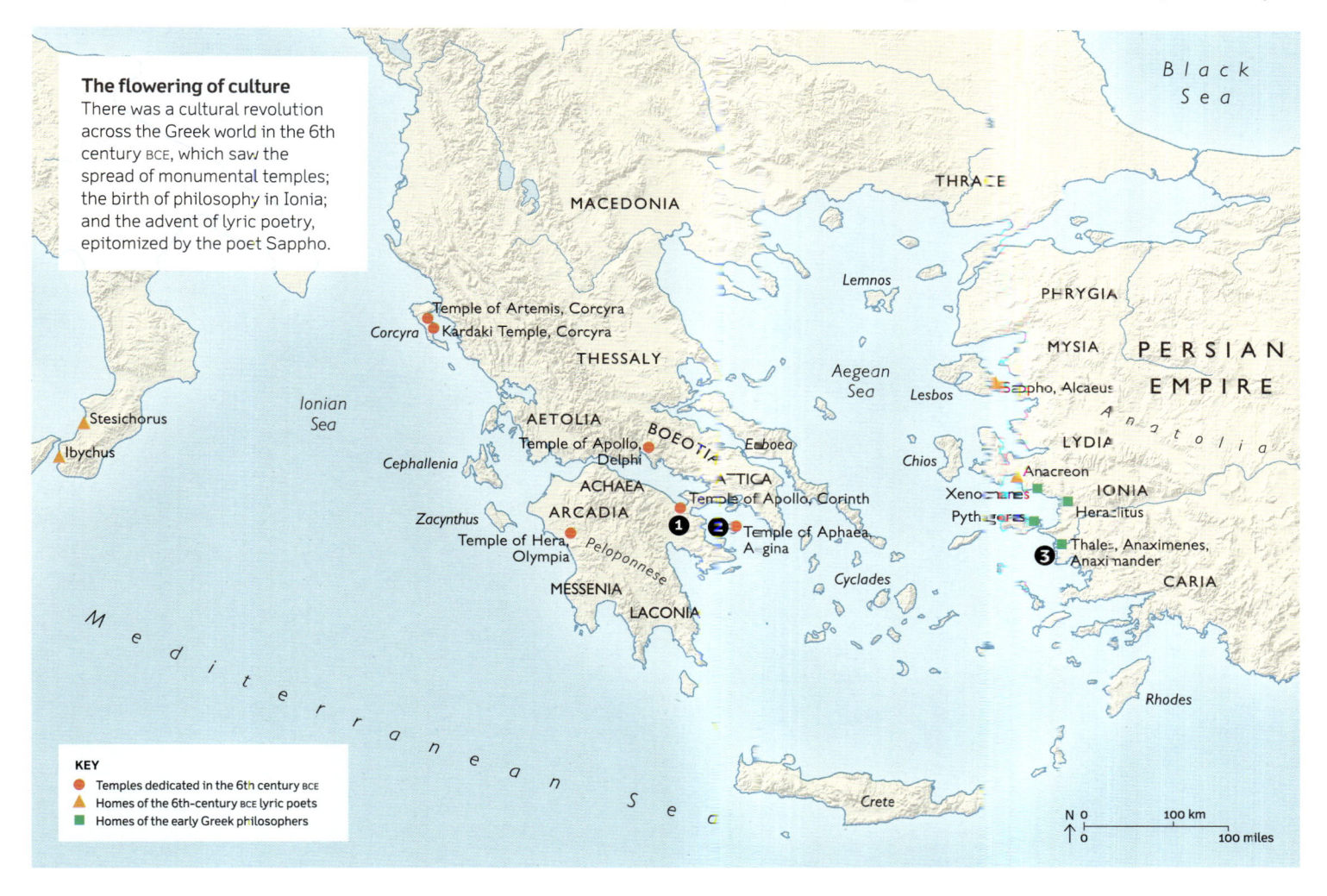

The flowering of culture

There was a cultural revolution across the Greek world in the 6th century BCE, which saw the spread of monumental temples; the birth of philosophy in Ionia; and the advent of lyric poetry, epitomized by the poet Sappho.

KEY
- ● Temples dedicated in the 6th century BCE
- ▲ Homes of the 6th-century BCE lyric poets
- ■ Homes of the early Greek philosophers

c. **550** BCE Sparta forms the Peloponnesian League

550 BCE Cyrus the Great founds the Achaemenid Empire of Persia

c. **540** BCE The Achaemenid Empire takes control of the Ionian Greek cities

c. **535** BCE An Etruscan and Carthaginian force expels the Greeks from Corsica

c. **527** BCE Pisistratus dies, and Hippias becomes tyrant in Athens

524 BCE The Greeks beat Italic forces at Cumae in southern Italy

510 BCE Spartan forces overthrow the Athenian tyrant Hippias

508 BCE Cleisthenes' reforms move Athens closer to democracy

Philosophers

Seeking answers to life's questions

A radically new approach to learning about the world developed in the 6th century BCE, sparked by the insights of thinkers in Ionia, whose critical questioning of dogma was the beginning of Greek philosophy.

Thales of Miletus is credited with setting the philosophical ball rolling with his quest to identify the principles that governed the natural world. He concluded that a single substance, the *arche*, embodied the fundamental nature of the world. Observing that water was ubiquitous and necessary, he reasoned that it must be the *arche*. He also established debate and rational argument as the foundation of philosophy.

Subsequent pre-Socratic (early Greek) philosophers took up the agenda that Thales had set. Some continued to adhere to monism, the idea that there is a single, constant substance governing the universe, but others took different views. Pythagoras (see p.115), for example, believed that the sole governing principle of the cosmos was number. Meanwhile, Heraclitus thought that fire was the *arche*, but disputed the notion of constancy, suggesting that everything flowed, and that "No man ever steps in the same river twice."

In the late 6th–early 5th centuries BCE, Parmenides of Elea espoused a radical form of monism, claiming that the cosmos was ruled by a rational unity, and that change and even motion were impossible. Zeno of Elea (c. 490–430 BCE) then illustrated this with his paradoxes, which challenged the notions of plurality, motion, space, and time.

△ **Thales of Miletus (c. 626–548 BCE)**
Recognized as the founding father of the Greek philosophical tradition, Thales rejected mythology in favor of rational thought to explain the universe. No writings by him have survived, and our knowledge of his life and work comes from later writers.

△ **Heraclitus (fl. c. 500 BCE)**
Known as the "weeping philosopher" for his melancholic disposition, Heraclitus offered a complex view of the universe, whose fundamental element he believed to be fire. Unlike his contemporary Parmenides, Heraclitus argued that the universe was characterized by conflict between opposites, and constantly in a state of flux.

△ **Empedocles (c. 494–434 BCE)**
As well as originating the notion of the four elements, Empedocles (pictured here as a young man) also developed a theory of metempsychosis, arguing that the soul transmigrated between people, animals, and even plants after death.

"Knowledge of the **fact** differs from **knowledge** of the **reason** for the **fact**."

ARISTOTLE, *POSTERIOR ANALYTICS*

Counterarguments to the idea of a single substance came from Empedocles, for whom the universe was composed of four material elements. Anaxagoras (c. 500–428 BCE), in his "everything in everything" theory, argued that there was a mixture of elements set in motion by the action of *Nous* (Mind), which created swirls of different density and proportion that produce the apparently separate material masses and objects that we perceive. Democritus named such basic elements of existence *atomos* (indivisible).

Socrates and after

While the main concern of early Greek philosophy was the physical universe, the arrival of Socrates (see p.187) brought a shift toward using the principles of reasoning to examine human behavior. This approach dominated the Classical period. Inspired by his critical questioning of conventions, Socrates' student Plato, and subsequently Aristotle, offered new perspectives on how we should understand the world and live our lives. They each developed a distinctive style of philosophy that encompassed ethics, epistemology (the theory of knowledge), and politics.

Among the thinkers attracted to Athens was Diogenes of Sinope, founder of the austere philosophy known as Cynicism. His work inspired the Stoicism of Zeno of Citium, which taught that practicing wisdom, courage, moderation, and justice would result in a well-lived life. It became the main philosophy of Hellenistic Greece and the Roman Empire.

△ **Democritus (c. 460–370 BCE)**
Democritus suggested that everything was composed of minute particles surrounded by empty space. These "atoms" were unchanging and eternal, but were always combining, separating, and recombining in different forms.

△ **Diogenes of Sinope (c. 412/403–324/321 BCE)**
Diogenes earned the epithet *Kynikos*, "doglike," from living according to his beliefs: a simple life in harmony with nature. His home was a large ceramic jar in the agora, and he sometimes went out with a lamp during daylight, explaining that he was looking for an honest man. His philosophy became known as Cynicism.

△ **Epicurus (341–270 BCE)**
In his materialist philosophy, Epicurus denied the soul's immortality. Since there was nothing after death, he argued, we should strive to live an ethical and therefore happy life avoiding the things that cause pain, and seeking those that bring pleasure.

Lyric Poetry

Songs from the Archaic Age

While the epic poetry that thrived from the 8th century BCE remained popular, the Archaic Age saw a flowering of shorter lyric forms across the Greek world. These poems addressed a range of human experience, as well as praising the gods.

The term "lyric poetry" is used to refer to a type of sung poetry that, in Greece, flourished between the 7th and 5th centuries BCE. It drew on a long tradition of popular song and the sung paeans, dirges, and wedding hymns mentioned by Homer in the *Iliad*. However, unlike the vast epic poems of composers including Homer and Hesiod, lyric poems were typically quite short and direct. They were also hugely diverse in nature, ranging from erotic poems and drinking songs—as seen in the works of Anacreon (c. 575–495 BCE)—to philosophical reflections. Meter, or rhythmic structure, rather than rhyme defined the different forms of lyric poetry, with patterns of long and short syllables producing rhythmic effect. Indeed, some poems were sung by groups, or choruses, sometimes with a dance; others were sung by individuals, who were often accompanied by instruments.

Love, celebration, and worship

Solo poetry often addressed love, yearning, absence, and loss (as in the work of Sappho, see pp.100–101)—from unfulfilled desire, through praise of a loved one's beauty, to despair at the end of a love affair. Political themes were also embraced—for example, celebrating military victories, and encouraging soldiers to fight bravely in battle. The poems were performed at both public and private events, including at symposia (see p.79).

Choral poetry created a spectacle out of words, music, and dancing, with themes that included praise of the gods, celebration of victory, wedding songs, and mourning for the dead. Many choral poems drew on the rich sources of Greek

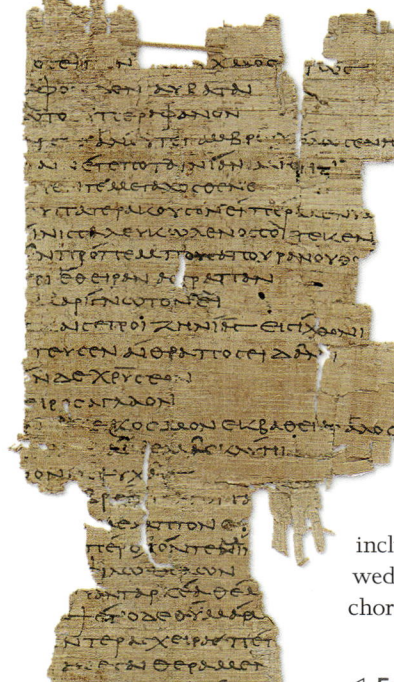

◁ **Fragment of Bacchylides**
This fragment of a 2nd-century CE scroll contains sections of Bacchylides' (c. 510–451 BCE) 17th dithyramb (choral poem), which features King Minos and Theseus.

△ **Musical accompaniment**
Shown on this 4th-century BCE vase painting is a musician playing an aulos—a type of reeded flute that was often used to provide musical accompaniment to lyric poetry.

myth known to the earlier epic poets, weaving these stories into the narrative. Choral poetry was an important feature of religious ceremonies at public festivals, forming part of the worship of the gods.

One of the most highly acclaimed lyric poets is Pindar (c. 518–439 BCE), whose choral odes celebrated the victories of athletes in the four Panhellenic sporting events, including the Olympic Games. His poetry combined praise of the gods and the victor, their family, and homeland with allusions to myth and the heroic exploits of former times.

In the 3rd century BCE, scholars at the great library in Alexandria, Egypt, compiled a list of nine major lyric poets from across the Greek world whose work they considered to be preeminent. These were Pindar, Anacreon, Sappho, Bacchylides, Stesichorus, Alcaeus, Alcman, Ibycus, and Simonides. The Nine were just a small sample of those who wrote lyric poetry. Much has been lost because the poems that have survived exist only in fragments, though occasional discoveries continue to shine new light on the genre.

◁ **Muse with kithara**
This 2nd-century BCE relief depicts a kithara, a harp-shaped instrument with tortoiseshell sound box that often accompanied performances of poetry in ancient Greece. It is played here by one of the nine Muses, goddesses who inspired writers, musicians, and other artists in their craft.

The seven strings of the kithara were played with both hands

One of the Muses is represented here—most likely Calliope, Muse of poetry, or Terpsichore, Muse of dance and chorus

THE LYRE **IN MYTH**

According to Greek mythology, the god Hermes was the inventor of the lyre. On the day of his birth, he was said to have killed a tortoise he found and strung its hollow shell with sheep-gut to create the first lyre. He then tracked down the sacred cattle belonging to Apollo, stole 50 of them, and sacrificed two to the gods. Apollo was furious at the theft, but apparently put aside his anger when he heard Hermes playing the lyre. Entranced by its sweet music, Apollo offered to trade his cattle for the instrument and a promise from Hermes never to steal from him again. Apollo was god of music and poetry, with the lyre as his symbol.

APOLLO WITH HIS LYRE

Sappho

The lyric poet of Lesbos

One of the nine great lyric poets, Sappho was a composer of intense, sensual, and passionate songs, most of which survive only in fragments. Much has been written about her but little is reliably known.

There is an apparent wealth of information about Sappho, much from her own work, which names family members, including a daughter, a husband, and brothers. Herodotus states that she was from Mytilene on Lesbos, and other ancient sources link her with her countryman Alcaeus and other poets, and the Mytilenean tyrant Pittacus. According to one tradition, she died by suicide because of her unrequited love for Phaon, a ferryman.

Yet none of this information is reliable. We do not even know for certain that she was from Lesbos. The autobiographical details in her songs may represent her adoption of a persona rather than any actual personal circumstances or experiences.

Sappho's poetry

We do know, however, that Sappho was so revered in the ancient world that Plato called her the Tenth Muse. We also possess the full text of one surviving poem, a hymn to Aphrodite, along with some long fragments and many shorter ones. Sappho was among the earliest ancient poets to use the first person, and her poems typically deal with intense feelings for other women, including those she desires and whose absences she grieves. These surviving texts include hymns, laments, and songs that may have been composed for weddings, festivals, and symposia. There they would have been sung to music, now lost, probably composed by Sappho herself.

Much of what survives typically presents multiple viewpoints and often subverts dominant male perspectives. For example, Sappho's Helen of Troy (fragment 16) is not a possession transferred between men, but a woman who makes her own choices. Here, perhaps, we glimpse the real Sappho—an empathetic, independent, and talented artist.

◁ **Alcaeus and Sappho**
This Attic red-figure kalathos, which dates from c. 570 BCE, shows Alcaeus holding a lyre and paying homage to Sappho.

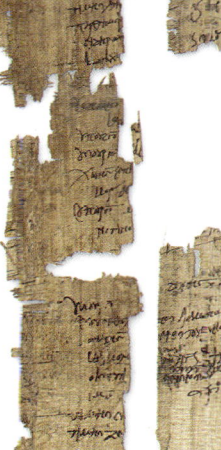

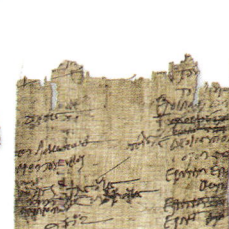

▽ **Sappho's song**
Written in Sappho's Aeolic dialect, these fragments of her poetry date from the 2nd–4th centuries CE. They mention the poet's—perhaps imaginary—brothers.

"Again **love**, the **limb-loosener**, rattles me bittersweet, irresistible, a **crawling beast**."

SAPPHO, FRAGMENT 15

c. 620 BCE Birth of the poet Alcaeus

c. 600 BCE The tyrant Pittacus becomes prominent in Mytilene

c. 570 BCE Suggested date for Sappho's death

c. 350–275 BCE The scholar Chamaeleon writes his treatise *On Sappho*

c. 610 BCE Suggested date for Sappho's birth

c. 580 BCE Death of Alcaeus

c. 425 BCE Herodotus tells us Sappho had a brother called Charaxus

c. 975 CE Earliest biography of Sappho in the *Suda*, a Byzantine encyclopedia

Remaking the Sanctuary

From mudbrick to marble

Within around a century from c. 650 BCE, Greek temple sanctuaries evolved from small buildings of mudbrick and thatch to enormous colonnaded structures of marble, elaborately carved with narrative friezes.

△ **Heraion of Samos**
The only column remaining of the Temple of Hera on Samos was left after the site was quarried for stone in the Byzantine period.

Temple sanctuaries were a defining feature of the emerging Greek city-states in the 9th century BCE. Originally simple shrines in groves or caves, where animal sacrifices were made to the gods, they had at most portable altars and a collection of stones marking the boundary of the *temenos*, the sacred space.

By the 8th century BCE, small temples of mudbrick, wood, and thatch were being built. These had a single rectangular hall, or naos, in which the central shrine, or cella, housed the cult statue. Evidence of the earliest ornamentations survives from a later Temple of Apollo at Thermon in Aetolia, which contains ten decorated terra-cotta panels dating to 630–620 BCE. Around that time, temple sizes increased, with the appearance of the *hekatompedon* or "hundred-foot" temple, such as that dedicated to Hera on Samos, which measured 108 ft (33 m) by c. 20 ft (6 m) and featured an early colonnade of wooden columns to support its roof. Unable to support a large, heavy roof, these temples were necessarily narrow.

The invention of clay roof tiles in Corinth in the 7th century BCE permitted the development of larger temples of stone. These retained colonnades, now also of stone, which helped spread the weight and became

△ **Medusa metope**
This carved panel is a 6th-century BCE metope from the frieze on Temple C in Selinus, Sicily; it shows the hero Perseus, supported by Athena, beheading the Gorgon Medusa.

a key feature of almost all temples of the Classical era. The triangular sloped ends below the roofs and the band above the columns came to be decorated with elaborate sculpted friezes.

Since stone—particularly high-quality white marble, such as that from Paros, Naxos, and Mount Pentelicus (near Athens)—was readily available, the new-style sanctuaries spread rapidly. Such temples appeared even on the fringes of the Greek world, for example at Selinus on Sicily, where Temple C, dedicated to an unknown deity, was built around 600–550 BCE.

The temples became a badge of civic pride, signaling the power of the *poleis* that constructed them. They received gifts, prompting the construction of smaller templelike treasuries to house these votive offerings. From the 4th century BCE, however, the monumentalization of the sanctuary waned. By that time, most cities that could afford stone and marble temples already had many of them, and new ones were largely replacements for earlier ones that had been destroyed, for example by fire. Although almost no temples have survived intact, the ruins of these monumental buildings remain an impressive reminder of the heights of Greek architecture.

GREEK COLUMNS

The marble columns of Greek temples evolved into three distinct forms. The Doric (most famously used on the Parthenon) was the plainest, with a bulky shaft with 20 grooved flutes, an unadorned capital (top section), and no base. The Ionic, which appeared along with the Doric around 600 BCE in eastern Greece, had volutes (scroll-like decorations) on the capital, and a molded base. The later Corinthian was the most ornate, with capitals decorated with scrolls and acanthus leaves.

DORIC　　**IONIC**　　**CORINTHIAN**

"It is an **extraordinary place** ... so **light** and **aerial**, so **pure** and in **tune** with the **sky**."

BRITISH AUTHOR LAWRENCE DURRELL ON THE TEMPLE AT LINDOS, *THE GREEK ISLANDS*

Acroterion (pediment ornament) in the form of the goddess of victory, Nike

Heracles argues with Apollo over the Delphic tripod, while Zeus (in the center) tries to stop them

Frieze depicting a council of the gods deciding the fate of Greeks and Trojans

One of two caryatids that support the front portico in place of Doric columns

Kore figure bearing an offering

◁ **Painted beauty**
Greek sanctuary buildings would have been painted with bright colors to enhance the decoration, as shown in this reconstruction of the Siphnian Treasury.

Gods versus Giants
This detail from the north side of the marble frieze that
encircled the Siphnian Treasury at Delphi depicts a scene
from the Gigantomachy (the battle between the Olympic
gods and the Giants). To the left, a beautifully carved lion
takes a bite from a Giant's midriff. Advancing right into
battle are the divine twins Artemis and Apollo, children
of Leto and Zeus. Both were expert archers, and the
figure of Apollo is wearing a quiver. Fleeing the twins
is a Giant named Ka[n]tharos; another, named Ephialtes,
lies on the ground.

The Rise of Sparta

Power in the Peloponnese

After centuries of warfare with its neighbors—the Messenians, Arcadians, and Argives—Sparta secured control over the Peloponnese to become one of Greece's two dominant city-states, along with Athens.

Over the course of around 500 years, through a potent mix of conquest and cooperation, Sparta developed from its humble origins into a major power of the Archaic Age.

The first traces of settlement in Sparta's homeland, in the inland plain of the Eurotas River in the southern Peloponnese, date to around 1000 BCE and the appearance of four small villages. These had merged by the 8th century BCE to form the tiny kingdom of Sparta. Around 750 BCE, during the reign of its dual kings Archelaos and Charillos, Sparta annexed Amyclae just to the south, the former site of a small Mycenaean palace.

Growing power

Seeking to expand further but faced with stronger powers—Arcadia, and in particular Argos—to its north, the nascent Spartan state advanced instead from its Laconian heartland, beginning a war with Messenia to the west around 743 BCE. During the war, the Spartans enslaved the people of Helos, possibly for not supporting it against Messenia, and this may have given rise to the term "helots." The Messenians were finally defeated around 720 BCE. They were reduced to serf status, which provoked unrest and a revolt c. 670 BCE. The Messenians held their own until the Spartans bribed the Arcadians to withdraw their support. Though the Messenians fought an 11-year guerrilla campaign from their stronghold at Mount Eira, once again they were vanquished. Sparta was defeated by Argos at Hysiae around 669 BCE, and this stemmed its expansion for a while, but the Spartans turned against the Arcadians once more in 570 BCE, fighting

◁ **Spartan warrior**
This bronze figurine of a Spartan soldier, wearing a Corinthian-type helmet with a large plume, was found at the Sanctuary of Apollo Korythos at Longa, Messenia, and dates from c. 550–525 BCE.

△ **Laconian artwork**
The yellowish-white ground on this 6th-century BCE tondo, depicting the Greek heroes' legendary hunt for the Calydonian Boar, is typical of Laconian vase painting.

a decade-long war against the city of Tegea. Inspired by a Delphic oracle that told them they would have "Tegea to dance upon ... and a fair plain to measure out with the rod," the Spartans brought rods and chains for measuring, but were soundly defeated by the Tegeans (who placed the captured chains in their temple to Athena). When a second oracle told them that if they wished to defeat Tegea, they should steal the remains of Orestes, the Spartans sent a spy who did so. Victorious in the battle that followed, the Spartans finally forced Tegea into an alliance.

Emboldened, Sparta turned against Argos. At the Battle of the Champions, fought to the death between 300 hand-picked warriors on each side in 546 BCE, both sides claimed victory: the Argives said their two surviving champions meant they had won; the Spartans retorted that the two Argives had fled

◁ **The growth of Sparta**
Sparta grew to control the southern half of the Peloponnese by the mid-6th century BCE. By the century's end, it had also gained the support of the northern half and of the Isthmus of Corinth, which linked the Peloponnese with Attica.

▽ **Spartan ivory**
Found at the Sanctuary of Artemis Orthia, built c. 700 BCE and one of the most important religious sites in Sparta, these figurines of idols date from the 7th century BCE.

the field, leaving the mortally wounded Spartan Othryades as victor. In the aftermath, the Spartans gained control over Kynouria, on the eastern coast of the Peloponnese. Now the region's principal power, Sparta was able to build the first great alliance of Greek city-states, the Peloponnesian League, from around 550 BCE.

Beyond the Peloponnese

The Spartans used their position to interfere in several other Greek city-states, acting against regimes ruled by tyrants such as Aeschines of Sicyon, who was expelled in the mid-6th century, and intervening against Polycrates of Samos around 522 BCE. Sparta even meddled in Athens, when King Cleomenes I marched north in 510 BCE (see pp.117) to overthrow the tyrant Hippias and install a Spartan client, Isagoras, in power. The whole affair ended badly, as Isagoras was overthrown, but it was a sign of Sparta's growing willingness to project its power outside the Peloponnese. Traditionally, the Spartans had not done so: their only colonizing venture had been the foundation of Taras

(now Taranto in southern Italy) in 706 BCE, and when Croesus of Lydia sought an alliance against the Persians in 546 BCE, Sparta had agreed, but sent no aid. Yet even now, the Spartans primarily acted to secure their position in the Peloponnese, with Cleomenes launching yet another invasion of Argos in 494 BCE and, at the Battle of Sepeia, inflicting such huge casualties that Argos was finally neutralized as a threat. By the time the Persians invaded Greece in 492 BCE, it was clear they needed to defeat Sparta.

> "Be **stout hearted** and **great hearted**, and when you are **fighting** against men **don't dwell** on **how great life is**."

SPARTAN POET TYRTAEUS, FRAGMENT 10

Spartan Society

The way of the warrior

Sparta acquired a reputation among other Greek states for its single-minded devotion to war. Although much of Spartan life and its laws reinforced a warrior ethos, in reality its society was more nuanced.

The Spartiates, the aristocratic male citizens of Sparta, were a force to be reckoned with. They stood at the summit of a hierarchical system that evolved slowly through Sparta's conquest of its neighbors (see p.106). As the original Spartans, the Spartiates had full political rights, and provided the warriors and rulers. Spartan women on the other hand lacked political rights, but were allowed to inherit and own land and run businesses, and were taught that their contribution to society was valuable. The *perioikoi*, descended from those who submitted to the Spartans, were free but without civic rights, while the helots, the conquered Messenian serfs, had few rights. Foreigners were generally not welcome in Sparta, which regularly banished non-Spartans.

The Spartans later ascribed much of their social system to the semi-mythical lawgiver Lycurgus (see p.75), though its details probably developed over time. Political authority was diffuse. Sparta had two hereditary kings, whose principal roles were as chief priests and military commanders. Alongside them were the *gerousia*, a council of elders, composed of 28 men over the age of 60, who were elected for life by the *ekklesia*, the Spartan assembly, which was open to all male Spartiates. They acted as royal advisors, judged criminal cases, and selected issues on which the *ekklesia* voted at its monthly meetings. A further brake on royal power was provided by the ephors, five officials elected for a term of a year, who ran the *ekklesia* and judged civil cases.

The Spartan regime

Sparta's kings were most powerful in wartime, though even then they had to be accompanied on campaign by two ephors. Much effort was expended in ensuring Sparta was ready for war. Babies who were considered weak were allegedly hurled into a chasm at Mount Taygetos, although there is little evidence for this. From the age of seven, Spartiate boys entered the *agoge*, a system designed to produce able warriors. Their schooling was harsh, and pupils were often whipped by their older male mentors, but they studied reading, writing, and music, as well as training in the gymnasium. Some clearly developed an appreciation for art, creating a demand for the high quality of painting found on Spartan ceramics, which were created by the members of the *perioikoi*.

At age 20, Spartiates joined the *syssitia*, a communal system in which they lived and dined together on plain food such as cheese, figs, and bread. This reinforced the bond that they felt as *homoioi* (equals). Unusually for a Greek city-state, girls were also educated, in poetry, music, and dance. As adults, they had more independence than women elsewhere and were able to leave their houses freely and exercise in the gymnasia. A few could even own and train horses

△ **Female athlete**
Displaying the skill of Spartan metalworkers and the relative freedom of female Spartans, this bronze statuette of a running girl dates from c.520 BCE.

▷ **Laconian plaque**
This 3rd-century BCE funerary relief from Aphyssou in Sparta shows a man, probably the deceased, with a drinking cup and a rising snake, a guardian of the Underworld and symbol of rebirth and immortality.

◁ **Spartan style**
Laconian pottery painters favored mythical and heroic scenes on tondos. Dating from c. 550 BCE, this example depicts a male figure—a hero or god—followed by a winged figure, perhaps representing victory.

The elongation seen on the horse's legs is typical of Spartan style

Waterfowl, a common motif on Greek pottery

SPARTAN ART

Sparta produced high-quality pottery and ivories (which were uncommon in Greece). It also had access to highly skilled bronze-workers, who created ornate vessels, votive statuettes, and mirror-stands. Dating from c. 550 BCE, the stand below depicts a girl who has griffins sprouting from her shoulders. Most of the surviving Spartan art dates to the 6th century BCE; production trailed off at the start of the Classical period.

for racing. Indeed, the first recorded female victor in the Olympic chariot race was a Spartan woman, Cynisca (daughter of King Agesilaus II), whose team won in 396 BCE.

To support themselves, male Spartiates relied on the klaros, an allocation of land sufficient to provide for one family. This was worked by helots, which left the Spartiates free to train and participate in religious rituals. The Spartans were particularly devoted to Apollo, who was honored in three annual festivals, notably the Karneia, which was held in August.

Over time, the Spartan system changed. Royal power declined, and the number of Spartiates fell, through losses in war and the inability of many to pay the necessary financial contributions to the syssitia. Increasingly, Sparta's army had to rely on the periokoi and on mercenaries, so that by the time of its defeat at Leuctra in 371 BCE (see pp.204–205), only a quarter of the army, some 700 hoplites was composed of Spartiates. Sparta's division of power and its education system, designed to produce warriors who would defend but not dominate the state, had finally failed.

Monuments of Youth

The human form in Archaic Greece

In the late 7th century BCE, Greek artists broke new ground by making statues on a bigger scale than ever before. These life-size or even larger stone figures, often brightly painted, were offered to gods at sanctuaries or acted as grave markers. They became increasingly lifelike and more skillfully made as the 6th century BCE progressed and as developments in bronze casting opened up new design possibilities.

Young male figures, called *kouroi*, are shown naked, while statues of young women (*korai*) are clothed and often hold an offering in one hand. They share an upright, forward-facing pose, with the feet together or one slightly advanced, and the arms generally held close to the body. This pose was probably inspired by Egyptian sculptures, but the Greeks went a step further and made their stone statues freestanding. They were thus technically demanding to produce, because they had to support their own weight.

Purpose and progress

The statues represent youthful, generic figures, rather than individuals. This can make it difficult to know the role of a particular *kouros* or *kore* in its ancient Greek context, and whether it represents a god or a mortal. Some statues have been found with inscriptions that explain who had them made and why. For example, one *kouros* from Boeotia has the inscription, "Amphias made this dedication from the tithes to the Far-Shooter [Apollo]." Those used as grave markers often name the deceased person.

△ **Egyptian influence, c. 600 BCE**
Found in Attica, this *kouros* has proportions similar to contemporary Egyptian statues. He is highly stylized and almost symmetrical, with anatomical details engraved into the stone. His eyes are over-large, and his braided hair makes a geometrical pattern.

△ **Archaic smile, 570–560 BCE**
The face of this *kore* from Keratea, Attica, has the small smile that was widely adopted in the second quarter of the 6th century BCE. Her hair and the folds of her drapery are stylized. Her arms are angular, with one hand close to her body, her thumb tucked inside her mantle, while the other holds a pomegranate as an offering.

△ **Realistic elements, 550–540 BCE**
This *kore* from Myrrhinus, Attica, was a grave marker for a girl or woman called Phrasikleia. The soft draping of the *kore*'s clothing and her jewelery and elaborate hair reflect stylistic developments of the mid-6th century BCE.

"Stay and mourn at the monument for dead Kroisos."

INSCRIPTION ON THE BASE OF A *KOUROS* FROM ANAVYSSOS, ATTICA

The statues show a clear progression over the 6th century BCE. Early figures were highly stylized, with over-large eyes and a beaded pattern for the hair. *Kouroi* had muscles incised rather than modeled on their bodies, and *korai* had thick, heavy drapery that gave little hint of the shape of the body beneath. From around 575 BCE, sculptors introduced a small "Archaic smile," which was an attempt to suggest their subject was infused with life and give the face a more human expression. As time went on, the proportions of the face and body became more lifelike, and their planes more rounded. The treatment of clothing on *korai* began to skillfully represent intricate folds and layers. Hairstyles became varied and elaborate, and the poses more relaxed.

By the mid-6th century BCE, technical abilities had advanced to the point where full-scale statues could be made from hollow bronze. This allowed for the creation of freer, more natural poses, with arms held away from the body.

Working in bronze

Bronze statues began with a model made of clay, which was then coated in a thick layer of wax. The artist then layered a clay mold on top, melted the wax away, and filled the gap between mold and model with molten bronze. Once cool, the mold was taken away and the statue was smoothed and finished. It was a tricky technique, and creators often made statues in several pieces then joined them together.

△ **Molded muscles, c. 530 BCE**
A grave marker for the fallen warrior Kroisos, this *kouros* from Anavyssos, Attica, has more realistic proportions and anatomical details than earlier *kouroi*. The stone is shaped to represent muscles; the face is gently rounded.

△ **Cast-bronze god, c. 530–520 BCE**
The pose of this statue of Apollo from Piraeus, near Athens, is looser than in contemporary stone statues, reflecting the increased freedom that working in bronze offered. Apollo's head is slightly turned and his arms are held forward, away from his body, with one hand outstretched while the other once held a bow.

△ **Rich details, 530–520 BCE**
Found at the Athenian Acropolis, this *kore* holding a quince has the skillfully carved folded and draped clothing typical of statues created in the late 6th century BCE. Elements remain of the elaborate patterning that once covered the garment, painted in red, blue, and green.

Early Athens

Sprung from the land

Rooted in myth, the stories that the Athenians told about the earliest beginnings of Athens emphasized their connection to the land of Attica and the divine favor that supported the growth of the city.

Inhabited from the Neolithic period and once an important Mycenaean center, Athens had become a prominent city by the end of the Archaic period. The story of its path to dominance was rooted firmly in the earth of Attica and in myths that connected kings, heroes, and gods to explain the past and show how it had led to the present.

Cecrops was the legendary first king and founding father of the city that would come to be known as Athens. The ancient Athenians considered him to be an autochthon (see box opposite), a mythical figure who had no human parents but sprang directly from the earth. His physical form, as half-man, half-snake,

△ **Erichthonius discovered**
This 17th-century painting by Peter Paul Rubens shows Cecrops's daughters opening the box in which Athena had hidden Erichthonius with a snake to keep him safe.

▷ **Goddess and king**
This 2nd-century CE Roman copy of a Greek statue from the 2nd–1st centuries BCE shows Athena holding the infant Erichthonius.

emphasized this close connection with the soil of Attica. The myth encapsulated a concept of strength and indigenity that the Athenians used to justify their dominance in Greece. This sense of superiority was strengthened by the city's connection with the goddess of wisdom.

In the reign of Cecrops, myth tells how the goddess Athena held a competition with Poseidon to decide who would be the patron god of the city. Poseidon struck the rock of the Acropolis with his trident and made a well of salt water. Athena planted an olive tree to mark her ownership. The people judged the olive tree to be a far more useful gift than salt water, and declared Athena the winner of the contest. Scholars debate whether Athens was named after her or she was named after Athens.

The Athenian king Erichthonius was said to have been born from the semen that fell from the smith-god Hephaestus to the earth after he attempted to rape Athena. Adopted by Athena, Erichthonius was credited with founding the yearly Panathenaea festival dedicated to her.

> "The **lineage of Theseus**, on the **father's side**, goes back to **Erechtheus** and the first **children** of the **soil**."

PLUTARCH, *LIFE OF THESEUS*

Phaea the witch with her sow, which terrorized Crommyon, in northern Greece

Theseus dragging the vanquished Minotaur from the Labyrinth

Theseus fighting the bandit Sinis Pityocamptes ("the pine-bender")

Theseus capturing the Cretan Bull, said to have fathered the Minotaur

The myth of Erichthonius's descendant Erechtheus, who secured an Athenian victory over the city of Eleusis, and Eumolpus, a legendary king of Thrace and son of Poseidon who had taken refuge there, no doubt speaks of the growing power of Athens in the Greek "Dark Age". However, according to Athenian legend, it was the Bronze Age hero Theseus (a descendant of Erechtheus) who was responsible for the *synoikismos* that turned Athens into a powerful city-state. He drew together 12 cities in Attica in a political union, creating a single state with Athens at its center.

From kingship to oligarchy

According to Athenian tradition, in the late 12th century BCE, the Erechtheid dynasty was replaced by a short-lived Melanthid dynasty. Athens' last king was Codrus, who ruled until c. 1068 BCE, after which Athens became an oligarchy. According to the 4th-century BCE *Constitution of the Athenians*, the powers of the hereditary kings devolved to three *archontes*

(rulers). These were the *basileus* (responsible for religious duties), the *archos* (the civilian head of state), and the *polemarchos* (who commanded Athens' army). By the 6th century BCE, Athens was ruled by nine annually appointed archons (magistrates), all elected by and from the aristocracy. By then, however, Athens' citizens were demanding more say in the city's politics (see p.118)

△ **The deeds of Theseus**
This Attic red-figure kylix from c. 440–430 BCE was found in Vulci, Italy. It shows the Athenian hero Theseus, and some of his "labors," including (in the center) his victory over the Minotaur.

BORN FROM **THE EARTH**

Cicadas, which emerge from the soil as "earth-born" nymphs, were symbols of autochthony (the idea of being born from the earth) in ancient Athens. The Athenians' belief that they were descended from a line of kings who were literally born from the soil of Attica was central to their identity. The historian Thucydides notes that some wealthy Athenians wore cicada ornaments in their hair to mark their pride in this deep connection. Autochthony was used not only by the Athenians but also by groups in Boeotia and the Peloponnese to help justify territorial claims.

TERRA-COTTA CICADA

Pythagoras of Samos

Charismatic philosopher and community leader

Believed to be the first to call himself a philosopher, a "lover of wisdom," Pythagoras was a polymath whose metaphysical, mathematical, and sometimes mystical ideas were influential in Classical Greek philosophy.

Despite his great renown, almost nothing is known for certain of Pythagoras's life. He left no written teachings, but a general picture of the man and his ideas can be gleaned from accounts by his students and contemporaries, although these have come to us through later writers and may be unreliable legends.

There is no doubt, however, of the existence of Pythagoras, a native of the Ionian island of Samos. Coming from a wealthy family, he would have been well educated, and is likely to have traveled to Babylon or Egypt to study as a young man. At the age of about 40, Pythagoras left Samos for Croton, a Greek colony in southern Italy. There, he set himself up as leader of a school of mathematics and philosophy.

His students, the Pythagoreans, lived communally according to a lifestyle advocated by Pythagoras that embraced vegetarianism, pacifism, and the humane treatment of all living things.

Pythagoras's world view
Central to Pythagoras's philosophy was a sense of harmony, order, and interconnectedness. He believed, for example, in metempsychosis, the transmigration of the immortal soul after death from one body to another. In addition, he put great importance on the role of mathematics, and numbers in particular, in his interpretation of the physical world. He argued that the cosmos is ordered mathematically, and that the movement of heavenly bodies created a "harmony of the spheres" that corresponded to the mathematical ratios of musical notes.

Pythagoras and his followers initially had some political influence in Croton, but it seems that he faced hostility from supporters of democracy and was either killed or, more probably, hounded out of the colony and headed north to the city of Metapontum, where he died shortly afterward.

△ **Pythagoras at work**
In this 15th-century miniature, Pythagoras is shown at work on his theory about the mathematical relationship between the frequencies of different notes of the musical scale. His work underpins the tuning systems of Western music.

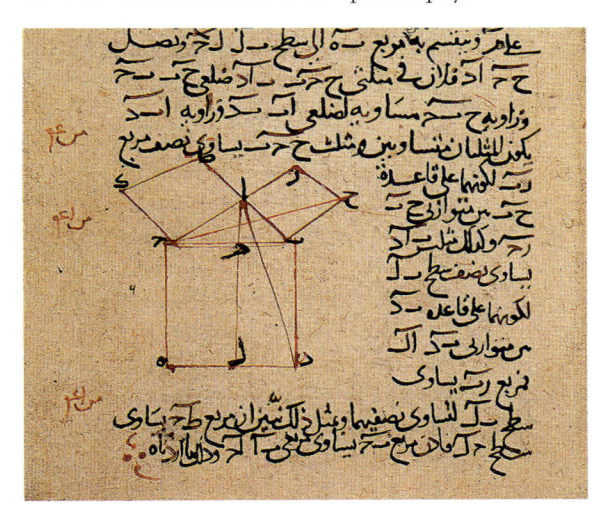

◁ **Pythagoras's theorem**
This drawing from a 13th-century Arabic manuscript shows "Euclid's Windmill," a proof of the theorem credited to Pythagoras that the square of the longest side of a right-angled triangle is equal to the sum of the other two sides.

Democratic Revolution

Oligarchy overthrown in Athens

In the wake of social unrest during the 7th century BCE, the renowned Athenian lawmaker Solon introduced a series of reforms that marked the beginning of a democratic revolution in Athens.

As rival aristocratic clans vied for dominance in Attica, the region of Greece with Athens as its urban center, resentment grew among its inhabitants, who wanted a greater say in the government of the area. Around 622 BCE, Draco, an Athenian lawgiver, instituted a notoriously strict legal code—which included the death sentence for most offences—in an attempt to quell the unrest, but it had limited success. It was only when Solon (see opposite) was appointed as archon (chief magistrate) that a lasting way to restore order was found.

At the beginning of the 6th century BCE, Solon took an important step in appeasing the protests by ending the practice of debtors having to surrender their estates and even becoming enslaved to their creditors, and immediately canceling existing debts. He brought in reforms that gave more Athenian citizens the right to participate in the political process—a right previously reserved for the aristocracy. These shifted control of the political agenda from the Areopagus, a council of aristocratic ex-archons that chose the city's archons, to the *boule*, composed of selected citizens from the four *phylai* (clans) of Athens. In addition, Solon instituted the *ekklesia*, an assembly that was open to all free adult male citizens. With these reforms, Solon introduced democratic principles, but it would be some decades before Athens achieved a true and lasting democracy.

There were setbacks in this process too: the aristocracies continued to fight for power, and in the 560s BCE, an aristocrat called Pisistratus seized control of Athens, exiling Solon and members of the powerful and pro-democracy Alcmaeonid family. Many in Athens mourned the loss of democracy, but as tyrant, Pisistratus kept several of Solon's reforms and continued the process of diminishing the power of the aristocracy. His populist policies gained the support of the lower classes in particular, but this was not enough for him to hold on to power: twice he was ousted and exiled by the pro-democracy faction, each time returning as tyrant some years later. He ruled until his death around 527 BCE, when he was succeeded by his sons, Hippias and Hipparchus.

The end of tyranny

Hippias's and Hipparchus's time in power began well, with Athens experiencing a period of prosperity. A turning point came in 514 BCE, when Hipparchus was assassinated by two lovers called Harmodius and Aristogeiton, apparently motivated by a personal grievance rather than political reasons. The two were executed for their crime but popularly hailed as the "Tyrannicides," and their action set in motion the Athenian Revolution that brought about true democratic reform.

The remaining tyrant, Hippias, reacted by becoming more despotic, imposing harsh taxes and executing or exiling a large number of citizens. This triggered unrest in the city, and in his quest to maintain control, he sought an alliance with Persia, further angering his opponents. Encouraged by the head of the Alcmaeonid family, Cleisthenes, and driven by the Delphic Oracle's instructions to "Free Athens!"—but also, no doubt, by his own ambition—

△ **Athenian coin**
The head of Athena adorns the obverse of this silver drachm from 510–490 BCE, the early years of democracy in the city-state.

▽ **Athenian tyrant**
Painted by French artist Jean-Auguste-Dominique Ingres, this early 19th-century neoclassical painting depicts the tyrant Pisistratus.

"**Freedom** is the **sure possession** of those alone who have the **courage** to **defend** it."

PERICLES, ACCORDING TO THUCYDIDES

King Cleomenes I of Sparta led an army into Attica in 510 BCE. Hippias fled, and an oligarchy under an aristocrat named Isagoras was installed.

In 508 BCE, Athens' citizens revolted against the Spartan-imposed oligarchy. They eventually besieged its members on the Acropolis for three days. Cleomenes and Isagoras were finally allowed to flee, but around 300 of their supporters were executed. The exiled Alcmaeonids were called back to Athens, and Cleisthenes was made archon. Once in power, he improved participatory democracy, ensuring fairer representation of the citizenry across the Attic region by increasing the number of *phylai* to ten.

Despite attempts by Sparta to restore Hippias as tyrant, Athens retained its democratic constitution and continued to refine its democracy through the 5th century BCE. Other than a short period in 413 BCE, when an oligarchy seized control, and the year-long rule of the Thirty Tyrants installed in 404 BCE (see pp.188–189), Athenian democracy lasted until the Macedonians conquered Athens in 338 BCE. Even then, the city retained many of its democratic institutions.

SOLON

Born in Salamis in about 630 BCE, Solon came from an aristocratic Attic family. He wrote poetry for pleasure and became a prominent Athenian politician during the turbulent period at the end of the 7th century BCE. He was appointed archon (chief magistrate) in 594 BCE, and the legal reforms he introduced paved the way for democracy, and a "golden age" in Athens. Having instituted the reforms, however, he retired from public life, and left Athens to travel abroad. He returned some ten years later to find the fledgling democracy under threat and became actively involved in politics again. Solon died at the age of 80, shortly after a populist coup led by his old rival Pisistratus in the 560s BCE.

Sword hilt, all that remains of the sword that the statue once held

Early Classical style favored short, stylized hair and an impassive, almost masklike face.

◁ **Tyrannicide**
This 2nd-century BCE Roman copy of a Greek original from c.477 BCE is of Harmodius, hero of democracy. The original replaced a statue that Cleisthenes had commissioned, and that the Persians stole in 480 BCE.

Athenian Democracy

Political rights for citizens

After overthrowing its aristocratic oligarchy in the Athenian Revolution, Athens adopted a form of democratic government that offered the citizens of Attica a chance to be directly involved in the city-state's decisions.

△ **Jury ballots**
Jury members used bronze disks, such as these from c. 300 BCE, to indicate their decision in a trial: ballots with a pierced axle for guilty, a solid axle for acquittal.

The democracy that emerged in ancient Athens is widely regarded as the model from which our modern democracies evolved, but it is likely that similar types of popular government existed in many of the major city-states. The Athenian system, however, was perhaps the most sophisticated and certainly the best documented, as Classical Greek writers, including the author of the *Constitution of Athens*, left descriptions of its history and institutions.

The heart of power

Considered the sovereign institution of Athens, the *ekklesia* met 40 times a year, originally in a dedicated auditorium on the hillside of the Pnyx. Here, the citizens had the final say on matters of governance. They had the authority to write laws, to determine foreign policy, and to act as a court of appeal. Voting was by a simple majority with a show of hands.

All free, male citizens of Athens were entitled to attend and vote in the sessions, but in practice this included only a minority of the inhabitants of the *polis*. Citizenship was restricted to property-owning men over the age of 18 who had completed their military service, and so excluded lower-class workers, women, and the enslaved. It also excluded Athens' resident foreigners, or *metikoi* (see pp.198–199). The

◁ **Sortition system**
Kleroteria, such as this example from c. 300 BCE, were filled with tokens (*pinakia*) and used to select citizens for the *boule* and for jury duty.

number of citizens was thus reduced to 10–20 percent of the population. Among the *ekklesia*'s regular duties was the yearly decision on whether to hold an ostracism—a vote to banish one citizen for ten years. If agreed, each citizen was able to submit an ostracon, a pottery shard that they marked with the name of the person they hoped to exile. As long as 6,000 such votes were made altogether, the person whose name appeared the most was ostracized.

The *boule*, the "Council of Five Hundred," was responsible for the day-to-day governance of the *polis* and oversaw the running of Athens' democracy as a whole, including setting the agenda of the *ekklesia*. It met daily and was made up of 50 citizens selected from each of the ten *phylai* (clans) to serve for one year. These representatives were chosen by sortition, that is, selected by lot, which was considered more democratic than election, as votes could be influenced by money or skillful oratory.

The judiciary

Working alongside the *boule* and the *ekklesia* were the judiciary institutions. These included the *dikasteria*, popular courts that decided verdicts and sentences for cases brought to them by citizens. Jurors were selected daily by lot from a pool of citizens over the age of 30 to preside over the cases. After listening to the prosecutor and the defendant, the jury would vote by secret ballot on the accused's guilt. The democratic reforms of Solon and Cleisthenes (see p.116–117) had restricted the role of the Areopagus council, but it continued to function as a judicial council and a court trying the most serious crimes.

▽ **Constitution of Athens**
Attributed to Aristotle and composed c. 325–300 BCE, the *Constitution of Athens*, seen here in a 1st-century BCE papyrus, described the constitution's development and the contemporary workings of the government.

△ **The Pnyx**
Painted by German artist Rudolf Müller in 1863, this scene offers a view from the hill known as the Pnyx, with the Acropolis in the background to the east. The *ekklesia* met regularly on the Pnyx, where there was an auditorium that had space for up to 6,000 people. At some point, certainly by the 1st century BCE, the assembly meetings were moved to the Theater of Dionysus.

A romantic depiction of the ruins of the Acropolis, topped by the Parthenon, lit by the morning sun

The ruins of the speaker's platform (*bema*), which was quarried out of the bedrock of the hill

"**Athens' constitution** is called a **democracy** because it **respects** the **interests** not of the **minority** but of the **whole people**."

PERICLES, FUNERAL ORATION

Athenian Agora

More than a marketplace

Located halfway between Athens' main gate and the Acropolis, the Agora was the city's beating heart. Athenian citizens thronged here to address political and legal matters, conduct business, shop, philosophize, and socialize.

As Athens rebuilt after Persian sackings in 480 and 479 BCE (see pp.172–173), stately civic buildings sprang up around the open square, many to support the new democracy. The *boule* and its executive committee benefitted from a new meeting house (New Bouleuterion) and headquarters (Tholos), respectively; the Old Bouleuterion became the city archives. Colonnaded stoas served as commercial and administrative spaces, providing shady places to walk, talk, and run the city's affairs; the Royal Stoa was seat of the Archon Basileus (King Ruler). A complex of law courts evolved east of the Panathenaic Way, while sacred spaces included the Altar of the Twelve Gods, from which all distances from Athens were measured.

The Agora hosted everything from cavalry inspections and races to ostracism votes. Above all, it was a thriving marketplace, catering to citizens' every need: fresh produce, home textiles, wood, clothing, perfume, animals, and even people. Although the majority of noncitizens were excluded from the Agora, there were lower-status women and foreign-born residents among the merchants and visitors, and enslaved people went there to shop for their households.

KEY

1	Stoa Poikile/Painted Stoa	7	Panathenaic Way	13	Old Bouleuterion
2	Altar of Aphrodite Ourania	8	Parthenon	14	New Bouleuterion
3	Law court	9	Southeast Fountain House	15	Tholos
4	Altar of the Twelve Gods	10	South Stoa	16	Residential/artisans' district
5	Stoa Basileios/Royal Stoa	11	Aiakeion	17	Hephaisteion
6	Stoa of Zeus Eleutherios	12	Eponymous Heroes		

THE AGORA **THROUGH TIME**

Long used as a cemetery, the site of Athens' Classical Agora was marked out as a public space in the late 6th century BCE, with the first Bouleuterion built in 508/507 BCE as the new democracy took shape. After the flurry of building in the 5th and 4th centuries BCE, the Agora was next redeveloped during the Hellenistic period, gaining grand new stoas for commercial purposes. It acquired its fullest form in the 2nd century CE, when Roman sponsors, recognizing Athens as a hub of culture and learning, added temples, a library, and a great concert hall at its center.

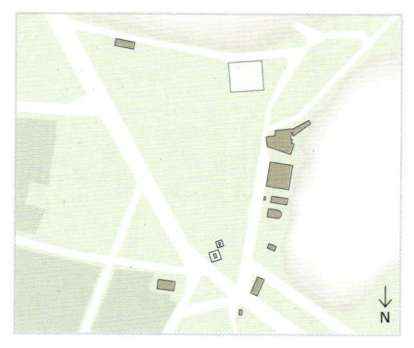

EARLY AGORA, C. 500 BCE

ROMAN AGORA, C. 150 CE

This names Themistocles as son of Neocleos

Themistocles came from Phrearrhi

Potsherds were used like modern scrap paper

△ **Ostraca**
Ostracisms, at which citizens could vote another citizen into exile, took place in the Agora. More than 2,000 ostraca have been found naming Themistocles, an Athenian politician ostracized around 470 BCE.

▽ **The hub of Athens**
This illustration depicts the Agora around 400 BCE, soon after the construction of the New Bouleuterion and other public buildings that reflected Athens' wealth and mode of democratic governance.

△ Southeast Fountain House
Women fetched water from the Fountain House as one of their domestic duties. Since respectable women were not permitted in the Agora, they visited around dawn to avoid being seen by men.

△ The Eponymous Heroes
The Monument of the Eponymous Heroes depicted the founders of Cleisthenes' ten *phylai* of Athens (see p.117). Citizens gathered here to read public notices, such as proposed legislation, posted below their *phyle*'s statue.

Greek Pottery

Style, form, and function

Flourishing from the 1st millennium BCE and created in a wide variety of forms, Greek pottery served both utilitarian and ceremonial purposes. Its decoration ranged from the geometric to the figural, encompassing themes from mythology and everyday life and such techniques as black- and red-figure painting and relief work.

△ **Protogeometric tripod**
Found at the Kerameikos necropolis in Athens, this tripod has the abstract decoration typical of the Protogeometric period (1050–900 BCE).

The lid's handle is decorated with a miniature version of the box

Buff-colored clay decorated with reddish paint and an inscription incised into the surface

Flowing, curved animal motif

Handles painted with clay slip that turned black on firing

Athena standing with shield and spear, as always seen on such prize vases

△ **Geometric pyxis**
This lidded box, or pyxis, dates from 800–760 BCE and is decorated in the Geometric style that characterized Greek pottery from 900–700 BCE. Such boxes were used to store personal items.

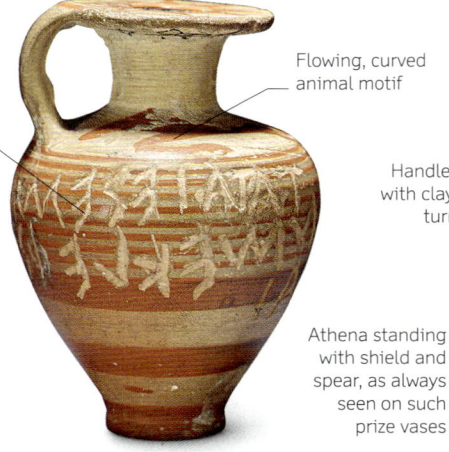

△ **Proto-Corinthian aryballos**
This jug, used for perfumed oil, is from c. 670 BCE. Corinth's potters adopted flora and fauna motifs influenced by the art of the Eastern Mediterranean.

◁ **Corinthian krater**
This wine-mixing vessel produced in Corinth c. 600–575 BCE has the animated, rounded figures typical of pottery made in the city in the 7th and 6th centuries BCE.

△ **Prize amphora**
This amphora from c. 530 BCE, painted using the black-figure technique, was designed to be filled with oil from olive groves sacred to Athena and given as a prize in the Panathenaic Games.

Woman's face, roughly sculpted by hand by the potter

◁ **Two-faced kantharos**
This drinking cup features two faces—of a woman, possibly a maenad, and of a satyr. It was produced by an Athenian artisan around 500–490 BCE, when such human-head vessels were fashionable.

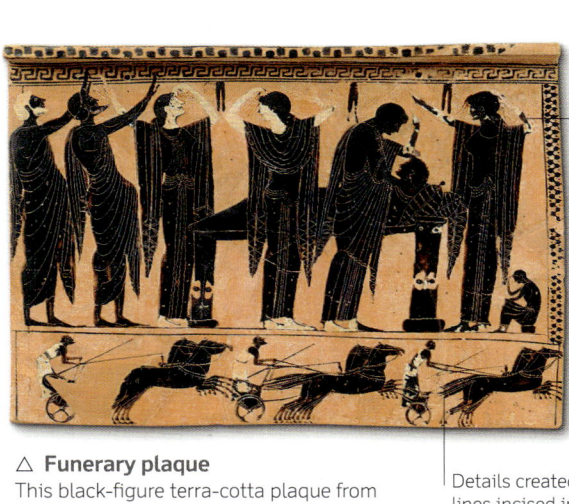

Mourners, their arms raised in an expression of grief

△ **Funerary plaque**
This black-figure terra-cotta plaque from 520–510 BCE shows mourners laying out the dead above a chariot race scene.

Details created by lines incised into the painted slip

▷ **Classical chous**
This small wine jug, from c. 410 BCE, is just 3½ in (9 cm) tall. Associated with the Dionysian Anthesteria festival, in which children played a major part, it is decorated with two boys.

Red-figure painted cow

△ **Herdsman's cup**
From c. 470–460 BCE, this hoof-shaped terra-cotta cup is painted with a scene whose details—the herdsman's fur cloak and warm hat—hint at real knowledge of country life.

Runners taking part in a foot race

Polydeuces or Castor, who were venerated as gods in Sparta

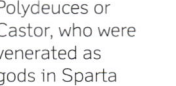

▽ **Pergamene beaker**
Created in Pergamon, in Asia Minor, in 125–75 BCE, this beaker was decorated with mold-made clay appliqués of ivy leaves and berries, before being dipped in red clay slip and fired.

A sketchily painted dining couch with coverlets

◁ **Cult vessel**
Showing the twin brothers Castor and Polydeuces riding to a feast, this black-figure lekythos from c. 500 BCE reflects the belief that gods could be entertained like human guests.

◁ **Panathenaic trophy**
This Attic black-figure amphora was produced in 333–332 BCE as a prize for a winner at the Panathenaic Games. Such prizes were always decorated with the competition for which they were awarded, in this case a foot race.

△ **Place of worship**
The Temple of Athena at Poseidonia, in southwestern Italy, was built c.500 BCE. Votives found at the site include figurines of Athena in the guise of a nurturing goddess holding a child, and of an armed warrior.

A Greater Greece?

The Greeks in southern Italy

From the 8th century BCE, Greek traders had made their homes in southern Italy, building successful colonies that in turn drove further colonization and that threatened to outshine the city-states of Greece itself by the 6th century BCE.

Southern Italy and Sicily had obvious attractions for Greek colonizers: there was plenty of cultivable land, and it was the ideal base for onward trade to the Greek emporia in France and Spain, and within Italy. By the 6th century BCE, the Greek cities in Magna Graecia (Great Greece, the name given to southern Italy and Sicily) dominated the region.

The Greeks first settled in southern Italy around 775 BCE, where traders from Euboea set up an *emporion* (trading center) on Pithecusae, off the Italian coast

near Naples, and a more substantial *apoikia* (a colony connected to the mother city) at Cumae, on the mainland. Around 720–700 BCE, settlers from the Peloponnese established colonies at Sybaris, Croton, and Metapontum, while the Spartans established Taranto in 706 BCE. The first colony in Sicily was Naxos, founded around 735 BCE. More colonies followed, including the greatest of them all, the city of Syracuse (see pp.128–129). The Greek settlers encountered several groups in southern Italy,

"In **one word,** the whole of **Italy** is **rich**."

STRABO, *GEOGRAPHIES*

including the Ausones, the Oenotrians, and the Iapygians (themselves divided into three groups). Archaeological evidence points to Greek goods and ideas having penetrated these groups quite early on, and by the 6th century BCE, many had become Hellenized, adopting elements of Greek culture, religion, and language.

Trade and wealth

The Greeks also came into contact with the Etruscans (see below), who they called "Tyrrhenians" and dismissed as pirates. Yet they were only too willing to trade with them, since the Etruscans had become rich from mining and working their immense reserves of copper, silver, iron, lead, and tin, and were hungry for Greek luxuries. Some Etruscan cities were subsequently Hellenized. Spina, for example, at the mouth of the Po River in northeast Italy, had been founded and populated by ethnic Etruscans, but by

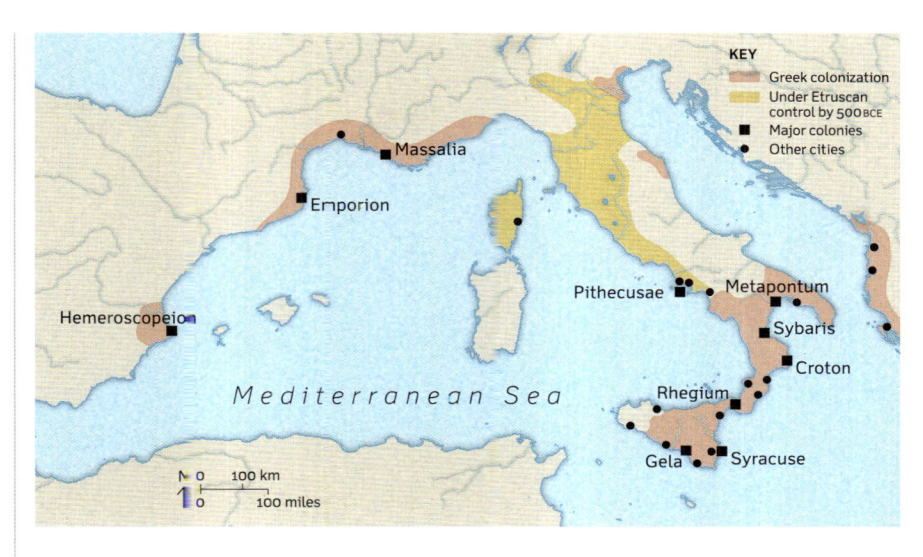

the late 6th century BCE was linguistically and culturally Greek. Spina even maintained its own treasury at the Sanctuary at Delphi.

By the 6th century BCE, the cities of Magna Graecia on the Ionian coast had developed into wealthy centers that attracted the best artists and whose large, ornate temples threatened to outshine those in Greece itself. Indeed, the colony of Sybaris was so steeped in luxury that it gave the English language the word "sybaritic," which refers to something characterized by pleasure, self-indulgence, and sensuousness.

Expansion and conflict

Eager to grow their power, the cities turned their attention to expansion. Many founded colonies themselves: Naples was established around 600 BCE by migrants from Pithecusae; Poseidonia (later renamed Paestum by the Romans) was settled from Sybaris. Almost inevitably, this led to conflict between the major cities. At some time between 550 BCE and 510 BCE, an alliance of Metapontum, Sybaris and Croton overcame the colony at Siris, on the Sinni River. Around 510 BCE, Sybaris was itself razed during a conflict with Croton. In the mid-5th century BCE, Croton became hegemon (leader) of the Italiote League, created to counter the power of the cities of Thurii and Locri, also originally Greek colonies.

The growing power of the cities also attracted the attention of external forces. Around 540 BCE, Carthage brought the Phoenician cities in Sicily under its hegemony, and helped prevent Greek expansion westward. In 524 BCE, the tyrant Aristodemus of Cumae successfully fought off a coalition of Etruscans, Daunians (an Iapygian group), and Ausones seeking to capture the city. Ultimately, the Greeks could not retain control of their southern Italian territories, and by 200 BCE, Magna Graecia was under Roman control.

△ **The western colonies**
This map shows the spread of Greece's colonies and influence in the Western Mediterranean, where the Greeks dominated southern Italy and Sicily and Greek settlers reached Spain.

▽ **Mirror handle**
Found in Sicily, this 4th/3rd-century BCE handle for a mirror may have been made by a Greek, an Etruscan, or another indigenous artisan.

THE **ETRUSCANS**

The most important of the indigenous peoples in pre-Roman Italy, the Etruscans flourished from the 9th to the 4th centuries BCE, when they were subsumed by the Roman Republic. The Etruscans were known for their sophisticated art and heavily influenced early Rome, but they also shared influences with the Greek colonies in southern Italy. This could result in hybrid creations such as the cup below, whose shape is Etruscan, but whose "phallus bird" motif was popular in Athenian painting in the 6th and 5th centuries BCE.

> "The **diver** dives **alone**. There is present all the **intensity** of the **moment** of **death**."

AMERICAN ARCHAEOLOGIST R. ROSS HOLLOWAY

Border with palmette and scroll corners

The Tomb of the Diver

A remarkable survival

The Tomb of the Diver once belonged to a small necropolis at Tempa del Prete, located around 1 mile (1.5 km) south of the ancient city of Paestum in the Greek colony of Poseidonia, now in Campania, southern Italy. The tomb dates to the early part of the 5th century, around 470 BCE, and was discovered by Italian archaeologist Mario Napoli in 1968. It is formed of five large limestone slabs set in a bedrock base and contained the remains of a young man. He was provisioned in death with a two-handled lekythos (oil flask) and a *chelys* (a tortoiseshell lyre), and surrounded by fresco scenes.

The tomb has been identified as the work of several hands: the technically accomplished and expressive painter of the north, east, and west walls and the cover slab; the less skilled painter of the south wall; and an apprentice.

A leap of faith

The frescoes offer a fascinating insight into the beliefs about death and the afterlife during this period. The tomb is named for the scene found on the interior of the cover slab. Executed in "true" fresco, in which the paint pigment mix is applied to wet plaster and becomes fixed in place when the plaster dries, it depicts a nude man diving from a cliff into the water below. He passes a tower on his descent; sparely illustrated olive trees mark the cliff and shore, and the whole is framed by a border with palmettes at the corners. The dive and the diver's inevitable immersion are thought to represent death; the tower, protection; and the far shore, a promise of safety.

The walls of the tomb depict an aristocratic male drinking party, or symposium, and place the dead man at the center of a revelry intended to last for eternity. On the north and south walls, guests recline on couches; one throws his wine lees at a target; others carry lyres or play the aulos (double flute). The west wall depicts the departure, or perhaps arrival, of two further attendees preceded by a young female flautist. On the east wall, a serving boy stands by a table upon which sits a large krater.

A long tradition

The Tomb of the Diver was part of a tradition of tomb painting on the Greek mainland and in the Etruscan tombs of Magna Graecia, at sites such as Tarquinia and Veii. A large number of tombs around Paestum preserve scenes illustrating contemporary ideas concerning religion and death like those found in the Tomb of the Diver. These paintings were perhaps commissioned by an aristocratic family in recognition of a young life unfulfilled. While the Tomb of the Diver was part of this tradition, it is an exceptionally rare archaeological find, being the only known such tomb to have survived in its entirety.

△ **Grave slab**
The slanting border on the right-hand side of the tomb's roof may have been a modification necessitated by damage to the slab.

An olive tree, mirroring depictions of olives on Greek painted pottery

Green paint, one of five colors used: black, red, blue, green, and white

The eponymous "diver," diving past a tower into the water

The cover spread over two couches is likely an apprentice's mistake

Black outline and musculature added after the colors

△ **Stone tomb**
This shows the tomb as it looked when excavated. Built of limestone slabs, it measured approximately 7 ft (2.2 m) by 3 ft 7 in (1.1 m) by 2 ft 8 in (0.8 m).

△ **The north wall**
One of two scenes depicting reclining symposiasts, the painting on the north wall shows revelers in conversation, playing music, and engaging in games of skill.

The Rise of Syracuse

Dominance in Sicily

Sicily proved a land of opportunity for its Greek settlers. Nowhere was the opportunity grasped more firmly than in Syracuse, which became a wealthy, forward-looking city, albeit one subject to cruel and autocratic rule.

Syracuse was one of the first Greek colonies to be implanted in Sicily, on the eastern half of the island, in the 8th–7th centuries BCE, along with the cities of Zancle, Naxos, Leontini, Catana, Megara Hyblaea, and Gela. Before the Greeks' arrival, the island, from east to west, was inhabited by the Sicels, who had lived in eastern Sicily since the Iron Age; the Sicani, who perhaps came from Iberia; and the Elymians, migrants from Italy. To the west, there were also several trading colonies founded by the Phoenicians of North Africa after c. 900 BCE.

By the 5th century BCE, the rulers of Syracuse had successfully maneuvered through inter-city rivalries, and internal and external threats, to establish the city as the dominant power in Sicily and southern Italy.

The city's beginnings

Syracuse was founded around 734 BCE by settlers from the town of Tenea, outside Corinth. Even before they left, their leader, Archias, had reputedly planned the city they were going to found. Arriving on the tiny island of Ortygia, just off Sicily, they soon built a wealthy city that spread more than half a mile (1 km) onto the mainland. It had a large rural hinterland that was owned by the ruling aristocracy of Syracuse, the *gamoroi*, and largely worked by the Sicels.

△ **Winged Gorgon**
A common motif for Sicilian artisans, the Gorgon Medusa is shown holding one of her children, the winged horse Pegasus, in her right hand in this 7th-century BCE relief from Syracuse.

From the 7th century BCE, Syracuse was prosperous enough to found its own colonies in Sicily, such as Akrae (664 BCE), Kasmenae (643 BCE), and Camarina (599 BCE). The remains of Syracuse's 6th-century BCE temples dedicated to Apollo, Olympian Zeus, and Athena also point to a thriving culture.

Growing power

The cities in Sicily faced the same issues of political violence and rivalry that troubled the colonies in southern Italy, and indeed the cities of Greece itself. Syracuse was in near constant dispute with Camarina, for example. Syracuse destroyed Camarina in 533 BCE and again around 484 BCE, after it had been rebuilt with the help of the city of Gela. Founded by Cretans and Rhodians in 688 BCE, Gela became the most powerful city in Sicily under its tyrants Cleander

MYTHICAL CONNECTIONS

According to Greek myth, the nymph Arethusa turned into a freshwater stream to escape the unwanted attentions of the river god Alpheus. Helped by Artemis, she fled the Peloponnese for the west. Flowing in headlong panic across the Ionian Sea, she surfaced as a freshwater spring on the island of Ortygia, off Sicily's southeast corner. This was where Syracuse was founded. Legend says that her path through the sea has been marked ever since with a stream of fresh water.

DECADRACHM OF ARETHUSA FROM SYRACUSE

◁ **Sicilian drama**
Originally built in the
5th century BCE and rebuilt
between 238 and 215 BCE,
the Greek theater on the
Temenite Hill overlooking
Syracuse is the largest in
Sicily. The seating area had a
diameter of c. 460 ft (140 m)
and had 67 rows of seats.

▽ **Etruscan booty**
Captured at the Battle of
Cumae, this bronze helmet
is inscribed in Greek script
with "Hieron, son of
Deinomenes, and the
Syracusans, [dedicated]
to Zeus Etruscan [spoils]
from Cumae".

(r. 505–498 BCE) and Hippocrates (r. 498–491 BCE).
Soon after Hippocrates' death, a formidable soldier
named Gelon seized control of Gela from Hippocrates'
sons in a military coup. In 485 BCE, when the people
of Syracuse rebelled against the *gamoroi*, exiling them
from the city, Gelon intervened. The *gamoroi* were
back within weeks with Gelon's assistance and Gelon
himself became Syracuse's tyrant. He handed control
of Gela to his brother, Hiero. In 483 BCE, Gelon went
on to overthrow the leaders of Megara Hyblaea and,
according to Herodotus, enslave the population.

Tyranny and triumph

Under Gelon's brutal rule, Syracuse prospered. As
tyrant, Gelon instigated a major building program,
and forced half the population of Gela to move to
Syracuse. He also strengthened his position by
recruiting a large army of mercenary troops from the
local Sicel population and from Greece—all of whom
gained citizenship of Syracuse—and by building up
Syracuse's naval strength. Meanwhile, he made a
strategic marriage to the daughter of Theron, tyrant
of the southwestern Sicilian city of Akragas, which gave
him an important ally. It was with Theron's support
that Gelon went on to successfully repel an attack
by the Carthaginians.

The Greeks coexisted fairly peaceably with Sicily's
Phoenician colonies until the 5th century BCE, when
the Phoenician city of Carthage began to assert its
control over the Western Mediterranean. Seeing Gelon
and Theron threatening to take over all of Sicily, in
480 BCE Carthage sent a force to support Terrilus,
the tyrant of Himera who had been deposed by
Theron. According to tradition, on the same day
as Athens' triumph at Salamis (see pp.152–153),
a force led by Gelon and Theron defeated the
Carthaginians in battle on land and at sea.

Gelon died in 478 BCE. He was succeeded by his
younger brother Hieron, who also made a strategic
marriage, with the daughter of the tyrant of the Greek
city of Rhegium, in Calabria, Italy. His victory over
the Etruscans at the naval Battle of Cumae (474 BCE)
made Syracuse the main power in Magna Graecia.
Under Hieron, the city continued to flourish and by
415 BCE, it was as big as Athens.

"The **largest** of **Greek cities** and the most **beautiful** of **all cities**."

ROMAN HISTORIAN CICERO, *IN VERREM*

A pair of mules pulling a second cart

The bridal couple traveling by cart as a mark of honor

Wedding guest arriving on foot

Travel and Transportation

By land and sea

Travel was integral to the life and culture of the Greeks. As traders, they traced the limits of their known world. Even within Greece itself, they often went on journeys, traveling to social or cultural events or visiting shrines.

Greek culture was fundamentally outward-looking. Trade made travelers of many Greeks, because produce had to be taken to market, and luxuries imported from overseas. Similarly, the frequent wars of the ancient world saw many citizens traveling far and wide in the service of their *polis*. Even the tales of the Greek heroes (see pp.42–43), including Odysseus, Theseus, and Jason, often involved adventures in far-off places. The Greeks also took pride in their common "Greekness," nurturing it through travel to religious sanctuaries such as Delphi and festivals such as the Panathenaea, while skilled craftspeople, actors, writers, and medical experts often traveled for work.

Crossing the waters

To be a Greek citizen was to travel, and the sea provided the easiest way to reach both Greek *poleis* across the Mediterranean and the coastal city-states of Greece itself. With no passenger ships, travelers had to make their journeys aboard cargo ships. The classic Greek galley, its big square sail supplemented by banks of oars, and with a ram at the bow, was a fighting vessel, capable of considerable speed in short, attacking bursts. But oars also offered a useful

THE **DIOLKOS**

Built in the 7th century BCE, the Diolkos was a paved road that allowed ships to be portered, by being towed, across the Isthmus of Corinth from the Gulf of Corinth to the Saronic Gulf. The route saved a 210-mile (340-km) voyage around the Peloponnese. Writing of the road in the 5th century BCE, Thucydides tells how the Spartans "got ready hauling machines to carry their ships ... to the sea on the side of Athens, in order to make their attack by land and sea at once."

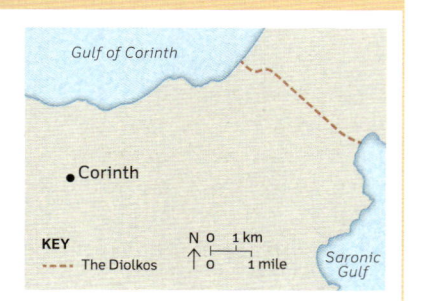

Gulf of Corinth

• Corinth

KEY
----- The Diolkos

N 0 1 km
↑ 0 1 mile

Saronic Gulf

Woman with torch waiting in the groom's house

▷ Wedding procession

This black-figure painted scene from a terra-cotta lekythos made by a potter named Amasis shows a bride, a groom, and their guests traveling on foot and by cart to a wedding.

maneuverability that was much needed in confined coastal waters, as well as insurance against any lack of wind. From around 500 BCE, larger Greek freighters also combined oar- and sail-power, though smaller vessels went solely under sail.

Seafaring was hazardous. Along with the risk of storm and shipwreck, certain coasts were home to pirates, who waylaid vessels, capturing passengers and crews, as shown by the story of Dionysus and the pirates (see right). Ironically, the Greeks were among the customers for those the pirates enslaved along the way. Mythical creatures such as the whirlpool called Charybdis, the monster Scylla, and the Sirens—all encountered by Odysseus—gave form to sailors' fears.

Over the land

Traveling over land was of course possible, if time-consuming, expensive, and arduous. While members of the elite might ride on horseback or in carriages, the majority of Greeks walked. Mules and donkeys were used as pack animals, and wagons, drawn by oxen, were widely used for haulage. A network of roads crisscrossed Greece, which the Greek writer Aeschylus attributed to the god Hephaestus's many children, who tamed "the wildness of the untamed land." In recent years, archaeologists have found regular ruts, carved out purposefully to consistent

> ## "[Periphetes] carried an iron club, with which he dispatched the passers-by."

PSEUDO-APOLLODORUS ON THE BANDIT PERIPHETES

gauges, like tram tracks, which appear to have been used to guide heavy wagons over rugged ground. Ferrymen helped travelers cross Greece's rivers.

The land often remained "untamed," however. Bandits were a major hazard in many places, and even made their way into myth. As he traveled from Troezen to Athens, the hero Theseus was said to have killed two bandits called Periphetes and Sinis Pityocamptes, who terrorized the Isthmus of Corinth.

Travelers also faced the pitfalls of overpaying for food and accommodation in unfamiliar places, or falling foul of local customs. Writing in the 3rd century BCE, Heraclides Creticus provided a travel guide that might have helped travelers avoid trouble, reviewing the state of the roads and the negative and positive characteristics of the cities and peoples of Greece. He found the road to Athens a "pleasant one," but the city itself "dry and ill supplied with water"; the inhabitants of Attica, he warned, were "gossiping, slanderous, given to prying into the business of strangers," while Oropia (a district in Boeotia) was a "nest of hucksters."

△ Sea terror

This terra-cotta relief was made c. 450 BCE on the island of Milos. It shows the sea monster Scylla as a combination of fish, woman, and dogs.

▽ Dionysus's escape

This black-figure kylix was painted by Exekias of Athens around 535 BCE. It tells the story of Dionysus's capture by pirates, and the vines he had entangle the ship, which caused the pirates to flee.

Vines growing around the ship and above Dionysus

Sail shown realistically, bellying out and filling with wind

Naval Warfare

War among the waves

Naval battles were fundamental to war from the late Archaic period and, while the hoplite dominated land warfare, some of the ancient Greeks' largest battles, and greatest losses, were experienced at sea.

With few ships having survived, evidence for the history of naval warfare in ancient Greece comes largely from paintings and literature. These tell a story of technological development that reached new heights with the first triremes in the mid-6th century BCE.

The Bronze Age certainly saw skirmishes at sea, but there is relatively little evidence for naval "warfare." Although fresco and pottery scenes preserve images of armed men on ships, and dead men at sea, many probably represent troops departing to, or returning from, battles fought on distant shores. Spears, javelins, and other projectile weapons could have been used in ship-to-ship action, and very late in the period, there are depictions of close-quarters combat on deck. However, such technology and tactics would have served against opportunistic pirates and raiders as much as they did against adversaries in battle.

△ **Secret weapon**
Decorated with Greek symbols, the Athlit ram was probably made for the fleet of Ptolemy V or Ptolemy VI in the 2nd century BCE.

> # "Bronze will come together with bronze, and Ares will redden the sea with blood."

ORACLE ON THE BATTLE OF SALAMIS

Naval warfare was, for the most part, a development of the Early Iron Age (c. 1100–750 BCE) that went along with the emergence of new types of ship, such as the pentekonter. With at least 50 oarsmen, these were heavy vessels. They were built for war and trade, but were equipped with simple wooden rams at the prow that, albeit rarely, facilitated ship-to-ship engagement.

▽ **Deadly elegance**
This early 3rd-century BCE fresco from Nymphaion, a Greek colony in Crimea, shows a Greek trireme—its prow ram and prow head visible to the right.

There were also smaller triakonters, with a complement of 30 oarsmen, although later sources record that they served as troop-carriers for coastal raids or as reconnaissance ships.

The powerful trireme (from the Greek for "three-fitted") emerged around 650 BCE. A long, narrow warship, it was faster and more maneuverable than both its predecessors and its contemporaries. A complement of 200 men, including 170 oarsmen spread across three banks, acted in place of ballast (weight providing stability). The trireme's light weight made it vulnerable in rough seas, and a lack of storage space necessitated daily resupply, but it was a ship designed for war and—armed with a bronze prow ram that was far more effective and far less prone to damage than a wooden one—it was very capable.

The trireme in action

Prior to battle, the trireme could be further stripped down to improve acceleration. This included the removal of the mast. Drummers or flautists kept the oarsmen's strokes to time, and historical records suggest that the trireme could reach a maximum speed under oar of around 7 knots, or 8 mph (13 kph). While the men onboard included a small contingent of soldiers, known as marines, it was the ship's prow ram that served as the trireme's main offensive weapon.

In battle, a trireme crew would try to pass an enemy ship at close quarters, shattering its oars to immobilize the ship and injure its crew. Alternatively, the crew would aim to breach an enemy vessel by ramming it below the waterline. Among the maneuvers employed to achieve this were breaking through the line of enemy ships (*diekplous*) or sailing around the enemy ships (*periplous*) to reach a better position from which to attack their flanks. These tactics could be countered by, for example, forming ships into tight circles or inserting smaller vessels into the gaps between the warships.

With ships frequently damaged or sunk, war was an expensive business, and funding a fleet and its crew an ever-pressing concern in ancient Greece.

△ **Escape ship**
The painting on this 8th-century BCE krater from Thebes is sometimes thought to show Ariadne (far left) escaping Crete with Theseus after he slayed the Minotaur. The two rows of oarsmen are shown stacked one above the other.

The shortest oars were on the lowest bank

▷ **Section of a trireme**
The trireme had three banks of oarsmen: thalamians (lowest), zygians (middle), and thranites (upper). The oarsmen were staggered to maximize the number of oars.

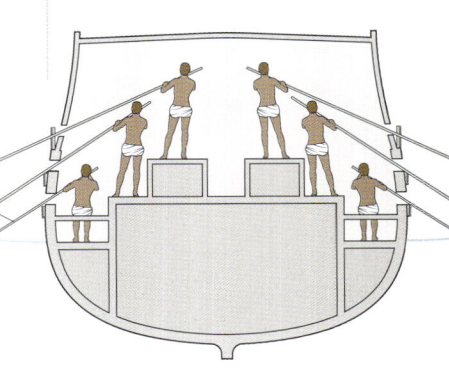

Enslavement

Oppression in ancient Greece

Greece was one of the earliest-known enslaving societies in history. Enslaved people made up a large proportion of the population in most states and performed vital economic roles, despite having few legal rights.

△ **Enslaved girl**
This marble grave stele, c. 400–390 BCE, depicts a young free woman (right) and an enslaved girl holding a jewelery box. The girl's status is indicated by her unnaturally small size in comparison to her enslaver.

Enslaved people were an integral part of ancient Greek society, even though most were denied its privileges. They were recorded as far back as Mycenaean times, in the 14th century BCE, working in homes and as shepherds and weavers. From around the 9th to the 8th centuries BCE, enslaved people were most often war captives, taken from their homes and subjugated.

The brutality of enslavement

From the 7th century BCE, greater interchange via trade and the emergence of the idea of a wider body of citizens (as opposed to aristocrats) with rights worsened the plight of those with neither economic resources nor citizenship. By around the same time, chattel enslavement had emerged, which allowed for people to be bought, sold, and leased as "possessions." Aside from through warfare, enslaved people were acquired through trade with areas on the margins of the Greek world, especially Scythia and Thrace, and by birth to enslaved parents.

The enslaved population was huge—in Athens it was about a third of the total population. Many enslaved people were forced to work in domestic settings, some worked as agricultural laborers, and large numbers worked as artisans, doctors, teachers,

△ **Ticket to freedom**
Manumission statements, recording the liberation of enslaved people, are inscribed on this stone at the 4th–3rd centuries BCE Greco-Roman theater in Butrint, southern Albania.

and even bankers. Those in such highly skilled positions were paid some money. However, others worked in appalling conditions in quarries and the state silver mines of Laurium. All enslaved people were unable to own property, vulnerable to sale, and denied legal rights—including the right to legal action.

In Sparta, most enslaved people were helots, who descended from the Messenians (see p.106). The Spartans allowed the helots to inherit land, but treated them brutally, provoking an uprising in 465 BCE. The outcome of this rare example of large-scale resistance to enslavement in ancient Greece is unknown.

Some enslaved people absconded: after Athens' defeat in the Peloponnesian War in 404 BCE, 20,000 people enslaved by the city are said to have escaped. Generally, however, the only path to freedom was manumission, whereby an enslaved person could buy their liberty by paying their enslaver a sum equal to the price they would command if sold to a new enslaver; for a highly skilled enslaved person this could amount to three years' wages. Enslavement persisted through Classical times, and when the Greek states lost independence in 146 BCE, it was to Rome, another society that kept the inhuman practice alive.

GREEK VIEWS **ON ENSLAVEMENT**

Greek views on enslavement seem to have hardened from the 5th century BCE, as the wars against Persia heightened prejudice against non-Greeks and, among the Athenians, against those living in non-democratic societies. In the 4th century BCE, Aristotle considered enslavement to be a natural state endured by those of lesser physical or intellectual capacity than the free. Centuries before, Homer suggested that enslavement took "half the goodness out of a man," making him "inferior." Among the few critics of enslavement was Alcidamas of Aeolis, a rhetorician who argued in the 4th century BCE that all men were born free.

AKROTIRI FRESCO OF A SERVANT

A woman takes a basket of clay for transportation to the kilns

This oil lamp provides essential light for the clay pit

A man uses a pickax to chisel away sections of clay from the wall of the pit

△ **Hard labor**
This 6th-century BCE plaque from Corinth shows people quarrying clay for roof tiles and pottery. Such grueling work was often performed by enslaved people.

A young person gathers the excavated clay into a basket; impurities such as shells and small rocks would be removed at the pottery workshop

"**God** made all **men free**. **Nature** has made **nobody** a **slave**."

ALCIDAMAS OF AEOLIS

Artists and Craftspeople

Transforming raw materials

Ancient Greek artists and craftspeople were sometimes held in disdain, owing to the demanding and dirty nature of their work, but were often talented and highly skilled, producing some of the world's most magnificent objects.

△ **Woman at work**
Evidence from workers' signatures suggests that craft studios in ancient Greece were male-dominated environments. This workshop scene from the 5th century BCE is unusual in that it depicts a woman at work, most probably decorating the handle of a pottery vase.

Almost all durable goods in ancient Greece were created by skilled craftspeople. The Greeks used a single word, *banausoi*, to refer to this talented group of non-agricultural workers. Most of them lived in cities, where they worked in metal, leather, wood, glass, clay, ivory, stone, textiles, and other materials to produce a range of objects, from shoes, agricultural tools, and musical instruments to impressive freestanding statuary and exquisite painted pottery. Many of the surviving objects they created are now considered spectacular works of art.

Artists and craftspeople included men and women, enslaved and free people, citizens and immigrants. Their circumstances and status would therefore have been hugely varied. Some would have led comfortable lives as prosperous small-business owners, while others would have been impoverished, exploited, and trapped in demanding and sometimes dangerous jobs. It is unlikely that they would have identified themselves as a single, unified community. The wealthy, aristocratic authors of ancient texts were

◁ **Bronze armorer**
A craftsman is shown working on a Corinthian helmet in this 8th–7th-century BCE bronze sculpture. His right hand would probably once have held a mallet.

often contemptuous of this group of people, so very little about them can be gleaned from textual sources. However, the workers themselves left evidence of their existence through the objects they made and the environments in which they worked.

Self-representation

When ancient craftworkers described themselves by means of inscriptions, they used specific descriptors for their task or skill, such as "metalworker," rather than just "craftsperson." Numerous objects, including sculptures, engraved gems, vases, and pots, were also signed by the people who made them. Their names provided additional information about them: perhaps a hint as to what part of the world they came from or sometimes their family relationships.

Occasionally, two or more signatures are present on Greek artifacts, revealing not only that, for example, the making of a pot and the decoration of it were separate tasks—providing evidence of division of labor—but also that both skills were valued. The main reasons for signing would have been much the same as for artists today: to reflect pride in their work and to ensure people knew who had created it. Some signed objects were placed in temples as offerings to the gods, thereby demonstrating the maker's piety and providing the opportunity to exhibit in a public place.

Signatures on objects were more common in Greece than in other ancient cultures, which may also suggest that, despite the disdain of lofty authors, some Greek artisans were seen as possessing admirable skills, and having their name on a work could add to its value.

WORKING WITH **CLAY**

Clay was put to multiple uses in ancient Greece—from building construction to magnificent pottery and sculpture. It was readily available, and most areas had beds of clay that were able to support local pottery industries. The clay was first dug out of the ground, then mixed with water—larger particles were left to settle out. All usable clay was then poured off and left to dry until ready to be shaped. It could be formed by hand, or with specialized tools. Most pots were made on a potter's wheel, turned by an assistant, and decorated before firing with a clay slip. Complicated three-dimensional shapes, such as figurines, could also be produced in large quantities by pressing clay into molds that had been shaped on a hand-modeled original. Details could be touched up by hand and figurines were painted after firing.

CLAY MOLD

A piece of leather cut to form the sole of a boot

A shoemaker's cutting tool

The *diphros*, or stool, was easy to carry

This *trapeza*, or table, has an under-shelf and two side slits

A cubical wicker basket sits at the shoemaker's feet

△ **The shoemaker**
This detail from a kylix from 480–470 BCE offers a glimpse inside a shoemaker's workshop in ancient Greece. It shows the craftsman—sitting on a cushion at his table and surrounded by some of the tools of his trade—cutting out a strip of leather that he will later fashion into a pair of shoes or boots.

4

Classical Athens and Sparta

500–400 BCE

A Century of Conflict

The 5th century BCE was a remarkable period in Greek history. Bookended by two of the best-known conflicts in ancient Greece—the war with the Persian Achaemenid Empire and the Peloponnesian War—the century also saw significant developments in culture and philosophy that had a profound impact on Western culture. At the center of this were two of Greece's greatest cities, Sparta and Athens, which were tied together by their Greekness, but pulled apart by their very different political systems and ways of life.

Fighting for power

Angered by the Ionian cities' revolt against his rule, in 492 BCE the Persian king, Darius I "the Great," launched an invasion of Greece. It faltered amid storms that sent the Persian fleet back to Asia. After Sparta and Athens refused Darius's demands for earth and water, the traditional symbols of submission, Darius sent another expedition, far larger than the first, to Greece in 490 BCE. Athens successfully fended it off, securing an unexpected victory at the Battle of Marathon. Ten years later, Darius's son Xerxes returned to Greece with an invading force to avenge his father. Although they were defeated at Thermopylae (480 BCE), the Greeks joined together to defeat the Persians at sea at the Battle of Salamis (480 BCE), and on land at Plataea (479 BCE).

Over the next decades, Athens and Sparta consolidated their power: Athens presiding, often with a heavy hand, over the Delian League, an extensive maritime empire around the Aegean Sea; Sparta establishing itself as the predominant power in mainland Greece and the leader of the Peloponnesian League. In 460 BCE, the First Peloponnesian War broke out between them. Neither side was able to force a conclusive victory, and the leagues made peace in 446 BCE. However, in 431 BCE, for a range of reasons much debated by historians both ancient and modern, war broke out between the two power blocs for a second time.

The balance tips

This Second Peloponnesian War finally ended in 404 BCE with a Spartan victory. That it was Sparta that won may seem surprising, given that the Athens of the 5th century BCE is often hailed as the epitome of the ancient Greek city. Its democratic system—highly inclusive as long as one was an adult male citizen rather than a female of citizen class, a resident foreigner of any gender, or an enslaved person—has been regarded as a lesson both to ancient Greece and to subsequent Western civilizations. Athens was also the home of Socrates and of Pericles, under whose leadership the city, and most notably the Acropolis, was magnificently albeit controversially beautified. It was the home too of the tragedians Aeschylus, Sophocles, and Euripides, and of the comic playwright Aristophanes, whose plays celebrated but also lampooned the greatness of the city, its prominent inhabitants, and even the goddess Athena herself.

Yet, for all its cultural triumphs, Athens had pushed its imperial agenda too hard. It had lost allies, and found itself ultimately unable to withstand Sparta, which was bolstered by Persian support. In the war's wake, Athens lost its fleet and empire to Sparta and temporarily lost its democratic system, which was replaced with a Sparta-imposed oligarchy.

◁ **Gold rhyton from the Achaemenid Empire**

499 BCE The Ionian Revolt against Persian rule begins

492–490 BCE The first Persian invasion of Greece, by Darius

480–479 BCE The second Persian invasion of Greece, by Xerxes

478 BCE The Delian League established under Athens' leadership

460–446 BCE The First Peloponnesian War between Sparta and Athens

454 BCE The Delian League's treasury moves from Delos to Athens

1 Acropolis of Sardis, sacked in the Ionian Revolt

2 Greek burial mound on the plain at Marathon

3 The pass at Thermopylae

War with Persia 492–479 BCE
The Achaemenid Empire was determined to subdue Greece at the beginning of the 5th century BCE. The Greco-Persian Wars saw some of the ancient world's best-known battles, including Marathon and Thermopylae.

KEY
- Achaemenid Empire
- Persian vassal states
- Greek allies
- Greek neutral states
- → Darius's first campaign 492 BCE
- → Darius's second campaign 490 BCE
- → Xerxes' invasion 480–479 BCE
- ◆ Key battles with date

447 BCE Pericles instigates a building program in Athens

429 BCE Pericles and hundreds of citizens die of plague in Athens

415 BCE Athens begins an expedition against Syracuse in Sicily

405 BCE The Spartans defeat the Athenian fleet at the Battle of Aegospotami

431 BCE Second Peloponnesian War breaks out

421 BCE The Peace of Nicias offers only a short break in the Peloponnesian War

412 BCE Sparta and Persia make peace with the Treaty of Miletus

404 BCE Sparta declares victory in the Second Peloponnesian War

The Ionian Revolt

Greco-Persian conflict in Asia Minor

In 499 BCE, the Ionian city of Miletus rose up against the Achaemenid Empire, sparking a general revolt against Persian rule in the region that led to the introduction of democracy in the Greek cities of Asia Minor.

The Greek citizens who lived in the coastal cities and islands of Asia Minor had been compliant subjects of the Persian Achaemenid Empire for nearly 50 years when the Ionian Revolt erupted in 499 BCE. The revolt's apparent aim, and ultimate result, was the introduction of democracy, but its origins lay in the thwarted ambitions and shifting loyalties of the ruler of the city of Miletus, a man named Aristagoras. To maintain power across the vast empire, the Achaemenids employed local satraps (governors), who in turn appointed Greek tyrants to rule the Greek cities. Since 512 BCE, Aristagoras had controlled Miletus as the regent for the city's tyrant, his uncle Histiaeus.

Aristagoras's gamble

When, in 500 BCE, the people of Naxos toppled the island's ruling elite, Aristagoras saw a chance to assert his power by reinstalling the deposed regime and bringing Naxos island under Miletus's control. With assistance from Artaphernes, the Persian emperor Darius I's brother and satrap in Lydia, Aristagoras launched an expedition to Naxos. The Naxians, however, quickly chased the invaders back to Miletus.

△ **Culture clash**
A hoplite (right) is shown fighting a Persian warrior, identifiable by his distinctive Persian trousers and headgear, in this red-figure kylix from c. 460 BCE.

△ **Persian chariot**
Found in the Achaemenid capital, Sardis, now in Türkiye, this 6th-century BCE carved relief depicts Persian warriors on a chariot along with a golden falcon, a symbol of the empire.

Now in the city with a considerable force still under his control, and fearing that he would be removed from power, Aristagoras turned on the Achaemenid Empire. He declared Miletus a democracy and called for an uprising against Persian rule.

The revolt spread quickly through the Ionian cities, many of which were tired of rule by foreign kings and their Greek collaborators. In 498 BCE, Athens and Eretria (a city in Euboea) responded to the Ionians' plea for help and sent an expeditionary force to Ephesus. From there, the Greeks struck inland and set fire to Sardis, the Achaemenid capital. On their return to Ephesus, however, the Greeks were routed by the Persian cavalry. Cyprus, Greek colonies along Propontis (the Sea of Marmara) and the Hellespont (the Dardanelles Strait), and Ionia's neighbors, the Carians, joined the rebellion, prompting the Persians to mobilize three armies.

The Persians made swift progress in the Hellespont and Propontis, and nearly broke the Carians at the battles of the Marsyas and Labraunda in 496 BCE. However, the Carians destroyed the Persian forces

THE ACHAEMENID EMPIRE

In the 6th century BCE, Cyrus the Great turned the Persian Achaemenid kingdom of Anshan (a city in southwest Iran) into an empire. He overthrew the Median Empire around 550 BCE, subjugated the Lydian Empire in the 540s BCE, and claimed the Babylonian Empire in 539 BCE. At its greatest extent, under Darius I (r. 522–486 BCE), the Achaemenid Empire covered 2 million sq miles (5 million sq km) from Anatolia and Egypt through West and Central Asia to northern India.

RELIEF OF PERSIAN GUARDS FROM PERSEPOLIS

> ## "Of the **Persians** there **fell** as many as **2,000 men**, and of the **Carians 10,000**."

HERODOTUS ON THE BATTLE OF THE MARSYAS, *HISTORIES*

△ **Achaemenid griffin**
Found in the Achaemenid Palace of Darius I at Susa, now in Iran, this relief of a griffin in glazed brick is from the 5th century BCE.

at Padusus that year. While the Persians regrouped, their campaign in Ionia and Aeolia stalled. The Persian army and a huge fleet finally moved on Miletus in 494 BCE. The Ionians gathered their ships and headed to Lade, an island off Miletus, to "fight for Miletus at sea." There, around 70,000 allied Greeks in 353 ships (largely from Samos, Chios, and Lesbos) faced 600 Phoenician vessels under the command of the Persians. According to Herodotus, the Greek fleet was deserted by the Samians, with whom Persia had made a secret deal, just as battle was joined. The ships from Lesbos then fled, leaving the Chian ships to fight on, sustaining huge casualties. After the battle, Miletus fell after a short siege, and the Persians regained control of Asia Minor by the end of 493 BCE.

In the wake of the revolt, Darius sanctioned the installation of democracies in many of the Ionian cities. He reserved his anger for Miletus, whose people he enslaved, and Athens and Eretria, whose interference had threatened to destabilize his empire.

The Invasion of Darius

Persia puts Greece under pressure

In 492 BCE, the Persian king Darius I ("the Great") launched an invasion of Greece. While the invasion successfully extended Persian control into Macedonia and the Aegean, the Greeks' victory at Marathon saved much of Greece.

There were several reasons behind the Persian invasion of Greek territory in 492 BCE, including Darius I's ambition to extend the Achaemenid Empire into Europe and the Aegean. However, the main impetus was Darius's anger at Athens and Eretria, whose support for the Ionian Revolt (see pp.142–143) and destruction of Sardis had struck at the heart of his empire. While Darius failed to subjugate most of Greece over the two years of the invasion, his forces did extend Persian control and remain strong enough to fight another day.

The first phase of the invasion was led by Darius's son-in-law Mardonius. Making his way toward Athens, he installed democracies in the Ionian cities, re-subjugated the northern Greek region of Thrace, and took total control of Macedonia, which was already a vassal state of Persia. After the Persian fleet was devastated in a storm off Mount Athos, preventing further military action, Darius turned to diplomacy in 491 BCE. He sent ambassadors to

◁ **Hero's helmet**
This bronze helmet is inscribed with the words "Miltiades offers his helmet to Zeus" and is thought to have belonged to the Athenian general Miltiades, who fought at Marathon.

the Greek cities demanding from each earth and water, the ancient traditional symbols of submission. The cities capitulated, with the exception of Athens and Sparta, who not only refused, but executed the ambassadors.

In response, in 490 BCE, a huge invasion force—said to be 600 triremes according to the main source for the conflict, Herodotus—set sail. It was led this time by the Persian commander Datis, and Darius's nephew Artaphernes. Reaching the island of Rhodes, the Persians tried, and failed, to take Lindos. Then they sailed to the Cyclades, where they took and burned Naxos, and seized the sacred island of Delos—where they made sacrifices to Apollo—without violence. From the Cyclades, the Persians headed to Euboea, where they besieged and finally destroyed the city of Eretria and enslaved the population.

Defeat at Marathon

The fleet sailed down the coast of Attica before landing around 25 miles (40 km) from Athens, at the Bay of Marathon. This location was chosen on the advice of Hippias, the Athenian tyrant who had been ousted twenty years previously (see p.116–117) and was hoping to be reinstated as a Persian "puppet."

◁ **Darius the Great**
Persia's king, Darius I, commonly known as "Darius the Great" is depicted seated and receiving supplicants in this detail from a bas-relief from the Imperial Treasury at Persepolis in Iran.

> ## "The Athenians hung upon the runaways and cut them down, chasing them all the way to the shore."

HERODOTUS, *HISTORIES*

△ **Athenian treasury**
According to Pausanias, a 2nd-century CE writer, the Athenians used spoils from the Battle of Marathon to build this treasury (now reconstructed) at Delphi, although scholars date the temple to between 510 BCE and 480 BCE.

As the Athenians prepared to meet the Persians at Marathon, a herald named Pheidippides was dispatched to run to Sparta, a distance of around 150 miles (240 km), to seek help. The Spartans refused, because they were celebrating the festival of Apollo Karneios, making military action impossible. The 10,000 Athenians thus prepared to face a Persian army of around 15,000 men supported only by a 1,000-man contingent from the city of Plataea in Boeotia. The Athenian commander Miltiades ordered the Greek phalanx forward at a run, and the Persian flanks collapsed. In the center, the Persians broke through but then the Greek flanks closed in, and the Persians were routed. They fled to their ships, which set off along the coast to Athens. Rushing back to the city by land, the Athenians managed to repel the Persian fleet, and it returned to Asia Minor.

Darius began preparing for a new invasion, which he planned to lead himself. However, in 486 BCE, he died at the age of 64—his involvement in quelling a revolt in Egypt having damaged his health—and his son Xerxes was left to take revenge on Greece.

History and Historians

An enduring legacy

The origins of the Greek historical tradition lie around 750 BCE in Homer's *Iliad*, an account of a semi-mythical event—the Trojan War—by an author of uncertain identity. Yet Homer's epic poems played a crucial role in later Greeks' consciousness of their cultural unity, inspiring writers such as Eumelus of Corinth, who wrote a verse history of his home town in the 7th century BCE.

A new spirit of inquiry

The 6th-century revolution in thought in the Greek cities of Ionia (see pp.96–97) inspired a wider and more critical sense of historical inquiry. Hecataeus of Miletus (c. 550–476 BCE) wrote the *Periodos Ges* (*Journey Round the World*), describing the Mediterranean lands and their history, while a series of chroniclers wrote small-scale histories of their regions. These paved the way for Herodotus of Halicarnassus (see pp.148–149), whose work is the first substantial surviving prose history; his conscious use of sources set him apart from his predecessors. Around the same time, Hellanicus of Lesbos (c. 480–395 BCE) was the first to create the basis for a scientific chronology.

By far Herodotus's most famous successor was Thucydides. His *History of the Peloponnesian War* covered the conflict between Athens and Sparta to 411 BCE. He used direct eyewitness accounts to try to understand the motives of the warring parties without reference to the gods. However, Thucydides also gave his characters wholly fictional speeches.

△ **Homer (c. 8th century BCE)**
Homer is traditionally named as the author of the *Iliad* and the *Odyssey*, which dealt with the Trojan War and its aftermath. However, "Homer" may in fact represent a group of poets that produced these epic poems sometime around 750–700 BCE.

△ **Hellanicus of Lesbos (c. 480–395 BCE)**
Hellanicus devised a dating system using the cycles of the Olympic Games, the succession of priestesses in Argos, and the ruling ephors (magistrates) of Sparta. With this, he created a scientific chronology that enabled comparisons of the dates of events in different cities. A fragment of one of his works, *Atlantis*, is shown above.

△ **Thucydides (c. 460–400 BCE)**
An Athenian general in the Peloponnesian War, Thucydides championed a rational approach to history in his account of the war, attempting to exclude material he could not confirm himself. "My work," he claimed, "was done to last forever."

"I write what seems to me to be true; for the Greeks have many tales which, as it appears to me, are absurd."

HECATAEUS OF MILETUS, *PERIODOS GES*

Thucydides was followed by historians such as Theopompus of Chios (c. 380–318 BCE), whose *Hellenica* continued Thucydides' unfinished history of the Peloponnesian War. Theopompus also began to focus on the stories of notable men such as Alexander the Great. Cleitarchus continued this trend, writing his own biography of Alexander; he may have accompanied the Macedonian army on campaign.

Greek historiography diversified in other ways, with regional histories such as the *Makedonika* by Marsyas of Pella (c. 356–294 BCE), covering Macedonia's development down to 331 BCE, and Timaeus's (c. 345–250 BCE) 38-volume history focusing on his native Sicily and Magna Graecia, the Greek settlements in southern Italy.

In the late 4th century BCE, the author Duris of Samos (c. 350–281 BCE) pioneered "tragic history," which exhibited a new concern for morality over accuracy and often used rhetoric to heighten readers' reactions. It was in contrast to Polybius (c. 200–118 BCE), whose forensic examination of the causes of the Roman conquest of Greece, along with his criticism of predecessors who privileged stylistic devices over historical accuracy or resorted to divine explanations, made him a worthy successor to Herodotus and Thucydides. It is to Polybius that we owe our knowledge of many Greek historians whose work survives only in fragments or as quotations in texts such as his *Histories*. Later historians, such a Diodorus Siculus and Plutarch, often plundered his work.

△ **Theopompus of Chios (c. 380–318 BCE)**
Born on Chios, Theopompus spent much of his life in Athens and Egypt. His *Hellenica* continued Thucydides' work on the Peloponnesian War, and his *Philippica* was the first of the major biographies of the Macedonian ruler Philip II (shown above).

△ **Polybius (c. 200–118 BCE)**
A general in Greece's Achaean League (see pp.256–257), Polybius was taken to Italy as a hostage to ensure the League's loyalty to Rome in 167 BCE. His status gave him access to elite Roman political and military circles, allowing him to analyze Rome's success and chronicle Greece's absorption into the Roman world.

△ **Plutarch (c. 46–after 119 CE)**
Born in Chaeronea, in Boeotia, Plutarch was a philosopher and historian best known for *Parallel Lives*, his collection of 23 paired biographies that compared important Greek and Roman figures, such the Spartan general Lysander and the Roman general Sulla.

◁ **The "Father of History"**
A 2nd-century CE Roman copy in marble of a Greek bronze statue of Herodotus from the early 4th century BCE, this bust was found in Benha, Egypt, and reflects the admiration the Romans felt for Herodotus and other Greek writers.

Trimmed hair was a 5th-century BCE innovation

"In Herodotus, the **father of history** ... there are a **countless number** of **legends**."

ROMAN HISTORIAN CICERO, *LAWS*

Herodotus

Historian, geographer, and storyteller

Author of the first major work of narrative history, Herodotus has been both lauded as the "Father of History" for his attempt at objectivity and labeled the "Father of Lies" for his inclusion of many outlandish anecdotes.

Herodotus's great literary achievement, his nine-book *Histories*, tells us much about a turbulent period that accompanied the Persians' two invasions of Greece in the early 5th century BCE, but little of his own life. We do know that Herodotus was born around 484 BCE in the Ionian Greek town of Halicarnassus (now Bodrum in western Türkiye). At the age of around 24, he was exiled to Samos when the tyrant Lygdamis II took power in Halicarnassus. He only returned when Lygdamis was overthrown, around 454 BCE. He remained in his home town for about ten years before emigrating to the Athenian colony of Thurii, in southern Italy.

By then, Herodotus was already writing the *Histories*. Indeed, by 445 BCE, he already had enough material to "read his books" to the Athenian Council. He finished writing sometime after 430 BCE.

The first historian

Herodotus took an innovative approach to history. He was the first to reject explanations of events based on the actions of the gods and instead seek empirical evidence for why people acted as they did. He traveled widely, and there are references in his work to first-hand evidence collected in the Eastern

Mediterranean, Libya, Egypt, and Scythia. He also carefully recorded the geography, folklore, customs, and traditions of the Greeks and their enemies. However, Herodotus's express purpose was to explain the causes of Greece's war with Persia and analyze the course of the campaign. His critique of the events led the Roman orator Cicero, writing in the 1st century BCE, to call Herodotus the "Father of History."

Yet some of the material Herodotus included, such as the claim that there were ants the size of foxes in Persia, led the historian Plutarch to dismiss Herodotus as the "Father of Lies." Still, Herodotus's attempt to make a *historie* (an inquiry) founded on the actions and motives of people, rather than gods, makes him the first great historian.

△ **The Histories**
This 15th-century CE Italian edition of Herodotus's work was translated into Latin by scholar Lorenzo Valla and has a portrait of the author by miniaturist Francesco Rosselli.

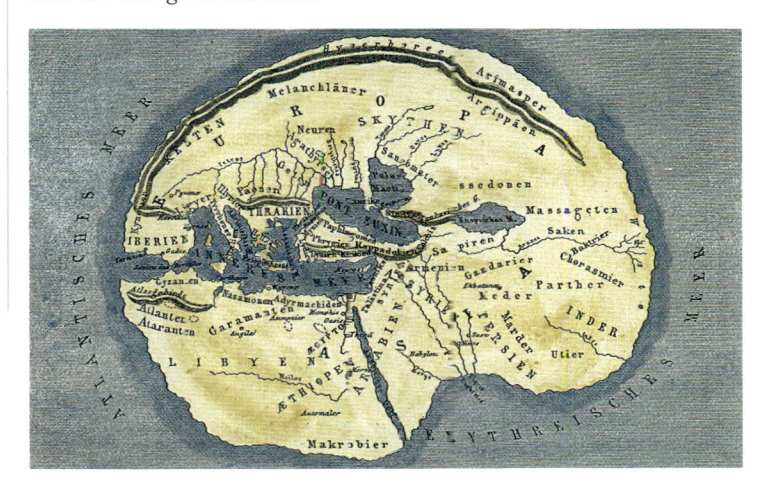

▷ **The world according to Herodotus**
This map reconstructs how Herodotus may have viewed the world as known to him: centered around the Mediterranean Sea and with all landmasses surrounded by an ocean.

492 BCE Persia's Darius I invades Greece; Xerxes' invasion follows in 480 BCE

460 BCE Herodotus is exiled from Halicarnassus to Samos

C. 445 BCE Herodotus gives a public reading of some of his work in Athens

430 BCE Last datable event in the *Histories*: the execution of two men from Tegea in Athens

C. 484 BCE Herodotus is born in the Ionian city of Halicarnassus (Bodrum)

C. 454 BCE Herodotus returns to his home town, Halicarnassus

C. 444 BCE Herodotus migrates to the new colony of Thurii in southern Italy

C. 425 BCE Herodotus dies in Thurii

△ **The Hot Gates**
In this enormous painting by French artist Jacques-Louis David (1814), the Spartans, including Leonidas (center), are shown preparing for battle with the Persians at Thermopylae (the Hot Gates), named for nearby thermal springs.

The Invasion of Xerxes

Revenge and retreat in the Second Persian War

The armies of the Achaemenid Empire came close to physically destroying Athens in 480–479 BCE, but their ultimate failure to crush the Greeks marked the moment at which Greece's values were seen to triumph.

The Persian invasion of Greece in 480 BCE came after ten years of preparation on both sides following Darius I's failed invasion (see pp.144–145). When the expedition finally began, Xerxes expected the Greeks to immediately capitulate in the face of his vast army. Instead, he found himself pitted against a determined military coalition of 31 Greek states led by Sparta. After making a heroic stand at Thermopylae, the Greeks secured victories at Salamis and Plataea to drive the Persians out in little more than a year.

Returning to Persia after his defeat at Marathon in 490 BCE, Darius had begun planning his revenge on Greece. When he died in 486 BCE, his son Xerxes took over and began preparing for a new invasion. According to Herodotus, Xerxes swore to "bridge the Hellespont [the Dardanelles Strait] and march an army through Europe into Greece." This he did by creating a floating bridge that rested on two rows of more than 300 ships and was fastened by rope cables. To smooth the invasion's progress, the Persians also set up supply depots along the Aegean coast, bridged the Strymon River in northern Greece, and had a canal dug across the Athos peninsula, off whose stormy southern cape Darius had lost a large part of his fleet in 492 BCE.

In April 481 BCE, Xerxes left his capital, Susa, and marched to Sardis in Anatolia, where his army was gathering. According to Herodotus, Xerxes had around 1.7 million fighters, drawn from across his empire, although the true number was more likely between 100,000 and 250,000.

The Greeks were also making preparations. In Athens, the statesman Themistocles was attempting to convince his fellow citizens that they needed to turn the city into a major naval power in readiness for the return of Persia's forces. When a new seam was discovered at the state silver mines of Laurium in 483 BCE, Aristides, a much-respected veteran of the Battle of Marathon, called for a cash handout to citizens. Themistocles instead demanded that the money be spent on ships. He won the argument, and by 480 BCE, Athens had a fleet of more than 200 triremes. In 481 BCE, 31 states came together in the Panhellenic League, whose allied forces both on land and at sea would be led by Sparta. The League also issued a warning that any who collaborated with the Persians would lose their

LEONIDAS

Born around 540 BCE, Leonidas was the son of Anaxandridas II, a member of Sparta's senior royal dynasty, the Agiads, who had ruled in Sparta since the 10th century BCE. His mother was Anaxandridas's first wife, but by the time Leonidas was born, his father had taken a second wife, and her first-born son, Cleomenes I, became king in 524 BCE. Leonidas succeeded his half-brother to become one of Sparta's kings in 490 BCE, co-ruling with King Leotychidas. A widely respected military general, Leonidas was chosen to lead the Greek resistance to Xerxes' invasion. The stand that he made at Thermopylae gave Leonidas (and the 300 Spartans who perished with him) legendary status as a symbol of courage and self-sacrifice.

"Come and take them."

LEONIDAS'S RESPONSE TO XERXES' DEMAND FOR HIS WEAPONS

lands. But the Athenians also received their own warning, from Delphi's Oracle: "Leave home, town, and castle and do not stay."

In early 480 BCE, Xerxes' army, supported by perhaps 1,200 ships, began its invasion, crossing the Hellespont into Thrace and slowly making its way through northern Greece and into Thessaly.

The Battle of Thermopylae

Initially, the Greeks' strategy was to hold the Tempe Pass at Mount Olympus. However, they swiftly abandoned this plan in favor of holding a line at Thermopylae, a narrow pass on the Gulf of Maliakos in central Greece, about 90 miles (140 km) northwest of Athens. There, the Spartan king Leonidas waited with an elite of 300 Spartiates and more than 6,500 hoplites, while 200 Greek triremes gathered at nearby Artemisium to take on the Persian fleet.

The Persians reached Thermopylae in August. After waiting four days, assuming the vastly outnumbered Greeks would withdraw, Xerxes ordered a direct assault on the Greeks. The hoplites stood firm, repelling first the Persian heavy infantry, then the Persian royal guards, the 10,000 Immortals. They held the pass for three days, until a local shepherd named Ephialtes showed the Persians a path through the hills that led them to the rear of the Greeks. According to historian Diodorus Siculus, Leonidas was keen to win a "great garland of victory" for himself and Sparta. He dismissed the other Greek forces, and he and 300 Spartans were slaughtered as they made a last stand »

△ **Xerxes and Darius**
Xerxes (seated) with Darius standing are shown at the height of the Achaemenid Empire in this relief from the Apadana, the audience hall, in the palace at Persepolis.

△ **Warrior king**
A Persian king, dressed in striped trousers, drives a spear into a Greek hoplite, holding a shield and wearing only a Corinthian helmet, in this seal carved from banded agate around 450 BCE.

▷ **Victory at Salamis**
This map shows the narrow strait at Salamis, in which the Persians were trapped when the Greeks emerged from the two bays in which they had been sheltering.

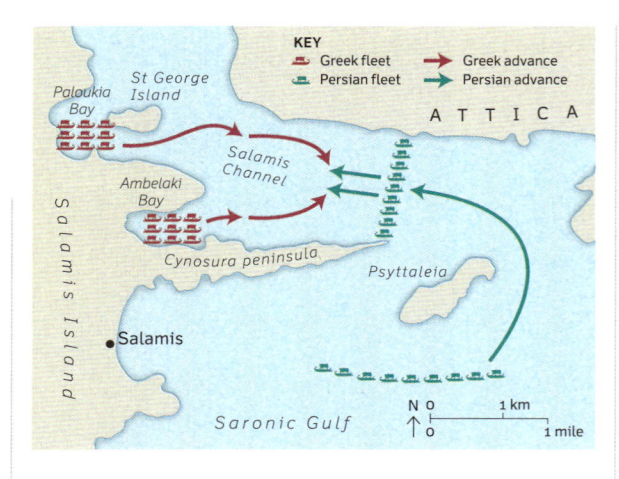

▽ **The Battle of Salamis**
This 1858 German painting by Wilhelm von Kaulbach shows Xerxes (seated on the left) and the Greek leaders (right) watching the drama of the naval battle unfold.

As Xerxes moved toward Thermopylae, the Greek fleet engaged the Persian fleet in the Straits of Artemisium, off the coast of Euboea. Herodotus claimed that the Persian invasion fleet had 1,200 triremes, but that it lost around a third of these in storms off the Greek coast, and that a further 200 ships were wrecked as they attempted to sail down Euboea's east coast to outflank the Greeks at Thermopylae. That still left 600 ships to face Greece's 200 triremes at Artemisium. Even allowing for some exaggeration from Herodotus, the Greeks were clearly outnumbered. For two days, they engaged the Persians in the afternoon and early evening, so they could withdraw if necessary. On the third day, however, the Persians sailed out at midday to meet the Greeks. In the ensuing battle, the Greeks lost so many ships that they were close to withdrawing. When news reached them of the events at Thermopylae, the Greek fleet fled southward to Salamis, an island east of Piraeus, with the Persians in close pursuit.

The tide turns

Fresh from their victory against the Spartans at Thermopylae, Xerxes' troops descended on Attica, burning and destroying as they went, and were soon threatening the city of Athens. Themistocles evacuated most of the Athenians to Piraeus, from where they embarked for the island of Salamis and the cities of Aegina and Troezen. The Persians rampaged through the city, destroying the city's temples, razing the Acropolis, and killing the few Greeks who had remained, including priests and priestesses.

Themistocles rejected the idea of retreating with the Greek forces to the Isthmus of Corinth. He instead convinced his co-commanders to adopt a plan that he hoped would see the Persian fleet destroyed. He sent his personal servant, an enslaved Persian named

△ **Elite warriors**
The garments worn by the guards in this relief from the Palace of Darius in Susa match ancient authors' descriptions of those worn by the Immortals.

Sicinnus, to tell Xerxes that the Greeks were divided and Themistocles himself wanted to help the Persians. Acting on Themistocles' instructions, as day broke, Xerxes sent the Egyptian contingent of his fleet to block the western exit from the strait at Salamis, where the Greek fleet was sheltering. The rest of the fleet then entered the eastern end of the strait, intending to capture the Greek fleet, which seemed to be making itself ready to flee westward.

In reality, the Persians had sailed into a trap. The Greek ships surged forward to attack the Persians, now too tightly packed in the strait to maneuver properly. By the afternoon, the Greeks had inflicted a devastating defeat on Xerxes.

Victory at Plataea

After Salamis, Xerxes decided to return to Asia with the main body of his army. He left behind a small force under his cousin Mardonius to complete the conquest. With winter approaching, Mardonius withdrew his men to Thessaly, and returned to Attica only in mid-479 BCE. In the interim, the Athenians had returned to their city and begun rebuilding it.

However, fractures were starting to appear in the Greek alliance, as some argued that Attica should be abandoned to the Persians while the Greek forces remained behind the Hexamilion Wall across the Isthmus, which protected the Peloponnese. That spring, the Athenians rejected Xerxes' offer of peace, declaring that they could not break with their fellow Greeks because, in the words of Herodotus, they were

"The **master** of the **sea** must be the master of the **empire**."

THEMISTOCLES, QUOTED BY CICERO

"one in blood and one in language." However, after Athens was sacked for a second time in June 479 BCE, the Athenians warned their allies that they might be forced to accept Xerxes' offer and join the Persian cause.

The threat worked, and a Spartan force under Pausanias—regent for Leonidas's infant son—along with warriors from several other Greek cities joined Athens' hoplites to meet the Persians near Plataea, on the border between Attica and Boeotia, in 479 BCE.

Mardonius had around 100,000 men under his command, outnumbering the 40,000 Greek soldiers, but he was wary. Thermopylae had shown the damage that a small force of heavily armed hoplites could do. Rather than challenge the Greeks directly, Mardonius sent the Persian cavalry to threaten their supply lines. The Greeks had begun to withdraw toward Plataea when the Persians captured their water supply. Seeing the enemy on the move, Mardonius ordered an attack. In the battle that followed, the Persians were routed by the disciplined ranks of the hoplite phalanxes. When Mardonius was killed, the Persians fled to their camp, where they were slaughtered by the Athenians.

According to Herodotus, Greece's victory over the Persians was cemented that same day at Mycale, in Anatolia, where the Greek fleet defeated the Persian fleet. It was a victory that, for Herodotus, represented both divine punishment for the arrogance of Xerxes and the triumph of Greek unity and independence over the forces of despotism.

△ **From the ruins**
This marble statue, which is known as the Moscophoros (Calf-bearer), dates to the 6th century BCE and was excavated from the debris of Persia's destruction of Athens in 480 BCE.

ARTEMISIA, **QUEEN OF CARIA**

Artemisia I was queen of the Persian satrapy of Caria, in Anatolia, having taken the throne when her husband died around 480 BCE. She is most famous for her role in the Battle of Salamis, in which she supported the Persians. In tactical discussions with Xerxes and his other naval chiefs, she alone counseled caution with regard to Themistocles' ultimately duplicitous offer of help. Indeed, she also questioned whether Xerxes needed to engage in any further naval conflict at all, given that most of the Greek mainland was already his. Xerxes did not take Artemisia's advice, but he was delighted by her honesty. He was also impressed by her skill and courage in the Battle of Salamis, in which she took command of her own ships.

Consulting the Oracle

Divination in ancient Greece

Greeks of all social classes consulted oracles to solve their problems, in both public and private life. Oracle sites were scattered throughout ancient Greece, but the most celebrated of all the oracles was that of Apollo at Delphi.

△ **The omphalos**
This Hellenistic marble omphalos stone from Delphi is believed to be a copy of the original stone that was kept at the site. The stone's decoration is thought to represent the woolen net that once held the omphalos.

▽ **Oracle tablet**
In the question inscribed on this 6th-century BCE lead tablet from the Oracle of Zeus at Dodona, the supplicant asks to which god he should pray to ensure his wife bears "useful children."

The word "oracle" (from the Latin *orare*, to speak) refers to the priests or priestesses who received revelations from the gods and to the places where those revelations were made. There were famous oracles of Zeus at Dodona (in Epirus), Olympia, and Siwa in Egypt. Asclepius, god of healing, had oracles at sanctuaries including Epidaurus, while the hero Amphiaraus had an oracle at Oropos in Attica, the goddess Demeter at Patras, and the god Pan on Mount Lykaion. The most widely consulted god was Apollo (as god of prophecy), who had oracles on Delos and at Didyma, Claros, and, most famously, Delphi.

Practices and rituals

There was a wide variety of oracular practices. Patients consulting Asclepius often stayed overnight, hoping to receive a cure from the god in their dreams. At Dodona—where the supplicants' questions were often of a personal nature, relating to stolen property or marriage partners—the priestess interpreted sounds such as rushing streams and whispering leaves. Most questions regarding high politics went to the more prestigious Oracle of Delphi. It was said that Sparta's legendary lawgiver Lycurgus (see p.75) consulted the oracle before reshaping Sparta's constitution along military lines.

The pronouncements made by the Delphic Oracle were notoriously ambiguous. As Xerxes' army approached Athens during the war with Persia in the early 5th century BCE, the Oracle advised the Athenians to flee and, later, to rely on a "wooden wall." Some thought this meant a palisade, but the Athenian general Themistocles persuaded them the Oracle meant Athens' fleet of wooden ships.

△ **Egypt's oracle**
The Temple of the Oracle of Zeus Ammon (above) was at the oasis of Siwa, in the Western Desert area of the Sahara, near the Egypt–Libya border.

Those who came to Delphi to ask questions faced elaborate rituals. Petitioners drew lots to determine who would be seen first. Consultations could be held on the seventh day of the month. The petitioner only brought a sacrificial animal, which was sprinkled with water: if it trembled, the ceremony could proceed; if it did not, the petitioner was sent away. The Pythia, priestess of the shrine, then cleansed herself in the Castalian Spring, nestled in a ravine at Delphi. She entered the *adyton*, an area within the temple's inner chamber that contained the omphalos, the stone denoting the center of the world. There, she climbed onto a sacred tripod and chewed leaves from a laurel tree dedicated to Apollo.

Ancient accounts of what happened next vary, but the historians Plutarch and Pausanias say the Pythia was inspired by vapors arising from a cleft in the rock and would then speak words, frequently unintelligible, which were interpreted by temple priests and set down in hexameter verse. Others were more skeptical, and the Athenian leader Cleisthenes (see p.117), was said to have once bribed the priestess to give an answer that would suit his purposes.

A Fury with snakes in her hair hovers above the sanctuary, ready to seize Orestes

The tripod on which Apollo's priestess sat to deliver oracles

Apollo, chief god of the sanctuary, shields Orestes from one of the Furies (to his right)

Orestes kneels before the tripod and the omphalos (left), as he seeks refuge from the Furies

The goddess Athena, protector of Orestes, assures him of her support

The omphalos, the navel-shaped stone said to mark the center of the world

"All **Attica** will be **taken**, Zeus grants Athens a **wooden wall** that shall alone be **untaken**."

AN ORACLE'S PROPHECY IN HERODOTUS, *HISTORIES*

◁ **Orestes and the Oracle of Delphi**
This red-figure vase, c. 350 BCE, shows the story of Orestes, son of the Greek king Agamemnon. Orestes is fleeing the Furies—vengeful divine beings who are intent on punishing him for murdering his mother, Clytemnestra. He seeks sanctuary with the Oracle of Delphi, where Apollo and Athena intervene on his behalf.

"Whoever has been **initiated** into the **Cabiri's rites** knows what I mean."

HERODOTUS, *HISTORIES*

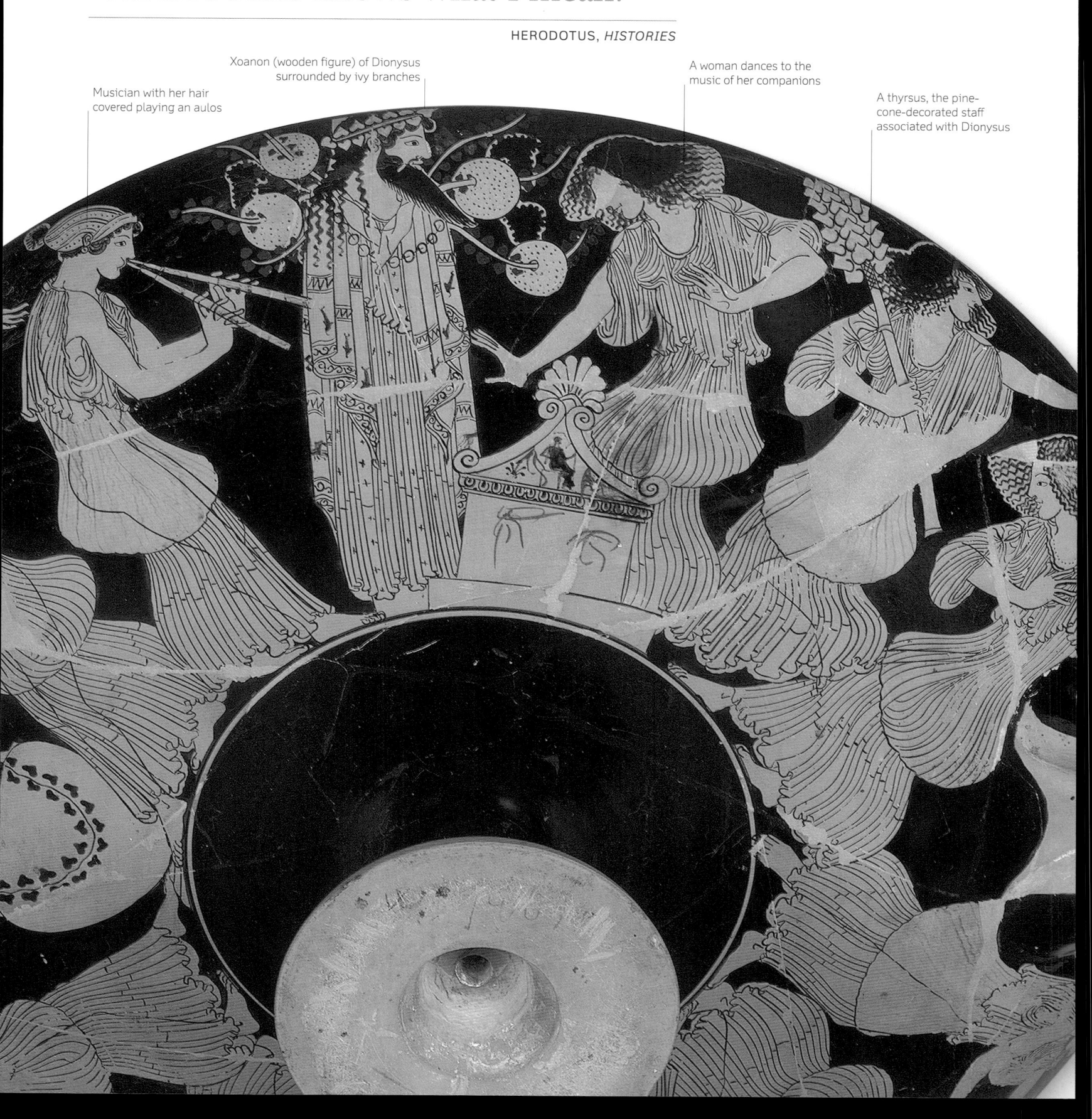

Musician with her hair covered playing an aulos

Xoanon (wooden figure) of Dionysus surrounded by ivy branches

A woman dances to the music of her companions

A thyrsus, the pine-cone-decorated staff associated with Dionysus

Religious Festivals

High days and holidays

There were no weekends in the ancient Greek world, but there were plenty of breaks from ordinary routines provided by regular festivals, which could take up as many as 120 days each year.

For the ancient Greeks, festivals were an opportunity to take time out of everyday life. Held in honor of particular gods, other divine entities, and heroes, these festivals ranged from public spectacles to secret rites, and could include processions, animal sacrifices, banquets, musical or dramatic competitions, and athletic events.

Relatively low-key festivals would last for a day; others could last for two days; and some were multi-day occasions. The Spartan Carnea, in honor of Apollo Carneius (of flocks and herds), for instance, took place over nine days. During this time military actions would be halted, as the Athenians discovered in 490 BCE when they sought and failed to secure Sparta's help ahead of the Battle of Marathon.

Many festivals would take place annually, on a set day or period of days in the religious calendar of a particular locality. Others, including the Isthmian Games in honor of Poseidon, the Nemean Games for Zeus, and a number of festivals of Dionysus, happened every two years. The principal Panhellenic festival, the Olympic Games held in honor of Zeus, took place every four years, as did the Pythian Games in honor of Apollo at Delphi. Meanwhile, at Athens, every fourth year would see a grander version of the Panathenaea, the city's major annual civic festival, during which Athens would throng with local people and visitors. Over several days, they would enjoy a huge procession to the summit of the Acropolis, where a hundred oxen would be

◁ **Dionysiac revel**
Dancing freely around the bowl, the women depicted on this drinking cup from 490–480 BCE are celebrating the Lenaea festival in honor of Dionysus.

sacrificed to Athena. There would also be a number of banquets and various competitive events, including running and chariot races, a men's beauty contest, boxing, and a regatta.

Among the Greek festivals were many that dated back to prehistory, but others were added later, and sometimes only to the sacred calendars of particular communities. In Athens, for example, a yearly festival of Pan was established after the Battle of Marathon, in response to the herald Pheidippides' claim that, on his return from Sparta to Marathon, he met Pan, who had asked him why the Athenians were neglecting him.

Public and private events

Festivals tended to be organized centrally, as part of a civic calendar, although some could be privately arranged. These included—in Athens at least—the Adonia, where groups of neighborhood women would gather to sing, dance, transform their rooftops into sacred gardens honoring Adonis (a lover of Aphrodite who had died in his prime), and perform a mock funeral procession for him. While festivals tended to be visible to onlookers, some would include rites performed in secret, often connected in some way with human, animal, or crop fertility. Meanwhile, mystery cults, such as those of Demeter and Persephone at Eleusis in Attica or of the Cabiri (see p.210) on Samothrace, included secret rites that could be witnessed only by initiates.

△ **Festival of Demeter**
Thesmophoria (1894–1897) by US painter Francis Davis Millet depicts a procession of women and girls celebrating the ancient fertility festival in honor of Demeter, which was popular throughout Greece.

▽ **Sacrifice**
Two altar boys stand with meat on spits while a priest pours a libation and Nike flies above on this Attic red-figure vase from 450–430 BCE.

The Athenian Empire

An oppressive alliance

The decade that followed Xerxes' invasion saw Athens cement its status as the self-appointed leader of the members of the Delian League. It soon turned the league to its own ends, crushing dissent to build an empire.

By 479 BCE, Xerxes' invasion of Greece (see pp.150–153) was over, but Greece's war with Persia was not. Seeking to plunder Xerxes' territory and free the Greek islands and coastal cities of the Eastern Mediterranean still under Persian rule, the Greeks decided to take the fight to Xerxes. Taking control of this enterprise, Athens gained the resources and power to dominate Greece and the Aegean, building an empire that came to threaten Sparta and turned the Greeks against each other.

Initially, however, the Greek forces were under the command of the Spartan general Pausanias, who led a force drawn from Sparta, Athens, and the Ionian cities in the conquest of Cyprus before ejecting the Persians from Byzantium in 478 BCE. Suspicious that Pausanias was conspiring with the Persians, the Ionians asked Athens to take control of the allied Greek forces.

The Delian League

Athens thus found itself as hegemon (leader) of the Delian League—an alliance of more than 150 Greek cities, including most of the Ionian and Aeolian cities in Asia Minor, and all but one of the Euboean cities. The League was inaugurated in 479–478 BCE at a

▽ **The ruins of Delos**
Delos in the Cyclades was the meeting place of the Delian League. The League's treasury was kept on the island until 454 BCE, when it was moved to Athens.

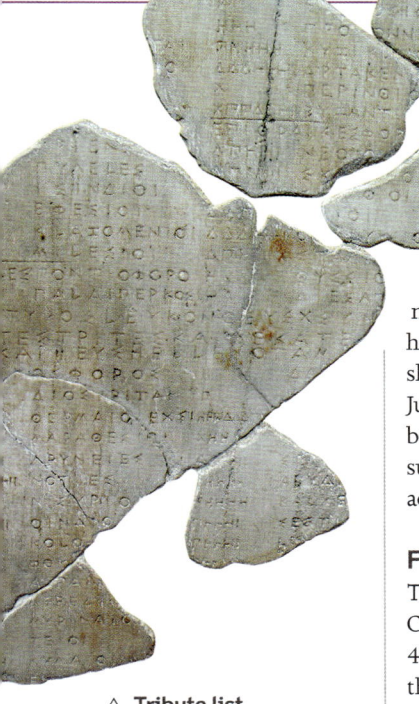

△ **Tribute list**
This stele records details of the portion of the annual tribute paid by members of the Delian League that was dedicated to the goddess Athena.

quasi-religious ceremony at Apollo's sanctuary on Delos, presided over by the Athenian statesman Aristides. Every year, each member of the League had to pay tribute in ships or in cash to finance the war with Persia. The initial revenues were enough to maintain 100 League galleys. Aristides was said to have been so fair in deciding how much each city should pay that he was nicknamed "Aristides the Just." Such justice was, however, short-lived. It soon became clear that Athens' rulers intended to use the subjects, ships, and tribute they had been handed to advance Athens' own interests.

From league to empire

The architect of this "Athens first" approach was Cimon, a statesman who came to prominence in the 470s BCE. In 476 BCE, as the League's *strategos*, he routed the Persians from Eion, a strategically important town in northern Greece; in 465 BCE, the Athenians attempted to colonize the town. Cimon's conquest of Skyros in 475 BCE also looked like imperialist expansion on Athens' part. The island had no strategic importance for the war with Persia, but it did lie on the route by which grain was shipped from the Black Sea to Athens. Athens also used the spoils from the League's victory over the Persians at the Battle of the Eurymedon in 467 BCE to rebuild its Acropolis.

Conflict between Athens and the League members inevitably arose. In 470 BCE, Naxos tried to leave the League, but remained after the Athenians blockaded the island. Five years later, Thasos rebelled when

△ **Athens' Long Walls**
Themistocles first proposed the building of walls to protect the route from Athens to its fleet at Piraeus following Xerxes' invasion, but construction did not begin until c. 460 BCE. The Long Walls helped turn Athens into an impenetrable fortress.

Athens founded a colony at Amphipolis in Macedonia to exploit silver mines already claimed by Thasos. The rebellion was subdued only after two years of fighting, and Athens began imposing severe penalties to discourage other independent-minded cities. The Delian League had become the Athenian Empire.

In 460 BCE, Athens began meddling in the Peloponnese, allying with Sparta's traditional enemy, Argos, and settling some of Sparta's rebellious helots on the Gulf of Corinth. When Megara withdrew from the Peloponnesian League and allied with Athens, because Sparta would not support it against Corinthian aggression, the Athenians helped the city build long walls (similar to those then under construction in Athens, see above) to its port at Nisaea that cut across the road through the Isthmus of Corinth and into the Peloponnese. This interference sparked the First Peloponnesian War, a sporadic conflict that lasted until 446 BCE, when the Thirty Years' Peace settled the spheres of Spartan and Athenian influence. By then the Greco-Persian Wars had ended, with Persia accepting Athens' hegemony over western Asia Minor and the Aegean.

> "The **Athenians** were **severe** and **exacting** ... applying the **screw** of **necessity**."
>
> THUCYDIDES, *THE PELOPONNESIAN WAR*

THE ISLAND OF **DELOS**

The small, rocky island of Delos in the center of the Aegean Sea was, according to the poet Callimachus in the 3rd century BCE, "the most sacred of all islands." It was famed as the birthplace of Apollo and Artemis. According to myth, after being raped by Zeus, the goddess Leto hid on Delos from Zeus's wife, Hera. She subsequently spent nine days and nights in labor before giving birth to Zeus's twin offspring. A sanctuary dedicated to Apollo was established at Delos in the 9th century BCE, and by the Archaic period it was attracting pilgrims from across Greece. As the center of the Delian League, Delos lent a Panhellenic, sacred air to what was essentially an Athenian-dominated economic and military alliance.

MOSAIC, DELOS ISLAND

▷ Pastas

The pastas, after which this type of house is named, was a long, covered space that normally opened onto the courtyard. It provided light, ventilation, and access to poorly lit rear ground-floor rooms, and was also used as a multifunctional work area.

Wooden pillars provided extra support

Work took place in the better-lit areas of the pastas

◁ Decorated plaster

A room (usually the andron) could be decorated in simple block color—such as the vivid red of this wall plaster fragment—or, more rarely, in multiple registers of color.

Roof space could accommodate beekeeping

Houses could incorporate rooms for business

A Greek Home

Domestic life in Classical Greece

The Classical Greek household, or *oikos*, was relatively modest in its design, and included special adaptations that took into account both the Greek climate and the expectations of contemporary social convention. Urban houses were typically constructed of mudbrick on top of a stone foundation, and had a pitched roof of terracotta tiles. While rural properties could be relatively large, urban houses were often restricted by their setting. There was no standard plan, but the need to accommodate day-to-day household activities and social norms meant that many houses, particularly within the same settlement, appeared similar.

A typical private house would include space for storage, crafts, and the preparation of food, though most rooms were probably multifunctional. Some rooms perhaps accommodated small-scale trade and industry. One room that certainly did not was the andron, or men's room, which would have hosted the domestic symposium, an elite drinking party. Women's rooms, or *gynaikonitis*, are noted by contemporary writers, often upstairs, but they are difficult to locate archaeologically and it is unlikely that much of the house would have been divided along gender lines.

The floor of the courtyard was often cobbled

A central courtyard provided light and ventilation

△ Olynthus house

Most evidence about Classical Greek homes comes from the city of Olynthus in northern Greece. At such sites as Olynthus, houses were arranged in close proximity on a street grid, so good neighborliness would have been key.

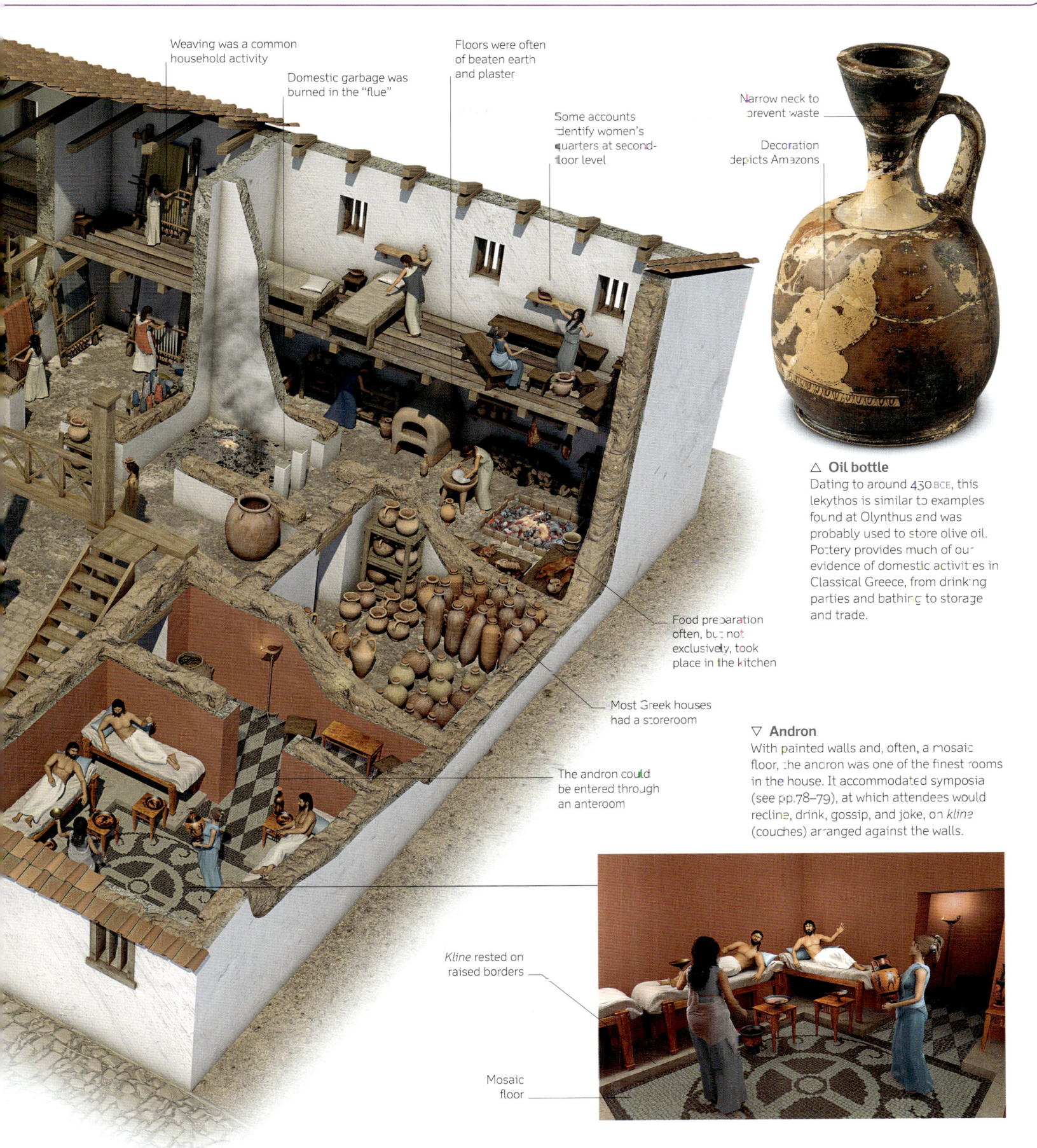

Weaving was a common household activity

Domestic garbage was burned in the "flue"

Floors were often of beaten earth and plaster

Some accounts identify women's quarters at second-floor level

Narrow neck to prevent waste

Decoration depicts Amazons

△ **Oil bottle**
Dating to around 430 BCE, this lekythos is similar to examples found at Olynthus and was probably used to store olive oil. Pottery provides much of our evidence of domestic activities in Classical Greece, from drinking parties and bathing to storage and trade.

Food preparation often, but not exclusively, took place in the kitchen

Most Greek houses had a storeroom

▽ **Andron**
With painted walls and, often, a mosaic floor, the andron was one of the finest rooms in the house. It accommodated symposia (see pp.78–79), at which attendees would recline, drink, gossip, and joke, on *kline* (couches) arranged against the walls.

The andron could be entered through an anteroom

Kline rested on raised borders

Mosaic floor

The Lives of Women

In and outside the house

Ancient Greek women, it is often said, led sequestered lives, confined to their homes. However, this characterization may be based on suppositions and generalizations about women's lives rather than on their lived experiences.

△ **Minoan priestess**
A priestess with rouged lips burns incense in this fresco from the 16th century BCE found at the Minoan site of Akrotiri on Thera (Santorini).

The traditional view of ancient Greek women as being hidden away in their homes, dependent on male relatives, is largely based on the perceived lives of citizen women in Athens in the Classical period. Yet the evidence, from Athens and elsewhere, points to women taking part in wider society, leaving their homes on many occasions and for many purposes, such as running errands, working, visiting friends, collecting water, visiting sanctuaries, performing duties as priestesses, and participating in festivals.

Among the events women might attend was the procession at the Panathenaea, the festival of "all Athenians." Here, a group of unmarried women of impeccable reputation would act as *kanephoroi* (basket carriers). With the wives and daughters of the metics as their attendants and the people of Athens following behind, they would walk through the streets and up the slopes of the Acropolis to the sanctuary of Athena. There were also several festivals attended only by women, such as the Haloa and the Thesmophoria (both for the goddess Demeter), and the midsummer festival of Adonia (see pp.156–157), where groups of women of all social statuses would gather together to honor Adonis.

Perhaps the most public role that a woman could play was as a priestess. Taking care of the temples and cult statues and performing prayers for the city and its people, priestesses were venerated for their service. Women were also highly visible at funerals and at the

◁ **Personal objects**
A woman styling her hair is depicted on this lid from a bronze box mirror from the late 5th century BCE.

processions that took place on the eve of a wedding with the bride, her mother, female attendants, and choruses of women. Even symposia, generally thought of as male-only events, provided another arena for female participation. It is often assumed that the women shown in paintings partying alongside men must be *hetairai*, a term usually translated as "courtesans" and suggesting engagement in sex work. However, the term covers a wide variety of women's situations: *hetairai* could be sex workers, but not necessarily; they could be dependent on a male relative or a guardian (*kyrios*), or—most importantly— they could be independent, acting as their own guardian.

Paintings on ancient Greek vases provide us with a range of possibly idealized images of ancient Greek women engaging in a variety of activities, including working as vase painters. Moreover, we know of a few female philosophers and poets (including Sappho, Nossis, Hipparchia, and Sosipatra) whose teachings, writings, or advice were important enough to be remembered by later writers.

▷ **Household craft**
A woman dressed in a chiton and himation pulls a skein of wool from her basket in this domestic scene from an oil flask from around 480–470 BCE.

> "Look at the **wise housewife** ... All hail, **blessed** among **women**."
>
> FEMALE HELLENISTIC POET NOSSIS, EPIGRAM

Narcissus motif; Persephone was gathering narcissi when she was abducted by Hades

Liknon, a winnowing basket used by priestesses in the Eleusinian Mysteries

Chiton carved with great detail, mirroring the details of Persephone's hair

△ **Private spaces**
The goddess Persephone—the mother of Dionysus according to some myths—opens the *liknon*, in which Dionysus was hidden, on this tablet from Persephone's sanctuary at Locri, Italy. The mirror hanging from the wall suggests a domestic setting.

Love, Sex, and Marriage

Intimate relations in ancient Greece

The art and literature of ancient Greece have left us many, often vivid, images of love, sex, and marriage. Their depictions of lust, longing, jealousy, joy, and violence continue to resonate into modern times.

Understanding Greek attitudes toward love, sex, and sexuality is not simple. Indeed, according to American scholar David Halperin, to many modern people, the ancient Greeks may seem "weird" when it comes to sex. Like other people of the ancient world, the Greeks would not have identified themselves using modern labels such as "gay" or "straight." Instead sexual status was expected to mirror social status. This meant that those at the top of the social hierarchy, such as adult male citizens in Athens, were expected to be dominant in their sexual relationships as well, whether with their wives, with sex workers (both male and female), with the people they enslaved, or with *pallakai* (concubines or mistresses). This hierarchy also extended to the complex and much debated practice of pederasty, which involved relationships between an adult man and a male youth that were seen to aid the social transition from youth to manhood.

This conception of sexuality in ancient Greece, however, leaves little room for the romance, desire, pleasure, and variety of experience expressed in many works of ancient literature and art. For example, the poetry of Sappho includes the assertion that "the most beautiful thing on the black earth is whom one loves." In the poetry of Alcman in the 7th century BCE, choirs of girls celebrate the beauty and erotic allure of their fellow girls. Meanwhile, some ancient Greek sources do appear to assume the existence of sexual preferences. In a speech on the nature of *eros* (love, lust) in Plato's *Symposium*, the comic poet Aristophanes recounts

◁ **Same-sex couple**
Relationships between men were a common motif on ancient Greek pottery, as shown in this drinking cup from 505–500 BCE depicting two pentathletes embracing.

◁ **Goddess of love**
Aphrodite rests her left foot on a swan, a symbol of good health, music, divination, and grace, in this marble statue from the 2nd century BCE.

that mortals were originally dual-formed, but were split into two because Zeus feared their power, leaving every resulting person longing for their lost "other half." Thus, any man who desired other men was, according to Aristophanes, once half of a double-male being; women who desired other women were originally half of a double-female being; and those who desired people of the opposite sex were once half of a part-male, part-female being.

Zeus was the deity who perhaps best encapsulates Greek ideas about sex, love, and marriage. For example, Zeus's dominance over the cosmos as its ruler is echoed in the violence he perpetuates against his wife, Hera. To stop her working against Heracles, Zeus binds and hangs Hera in the sky in chains, attaching anvils to her feet so she suffers agonizing pain. At the same time, Zeus's many extramarital relationships, often in the form of abductions and rapes, echo the sexual double standard present among ancient Greeks, where married men would be permitted—even expected—to seek a range of different sexual experiences or liaisons. Married women's sexuality, on the other hand, was closely guarded.

> "The **madness of love** is the **greatest** of **heaven's blessings.**"
>
> PLATO, *PHAEDRUS*

GETTING **MARRIED IN GREECE**

Arranged marriages were normal in ancient Greece, and transacted between the bride's *kyros* (controller), often her father, and the groom; the bride's consent was not required. Wedding traditions varied but typically centered on the bride. During the final days in her parental home, she would dedicate her toys to gods of marriage or childhood. On the wedding day, she would be ritually bathed and adorned. After a banquet, she would go in a procession by foot, cart, or chariot to the groom's house. There, the marriage would be consummated while friends of the bride and groom sang and danced outside.

GRAVE STELE WITH MARRIED COUPLE

The personification of the town of Eleusis, home to the Eleusinian Mysteries, which promised initiates good harvests and a happy afterlife

Strings hang down from an *iynx*, a wheel-shaped love-charm, held by Aphrodite

A tree from which a woman, perhaps a companion of Leda, plucks fruit

◁ **Divine desire**

This complexly decorated funerary vase from 330 BCE includes several scenes relating to love and sex. The top register shows Zeus with Aphrodite. She is accompanied by Eros (god of love). The register below shows a popular motif: the Spartan queen Leda's seduction by Zeus in the form of a swan. Around these central figures are others, including Astrape, who personifies lightning (top left); Hypnos, the personification of sleep (right of Leda); and two unnamed women.

"Faultless in form, in spirit, and also in the handling of arms."

AESCHYLUS, *SEVEN AGAINST THEBES*

The Riace Bronzes

Ancient warriors saved from the sea

This pair of bronze warriors emerged from the seabed in 1972 after they were discovered by Italian engineer Stefano Mariottini while he was scuba diving off the coast at Riace Marina, Calabria, in southern Italy. A rare survival from the Classical world, they most likely came from a shipwreck and were lost while being transported. Scholars date them to around the middle of the 5th century BCE, when the coastal area of Calabria was part of Magna Graecia and inhabited by Greek colonists. They may have been made in Greece or locally, in one of the colonies.

While many ancient bronze statues were melted down so their material could be reused, these survived in good condition, which has been improved by conservation treatment.

Technique and style

The statues represent two standing nude males, known as Statue A (shown standing on the left) and Statue B. They were cast in bronze in several pieces, which were then joined together. Their anatomy is detailed and finely modeled, down to the veins and sinews of the hands and feet, demonstrating what could be achieved in the medium of bronze.

The two men are similar in appearance and pose, but not identical. They both bear their weight on their right legs, with their left feet slightly advanced. They hold their right hands loosely at their sides, while their left arms are bent at the elbow and would have supported shields. Their heads turn to the right. Statue A appears younger, more ready for action. He has a proud and alert gaze. Statue B's expression and body suggest an older, more relaxed figure. Statue A's hair is more abundant and curly; its complex details would have been very difficult to achieve on a stone statue. Statue B's upper head is flattened and smoothed to more easily accommodate the helmet he once wore. It is difficult to know whether these variations were deliberate stylistic choices or the result of the statues having been made by different artists.

Mysterious identities

There have been many theories about the statues' identities. Their nudity suggests that they are heroic figures. Some scholars have identified them as Tydeus and Amphiaraus, warriors from Aeschylus's play *Seven Against Thebes*. Their similarity suggests they were made to be displayed together, maybe as part of a larger group. It is intriguing to imagine that more statues are waiting to be found.

▽ **Face of a warrior**
Statue A's face has added color from inlaid eyes, bronze eyelashes and lips, and silver teeth. His carefully combed mustache nearly covers his top lip.

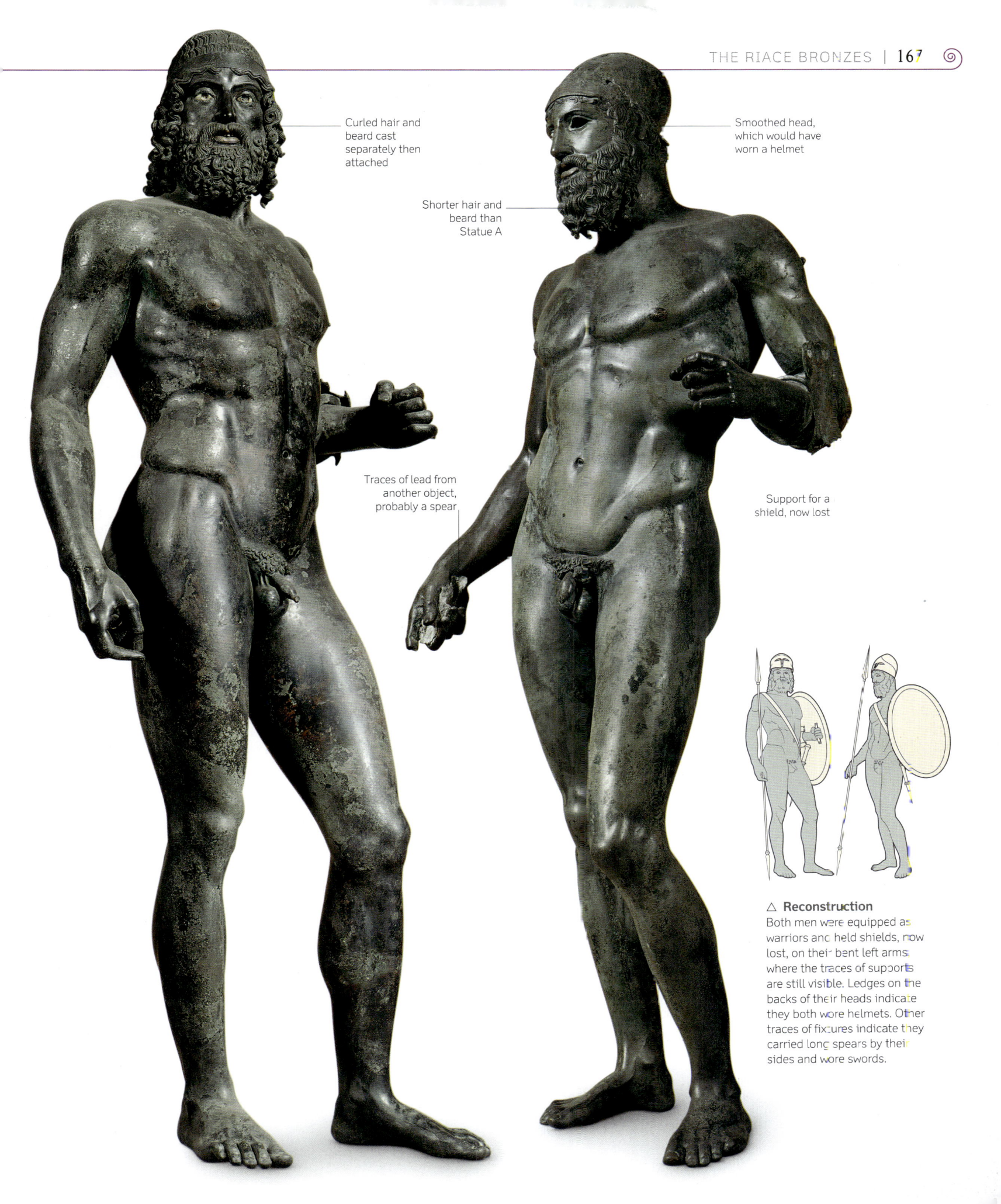

Curled hair and beard cast separately then attached

Smoothed head, which would have worn a helmet

Shorter hair and beard than Statue A

Traces of lead from another object, probably a spear

Support for a shield, now lost

△ **Reconstruction**
Both men were equipped as warriors and held shields, now lost, on their bent left arms where the traces of supports are still visible. Ledges on the backs of their heads indicate they both wore helmets. Other traces of fixtures indicate they carried long spears by their sides and wore swords.

▷ **Bust of Pericles**
This is one of several Roman copies
of a bronze bust of Pericles created
by the Greek sculptor Kresilas of
Argos, working in the 5th century BCE.
The base of the bust is inscribed
with Pericles' name. Another copy
has the additional inscription
"son of Xanthippus, Athenian."

A Corinthian
helmet indicates
Pericles' status
as a *strategos*

The bust reflects the
focus on proportion,
vitality, and harmony
typical of Classical
Greek sculpture

"We are rather a
pattern to others
than **imitators**
ourselves."

PERICLES, FUNERAL ORATION

Pericles

Popular politician and architect of Athens

A charismatic 5th-century BCE leader, Pericles transformed Athens with an impressive building program and political reforms before losing the Athenians' support with his poor management of the Peloponnesian War.

According to the historian Thucydides, the Athens of Pericles was "in name a democracy" but in reality "governed by its first man." This "first man" was born around 495 BCE to Xanthippus, a leading politician, and Agariste, a member of the aristocratic Alcmaeonid family. Before he rose to prominence, Pericles is known to have carried out the major public service of funding a dramatic chorus (for Aeschylus's *Persians*) and to have served as one of those elected to prosecute Cimon, then the most dominant politician in Athens, on charges of corruption.

Reforming Athens

Pericles was among the reformers who curbed the power of the reactionary, aristocratic Areopagus Council in around 461 BCE. In the years after this, Pericles emerged as a popular politician in Athens. He is credited with two measures that further weakened aristocratic power. First, he introduced pay for jurors, which widened access to participation in public life. Second, he created a law that undermined the common elite practice of forming marriage alliances beyond Athens by restricting citizenship to those whose fathers and mothers were both Athenian citizens. This law, however, apparently did not apply to his son by the metic Aspasia, from Miletus.

When the Greco-Persian Wars finally ended in 449 BCE, Pericles appears to have been instrumental in using the resources that had previously financed the war to advance Athenian interests. He began a costly, controversial building program (see pp.172), and established several cleruchies (dependent colonies where the settlers retained Athenian citizenship).

In 431 BCE, Pericles' policies led to the outbreak of the Peloponnesian War with Sparta. According to Thucydides, the famous funeral oration that Pericles gave commemorating the Athenians who had died during the first months of the conflict sought to encourage support for the war by glorifying Athens as the "school of Hellas." But Pericles' decision to not engage the Spartans as they approached Athens was so unpopular with the Athenians that they deposed him as *strategos* (general) in around 430 BCE. Pericles died the following year, perishing of the plague that spread though the overcrowded and besieged city.

△ **Ostracon of Pericles**
Pericles' initial popularity did not stop some citizens voting for his removal as *strategos* using pottery ostraca like the one above, inscribed with his name.

▽ **Patron of the arts**
This 19th-century painting by French artist Louis Hector Leroux shows Pericles and Aspasia on a visit to the sculptor Phidias's workshop.

Timeline

c. 495 BCE Birth of Pericles

472 BCE Pericles is the *choregos* (chorus-funder) for Aeschylus's *Persians*

461 BCE Pericles serves as one the elected prosecutors of Cimon

454 BCE Pericles leads Athens against Achaea, in the north Peloponnese

c. 451 BCE Pericles introduces his citizenship law

431 BCE Outbreak of the Peloponnesian War

447 BCE Building work begins on the Acropolis

429 BCE Pericles dies of plague during the Peloponnesian War

The Temple of Poseidon, Cape Sounion

Located around 43 miles (70 km) from Athens at the southern tip of the Attic peninsula, the temple at Cape Sounion was built in the time of Pericles, in 444–440 BCE. It originally had 38 columns rising 20 ft (6 m) into the air, of which 16 now remain standing, and a colossal bronze statue of Poseidon—the god of the sea and an important deity to the Athenians. The temple was built on the site of an earlier temple destroyed by the Persians in c. 480 BCE. Evidence points to activity at the site from the 8th century BCE, and Herodotus notes that the Athenians celebrated a quadrennial festival at Cape Sounion in the 6th century BCE.

The Athens of Pericles

A victorious city rebuilds

Pericles' 30-year tenure as Athens' leading statesman saw the city rebuilt after its destruction by the Persians. A number of building projects, most notably the Parthenon, left Athens and beyond with a magnificent architectural legacy.

In 480 BCE, Xerxes' invasion had been defeated, but Athens lay in ruins, its Agora and Acropolis burned by the Persians (see pp.150–153). The Greek city-states swore an oath to leave their destroyed temples as memorials to the dead, but work soon began on secular buildings. The Athenian general Cimon (c. 510–450 BCE) funded the Long Walls (see p.159), while around 475 BCE his brother-in-law Peisianax built the Stoa Poikile, a colonnaded walkway decorated by the artists Polygnotos and Mikas with paintings, including one of the Greek victory against the Persians at Marathon. Cimon helped establish the

Delian League of Greek city-states, and the funds contributed to this by its members provided Pericles, Athens' principal statesman from 461 BCE to 429 BCE, with the means to begin a much wider program of construction. The result was a series of impressive secular and religious buildings that projected Athens' image of itself as Greece's leading power.

The general population embraced the building work, which provided ample opportunities for employment. However, according to the historian Plutarch, Pericles' opponents disapproved of his use of the money from the Delian treasury, arguing that it

▽ **Temple of Hephaestus**
Built mainly from Pentelic marble, the ancient Temple of Hephaestus in the Agora in Athens is one of the best-preserved Greek temples because it was later used as a Christian church.

▷ **The Caryatids**
These figures on the Erechtheion represent the women of Caryae, doomed to hard labor after the town sided with the Persians in 480 BCE.

was insulting to use the money Athens' allies were paying to fund the ongoing war with the Persians to gild the city "like a wanton woman [who] adds to her wardrobe precious stones." In response, Pericles asserted that Athens owed its allies no account of how their money was being spent provided that it carried on the war on their behalf.

The earliest building Pericles commissioned was the Temple of Hephaestus (also called the Theseion from a mistaken connection with Theseus, the founder-hero of Athens), erected in the northwest of the Agora. The temple is decorated with lavish sculptures showing the Labors of Heracles and scenes from Theseus's life, including his battle with the 50 sons of Pallas, younger brother of King Aegeus of Athens. Pericles sponsored other buildings in the Agora, including the Stoa of Zeus Eleutherios, which symbolized the freedom of the city, and a new *bouleuterion*, or council house. However, Pericles' main work was on the Acropolis.

The Acropolis and beyond

With its soaring Doric columns of Pentelic marble and its huge size, the Parthenon (see pp.176–177) was the most impressive of the buildings on the Acropolis. Close by was the Propylaea, the monumental gateway at the western end of the Acropolis. South of this lay the small temple of Athena Nike (Athena of Victory) finished around 420 BCE, after the death of Pericles in 429 BCE. At the southeastern foot of the Acropolis, the Odeon of Pericles was built to host the musical contests of the Panathenaea.

Part of Pericles' plan for the Acropolis, but also not concluded in his lifetime, was the Erechtheion. Dedicated primarily to Athena, this incorporated several existing shrines and was built to an asymmetric plan that included multiple ground levels to accommodate the sloping nature of the site.

Pericles' construction works also extended beyond the city and into rural Attica. The Temple of Poseidon at Sounion (see pp.170–171) was built between 444 BCE and 440 BCE, and work began but was not completed on temples to Demeter at Thorikos in southern Attica. At Rhamnous in northeast Attica, a temple to Nemesis, goddess of revenge, was built that housed a large statue of the goddess by Agorakritos, a pupil of the sculptor Phidias. The Telesterion (the initiation hall of the cult of the Eleusinian Mysteries) at Eleusis was also reconstructed. Touching Attica's most far-flung demes, these works reflected Pericles' vision to not only restore Athens itself but make the entire *polis* unequaled in the grandeur of its monuments.

▽ **Ancient accounts**
This inscription, which dates from 408–407 BCE, records in detail some of the costs associated with the building of the Erechtheion.

"The **Propylaea** has a ceiling of **white marble** which in the **beauty** and **size** of the **stones** remains **supreme** even to my **time**."

PAUSANIAS, *DESCRIPTION OF GREECE*

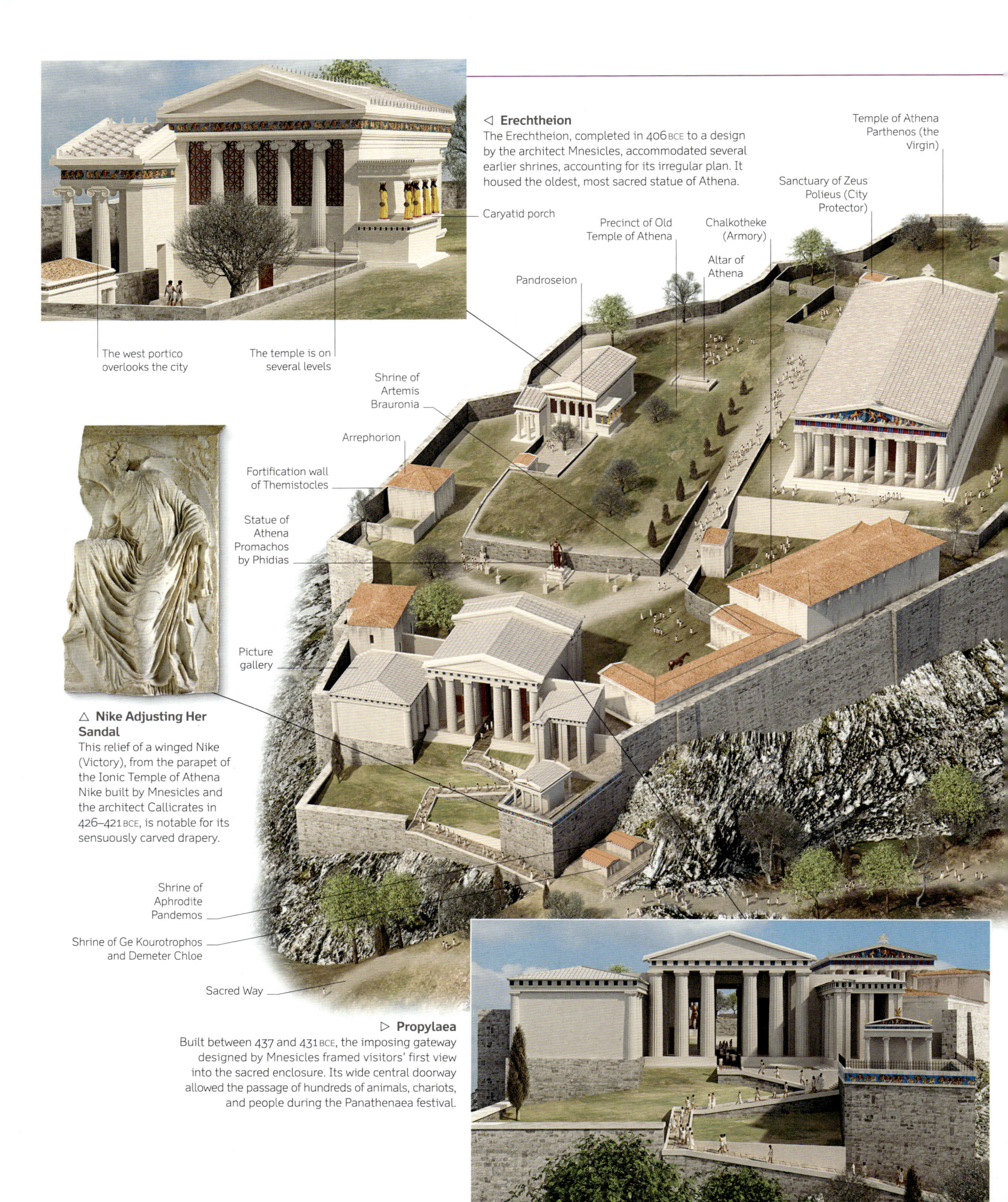

◁ Erechtheion

The Erechtheion, completed in 406 BCE to a design by the architect Mnesicles, accommodated several earlier shrines, accounting for its irregular plan. It housed the oldest, most sacred statue of Athena.

Temple of Athena Parthenos (the Virgin)

Sanctuary of Zeus Polieus (City Protector)

Chalkotheke (Armory)

Precinct of Old Temple of Athena

Altar of Athena

Pandroseion

Caryatid porch

The west portico overlooks the city

The temple is on several levels

Shrine of Artemis Brauronia

Arrephorion

Fortification wall of Themistocles

Statue of Athena Promachos by Phidias

Picture gallery

△ Nike Adjusting Her Sandal

This relief of a winged Nike (Victory), from the parapet of the Ionic Temple of Athena Nike built by Mnesicles and the architect Callicrates in 426–421 BCE, is notable for its sensuously carved drapery.

Shrine of Aphrodite Pandemos

Shrine of Ge Kourotrophos and Demeter Chloe

Sacred Way

▷ Propylaea

Built between 437 and 431 BCE, the imposing gateway designed by Mnesicles framed visitors' first view into the sacred enclosure. Its wide central doorway allowed the passage of hundreds of animals, chariots, and people during the Panathenaea festival.

Sanctuary of
Pandion

▷ **Theater of Dionysus**
This theater is the birthplace of Greek drama,
which evolved from hymn at Athens' Dionysia
festival (see p.180). It was here that the plays
of Aeschylus, Aristophanes, Euripides, and
Sophocles were first staged.

Fortification wall
of Cimon

The *skene* roof
provided additional
acting space

Staging devices were
stored in the *skene*

Dionysus and Xanthias, characters
in Aristophanes' *Frogs*

Odeon (concert
hall) of Pericles

Stage building, or
skene, of the Theater
of Dionysus

Temple of Dionysus

Sanctuary of
Asclepius

Temple of
Themis

△ **Sacred rock**
This illustration depicts the Acropolis as seen from
the west, overlooking the approach to the sanctuary.
It shows the site around 400 BCE, after the construction
of the gleaming marble buildings designed for Pericles
under the leadership of the sculptor Phidias.

The Acropolis

Cult center of Athens

Emerging as a sanctuary space in the 8th century BCE, Athens' lofty Acropolis soon
evolved into a thriving place of worship serving numerous cults. Small shrines
dotted its slopes, while temples and dedications, many of which were to Athena
and other deities and heroes, proliferated on the plateau. After the Persians devastated
the sanctuary in 480 BCE, the Athenians initially continued their worship amid the
ruins (see p.172). But in 447 BCE, the Acropolis became the centerpiece of Pericles'
grand redevelopment program: he commissioned the finest architects and sculptors
of the day to transform the sanctuary into an artistic embodiment of Athenian
greatness, one that celebrated its gods, people, culture, military victories, and
political status. The result was an ensemble of magnificent buildings combining
Doric and Ionic styles, which accommodated earlier shrines while paying the ultimate
homage to Athena, the city's patron and protector, in the form of the Parthenon.

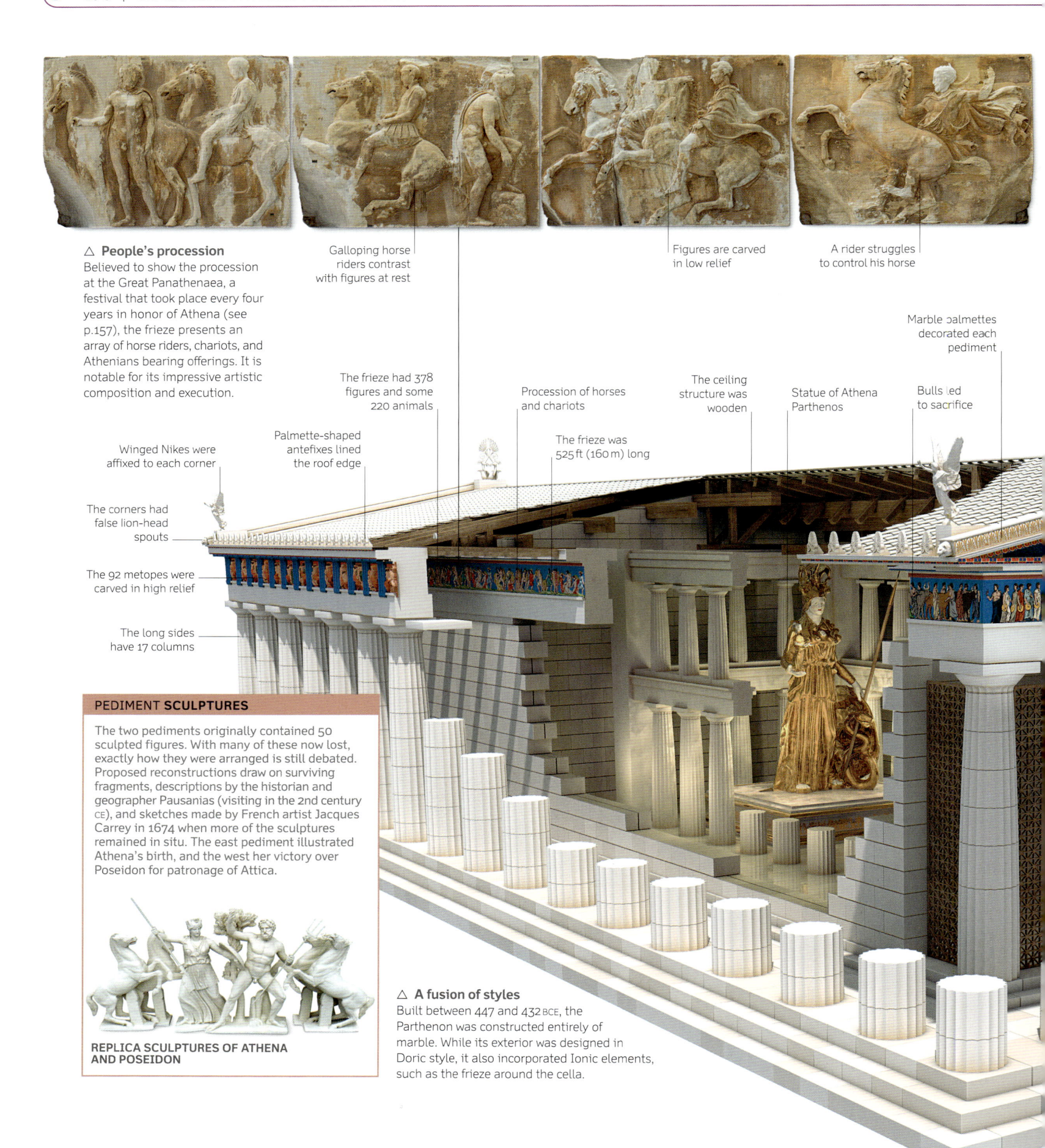

△ **People's procession**
Believed to show the procession at the Great Panathenaea, a festival that took place every four years in honor of Athena (see p.157), the frieze presents an array of horse riders, chariots, and Athenians bearing offerings. It is notable for its impressive artistic composition and execution.

Galloping horse riders contrast with figures at rest

Figures are carved in low relief

A rider struggles to control his horse

Marble palmettes decorated each pediment

The frieze had 378 figures and some 220 animals

The ceiling structure was wooden

Statue of Athena Parthenos

Bulls led to sacrifice

Procession of horses and chariots

Winged Nikes were affixed to each corner

Palmette-shaped antefixes lined the roof edge

The frieze was 525 ft (160 m) long

The corners had false lion-head spouts

The 92 metopes were carved in high relief

The long sides have 17 columns

PEDIMENT SCULPTURES

The two pediments originally contained 50 sculpted figures. With many of these now lost, exactly how they were arranged is still debated. Proposed reconstructions draw on surviving fragments, descriptions by the historian and geographer Pausanias (visiting in the 2nd century CE), and sketches made by French artist Jacques Carrey in 1674 when more of the sculptures remained in situ. The east pediment illustrated Athena's birth, and the west her victory over Poseidon for patronage of Attica.

REPLICA SCULPTURES OF ATHENA AND POSEIDON

△ **A fusion of styles**
Built between 447 and 432 BCE, the Parthenon was constructed entirely of marble. While its exterior was designed in Doric style, it also incorporated Ionic elements, such as the frieze around the cella.

The Parthenon

As Pericles' grand construction project took shape, the first building to rise from the ruins on the Acropolis was the Parthenon, a great temple dedicated to Athens' patron goddess, Athena. Incorporating columns from an earlier, unfinished incarnation of the Parthenon destroyed by the Persians, the new temple both acknowledged and defied that painful attack. Designed by the architects Ictinus and Callicrates under the supervision of the sculptor Phidias, this Parthenon was a masterpiece of precision construction and artisanship in the High Classical style, combining harmonious proportions with exquisite sculptural decoration. It became a potent symbol of Athens' power and status at that time.

WEST METOPES

SOUTH METOPES

NORTH METOPES

EAST METOPES

Key

1 Cella
2 Pronaos
3 Opisthodomos (Treasury)
4 East pediment: the birth of Athena
5 West pediment: contest for Attica
6 Frieze surrounding cella: Panathenaic Festival
7 Metopes around exterior colonnade: battle scenes

△ **Decorative scheme**
While the pediment scenes and frieze honored Athena, the metopes depicted four mythical battles. Alluding to the Greeks' recent triumph over Persia, these showed Greeks fighting Trojans in the Sack of Troy (north), Olympian gods fighting Giants (east), centaurs fighting Lapiths (south), and Greeks fighting Amazons (west).

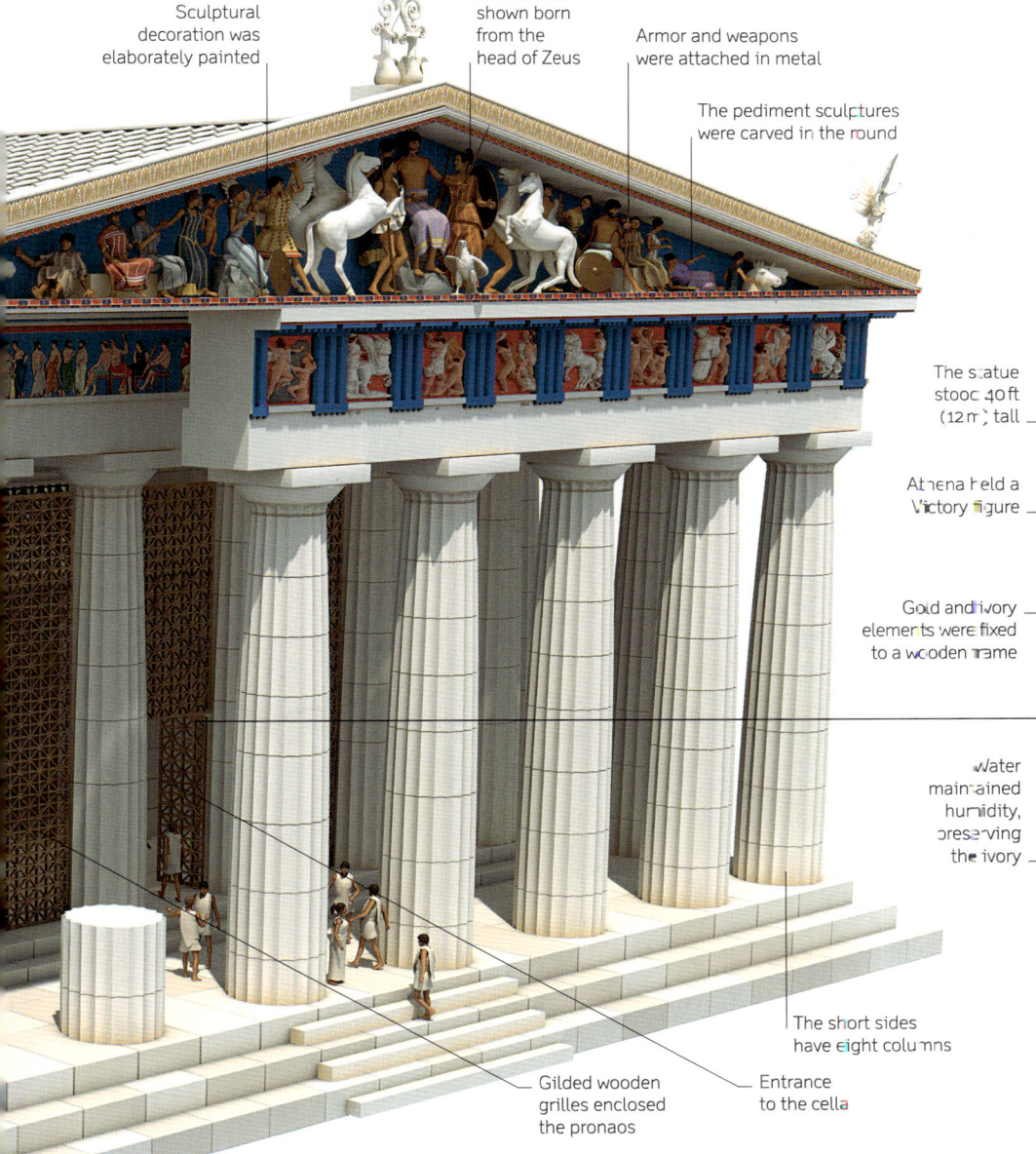

Sculptural decoration was elaborately painted

Athena was shown born from the head of Zeus

Armor and weapons were attached in metal

The pediment sculptures were carved in the round

Gilded wooden grilles enclosed the pronaos

Entrance to the cella

The short sides have eight columns

The statue stood 40 ft (12 m) tall

Athena held a Victory figure

Gold and ivory elements were fixed to a wooden frame

Water maintained humidity, preserving the ivory

△ **Statue of Athena**
The towering gold and ivory cult statue of Athena Parthenos, dressed for battle, was a masterpiece by Phidias. It was an instant tourist attraction, inspiring copies on which modern reconstructions are based.

Ancient Greek Theater

Actors, audiences, and performance spaces

Theater performances were a key element of social life in the ancient Greek cities, gathering together audiences of thousands to enjoy spectacles of dramatic, musical, and technical skill.

Early theaters were a far cry from the monumental spaces of later centuries, consisting only of an orchestra (dancing-place) of beaten earth and space for an audience, perhaps no more than a hillside. The first built theaters were made of wood and included temporary tiers of seats (*ikria*) erected only for days or weeks before being disassembled. Later tradition records at least one performance, a tragedy by Pratinas at Athens, in which these seats collapsed. By the late 4th century BCE, the design of the theater had developed considerably. Constructed of stone and sometimes with an audience capacity of 15,000 or more, theaters had become both grander and more complex than the early performance spaces.

Staging a play

Greek theaters were formed of several distinct elements. Formal entrances (*eisodoi* and *parodoi*) existed either side of the orchestra, and a small altar (*thymele*) that doubled as speaker's podium stood at its center. A structure called a *skene*, from which the modern word "scene" derives, stood at the back of the *logeion* (the stage) and served as a store for props and equipment, as changing rooms, and as scenery. The *ekkyklema* and *mechane* (machine) were key pieces of stagecraft. The *ekkyklema* was a wheeled platform that could represent a house, a temple, or similar interior. It also displayed dead characters (killed offstage, since onstage violence was prohibited). In Euripides' *Medea*, the *mechane* helped characters appear to fly or hover; in

△ **Dramatic mask**
This Sicilian terra-cotta model from the 2nd century BCE depicts the mask of a character from Greek drama.

Aristophanes' *Peace*, the *mechane* hauled one character, a farmer named Trygaeus, to heaven on a dung beetle.

All actors were male, even those playing female parts. The actors wore masks (*prosopa*, literally "faces") that helped audiences distinguish the character's gender, age, and social status, and important changes to their appearance or emotions. Made from strips of linen, leather, wood, or cork, the masks had holes for the eyes, a small aperture for the mouth, and sometimes an integrated wig. Costumes could include animal skin, feathers, and everyday dress. From the 5th century BCE, costumes became standardized to the part. For example, a short tunic fastened at one shoulder indicated an enslaved person, and a conical fur or felt hat marked a traveler. Costumes for Old Comedy (the comedies produced in Athens in the 5th century BCE) included padding and false parts that artificially exaggerated elements of the body, such as the belly and phallus, for comic effect. This padding was abandoned in the later 4th century BCE.

Involving actors, dancers, musicians, masks, and costumes, a Greek theater production was expensive. The state paid for the actors, who in the 4th century BCE were often well paid, and the playwright. A wealthy citizen, as *choregos* (chorus leader), was responsible for the recruitment, training, and costuming of the chorus members, whose function in Greek plays was to describe and comment on the main action. Admission was also costly. In the 4th century BCE, it cost an unskilled worker a day's wage, 2 obols, to attend the theater, although funds were available for the poorest, so they too could participate in what was a vital communal activity.

▽ **Playing to the crowd**
This hand-colored woodcut imagines how a performance at the Theater of Dionysus in Athens may have looked in the 1st century CE.

Volute handle decorated
with olive branch pattern

◁ **The Pronomos Vase**
Made in Athens around 400 BCE,
the Pronomos Vase is one of the
best-known artworks associated with
Greek theater. Among the figures on
side A of the vase are the chorus of
a satyr play, Pronomos the aulos
player, a *choregos* called Charinos,
and the playwright Demetrios.

Performer playing the character
Papposilenos (tutor to Dionysus)
dressed in costume and holding
his mask

Ariadne sitting on Dionysus's lap

Actor's mask for the
character of Heracles

An actor in satyr
costume practices
his dancing

▷ **Rural scene**
Side B of the vase depicts
Dionysus holding a lyre
and Ariadne with a torch
walking through rocky
terrain, along with satyrs,
maenads, and a panther.

Plays and Playwrights

The dramatists of ancient Greece

Only 40 or so complete ancient Greek plays survive, all from just four writers: Aeschylus, Sophocles, Euripides, and Aristophanes. Others survive in fragments, and for hundreds only the title alone remains. This diminished corpus is due to accidents of transmission and to the fact that plays were often staged just once, when they were entered into competition at the Dionysia or Lenaea festivals. Yet Greece's tradition set the stage for modern theater, and the Greek plays have retained their power by tapping into universal themes such as war, revenge, love, and humor.

The idea of the play as something separate from a song or ode is said to have been developed by a semi-legendary 7th-century BCE playwright named Arion of Lesbos. Actors followed later, when Thespis of Icaria is said to have included an actor (or "thespian")—who was set apart from the chorus and performed different roles—in his winning Dionysia entry in 534 BCE.

History, tragedy, and comedy

The first fragments of a play come from Phrynichus, who won the Dionysia between 511 and 508 BCE, and produced *The Capture of Miletus*, the first play with a historical background. Greece's history also influenced Aeschylus (c. 525–456 BCE), who grew up during the birth of democracy. His plays, including *The Persians*, *Seven Against Thebes*, and the *Oresteia* trilogy, reflect on the dilemmas and tragic choices of the powerful.

△ **The Capture of Miletus, 492 BCE**
Phrynichus's play targets the taking of Miletus by the Persians (shown above) in 494 BCE. The Athenians fined the author for his sympathetic portrayal of the Persians, but he regained favor with *Phoenician Women*, about Athens' victory at Salamis.

△ **Oresteia, 458 BCE**
Aeschylus's *Oresteia* tells the story of the murder of Agamemnon by his wife, Clytemnestra (above left), the vengeance of their son, Orestes, and his pursuit by the Furies (middle and right), tasked by the ghost of Clytemnestra with avenging her death. The *Oresteia* is the only ancient Greek trilogy to survive intact.

△ **Oedipus Rex, 435 BCE**
Sophocles' play relates Oedipus's attempts to escape a prophecy (depicted above) that he will kill his father and marry his mother. Fleeing Corinth, he kills a traveler (whom he later learns was his father) and marries the man's widow (his mother).

"Whom **the gods** love **die young**."

MENANDER, FRAGMENT 4

In the 5th century BCE, Sophocles (c. 496–406 BCE), an active politician as well as a 24-time winner in the Dionysia, introduced a third actor (Aeschylus was said to have brought in a second). This addition enabled Sophocles to put in place the multi-layered plots and deeper character development seen in his seven surviving plays, including *Antigone* and *Oedipus Rex*. With Euripides (c. 485–406 BCE), Greek tragedy became bleaker, when he—according to a quote attributed to Sophocles by Aristotle—showed men "as they are" and not "as they ought to be." His works, including *Medea* and *Trojan Women* are imbued with pessimism.

Greek comedy may have evolved from the raucous, earthy satyr-plays, often involving sexual innuendo and scatological humor, of which only *Cyclops* by Euripides survives. In his comedies, Aristophanes (c. 450–388 BCE) lampooned new ideas and cultural movements, using bawdy language, exaggeration, and satire in works such as *The Clouds* and *The Frogs*. His contemporaries included Cratinus (c. 520–423 BCE), one of whose surviving works is *Pytine* (*Bottle*), a retort to allegations of drunkenness.

The last play by Aristophanes, *Plutus* (388 BCE), foreshadowed New Comedy, signaling a shift to a less politicized drama that focused on stock characters and the private lives of the well-to-do. New Comedy's greatest exponent was Menander (342–291 BCE), of whose works *Dyskolos* (*Bad-Tempered Man*) is the best preserved. His plays helped transmit the dramatic art to the Romans.

△ **Bronze tragic mask**
Actors in ancient Greece typically wore masks, such as this bronze example from the mid-4th century BCE. Features on tragic masks were often exaggerated to indicate the traits of the character being represented.

△ **Medea, 431 BCE**
Euripides' (above) play tells of Medea's escape from Colchis, where she has helped Jason steal the Golden Fleece. She marries Jason, but he later spurns her for Glauce. Taking her revenge, Medea kills the children she had with Jason.

△ **The Frogs, 405 BCE**
The Frogs, by Aristophanes (above), satirizes other playwrights. Distraught at the state of tragedy-writing in Athens, the god Dionysus travels to Hades to bring Euripides back from the dead. After finding Euripides competing with Aeschylus for the title of best tragedian, Dionysus elects to take Aeschylus back with him.

△ **Dyskolos, c. 316 BCE**
In *Dyskolos*, Menander (above) tells the story of Sostratos, a rich young man, who falls in love with a village girl whose bad-tempered father, Cnemon, is opposed to the match. After falling down a well, Cnemon mends his ways and allows his daughter to marry Sostratos.

The Peloponnesian War

A struggle for supremacy

△ **Thracian soldiers**
Three young Thracian warriors dressed in caps called *alopekis* and cloaks known as *zeira* are shown in this red-figure krater from c.440–420 BCE. The Thracians were allies of Athens during the Peloponnesian War.

For nearly 50 years, Athens dominated Greece until, overreaching itself, it cast Greece into a struggle for primacy that lasted nearly 30 years and ended with Sparta emerging as Greece's most powerful city, and Athens in ruins.

Around 15 years into the Thirty Years' Peace agreed in 446 BCE, which brought an end to the conflict between Sparta and Athens known as the First Peloponnesian War (see p.159), the two sides were again at war. The roots of this Second Peloponnesian War lay in years of anger at Athenian bullying, and in the network of alliances that ensured events quickly escalated into a major conflict between Athens and the Delian League on one side and the Peloponnesian League—which was created c. 550 BCE, was led by Sparta, and included Corinth—on the other.

The crisis that provoked the war was an incident in 432 BCE in Potidaea—a Corinthian colony in southern Chalcidice and member of the Delian League. Fearful

> "A **great war**, and more worthy of **relation** than any that had **preceded** it."

THUCYDIDES, *THE PELOPONNESIAN WAR*

that the colony was about to rebel, as other League members that wanted to free themselves of Athenian domination had, Athens ordered Potidaea to pull down parts of its walls and send hostages to Athens. It then besieged the colony to enforce its demands. When the Corinthian fleet came to Potidaea's aid, the Athenian navy crushed it. The Athenian leader, Pericles (see p.169), began pressurizing Megara, which controlled the route through the Isthmus of Corinth, into an alliance by cutting off its supply routes.

According to Aristophanes (in his play *The Acharnians*, 425 BCE), the starving Megarians called on Sparta for help, precipitating the Peloponnesian War. However, the war's first historian, Thucydides, suggests the Spartans merely used Athens' treatment of Megara as a pretext for an attack. Whatever the truth, it is difficult to argue with Thucydides: "The growth of the power of Athens, and the alarm which this inspired in Sparta, made war inevitable."

The war began in 431 BCE, when Sparta's Theban allies took the city of Plataea. A few weeks later, Spartan forces launched a general invasion of Attica.

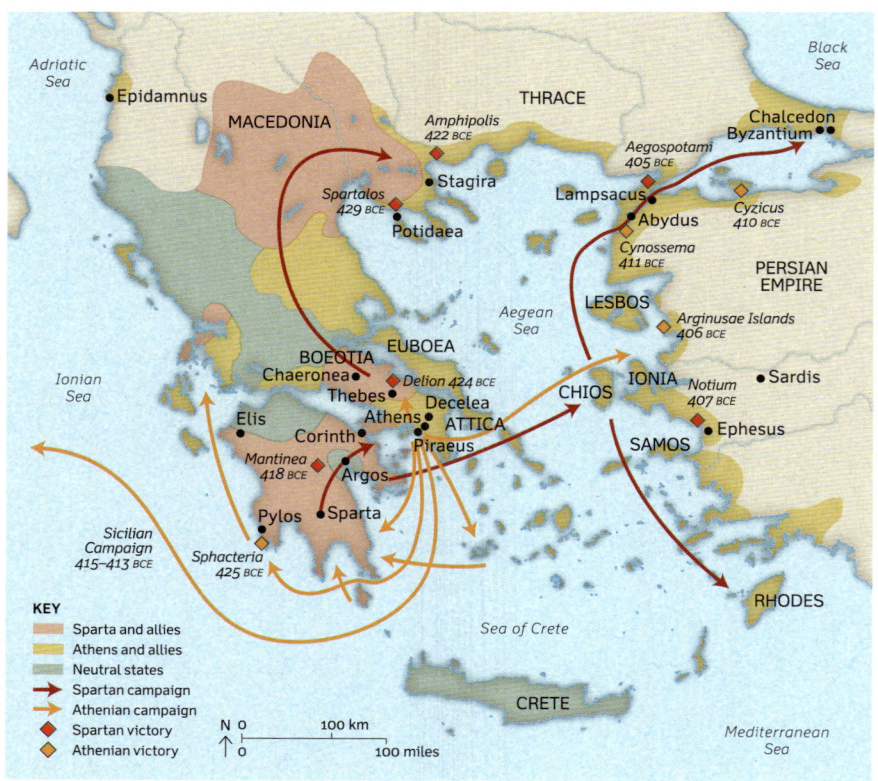

KEY
- Sparta and allies
- Athens and allies
- Neutral states
- ⟶ Spartan campaign
- ⟶ Athenian campaign
- ◆ Spartan victory
- ◆ Athenian victory

◁ **A wide-ranging war**
Alongside the Athenian and Spartan alliances at the beginning of the Peloponnesian War, this map shows the key campaigns and major battles of the war.

△ **Greek warrior**
This detail from a red-figure krater from 460–450 BCE shows a warrior wearing a plumed Attic-type helmet, widely used in the Peloponnesian War.

The menace to Athens was clear, and Pericles ordered all the Athenians, civilian and military, to retreat into the city rather than march out to meet the Spartans in battle. Thus, troubled only by occasional Athenian forays, the Spartans roamed freely, laying waste to the countryside. Athens' Long Walls (see p.159) protected the city's route to the sea, and the Athenians believed that they could wait out the Spartan assault.

Pericles' decision to bring the people from Athens' rural environs into the city itself, where they were crowded together in improvised encampments, turned out to be a huge mistake. When bubonic plague broke out in 430 BCE, Thucydides tells us that the overcrowded conditions made the epidemic far more damaging than it might otherwise have been. Athens' passive stance in the war had started out as a strategy, but it became a necessity for several months while the people suffered and some 30,000 died, including Pericles. Meanwhile, outside the walls, the Spartans went on ravaging the countryside, although they had to return home to tend their fields and vineyards between brief bouts of fighting.

Athens changes course

After Pericles' death in 429 BCE, Athenian thinking changed. Now under the command of Cleon, the Athenians established a base in the southwestern Peloponnese, at Pylos. In 425 BCE, the Spartans landed 420 hoplites on the nearby island of Sphacteria. However, an Athenian fleet arrived, scattering the Spartan ships and isolating the hoplites on the island. A party led by the Athenian general Demosthenes then landed on Sphacteria, forcing the Spartan soldiers to surrender. A significant defeat by any standards, Pylos was seen as a cataclysm in Sparta, where such capitulation was viewed with shame. »

▽ **The plague**
Painted by 17th-century Flemish artist Michael Sweerts, who lived through an outbreak of plague in Rome, *Plague in an Ancient City* links contemporary and historical experiences of the bubonic plague.

△ **Victor's laurels**
Discovered in a well-built 5th-century BCE structure within the walls of the Thracian city of Amphipolis, this gold laurel wreath was found with a silver urn said to hold the ashes of the Spartan hero Brasidas.

▽ **Trireme relief**
Ten nude oarsmen adorn this fragment known as the Lenormant Relief, which was found at the site of the Erechtheion in Athens. The relief dates from c. 410 BCE, in the last few years of the Peloponnesian War.

Toward a truce

The Athenians did not fare so well elsewhere. At Delium in Boeotia in 424 BCE, Sparta's allies, led by a Theban force under a general named Pagondas, defeated 7,000 Athenian hoplites—an invasion force led by a general called Hippocrates. In 422 BCE, the Spartan general Brasidas marched on Thrace, whose silver mines were vital in financing Athens' war, and successfully captured Amphipolis.

Both sides were by then exhausted, and an uneasy peace was agreed in 421 BCE. This was formally abandoned in 414 BCE, but fighting had continued anyway. Indeed, the largest land battle of the war, between around 9,000 soldiers on the Spartan side and 8,000 on the Athenian, happened at Mantinea in the central Peloponnese in 418 BCE. There, hoplites from Argos, which was a former ally of Sparta, fought on Athens' side against the Spartans and warriors from Tegea, a town in Arcadia.

Trouble in Athens

In 415 BCE, urged on by their statesman Alcibiades, the Athenians launched a disastrous expedition to take Sicily. They became bogged down in the siege of Syracuse, in which 40,000 Athenians were killed or captured. Alcibiades was forced to flee Athens and sought asylum in Sparta, where he began to advise the Spartans on strategy in the hope of being returned to power in Athens.

On Alcibiades' advice, the Spartans set up a fortified base in the village of Decelea, northeast of Athens. In doing so, they cut Athens off from its Attic hinterland and overland supply routes, including that which

> ## "There was even more **confusion** and **disorder** in Greece after the **battle** than before."
>
> XENOPHON ON THE BATTLE OF MANTINEA

brought silver from the mines of Laurium, around 30 miles (50 km) south of Athens. As a result, Athens had to wring yet more tribute from its increasingly exasperated allies. Meanwhile, the Peloponnesian League was building its naval strength after Sparta signed a series of treaties with Tissaphernes, the Persian emperor's satrap (governor) in Asia Minor. In return for funding for its fleet, Sparta acknowledged Persia's freedom to act not only in Asia but also in Greece, outside the Peloponnese. This was a blow to Athens and to the spirit of Greek solidarity, underscoring Athens' increasing isolation.

Picking up the narrative where Thucydides left off, the historian Xenophon summed up Athens' situation in 411 BCE: "The Athenians were now besieged by land and sea." Something had to give, and Athenian democracy imploded. In a coup allegedly stirred up by Alcibiades, members of the wealthy elite established an oligarchic regime known as the Council of Four Hundred, which welcomed the exiled leader home.

War on the waves

The Four Hundred were riven with division between moderate and extremist factions, but a narrow naval victory against a numerically superior Spartan fleet at Cynossema, off the coast of Asia Minor, in 411 BCE augured well for their ability to successfully continue the war. A more resounding win at Cyzicus by Alcibiades' Athenian fleet in 410 BCE boosted hopes further. It gave Athens control of the Hellespont (the Dardanelles Strait) and opened the way for the capture of Chalcedon and Byzantium. This upturn in Athens' fortunes brought a more democratic outlook, and the Four Hundred were replaced by a broader oligarchy, known as the 5,000.

The advantage in the war tilted back and forth. A fleet under the Spartan commander and king Lysander defeated the Athenians at Notium, near Izmir in modern Türkiye, in 407 BCE. The following year, however, Lysander's fleet was trounced by the

△ **Death of Alcibiades**
French painter Philippe Chéry's 1791 painting shows the assassination in 404 BCE of the Athenian general Alcibiades, killed in Persia at the request of Lysander.

Athenians at Arginusae, in the narrow strait just east of Lesbos. Sparta lost 70 ships to Athens' 25, but the Athenian triumph was tempered by the failure of the fleet's commanders to rescue the 5,000 crewmen whose ships were destroyed. Six senior officers were later executed for their neglect.

The Peloponnesian War's end was finally decided at the Battle of Aegospotami, off the northwest coast of Asia Minor, in 405 BCE, where a Spartan fleet under Lysander was threatening to block the Hellespont and prevent grain reaching Athens from the Black Sea. Athenian triremes rowed out to challenge Lysander for four days running, but the Spartan commander refused to engage. On the fifth day, as the Athenian ships dispersed, Lysander launched his attack and caught them unawares. The Spartans captured around 170 Athenian ships and executed at least 3,000 captives. Athenian naval power was broken, leaving Lysander to cruise the coasts of the Aegean, picking

off the remaining Athenian garrisons. Xenophon reports that Lysander gave the Athenian soldiers safe passage to Athens, knowing that overcrowding would see those in the city slowly starve. The Athenians welcomed their leaders' surrender in 404 BCE, hailing Greece's liberty, and leveling Athens' fortifications in accordance with the terms of the peace.

SPARTA AND PERSIA

Despite the invincibility of its armies, Sparta was at a severe disadvantage at sea. Athens had ruled the waves since Themistocles' day (see p.150). Without the help of the Persians, Sparta may never have prevailed against Athens. The Treaty of Miletus in 412 BCE brought peace between Persia and Sparta, and this connection was strengthened by Lysander's friendship with Cyrus the Younger, a son of the emperor Darius II. Darius gave Lysander the revenues from his cities in Asia Minor. With this money, Lysander was able to build a great Spartan fleet after the disaster of Arginusae.

**17TH-CENTURY PAINTING OF
CYRUS AND LYSANDER MEETING**

The Death of Socrates
In this detail from French artist Jacques-Louis David's 1787 painting, an old friend, Crito, holds Socrates' knee while a disciple hands the condemned philosopher a deadly cup of hemlock.

Socrates

The father of Western philosophy

Born in Athens at the beginning of the city's "golden age," Socrates laid the foundations of Classical Greek philosophy, shifting its focus from the physical world to matters of ethics.

Socrates was born in the second quarter of the 5th century BCE to Sophroniscus, a stonemason, and Phaenarete, a midwife. He initially followed in his father's footsteps, becoming recognized as a skillful sculptor. Then, serving in the Athenian army in the Peloponnesian War, he gained a reputation for courage at the battles of Potidaea, Amphipolis, and Delion. Socrates had no ambition to be a philosopher, but things changed when his friend Chaerephon told him that the Oracle of Delphi had proclaimed that there was no wiser man than Socrates. Shocked by this, Socrates set out to prove the Oracle wrong.

He spent his days from then on in the Agora in Athens, questioning people who were considered to be especially wise, discounting their reliance on conventional wisdom, and challenging their assumptions, in a form of argument now known as the Socratic method. The Oracle, he concluded, was right: the reputation of the wise was based on false knowledge, while he alone was wise enough to recognize that he knew nothing.

A man of principle

Socrates became a familiar sight in the streets of Athens. People mocked him for what they considered to be his unattractive and unkempt appearance, but he was revered by the young intellectuals of the city. Although he did not establish a formal school or leave any written teachings, he gathered around him a loyal following, including several who would go on to found their own schools and record his ideas for posterity. Among his students were Plato and Xenophon.

Socrates avoided active participation in politics, but was unafraid to take a stand against the authorities. As one of the *prytaneis* (presidents) who oversaw the trial of the generals accused of abandoning the bodies of the Athenian dead at the Battle of Arginusae (406 BCE), he alone stood against the motion to try them as a single group. He once defied the Thirty Tyrants (see p.188) yet was also know to consort with opponents of democracy such as Critias and Alcibiades.

Political motives may thus have been behind the accusation of impiety and corrupting young people leveled at him by the orators Lycon, Anytus, and Meletus in 399 BCE. After a day-long trial, Socrates was sentenced to death by drinking poison.

△ **Socrates' prison**
Shown here are the ruins of the prison at Athens' Agora, where Socrates is said to have been held after his trial until his death.

"For **wonder** is the **feeling** of a **philosopher**, and **philosophy** begins in **wonder**."

SOCRATES, IN PLATO'S *THEAETETUS*

c. **470** BCE Born in the Alopece suburb of Athens

425 BCE Socrates establishes himself as a philosopher in the Agora

407 BCE Plato joins the young followers of Socrates

399 BCE Socrates dies from hemlock poisoning after refusing to renounce his beliefs

432–422 BCE Socrates wins acclaim as a soldier during the Peloponnesian War

420 BCE Socrates marries Xanthippe, with whom he has three sons

404 BCE Socrates defies the Thirty Tyrants by refusing to authorize the execution of an innocent man

Tyranny in Athens

Democracy under threat

The Athenians' relief that the long Peloponnesian War was over was short-lived, as their supposed protectors—the Thirty Tyrants—turned out to be their oppressors, whose depredations were crueler than those of any enemy.

The Athenians had welcomed the end of the Peloponnesian War in 404 BCE (see pp.182–185), deeming their leaders' surrender, in the words of Xenophon, "the beginning of liberty to Greece." However, the Spartan commander, Lysander, immediately imposed an oligarchic regime known as the Thirty Tyrants in Athens, while a Spartan garrison occupied the Acropolis. Exhausted by decades of strife, the people of Athens were initially in no state to resist as the Thirty began stamping their authority on the city in the most brutal way. Perhaps as many as 1,500

people were killed and hundreds more sent into exile as the oligarchs began executing those who had argued against peace with Sparta and went on to target those suspected of more general dissent. However, the oligarchy lasted less than a year before it was overthrown and democracy restored in Athens.

Although the Spartans appointed thirty men to govern Athens, the government was in reality dominated by an inner group of extremists. At their head was Critias, a student of Socrates who may have been involved with the Council of the Four Hundred, an antidemocratic faction that held power briefly in Athens in 411 BCE (see p.184). Under Critias, the rule of the Thirty was corrupt, arbitrary, and capricious. He and his associates used their power to settle scores and enrich themselves. Trumped-up charges were brought to justify the harassment of individuals, along with the confiscation of their wealth. The Thirty abolished the popular juries and restricted citizens' rights to a roll of 3,000 men. When Theramenes, one of the moderates among the Thirty, tried to expand the franchise, Critias had him tried and executed.

Democratic rebellion

Among those exiled by the Thirty was Thrasybulus, a trierarch in the Athenian navy who had led resistance to the Four Hundred in 411 BCE. He took refuge at Thebes, and in early 403 BCE, armed and supplied by the city, he marched south to Attica with a small force. This had grown to 70 men by the time it seized the fort at Phyle, north of Athens. In the next months, more and more fighters, many of them mercenaries, joined the rebels. A first attempt by the Thirty to blockade the fort failed when a snowstorm forced their army back to Athens. The Spartan garrison then marched out to Phyle with the Athenian cavalry, but the force was routed by Thrasybulus's men in a surprise dawn attack. After his success, Thrasybulus marched to the fort at Munichia, northeast of Piraeus.

▽ **The Phyle campaign**
The democratic rebels led by Thrasybulus fought the forces of the Thirty and Sparta in central Attica, finally forcing the Thirty to concede at the Battle of Piraeus.

△ **Ancient Piraeus**
Created in 1890, this engraving imagines what Piraeus may have looked like in the 5th century BCE. From the Acropolis, Athens' Long Walls run down to Piraeus's largest harbor, Kartharos.

There, his forces routed the Spartan-oligarchic army in a battle in which Critias himself was killed. The next day, the Council of the 3,000 decided to exile the Thirty to Eleusis and elect ten men, one from each *phyle*, to govern.

Democracy restored

The democratic rebellion continued, and the ranks of Thrasybulus's army swelled with Athenians, and with metics and the enslaved, to whom he had promised democratic rights. The Ten called on Sparta for more help as the rebels threatened Athens. When the Spartan king Pausanias's army struggled to an unconvincing victory in the Battle of Piraeus, Pausanias cut his losses and urged Athens' leaders to come to terms with Thrasybulus and his democrats.

By late 403 BCE, democracy had been reestablished in Athens. But the divisions that had fractured the Thirty over who should have what rights remained, and the wounds inflicted by the Thirty's brutality would take a long time to heal. Even Thrasybulus found his support ebbing away, as Athens' citizens showed themselves reluctant to share their rights with the enslaved people and metics who had helped him restore democracy. Thrasybulus's influence in the Assembly waned as that of the more moderate—or less democratic—politician Archinus rose. Democracy had survived, but events had shown that it was fragile.

"What would they have to **suffer**, if their **punishment** should be **adequate** to their **actions**?"

LYSIAS'S SPEECH AGAINST ONE OF THE THIRTY, *AGAINST ERATOSTHENES*

5
Disunity and Order
400–323 BCE

New Powers Rise

The end of the Peloponnesian War in 404 BCE—and with it the end of the Delian League, through which Athens exerted its power—created an unprecedented opportunity for Sparta, and then Thebes, to recast the political landscape of mainland Greece. What followed was a long cycle of grievance, alliance, and war between the *poleis* that Macedonia would exploit for its own ends.

Sparta and Thebes

The end of the Delian League provided Sparta with the chance to realize its own imperialist ambitions. In most of the league's *poleis*, Sparta installed "dearchies," usually formed of ten loyal local oligarchs along with a garrison under a Spartan commander. Rather than ensuring stability, these rulers proved divisive agents of internal unrest, particularly in Athens (see pp.188–189). Sparta also attempted to exert its authority overseas, assuming responsibility for the protection of the *poleis* of Asia Minor. But its campaigns across the Hellespont achieved little.

Discontent with Sparta prompted Corinth, Thebes, and Argos, allied with Athens, to declare war in 395 BCE. Early Spartan victories at Nemea and Coronea rapidly gave way to a long grind of violence that ended only in 387 BCE. The resultant King's Peace, sponsored by the Persian Great King Artaxerxes II, brought the forced dissolution of the Theban-led Boeotian League.

Spartan maneuvering undermined the peace, and in 378 BCE war broke out between Thebes, allied with Athens, and Sparta. At the Battle of Tegyra in 375 BCE, a Theban force led by the generals Epaminondas and Pelopidas secured a victory that marked a tidal shift in Thebes's favor. Ultimate triumph came at the Battle of Leuctra in 371 BCE, in which more than half of the Spartan force was killed. It was perhaps an inevitable outcome given Sparta's reliance on military authoritarianism, its dwindling manpower, and its ignorance of the concerns of former allies who had helped it secure power on the promise of greater, not fewer, freedoms.

In 370 BCE, Thebes established the Arcadian League, and its new federal capital, Megalopolis, on Sparta's doorstep in the Peloponnese. However, internal divisions eventually saw league members and allies face each other at the second Battle of Mantinea in 362 BCE. In the aftermath, Thebes lost the initiative, and Athens took advantage of this to secure its own resurgence.

Macedonia's Empire

The Third Sacred War (356–346 BCE), which was engineered by Thebes against Phocis, provided Philip II of Macedonia with the opportunity to expand Macedonian interests and consolidate his power in northern Greece. The Fourth Sacred War (339–338 BCE) provided him with the chance to march his army south. At Chaeronea, in 338 BCE, his victory over a coalition army led by Thebes and Athens brought Greece under Macedonian control.

Philip's ambitious and sometimes ruthless son, Alexander III "the Great," went on to expand Macedonian control across the former Persian Empire as far east as India. His actions spread Greek culture further than ever before, and secured a legacy that would long outlast his death at Babylon in 323 BCE.

◁ **Alexander with the "horns of [the Egyptian god] Ammon"**

394 BCE Battle of Coronea; Sparta beats Thebes, Corinth, and Athens

371 BCE Thebes routs the Spartans at the Battle of Leuctra

359 BCE Philip II becomes king of Macedonia

379 BCE Epaminondas expels the pro-Spartan oligarchy from Thebes

362 BCE Epaminondas is killed at the Battle of Mantinea

353/352 BCE Philip drives the Phocians from Thessaly at the Battle of Crocus Field

❶ Ruins of Persepolis, conquered in 330 BCE

❷ Bull capital from the Achaemenid city of Susa

❸ Walls of Babylon, where Alexander died, 323 BCE

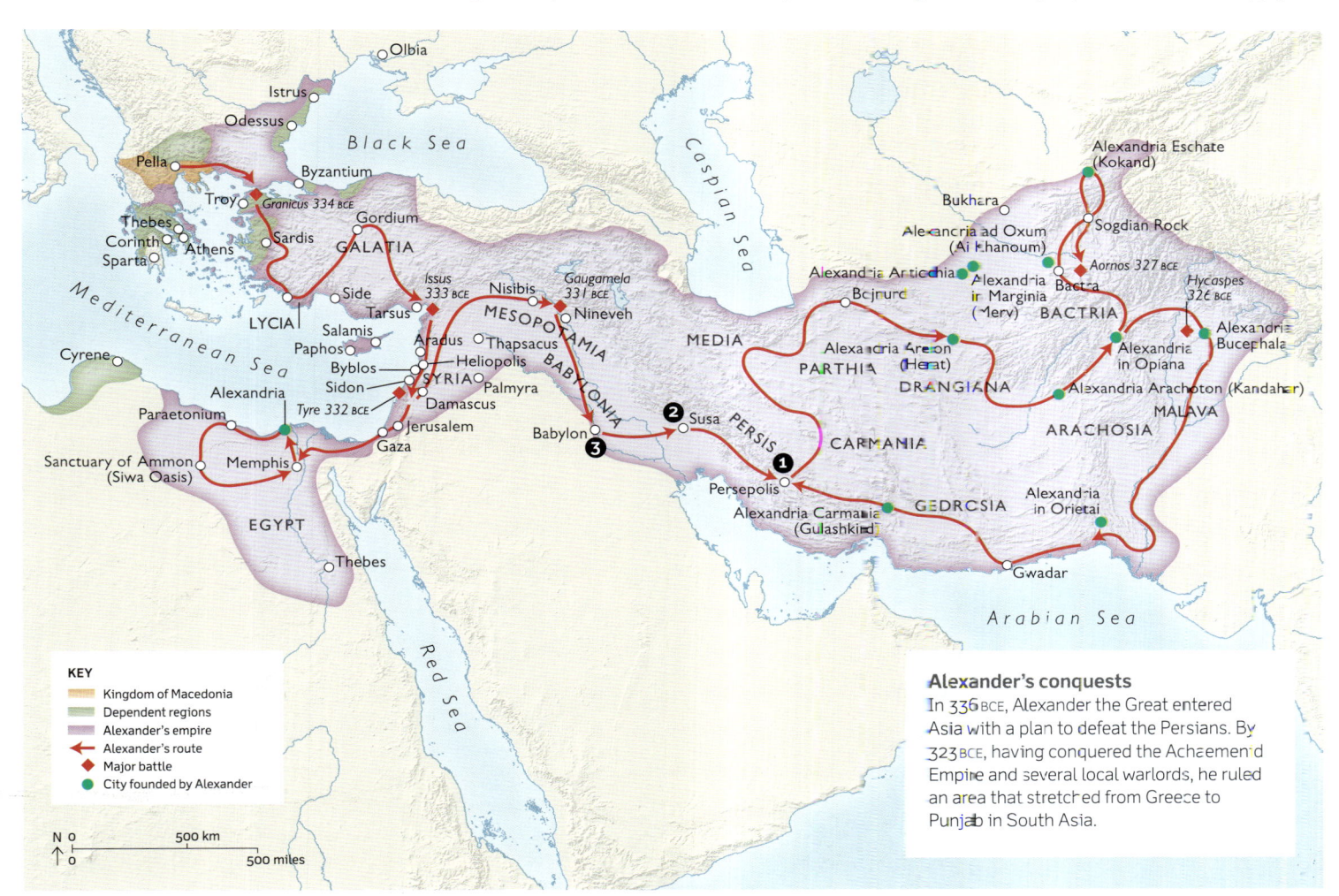

KEY

- Kingdom of Macedonia
- Dependent regions
- Alexander's empire
- → Alexander's route
- ◆ Major battle
- ● City founded by Alexander

N 0 ———— 500 km
0 ———— 500 miles

Alexander's conquests

In 336 BCE, Alexander the Great entered Asia with a plan to defeat the Persians. By 323 BCE, having conquered the Achaemenid Empire and several local warlords, he ruled an area that stretched from Greece to Punjab in South Asia.

338 BCE Macedonian victory at the Battle of Chaeronea

334 BCE Alexander defeats the Persians at the Battle of the Granicus

331 BCE Alexander routs the Persian army at Gaugamela

324 BCE Mass wedding of Persians and Macedonians held at Susa

336 BCE Alexander becomes king when Philip II is murdered

333 BCE Alexander battles the Persian emperor, Darius III, at Issus and wins

326 BCE Alexander defeats King Porus at the Hydaspes in Punjab

323 BCE Alexander enters the city of Babylon, where he dies

The Spartan Hegemony

Campaign and conflict in the age of Agesilaus

Victory in the Peloponnesian War propelled Sparta to supremacy among the cities of Greece and made it the major power in the Aegean. However, its ascendancy brought new challenges that drew the Greeks back into war with each other.

AGESILAUS II

Born c. 445 BCE with a disability affecting either his foot or his leg, Agesilaus went through the traditional Spartan education to become a valiant warrior and an astute strategist, respected by his soldiers in the Peloponnesian War. King from around 399 BCE, Agesilaus helped secure Spartan hegemony, but he also saw Sparta's influence wane before his death around 360 BCE.

As the dust settled on Athens' leveled walls (see pp.182–185), the Spartans found themselves with a ready-made empire. The states that had been subject to Athens now answered to Sparta, owing it tribute and support. In return, Sparta promised to protect their freedoms. However, it also installed new governing regimes that quickly descended into despotism: in Athens, the Thirty (see pp.188–189), and elsewhere, ten-man "decarchies" presided over by Spartan harmosts (military governors). According to Plutarch, the Spartan commander Lysander handed "power to his cronies, giving them absolute powers of life and death." In a similar way, he helped his lover, Agesilaus II, to become king when King Agis II died c. 399 BCE. With the cities it now occupied and its former allies feeling aggrieved by their treatment, Sparta soon found itself struggling to maintain control.

◁ **Pharnabazus II**
Showing a bust of the Persian satrap, this silver tetradrachm was struck under Pharnabazus II's authority in Cyzicus, Anatolia.

In 396 BCE, Agesilaus went on an expedition to Anatolia, where the Ionian cities were under threat from the Persian king Artaxerxes II for having supported the rebellion led by Cyrus the Younger (see p.185). Agesilaus tried to give his enterprise a Panhellenic air by going to offer a sacrifice at Aulis, a city belonging to Thebes in Boeotia, but Theban officials sent his party away. A supporter of Sparta in the Peloponnesian War, Thebes felt it had been unfairly treated in the division of the spoils—as did Corinth, another of Sparta's former allies. Several other cities also refused to help Agesilaus, claiming that their former alliance with Sparta had been purely defensive and they would not support a new war.

Rebellion in Greece

Agesilaus's campaign in Anatolia went well. The Spartans secured victories against the Persian satraps Pharnabazus II and Tissaphernes in Phrygia, and at the Battle of Sardis in 395 BCE. However, Agesilaus's army was recalled to Greece when Thebes began challenging Sparta's authority by fomenting war between its ally Locris and Sparta's ally Phocis.

To restore order, Lysander invaded Boeotia with King Pausanias, but he was killed during an attempt to besiege Haliartus, a Boeotian city, in 395 BCE. His death triggered the Corinthian War, in which Sparta faced Thebes, Corinth, Athens, and Argos, among others, all backed by Persia. Sparta seemed more

KEY

— Spartan hegemony 404–371 BCE

■ Boeotian territory during the Spartan hegemony

◆ Corinthian War battle

N 0   100 km
↑ 0   100 miles

◁ **Sparta's sphere of influence**
From 404 BCE, Sparta controlled Greece, the Aegean islands, and the trade route from the Black Sea via Byzantium, but it was threatened by a powerful coalition in the Corinthian War.

◁ **Nemean contest**
Found in Athens, at the Dipylon cemetery, this stele was created in the 4th century BCE for Dexileos. He was an Athenian cavalryman who died in the Battle of Nemea in 394 BCE, during the Corinthian War of 395–387 BCE, from which Sparta emerged victorious.

Dexileos is shown as a young man with no beard and wearing a chiton (tunic) and chlamys (cloak)

A Spartan soldier, his head turned up toward Dexileos, falls beneath the Athenian's horse

than a match for this alliance, scoring a decisive victory at Nemea (394 BCE). That same year, however, Sparta suffered a severe reversal at sea. At Cnidus, off southwestern Anatolia, the triremes of Pharnabazus II attacked and sank the entire Spartan fleet. A great showdown came at the Battle of Coronea (394 BCE), in Boeotia, where Agesilaus's army crushed the armies of Thebes, Corinth, and Athens.

The war rumbled on, and Spartan hegemony held in Greece, although it had to be buttressed by support from Persia, to which Sparta gave its possessions in Anatolia and the Eastern Aegean islands. In 388 BCE, the Spartan statesman Antalcidas blockaded the Hellespont with help from the Persian navy, starving Athens of its grain supplies and forcing it to agree to the King's Peace in 387 BCE. With Thebes and its allies defeated, the treaty left Sparta unchallenged in Greece, but it also left simmering resentments. In less than ten years, Sparta was once again at war with Thebes (see pp.204–205), and its authority would not survive beyond 371 BCE.

"[Agesilaus] steadily advanced, laying cities prostrate before him."

XENOPHON ON AGESILAUS'S CAMPAIGN IN ANATOLIA, *HELLENICA*

State Records

Commemorating significant events

Much of our detailed knowledge of daily life in the Greek world comes from inscriptions, often accompanied by sculpted images. The 4th century BCE was particularly rich in reliefs marking temple dedications and political decisions.

Ever since the art of writing was rediscovered in Greece in the 8th century BCE, people sought to permanently record important information. Some of the earliest examples of this revived literacy have survived as scratchings on pottery. However, as stone became a favorite medium for sculpture, partly under the influence of Egypt, from the 6th century BCE onward wealthy individuals and public bodies also began carving records and other communications with the populace in stone.

For mortals and gods

The durability of stone made it particularly well suited to public announcements. Inscriptions were also made on bronze, but far fewer examples have survived, since bronze is harder to work than stone and degrades faster. The information transmitted by both stone and bronze inscriptions varied enormously; examples include records of expenses, decrees, laws, lists of names, chronicles marking specific events, cult regulations, calendars, epitaphs, funerary reliefs, and lists of tribute.

The desire to ornament these public messages developed early on, and a tradition of relief work (decorating flat surfaces with raised images) grew from at least the 6th century BCE. The technique spread with the popularity of metopes, the rectangular stone panels that decorated the friezes in Doric buildings. By the 4th century BCE, there was strong demand for commemorative tablets and decree reliefs around much of the Mediterranean

◁ **Decree of the Triphylians**
Inscribed on this 4th-century BCE bronze tablet are the names of 13 people being granted citizenship of Macistus in Elis.

world. Typically, a square or rectangular metope-like panel would provide space for a symbolic sculpted image, perhaps showing a patron god or gods or else a symbolic figure of power and authority. The quality of the work was usually more than competent—a testament to the number of skilled craftspeople working in stone, including marble, at that time around the Greek-speaking world.

Not all reliefs were prepared for communicating with the public. Many wealthy individuals also commissioned stone tablets as votive offerings, designed to thank the gods—sometimes for recovery from an illness—or to placate them. There were so many of these that when someone expressed astonishment at the number on the Aegean island of Samothrace, the Cynic philosopher Diogenes is said to have replied: "There would have been far more, if those who were not saved had set up offerings."

Since 1825, scholars have been collecting and publishing all known inscriptions from the Greek mainland and islands, creating a rich source of material on life in ancient Greece and into the Roman imperial period.

> "**King Alexander** dedicated the **temple** to **Athena Polias.**"

INSCRIPTION AT THE TEMPLE OF ATHENA POLIAS

◁ **Treasury scribe**
This statue from c. 510 BCE is thought to depict one of the treasurers of the Sanctuary of Athena in Athens, the records of which were sometimes carved in stone.

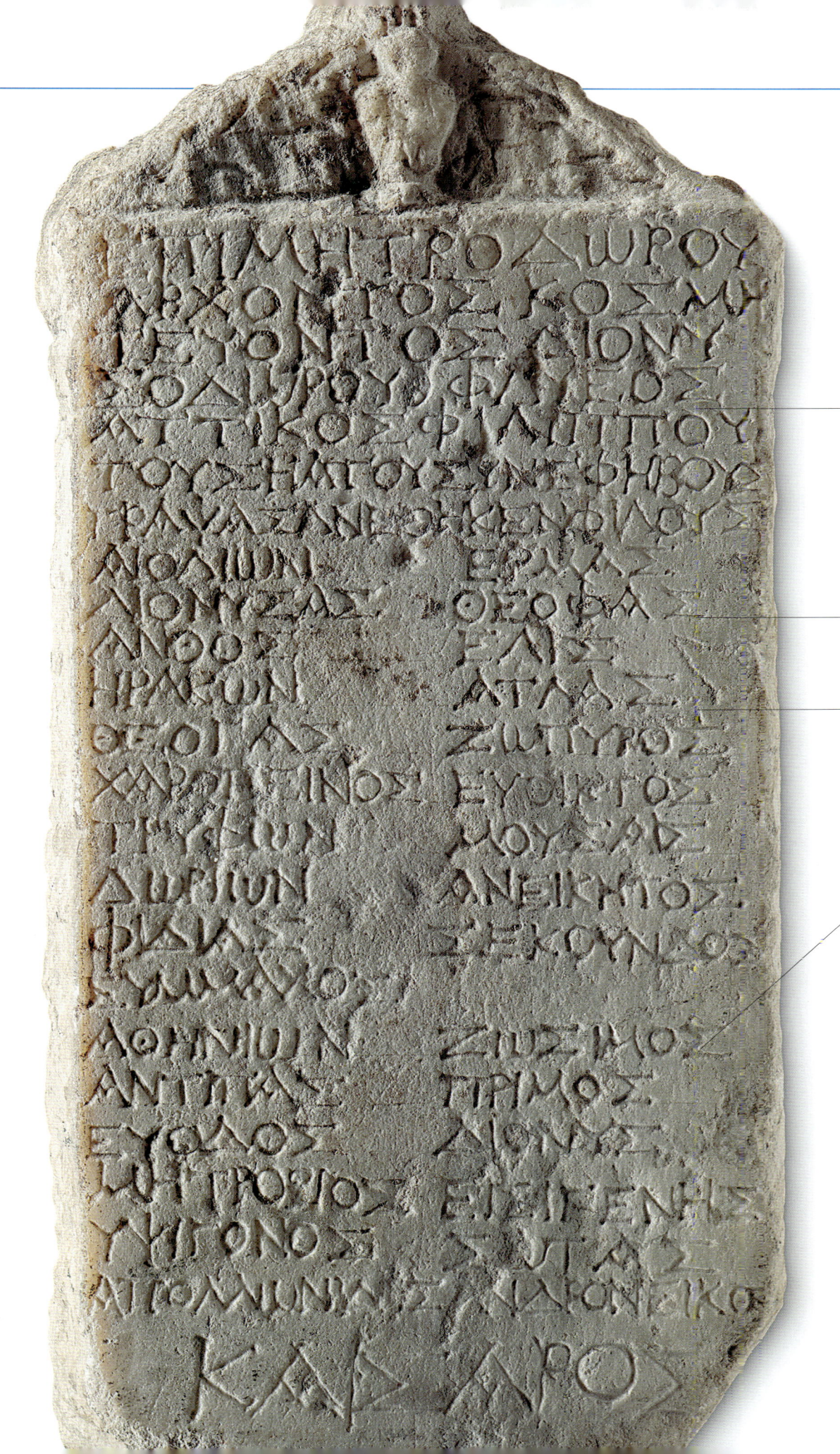

◁ **Ephebic list**
This inscription records the names of a group of friends who went through the Athenian *ephebeia* (military and civic training) in Emperor Claudius's reign (41–54 CE), which is referred to in the last line, reading "Of Caesar." The text provides the first evidence for the inclusion of noncitizens in Athens' education system in the early Roman imperial period.

The text names "Attikos, son of Philippos" as the one who commissioned the monument

The name "Theopas"; the ephebes are listed only by their given names, without their patronyms

One of nine citizens listed in the second column there are 16 in the first column

The names of noncitizens are listed separately

△ **Bronze chisel**
Masons used stone-carving tools very similar to this flat-ended chisel from c. 3200–2000 BCE—designed to apply detail and smooth surfaces—throughout antiquity.

▷ **Metic grave marker**
This marble stele was commissioned by the family of a woman called Hippostrate to honor her nurse Melitta. According to the inscription, Melitta's father was a metic with the status of an *isoteles*—someone who paid taxes equal to citizens and was exempt from metic tax.

Inscription reading "[Melitta] daughter of Apollodoros, *isoteles*"

Melitta (seated) gives an object to Hippostrate, depicted as a girl

Epigram composed by Hippostrate, honoring Melitta as a loved and "worthy nurse"

"If a **foreigner** lives with an **Athenian** woman ... he shall be sold, both **himself** and **his property**."

DEMOSTHENES, *AGAINST NEAIRA*

Foreigners in Athens

Life as a noncitizen

Few Greek city-states, with the exception of Athens, had large permanent foreign populations. In Athens, such noncitizens endured a series of legal disadvantages that placed their rights between those of citizens and enslaved people.

Few foreigners settled voluntarily in the Greek city-states. The Greek *poleis* did little to encourage immigration, and indeed, in Sparta, it was actively discouraged, and there were regular episodes of *xenelasia* in which all foreigners were expelled. Athens, however, was an exception, and housed a large population of foreign residents known as metics.

The metics

Emerging in the early 6th century BCE, the status of metic, or *metoikos* (from "*meta-*" meaning a change, and "*-oikos*" signifying a place of residence), gave foreign residents legal protections that were not available to *xenoi* (foreigners without status), who did not reside in the cities and were more transitory. This draw of metic status enabled Athens to attract workers, skilled artisans, and high-status experts such as orators, doctors, and even philosophers, including Aristotle. By 317 BCE, there were around 10,000 metics living in Athens.

The metics were at a legal disadvantage compared to citizens. They were obliged to pay normal taxes and serve in the army, but were not permitted to vote in the assembly, or to serve on juries. They could, however, give evidence and prosecute their own cases, but had to nominate a *prostateis* (a sponsor) to represent them in court. The penalty for murdering a metic was exile, while those who killed a citizen would be put to death, and metics could legally be tortured to extract confessions. Metics were also forced to pay the *metoikion*, a supplementary tax of twelve drachmas a year, as well as an additional levy of three obols to sell goods in the Agora. They were not permitted to hold state roles; they could not, for example, serve as priests, although they could take part in religious festivals such as the Panathenaea, where they acted as water-jug carriers. Metics were also generally forbidden to own property.

Metic status was hereditary, and this was reinforced by Pericles' law of 451 BCE (see p.169), which stated that an Athenian citizen had to have two Athenian citizen parents. A metic who married a citizen could be enslaved—as could one who failed to have a *prostateis*—and the state periodically purged its citizen list of those it believed were descendants of metics

Toward citizenship

Some metics did gain some of the advantages of citizenship. For example, *enktesis*, the right to own property, was often given as a reward for state service. Metics could also be granted *isoteleia*, equal taxation, which in practice meant exemption from the *metoikion*. Very rarely, metics were given citizenship. The banker Pasion, for example gained citizenship for donating five triremes to the state. When he died in 370 BCE, his land was worth 120,000 drachmas, and he owned a bank and a shield factory, despite having been born into enslavement. Life as a metic could be harsh, but it provided legal protections and opportunities for advancement for a fortunate few.

△ **Aspasia**
The wife of the Athenian ruler Pericles, Aspasia was a metic who was born in the city of Miletus c.470 BCE and moved to Athens. She is shown here in a Roman copy of a Hellenistic bust.

▽ **Metic goddess**
Bendis, shown standing (left) on this Apulian red-figure bell-shaped krater from c.380–370 BCE, was introduced to Attica by Thracian immigrants.

THE METIC **ORATOR LYSIAS**

Born around 445 BCE in Syracuse, Lysias moved to Athens when his father was invited there by Pericles. He studied rhetoric and, despite being a metic, rose to prominence for the speeches he wrote for lawsuits in the Athenian courts, 35 of which survive. Forced into exile during the reign of the Thirty Tyrants (see pp.188–189), he wrote a condemnation of them upon his return in 403 BCE. Famed for his plain, elegant style, he was included in the "Alexandrian Canon" of ten orators compiled by the Byzantine scholar Aristophanes in the 3rd century BCE.

Neaira

A former courtesan in court

The subject of a vivid though unreliable biography presented by her husband's rival, Apollodorus, Neaira worked as a *hetaira* before marrying and having a family. She was later accused of living illegally for many years as a citizen wife.

More is known about Neaira than most other Classical Greek women thanks to a detailed biography that set out her life from girlhood to middle age. However, this biography was narrated in a prosecution speech marking the latest stage in a feud between her husband, Stephanus, and his political rival and bitter enemy, Apollodorus. As such, what was said cannot be taken as reliable evidence for any aspect of her life.

To make his case that Neaira had been exercising Athenian citizen rights illegally, Apollodorus painted a picture of a woman who had allegedly been sold into sex work at a very young age before eventually setting up home with a man named Stephanus in Athens and passing herself off as a citizen wife

The case against Neaira

In his speech, Apollodorus never says where Neaira was born. Instead, he begins by describing her purchase as a young girl by Nicarete, a brothel owner in Corinth. She was later sold to two of Nicarete's clients, Timanoridas and Eucrates. When they each married, Neaira was allowed to purchase her freedom on condition that she leave Corinth. She managed this largely through the help of an Athenian client, Phrynion, with whom she moved to Athens. Fed up with abusive treatment at the hands of Phrynion and others, she later fled to Megara, taking with her some of Phrynion's property. Neaira returned to Athens, the narration continues, with Stephanus, who had spent time in her house in Megara. Apollodorus states

that they left for Athens along with a daughter and two sons, the latter of whom were enrolled into Stephanus's deme (suburb) and phratry (kinship group) and as citizens. When Phrynion brought a case to claim Neaira back, the court decided that she was in fact her own *kyria* (guardian), but also required her to divide her time between Stephanus and Phrynion.

Key to Apollodorus's case against Neaira decades later was that her daughter, Phano, had married Theagenes, the Archon Basileus (King Ruler), and had thus performed sacred civic duties that were the preserve of Athenian citizens. Should Neaira go unpunished for presenting herself and her children as being of citizen status, Apollodorus argued, the position of women entitled to the status would be imperiled. We do not know if Apollodorus won or lost, or the fate of Neaira.

△ **Greek hetaira**
This red-figure tondo from c. 490 BCE shows a Greek *hetaira* on a couch in the symposium with a guest playing a game of *kottabos*; wives were not allowed in the symposium.

▽ **Hetaira on trial**
This painting by French artist Jean-Léon Gérôme depicts Phryne, an ancient Greek *hetaira* who, like Neaira, was out on trial. Phryne was acquitted.

Children and Childhood

Growing up in ancient Greece

Life for children in ancient Greece could be a time of pleasure and innocence, or it could be a time of suffering. This dichotomy is perhaps best exemplified by the story of Astyanax. The *Iliad* depicts the deep love of the mythological Trojan couple Hector and Andromache for their infant son Astyanax. However, it also illustrates just how precarious the life of a child could be: when his now-widowed mother is taken captive after Troy falls to the invading Greeks, Astyanax is thrown to his death from the city walls.

Scholars used to believe that such was the extent of infant mortality in ancient Greece—with some figures suggesting that 30–40 percent of babies died within their first year—that parents would avoid forming close bonds with their children. But more recent studies have contradicted this view, analyzing frequent depictions (many on funeral stelae) of intimate family scenes where, for example, parents gaze lovingly at their children and mothers cradle their infants.

How life was experienced by children depended in large part on the identity of their parents. A child born to a married couple might be accepted into the family as a welcome new addition and brought up within the home. Meanwhile, illegitimate children, physically disabled newborns, or the offspring of female sex workers or enslaved women might be abandoned or exposed, that is left to die. In many parts of Greece, it appears to have been a child's father who decided whether or not a newborn should be reared. In Sparta, local elders decided a child's fate.

△ **Early milestones**
In Athens, babies were formally welcomed into the household and named at the Amphidromia festival five days after their birth. Another early marker for boys was when they were admitted into their father's phratry at their first annual Apaturia festival.

△ **Playing**
Boys and girls may have been brought up together until the age of seven. Games such as *ephedrismos* (involving a blindfolded player carrying another player on their back as they hunt for a stone) and knucklebones were popular, as were toys such as carved dolls and horses. Above is a painting of a young boy playing with a bird.

△ **Education**
The pathways of boys and girls diverged when it came to education. Boys were taught gymnastics, music, reading, writing, and mathematics, either in school or at home. Girls were usually taught household skills, dancing, and music.

"O billy-goat, [the children] **train** you to **race** like a **horse** round the **god's temple**."

HELLENISTIC EPIGRAM ON THE JOY OF CHILDREN AT PLAY

Whatever social strata they were born into, children served important functions. They were needed to bolster the workforce and to guarantee the familial line and inheritance. A citizen without a legitimate son might adopt a family member to become his heir. Sons were also expected to care for their aging parents, and marriageable daughters were a useful tool in diplomacy and business.

Adults in waiting

Many scholars have suggested that the ancient Greeks did not see childhood as a distinct phase in a person's life, but instead regarded it as merely something to be endured before adulthood began. This seems to have been Aristotle's view—he asserted that a child is no more than an incomplete adult. To an extent, the many childhood activities that were directed at preparing young people for their adult lives also support this analysis. Young women would be taught to become proficient wool workers, for example, while boys would be prepared for their future roles as citizen warriors via military training. Yet recent research on children's rites, such as those held at the sanctuary of Artemis at Brauron, suggest that the picture was more complex. The ancient Greeks may not have always conceptualized childhood in the way that we might, but children still passed through different stages on the way to adulthood, and Greek art shows us that they also had time to play on the journey.

△ **Psychro baby**
Found in Psychro Cave, a sacred site in eastern Crete in use from 1600 to 700 BCE, this Minoan bronze figurine is less than 2 in (5 cm) long.

△ **Religious duties**
Children took on religious roles—as temple servants, chorus members, and so on—perhaps from the age of about seven. For instance, girls might be basket carriers (*kanephoroi*) at festivals, as seen in the terra-cotta figure shown here.

△ **The end of childhood**
Marriage marked the end of adolescence for girls. Most girls were married at around 14 years old, and the ritualistic preparation of the bride (seen above on this pyxis from c. 440–415 BCE) marked the transition from the childhood household to the husband's household. Boys could continue their education until the age of 18.

△ **Becoming a citizen**
At 18, boys were considered adults and could participate in politics and the military. In many cities, they then undertook two years of military service. Along with ongoing lessons in politics, rhetoric, and culture, this formed part of their continuing development as citizens.

Thebes Ascendant

Boeotia breaks free

Tactical innovations and the charismatic leadership of Pelopidas and Epaminondas won Thebes important victories in the field, which allowed the city to throw off the yoke of Spartan domination and build a hegemony of its own.

△ **Symbol of Thebes**
Minted sometime between 379 and 338 BCE, this silver stater from Thebes features the distinctively shaped, handheld shield believed to have been used by Boeotian warriors.

▽ **Theban hegemony**
From 371 to 362 BCE, Thebes dominated Greece from its power base in Boeotia, with hegemony over an area that stretched even into the Peloponnese.

The leading city in Boeotia, Thebes grew into a major power in the first half of the 4th century BCE. Breaking Sparta's hold on Greece, Thebes enjoyed a brief period as hegemon, with control over Boeotia, much of central Greece, and the central Peloponnese.

The King's Peace that ended the Corinthian War (see p.195) had included a guarantee that the cities of mainland Greece would retain their autonomy. However, in 382 BCE, Sparta contravened the Peace when its army helped install a pro-Spartan, oligarchic regime in Thebes. The regime was overthrown in 379 BCE in a democratic coup, led by a Theban general and statesman named Pelopidas, and Thebes joined the second Athenian Confederacy—a maritime confederation of Greek city-states. Thebes was also leader of the Boeotian League—a federation of more than ten groups of sovereign cities and associated townships in Boeotia. As such, the city began to look like a more serious threat to Sparta. Agesilaus was also

△ **Theban ruins**
Situated west of Thebes, the ruins of the Kabirion, or Sanctuary of the Cabiri, were discovered in 1887, and housed several circular buildings such as that seen above.

still smarting from Thebes's insult at Aulis (see p.194). The threat increased as Pelopidas and his fellow commander, Epaminondas, began reorganizing Thebes's army and created an elite corps known as the Sacred Band. The scene was set for a new conflict between Sparta and Thebes.

In early 378 BCE, a Spartan force invaded Boeotia. The war started slowly, in a series of inconclusive skirmishes between which the Spartans, according to Xenophon, "plundered the Thebans" in raids that "devastated their land." Without doubt this increased the pressure on the Thebans, but Thebes itself remained untouched, and 377 BCE ended without the Spartans having landed any major blow.

Victory over Sparta

In 376 BCE, another Spartan expedition was stopped in the Cithaeron Mountains before it could even make it into Boeotia itself. At Tegyra in 375 BCE, the Thebans won a victory over a Spartan force that outnumbered them three to one. Peace talks in 371 BCE broke down, and that year, the Spartan king Cleombrotus, at the head of an 11,000-strong army, met Epaminondas,

KEY
- Thebes and allied states
- Athens and allied states
- Sparta and allied states
- Other Greek states

Map labels: Adriatic Sea, ILLYRIA, PAEONIA, THRACE, Black Sea, MACEDONIA, Thasos, Aenus, Sea of Marmara, Byzantium, Olynthos, Samothrace, EPIRUS, Passaron, Lemnos, Larissa, MAGNESIA, THESSALY, Aegean Sea, PERSIAN EMPIRE, Ionian Sea, ACARNANIA, Lesbos, AETOLIA, EUBOEA, Scyros, BOEOTIA, Chalcis, Chios, Thebes, ACHAIA, Corinth, Athens, Samos, Zacynthus, ARCADIA, ATTICA, Icaria, PELOPONNESE, Argos, Megalopolis, Cyclades, Sporades, Messene, Sparta, Naxos, Cos, LACONIA, Paros, Melos, Cythera, Rhodes, Sea of Crete, Cydonia, Knossos, Gortyn, Hierapytna, Crete, Mediterranean Sea

N 0 — 100 km
0 — 100 miles

Pelopidas, and 7,000 Theban soldiers at Leuctra, in Boeotia. Cleombrotus expected the battle to be easy. However, Epaminondas engaged the Spartan contingent of Cleombrotus's army with a huge phalanx composed of 50 ranks rather than the usual 8–12. With the Spartans occupied on the left flank, the Theban cavalry and hoplites crashed into the enemy's right flank, causing the Spartan lines to collapse. Cleombrotus was also killed in the battle.

Thebes was left as the dominant power in central Greece, but it was not done with Sparta. In 370 BCE, a Boeotian army invaded the Peloponnese, ravaging Sparta's Laconian heartland and liberating the communities that Sparta relied on for labor. Epaminondas also freed the helots in Messenia, who flocked to the newly founded polis of Messene. He persuaded the towns of Tegea and Mantinea in Arcadia, on Sparta's northern border, to found a new city, Megalopolis, which would act as the center of a new Arcadian League. With this, Epaminondas successfully contained Sparta.

Epaminondas died in the second Battle of Mantinea in 362 BCE. With Pelopidas having died on campaign in Thessaly in 364 BCE, Thebes was left without any great leaders, and its power began to fade, while Macedonia's fortunes rose (see pp. 222–223).

△ **Death of a hero**
This 19th-century plaster relief by French sculptor Pierre-Jean David d'Angers, shows the dying commander Epaminondas (seated) surrounded by Theban companions.

"The **Thebans** … were **massed** not less than **fifty shields** deep."

XENOPHON, *HELLENICA*

The Greek Way of Death

Tombs, monuments, and burial practices

Graves, their markers, and the goods found in them—as well as art and literature—provide a fascinating insight into the changing fashions and priorities of the ancient Greeks when it came to burying their dead.

Every society has its own approach to commemorating the dead and marking the end of life. For the ancient Greeks, a proper burial was paramount. In the *Iliad*, for example, the spirit of Achilles' friend (perhaps lover) Patroclus berates him for failing in his duty: "You were never neglectful of me while I lived, but now you are in my death. Bury me as quickly as can be, that I can pass through the gates of Hades." However, what proper burial looked like varied hugely across the Greek world and in different periods. Sites used continually over many centuries, such as the Kerameikos cemetery in Athens, offer an insight into burials from the Early Bronze Age (c. 3200–2050 BCE) to the 3rd century CE.

Funeral rites

In the Bronze Age, burial rather than cremation seems to have been universal, with the Mycenaeans burying their elite dead in beehive-shaped tholos tombs or shaft tombs—deep pits, lined with masonry and covered with planks. In the Iron Age, cremation seems to have replaced burial in southern Greece and Macedonia. The most common approach in Athens from 900 to 700 BCE was to cremate the body, and to place the ashes in urns, although this practice later gave way to both burials in graves and cremations performed in the grave itself. After 550 BCE, burials in graves or sarcophagi became more usual, although the Macedonians continued to favor cremation.

Greek burial rituals were usually divided into three parts, which were conducted by relatives of the deceased, typically women. The first part involved the laying out of the body (*prothesis*), during which

◁ **Humble offering**
Not all burial gifts were expensive, as this simple but elegant jug from the Angelopoulos plot, south of Athens' Acropolis, shows.

the body was anointed with oil, dressed, and placed on a bier in the house for a day of mourning. This was followed by the funeral procession (*ekphora*), where the men carried the body to the cemetery.

These processions became so opulent that the Athenian lawmaker Solon introduced laws in the 6th century BCE to curtail funerary expenditure, periods of mourning, and extravagant expressions of grief. The final part of the funerary rites was the interment or cremation of the body.

The Greek historian Diodorus's description of the funeral of Alexander the Great's companion Hephaestion—with its multitiered pyramid pyre, decorated with numerous gilt figures—suggests that Macedonian funerals, at least those associated with royalty, could be as extravagant as those of the Greeks.

Graves were often marked, and Greeks in the Geometric period (c. 900–700 BCE) favored huge vases decorated with scenes of mourning (see pp.66–67). From the 6th century BCE, life-size stone statues

△ **Painted tomb**
The ancient Macedonians had a strong tradition of tomb painting, as seen on this fresco from the tomb of an unknown aristocrat from the 4th century BCE at Agios Athanasios.

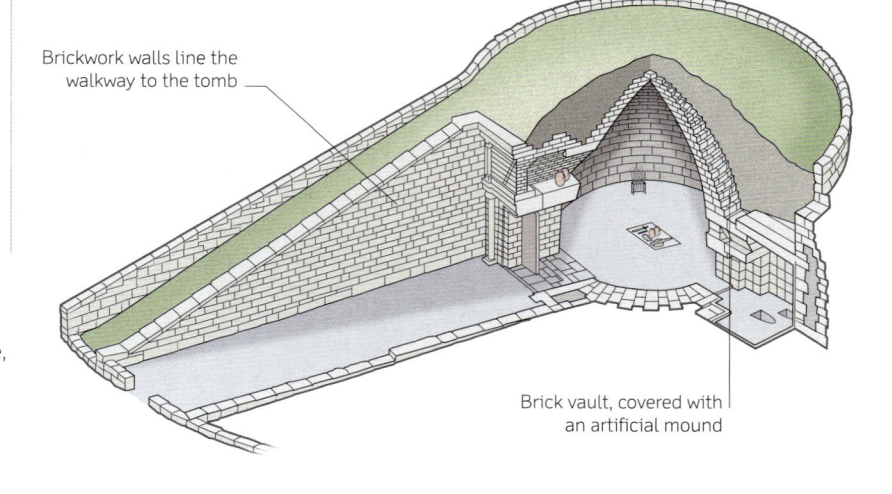

Brickwork walls line the walkway to the tomb

Brick vault, covered with an artificial mound

▷ **Beehive burials**
Depicted here is a tholos tomb built c. 1350–1250 BCE at Mycenae, and known since at least the 2nd century CE as the Treasury of Atreus, the legendary founder of Mycenae.

Macedonian solider wearing a chlamys, a short military cloak, and leather body armor

Large decorated shield held by a soldier wearing a helmet with large feathers

Sandals with laces that extend above the wearer's ankles

(*kouroi* and *korai*) representing young men or women appeared at graves, and stone markers or stelae were introduced in Athens, along with inscriptions commemorating the dead. These could be very elaborate in decoration and shape. Mainly made for men, they often bore carved scenes that depicted the dead person as an athlete or a warrior, and sometimes showed scenes representing the parting of the dead from the living. From around 430 BCE, stelae were carved or painted with a wide range of domestic scenes, in which women became more prominent. Emphasizing family relationships, these depicted the dead as they had been in life.

Funerary rites could include placing gifts in the grave or at the tomb to honor the dead or accompany them to the next world. The richness and value of these would vary according to the status of the dead person; they ranged from simple, domestic items such as vessels or spindle-whorls to jewelery and highly ornate vases that were not made for practical use.

> "When **parents die**, the most modest **funeral rites** are **the best**."

PLATO, *LAWS*

FUNERAL GAMES

Greek literature has several descriptions of magnificent funeral games held in honor of heroes. In the *Iliad*, Achilles (right) holds games for Patroclus (left), who had been killed by the Trojan warrior Hector. These include chariot and foot races, a boxing match, and archery, with prizes including strong oxen, cauldrons, horses, or "fair-belted women and gray iron." The participants also reminisce about funeral contests in which they have competed, including the games held for Oedipus at Thebes. In the *Odyssey*, Agamemnon's spirit recounts the contests of skill held in Achilles' honor.

The Mausoleum sat on an immense walled terrace

Royal Palace of Mausolus

◁ **A natural theatre**
The bay provided an impressive approach to the Mausoleum, which was located next to the Agora and complemented other of Halicarnassus's monumental structures, such as a theatre and a temple to Ares.

Marble lions faced each other

The Mausoleum at Halicarnassus

The original "mausoleum"

Mausolus (r. c. 377–353 BCE) was the king of Caria, which was then a satrapy of the Achaemenid Empire. Around 370 BCE, he refounded the city of Halicarnassus, making it his capital, and embarked on plans to build himself a grand tomb as its centerpiece. Wishing to draw on, and outdo, the temple-style tombs of earlier Anatolian kings, he commissioned two Greek architects, Pytheos of Priene and Satyros, to design a towering marble monument to honor his memory and that of his ancestors. He spared no expense, hiring four of the finest Greek sculptors of the day—Bryaxis, Leochares, Skopas, and Timotheos—to decorate it with elaborate scenes carved in the round and in relief. Although unfinished when Mausolus died around 353 BCE, it was completed by his sister-wife Artemisia II, and stood until the early 14th century CE, when it was toppled by an earthquake. Its sculptures and scale were so impressive that it was deemed one of the Seven Wonders of the Ancient World and, in time, the word "mausoleum" came to define any monumental tomb.

The columns were Ionic in style and 33 ft (10 m) tall

The walls, columns, and roof were made of Proconnesian and local marble

The burial chamber was below the podium

Visitors entered via a monumental gateway in the east terrace wall

The original bronze bit and bridle are still in place

◁ **Chariot horse**
This marble horse, restored from fragments, is one of four that once pulled the chariot driven by Mausolus and Artemisia that crowned the Mausoleum.

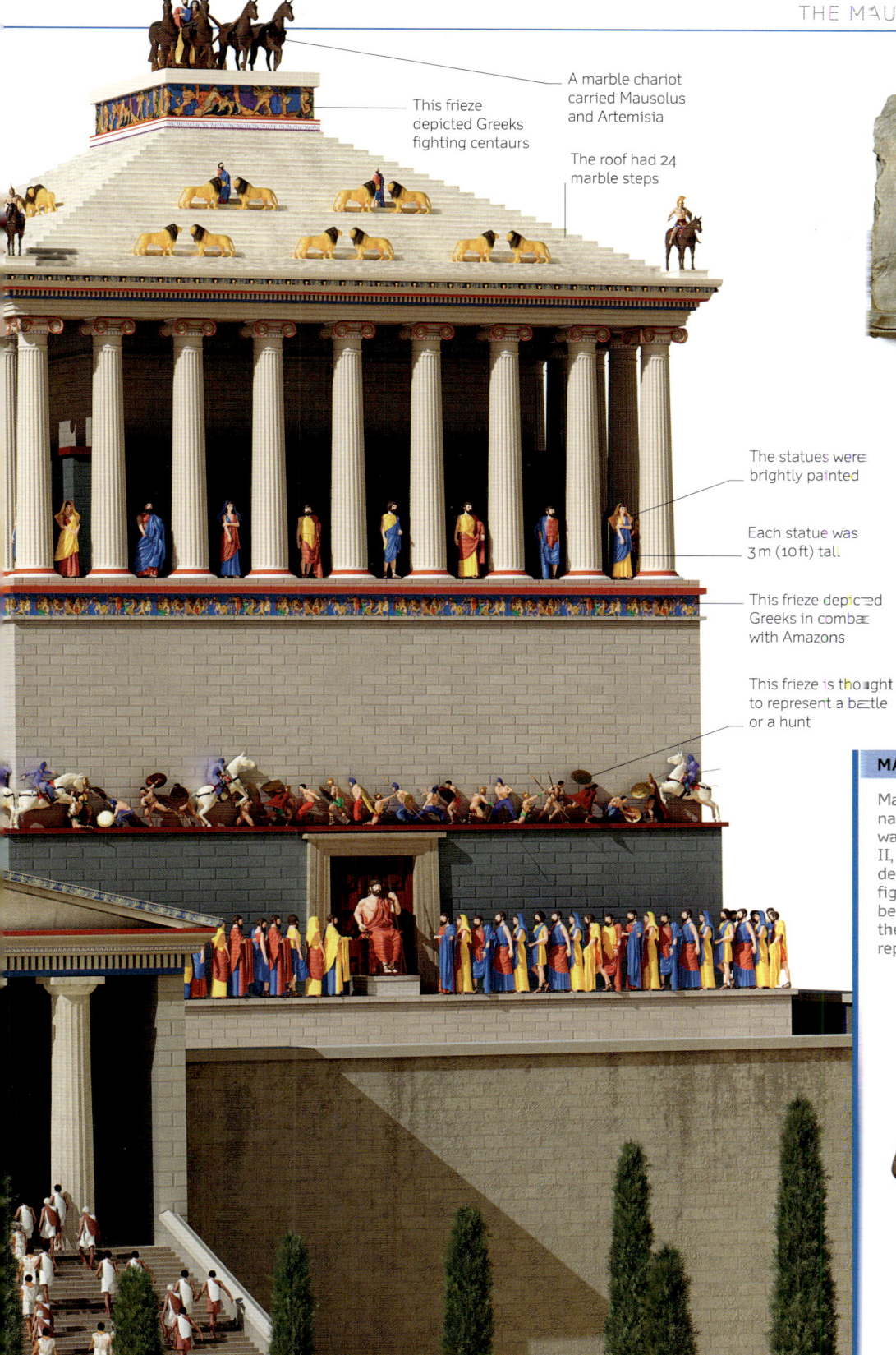

A marble chariot carried Mausolus and Artemisia

This frieze depicted Greeks fighting centaurs

The roof had 24 marble steps

The statues were brightly painted

Each statue was 3 m (10 ft) tall

This frieze depicted Greeks in combat with Amazons

This frieze is thought to represent a battle or a hunt

△ Amazon frieze

This relief is one of several surviving from a frieze that adorned the top of the podium. Designed by Pytheos, it depicts Greeks in fierce combat with female warriors known as Amazons.

◁ Interpretive challenge

Reconstructions of the Mausoleum are based on the few surviving archaeological remains and accounts by Roman writers. While the sculptural themes are known, the positionings of only the chariot, lions, and Amazon frieze are certain.

MAUSOLUS AND ARTEMISIA

Mausolus was a member of the Hecatomnid dynasty, named after his father, Hecatomnus. Although Caria was under Persian control, Mausolus and Artemisia II, who assumed the throne upon her husband's death, ruled with significant autonomy. These figures are two of the 36 over life-sized statues believed to have stood between the columns atop the Mausoleum's podium. They are thought to represent Hecatomnid family members.

The Afterlife

Attitudes to death

From vague conceptions of ghosts flitting about the Underworld to elaborate views concerning a blessed afterlife for those with a "passport for the dead," the ancient Greeks held a range of beliefs about life after death.

△ **Passport to paradise**
Inscribed gold sheets such as this example from the 4th century BCE were placed in graves and believed to protect the soul of the deceased on its journey through the Underworld.

Ancient Greeks appear not to have held uniform views concerning the afterlife. However, there seems to have been a widespread belief that the soul continued to exist once it had been conveyed by the god Hermes to the Underworld.

In the Underworld, the dead were thought to lead a vague and frightening kind of existence, detailed most elaborately in the *Odyssey*, where Odysseus tells of his encounter with apparitions who "fluttered about [...] with a grisly shout that made me quake with green fear." The exceptions were those who, in punishment for horrendous crimes, were condemned to an eternal ordeal in Hades. These included Sisyphus, fated to forever push a large boulder up a mountainside, and the husband-killing Danaids.

A better life after death

Initiation into mystery cults connected to several divine entities appears to have been thought to offer the promise of a blessed afterlife. These entities included the mysterious beings known as the Great Gods or Cabiri, the "Two Goddesses" (Persephone and her mother, Demeter), Dionysus (also known as Zagreus, Dionysus-Zagreus, Dio, and the "Bacchic One"), and Orpheus. The mysteries of these gods were located at sites across Greece, most prominently at Eleusis in Attica and on Samothrace.

Scattered pieces of evidence point to the existence of an ancient myth concerning inherited guilt and the promise of an afterlife among the Underworld gods. In this myth, it is proposed, the Titans dismembered and ate Dionysus, but the Olympian gods rescued his

▷ **Odysseus in the Underworld**
Flanked by his companions Eurylochos and Perimedes, Odysseus consults the shade (spirit) of the Theban king Tiresias, whose head is visible by Odysseus's foot.

▷ **Charon the ferryman**
This lekythos depicts Charon, the mythological ferryman who transported souls across the rivers Styx and Acheron to the Underworld.

still-beating heart and fed it to a mortal woman, Semele. She then nurtured the reformed Dionysus until she was fatally injured by a blast from Zeus's thunderbolt. Zeus took Dionysus from Semele's womb, keeping him safe in his thigh until he was born. Zeus also blasted the Titans, and humanity emerged from the embers.

Humans thus inherited the guilt of their Titan ancestors, but they also inherited a spark of immortality from the consumed body of Dionysus. As a result, thanks to Dionysus's mediation, some of the dead (presumably those initiated into the god's mysteries) would be equipped to travel through the Underworld toward the "holy meadows and groves of Persephone," in the words of one of the gold-leaf "passports of the dead" found in graves.

Vegetal decoration, used increasingly on works from Apulia from the mid-4th century BCE

Scene showing a battle between Greeks and Amazons

Perithous, who was trapped in the Underworld after trying to abduct Persephone

The judges of the dead: Triptolemus (in some versions Minos), Aeacus, and Rhadymanthys

The Danaids, doomed to seek to quench an eternal thirst by drawing water with sieves

◁ **The Underworld Krater from Altamura**
Created in Apulia, southern Italy, this elaborately decorated vase depicts several vignettes related to the Underworld, and to the fate of the dead. In the center sit Persephone and Hades being serenaded by Orpheus. Heracles holds the three-headed dog Cerberus, who guarded the Underworld's gates.

Sisyphus, a tyrant punished for his cruelty, with the boulder he was doomed to push for all eternity

Greek Medicine

Health and healing in the ancient world

The ancient Greeks were the first to devise scientific theories for the diagnosis and treatment of patients. These mainly centered on the idea that substances, or "humors," in the body must be kept in balance to ensure good health.

Like most ancient cultures, the early Greeks believed disease was a divine punishment, treatable by religious rituals. Yet descriptions of the treatment of war wounds by doctors such as Machaon, allegedly the son of the healing god, Asclepius, appear as early as Homer's epic poem the *Iliad*, c. 750–700 BCE.

In the 6th century BCE, the Greek philosopher and medical writer Alcmaeon of Croton argued that the body was subject to opposing forces (dry and moist, sweet and bitter), which if not in balance caused disease. He was also among the first to use dissection to investigate the body. His work, and that of the philosopher Empedocles of Acragas, was built on by Hippocrates of Cos (c. 460–375 BCE), credited with developing the theory of the humours—four substances (blood, phlegm, yellow bile, and black bile) that regulated the body.

△ Anatomy chart
This chart illustrates Galen's 2nd-century CE theory of the humors, with a balance of hot (*callida*) and dry (*sicca*) at the top, indicating a choleric or bad-tempered personality.

◁ Hygieia
The goddess of health and cleanliness, shown in this bronze statue from the 2nd–1st centuries BCE, holds traces of a bowl in her left hand.

Hippocrates also demanded close observation of symptoms, and used diet, medicines (which often utilized herbs), and exercise to reestablish the balance of humors. His students were required to make an oath in which they pledged to do nothing to harm their patients (a version of which is still taken by new doctors today).

Greek medicine diversified into competing schools of thought. The Empiricists, founded by Philinus of Cos in the 3rd century BCE, believed that doctors should treat visible signs of disease, without considering underlying causation. The Rationalists privileged causes over symptoms in diagnosis, while the Methodists, founded by Asclepiades of Bithynia around 50 BCE, believed that the body was simply a physical construct that could easily be put back into order with good hygiene, diet, and drugs.

Groundbreaking advances

Greek physicians made big advances in observing the body. Erasistratus of Ceos (c. 304–250 BCE) was the first to identify the difference between arteries and veins (but thought they carried "life force," not blood). Medicine flourished under the Roman Empire, with work such as that of Soranus of Ephesus at the start of the 2nd century CE, who wrote the earliest surviving text on gynecology. The most influential of all was Galen of Pergamon (129–216 CE), who united the Rationalist and Empiricist approaches to look both inside the body for underlying causes and outside it for symptoms in devising a treatment. His work on anatomy was flawed, but his understanding that knowledge of the human body was essential in treating disease underpins modern medicine.

Supplicants, probably the family of the patient, look on as Asclepius performs his healing work

▽ Healers at work

The figures on the right of this marble votive relief from c. 400 BCE are Asclepius, the god of medicine, and his daughter Hygieia. Asclepius is shown working to heal a patient, although it is unclear what ails her.

Asclepius places his hands on his patient's neck and shoulder

Hygieia stands nearby as her father's attendant

The sick patient sleeps while Asclepius treats her

△ Medical tool

A modern reproduction of a set of ancient Greek brass forceps is shown here. Instruments such as these were used to hold back tissue during surgery, or to extract fragments of bone or small tumors.

"I will use **treatment** to help the sick according to my **ability and judgment**, but never with a view to injury and **wrongdoing**."

THE HIPPOCRATIC OATH

Coinage

Identity and propaganda

Greek coinage reflected politics, religion, myth, nature, and daily life, employing a wide range of techniques to create some of the world's most beautiful and distinctive coins. Primarily used to facilitate trade, Greek coins also helped bolster the identity of individual city-states, mark victories, and assert authority.

Smooth shell; some examples were decorated

△ **Greece's first coin**
From c. 600 BCE, and perhaps earlier, Aegina issued coins with a sea turtle motif, representing the city's maritime power. A tortoise replaced the turtle at the end of the Peloponnesian War in 404 BCE.

△ **Wrestlers**
Perhaps alluding to local victors in the Panhellenic games, this coin was minted in Asia Minor, c. 430–350 BCE.

Nike heralds the victory with a trumpet

△ **Victory coin**
Nike stands on a ship's prow, on this coin minted from 306 BCE to mark Demetrius I Poliorcetes' victory at Salamis.

△ **Incuse coin**
This coin from Sybaris, Italy, c. 550–510 BCE, was stamped with one design, which was in relief on the obverse but set into the surface on the reverse. Such coins were hard to produce.

△ **Syracuse triumphant**
Weighing more than 1 oz (30 g), this decadrachm commemorated Syracuse's triumph over Athens' Sicilian expedition in 415–413 BCE.

Classical-shaped owl, with straight head and long body

△ **Athenian owl**
With the head of Athena on the obverse and an owl on the reverse, the Athenian owl tetradrachms were issued for more than 400 years from c. 510 BCE. The example shown here is from 450–406 BCE.

The Labyrinth from the myth of the Minotaur

△ **Minoan myth**
The reverse of this coin, minted in Knossos c. 350–300 BCE, draws on the myth of the Minoan Labyrinth. The obverse shows the goddess Hera wearing an ornamental circlet and necklace.

Portrait of Ptolemy II with Arsinoe II, his sister and wife

△ **Status symbol**
This gold octadrachm, minted during the reign of Ptolemy III Euergetes (c. 246–221 BCE), features portraits of Ptolemy I and Ptolemy II with their consorts.

△ **Symbols of resistance**
Issued when Thebes was under Spartan hegemony, this coin from 395–387 BCE features the Boeotian shield and Heracles, who is said to have freed the city from the overlordship of the legendary Minyans.

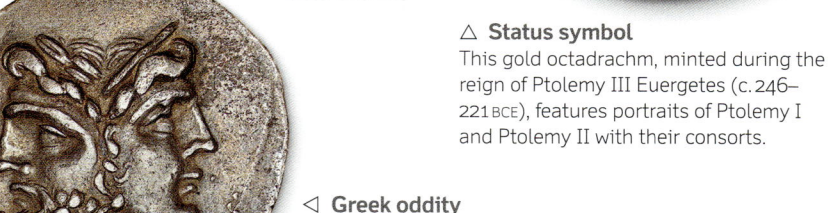

◁ **Greek oddity**
The Greeks had no equivalent for Rome's two-faced god Janus, but they did issue Janiform coins—often with conjoined male and female heads, as on this silver tetradrachm from c. 160 BCE.

△ Imitation and flattery
Issued in c. 85 BCE, this gold coin evokes the memory of Alexander the Great in its portrait of King Mithradates VI of Pontus as a semidivine conqueror with flowing hair. Its reverse honors Pontus's Persian roots.

Crescent and star motifs representing Persian deities

▷ Christ on coins
Christ first appeared on coins in the Byzantine Empire around 685–695 CE. With Islam then growing fast, the use of this image asserted Christian unity in the face of the new religion.

Latin inscription reads "Jesus Christ, King of kings"

◁ Dual deities
This tetradrachm was issued on Thasos around 146–50 BCE. The obverse shows a young Dionysus with ivy wreath; the reverse has Heracles with his club.

Skin of the Nemean Lion, killed by Hercules

▷ Cereal and cicada
Issued around 520 BCE, this stater reflects Metapontum's location in a barley-growing region in southern Italy.

Palm tree reflects the myth of Artemis's birth beneath a palm

Royal tiara or *kidaris* of the Persian kings

Stag, sacred symbol of Artemis

  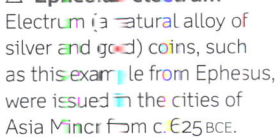 

△ The natural world
Flora and fauna frequently appeared on Greek coins, as seen on this coin from Ephesus around 390–380 BCE. The stag was sacred to Artemis, the city's patron goddess, whose priestesses were called "bees."

△ Persian overlord
Issued in Ionia in the 4th century BCE, this silver tetradrachm depicts Persia's Great King, indicating his control of the area.

△ Ephesian electrum
Electrum (a natural alloy of silver and gold) coins, such as this example from Ephesus, were issued in the cities of Asia Minor from c. 625 BCE.

△ Central Asian ruler
With a portrait of Demetrius I Anicetus, a Greco-Bactrian king, reflecting depictions of Alexander the Great, this coin was issued c. 200–190 BCE.

◁ Practical coin
This 11th-century CE gold coin from the Byzantine Empire is a scyphate, a thin coin whose cup shape meant that it could be stacked much more easily than flat coins with high-relief designs.

Orb and cross held by Emperor Constantine X

△ Cult object
Minted in Croton, Italy, this silver coin depicts the tripod at Delphi, sacred to Apollo, on which the Pythia sat to deliver the oracles.

Incuse figure of Poseidon

△ Greek god
Poseidon strides to the right with his trident raised on the obverse of this coin from Posedonia, Italy, c. 510–530 BCE; the reverse has an incuse design.

A cat, possibly employed to protect the cargo from rats, lies beneath the king's chair

A worker oversees the weighing process

△ **Supervising cargo**
This 6th-century BCE drinking cup shows Arcesilaus II, ruler of the colony of Cyrene, in modern-day Libya, watching workers weighing what may be silphium—a valuable medicinal and seasoning herb important to the local economy.

Workers store the bags ready for export

"The **wares** of the **whole world** find their way **to us**."

ATHENIAN STATESMAN PERICLES

The Greek Economy

Money and commerce in the Greek city-states

Agriculture, mining, and craft industries were the lifeblood of Greece's city-states, providing essential goods for their citizens and exports that helped generate the money needed to purchase both crucial imports and luxuries.

The economy of Greece was supported by a lively mix of international commerce and local trade that helped finance the city-states' expensive public works and ensured the comfort of their citizens.

Central to Greece's economic activities was agriculture (see pp.56–57). The vast majority of the population were involved in farming, growing enough food for their needs and then exchanging any surplus for goods they lacked. Greece's main crops were olives (whose oil was used in cooking, perfume, and lighting), grapes (used for wine), barley, and wheat.

Fishing was important too, and some coastal communities prospered from their abundant fisheries, trading in salted and pickled fish as well as marine byproducts, including a purple dye from sea snails that was used for textiles. Greece's craft industries (see pp.136–137), especially pottery and metalwork, were also a significant source of income. Mining (for silver, iron, gold, and copper) was pivotal in this respect—metals were used for numerous objects, from sculpture to tools and coins.

Economic development

Coins were introduced into Greece from Lydia around 600 BCE, facilitating business and the exchange of goods. By 500 BCE, each city-state was producing its own coinage. Among the best known are the Athenian silver "owl" drachmas, issued for around 400 years. Although there was no income tax, wealthy citizens were subject to a tax called a liturgy that subsidized city-states by financing public services, such as festivals, banquets, and military operations.

Greece's colonization of the Mediterranean meant it could easily trade its much sought-after products. For example, in return for olive oil, wine, and craft wares, it imported, among many things, linen, flax, and papyrus from Egypt. There was an eager market

◁ **Traders at work**
In this Attic black-figure painting of a textile shop on a wine jug from around 550 BCE, two men are shown weighing bolts of cloth.

within Greece for medicines and luxury goods, including spices, brought from the Mediterranean regions of West Asia. Marble was in demand for the construction of temples and statues, and quarries on the Aegean islands of Naxos, Paros, and Thasos did a thriving trade. The crucial import for Athens was grain. Estimates suggest that in the 4th century BCE, certainly half and possibly as much as 80 percent of its grain had to be imported, mostly from Black Sea ports. Laws were even put in place to protect supplies, including one prohibiting stockpiling.

Alexander's defeat of the Achaemenid Empire in 331 BCE (see pp.226–227) opened up overland routes that greatly increased trade with the civilizations to the east, and more luxury goods such as spices and precious gems entered Greece.

THE VIX TREASURES

In 1953, proof of the far-flung reach of Greece's trade in luxury goods came in the unlikely form of an excavated burial mound in the Burgundy region of north-central France. The goods laid to rest with its occupant—christened the Lady of Vix from the place the hoard was found—included an extraordinary bronze krater (shown here), said to be the largest ever recovered from Classical times. Standing 5 ft 4 in (1.64 m) high, it weighed 459 lb (208 kg). Drinking vessels, one of them dated to about 525 BCE, were also laid in the grave, suggesting that the burial took place around 500 BCE. Other mounds in the area have since unearthed Greek black-figure vases and bowls.

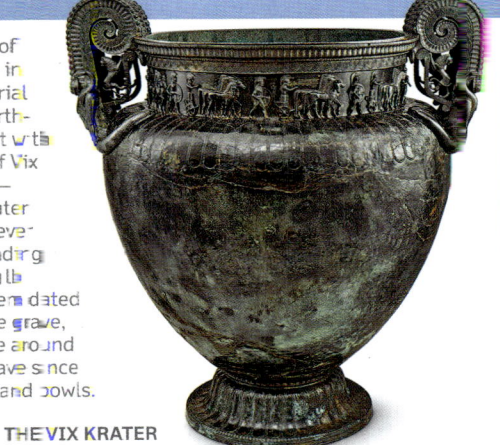

THE VIX KRATER

The Derveni Krater

Devoted to Dionysus

In the 1960s, archaeologists excavating the necropolis of the ancient Macedonian city of Lete, near Derveni in Thessaloniki, found this luxuriantly decorated krater in a tomb. Standing almost 3 ft (1 m) tall and weighing 88 lb (40 kg), it is made of bronze but, thanks to its high tin content, has a golden sheen. It was made between around 370 and 320 BCE and had been used as a funerary urn. Inside it were the burned bones of a young man and woman. According to an inscription on the krater's rim, the man was Astiouneios, son of Anaxagoras, from Larissa.

The krater is an extraordinary artifact. It is both a rare survival of Greek metalwork from the period and unique in its decorative exuberance. Most bronze vessels from the Classical era were decorated simply. By contrast, the Derveni krater offers a masterclass in metalworking, from its central repoussé (raised designs hammered out from the inside) frieze to its cast-bronze figures, silver and copper inlays and overlays, and construction from two sheets of metal.

Form and function

The maker of the krater carefully lined it with beeswax and a film of clay so it could function as originally intended—as a vessel in which to mix wine and water. They also chose the perfect decorative theme: the wedding of the god of drunkenness, Dionysus. What the artist then created was an extraordinarily coherent display of iconography that points to the krater's possible use in Dionysiac ritual.

Myths and meaning

The frieze that wraps around the body of the krater centers on Dionysus and his bride, Ariadne, and is rich with significance. Leaning back at his ease, one arm raised above a languid brow, Dionysus is shown resting his right leg in Ariadne's lap. Below the couple, two eagle-headed griffins tear into a young deer. Maenads, the god's female followers, cavort around them. One has a baby tossed over her shoulder—a reference to myths of Dionysus-induced infanticide. They are watched by Silenus, Dionysus's tutor. There is also a hunter, identified as Pentheus (who denied Dionysus's divinity and was torn apart by the women of Thebes in a Bacchic frenzy), with his foot on a fawn. Two of the maenads are also shown pulling a deer apart: the animal served as proxy for Pentheus in Dionysiac ritual.

On the handles, stylized vipers, symbols of rebirth, coil around the masks of figures associated with the Underworld, including Heracles, the river god Acheloüs, Hades, and Dionysus himself.

△ **The bride**
The caliber of the artist's work is clear in the lifelike draping of Ariadne's gown and diaphanous quality of her veil in this detail from the krater's central scene. Dionysus had found Ariadne on the island of Naxos and fallen in love with her.

Lion with slaughtered
lamb, symbolizing the
gods' cruelty

Frieze of
predator and
prey animals

Relief mask of
Heracles wearing
a lion's head

Viper, a symbol
of rebirth in
ancient Greece

Cast-bronze figure
of a tired maenad

Silver overlay
vine wreath

This maenad is carrying
a baby over her shoulder

▽ **Religious mania**
On the krater's reverse, maenads
dance and fall in exhaustion from
religious ecstasy. Below them a
lion and a female panther are
shown devouring a felled bull.

The figure of
Pentheus

Food and Drink

Sustaining a culture

Food was at the heart of religious, cultural, and social life in ancient Greece, not only providing sustenance but also helping to strengthen social bonds, and even placate the gods.

The diet of the ancient Greeks varied greatly according to region, social class, and season, but roughly equated to what today would be termed a Mediterranean diet: olive oil, wine, bread, grains, fruits, nuts, and legumes. Honey was the main sweetener. Meat and most fish were eaten only on special occasions, which could be frequent. Meals were usually cooked by women; in elite households, enslaved people made them. Most cooking was done in a courtyard or fireplace over an open fire, where food might be grilled or prepared in pots.

Material culture offers an abundance of information about drinking and eating habits. Greek vases were used to serve food or drink, and Greek pottery in general often depicts activities such as treading grapes, harvesting olives (see p.57), and sacrificing animals (see below). The utensils unearthed by archaeologists—mortars, braziers, strainers, pots, and so on—show the variety of ancient cooking techniques. Scientists can also analyze tiny seeds

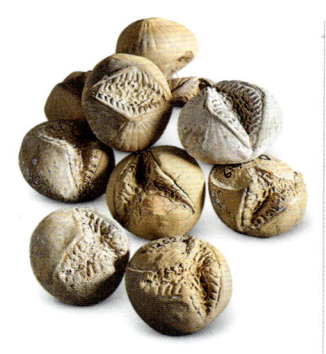

△ **Terra-cotta figs**
Found in the Fusco Necropolis near Syracuse in Sicily, these 5th-century BCE pottery figs were grave offerings, providing food for the deceased in the afterlife. Figs were a popular dessert; Athenaeus (see right) describes pairing them with fava beans.

◁ **Woman and girl cooking**
This terra-cotta statue from the Archaic period (c. 750–500 BCE) shows a woman and girl preparing food in a heatproof pot over an open fire.

to determine the types of plants people ate, residue on the inside of cooking pots to discover what foods they held, and marks on animal bones to determine how meat may have been cut and cooked.

The ancient Greek writers have also contributed to our understanding of culinary habits. The *Deipnosophistae* (*Sophists at Dinner*), for example, by the 3rd-century CE historian Athenaeus, presents a series of conversations held at a symposium (see p.79). It focuses on the lives of the leisured class, but also includes descriptions of the food and drink served at special events.

From banquets to street food

According to Athenaeus's text, at formal banquets guests reclined on couches and ate with their hands. Bread was accompanied by far less basic fare, and the highlight was usually fish. Rare species and large fish were expensive, so serving these was an opportunity to display wealth and generosity. The banquets were followed by a drinking party (where wine was mixed with water) and entertainment; beforehand, however, offerings were made to the gods. The gatherings described by Athenaeus were restricted to aristocratic men; ordinary Greek people enjoyed snacks from street vendors and eating together at home, in taverns, and at picnics.

Other ancient writers also often mention food. Some writers even parodied other writers who praised food. For example, in his humorous gastronomical work *Hedypatheia* (*Life of Luxury*), the 4th-century BCE poet Archestratus of Syracuse or Gela mocks the writing style of earlier poets and advises on what he considers the best food in the Mediterranean: fish.

SACRED FOOD

Most ancient Greeks rarely ate meat, but one of the main opportunities to do so was after animal sacrifice (as shown on this cup). Goats and sheep were the most commonly sacrificed animals, but cattle, pigs, birds, and other animals were also killed. After the sacrifice, a portion of meat was offered to the gods by preparing it and burning it on an altar. The rest could be butchered and cooked for people to enjoy. The act of sharing food with others and with the gods was an important part of any religious event. Roasting spits were used as currency and dedicated to gods.

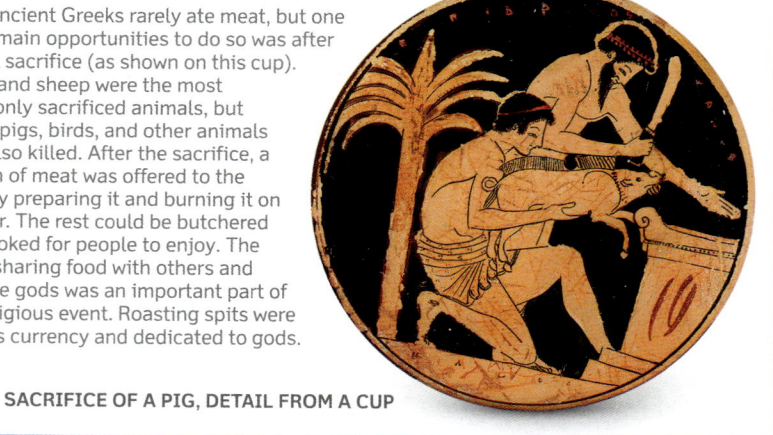

SACRIFICE OF A PIG, DETAIL FROM A CUP

The cockle shell was a symbol of Aphrodite, goddess of love

The torpedo fish was known to ancient Greek fishermen for its ability to inflict numbness

Bream and other large fish were considered a luxury

Shrimp, or prawns, glazed in honey are said to have been mentioned by the Greek poet Philoxenus of Cythera

△ **Terra-cotta fish plate**
Various fish, crustaceans, and shellfish are depicted on this painted terra-cotta fish plate from around 350–325 BCE and attributed to the Helgoland Painter. Such decoration is particular to southern Italian red-figure painting.

"Our **first** and **greatest need** is clearly the **provision** of **food** to keep us **alive**."

PLATO, *REPUBLIC*

The Rise of Macedonia

An empire in the making

Macedonia had begun to take on increasing importance in the Greek world during the early 5th century BCE. Under Philip II and his son, Alexander III, in the 4th century BCE, it would become head of a vast and unprecedented empire.

Outshone by the mighty city-states of central and southern Greece, the kingdom of Macedonia for a long time formed something of a socioeconomic periphery to the rest of Greece. That began to change after the Greco-Persian Wars, and in the 4th century BCE, Philip II (r. 359–336 BCE) transformed Macedonia into the hegemon of all of Greece.

Macedonia was rich in resources, including gold, as evidenced in the late Archaic cemeteries of Sindos, Aigai, Akanthos, and others. In the aftermath of the wars with Persia, Macedonia's wealth grew with the exploitation of silver mines near Lake Prasias under Alexander I (r. 498–454 BCE). His successor Perdiccas II's (r. 454–413 BCE) shrewd maneuvering, and Athens' reliance on Macedonia's resources, including timber, helped cement Macedonian power.

Under Perdiccas's successor, Archelaus (r. 413–399 BCE), Macedonia modernized. The king authorized the construction of fortresses and

◁ **The Lion of Chaeronea**
This monumental lion, today restored to a height of over 20 ft (6 m), was raised by Thebes above the mass grave of more than 250 members of the Theban Sacred Band who died fighting Macedonia at Chaeronea in 338 BCE.

◁ **Philip II of Macedonia**
This Roman bust does not show any of Philip's battle wounds, but he suffered several serious injuries, and the Athenian orator Demosthenes claimed he had been "wounded in every limb."

a military road network, and improved the organization of the Macedonian cavalry and infantry. He may have moved the Macedonian capital from Aigai (modern-day Vergina) to Pella on the coast, a more strategic location that offered better communication and oversight over key overland travel routes. There was increasing engagement with Greek culture. The artist Zeuxis was invited to decorate the new royal palace, and the sculptor Callimachus and the poet Euripides, who wrote *Archelaus* there, were guests.

Macedonia's ascent was halted by the assassination of Archelaus, possibly by a disaffected royal page, in 399 BCE. Five kings in six years preceded Amyntas III (r. 393–369 BCE), whose rule brought some stability and whose death sparked a further ten years of chaos.

When Amyntas's third son, Philip II, became king in 359 BCE, he inherited a kingdom on the brink of collapse, facing attack from without and within, and with a weakened military in near disarray. Philip had become a formidable tactician under the general Epaminondas during his three years as a hostage at Thebes, and as king he implemented sweeping military reforms (see pp.224–225) that strengthened

> "**Philip** … built up his **kingdom** to be the **greatest** of the **dominions** in **Europe**."
>
> DIODORUS SICULUS, *LIBRARY OF HISTORY*

his forces considerably. With political and economic alliances, and legitimization through military success, he would turn Macedonia into a superpower.

The conquest of Greece

In 358 BCE, Philip routed the Illyrians from the western frontier of Macedonia. Despite the loss of an eye at the siege of Methone, by 354 BCE, he had secured Macedonia's coast, with the exception of the Chalcidice peninsula. This he would subdue in 348 BCE, following the destruction of Olynthus, the peninsula's most powerful city.

Philip's role in bringing an end to the Third Sacred War (356–346 BCE)—which pitched the Delphic Amphictyonic Council (a religious league established to defend Delphi), along with Thebes and its allies, against a Phocian alliance that included Athens and Sparta—increased his reputation and influence. Athenian hostility toward Macedonia was stoked by the statesman Demosthenes. In 340 BCE, the threat of conflict became a reality when Philip seized the Athenian grain fleet at Byzantium and Athens declared war. This conflict between Athens and Macedonia was

soon swept up in the broader Fourth Sacred War (339–338 BCE), which provided Philip with the chance to march south. Fearing an invasion, Athens joined with Thebes in an anti-Macedonian coalition that met Philip and his army at Chaeronea in 338 BCE. Philip's victory there brought the submission of Greece, with the exception of Sparta (whose lands Philip went on to ravage and reduce), to Macedonian hegemony.

Stability within Greece allowed Philip to turn his attention to the conquest of the Persian Empire. However, his assassination by a bodyguard in 336 BCE destabilized Greece, and left his son, Alexander III "the Great," to reassert Macedonia's authority and fulfill Philip's ambitions.

△ **Royal tomb**
Tomb I of the Royal Necropolis at Aigai probably held one of Philip's wives and was decorated with a fresco depicting Hades' abduction of Persephone.

▷ **A king's casket**
Philip's cremated remains were first placed in this gold larnax, then in a stone sarcophagus in Tomb II of the Royal Necropolis at Aigai. His grave goods included silver vessels, ivory couches, weapons, and his great royal shield.

Macedonian Warfare

Reinventing the phalanx

Military reforms begun by Philip II of Macedonia created a well-trained, mobile force that, combined with the tactical genius of his son Alexander, defeated many opponents, from the heavy phalanxes of Greece to the vast armies of Persia.

Two Macedonian kings transformed Macedonian warfare. Philip II (r. 359–336 BCE) reorganized the army, enabling him to destroy the heavy phalanxes of the Greek city-states within two decades. The invasion of the Persian Empire by his son Alexander from 334 BCE then showed how the new army could adapt to defeat a numerically superior foe.

A new army

Philip created the *hetairoi*, "companions," an elite light cavalry unit with long lances and swords that, in a wedge formation, could break open a traditional phalanx. He also established a full-time, professional infantry, the *pezhetairoi*, or "foot companions." These were armed with a sarissa, a pike that was much longer than the Greek hoplite spear; smaller shields attached to the left arm allowed them to carry their sarissas with both hands. They were formed into a much deeper phalanx, with 16 files (columns) of 16 men. This created the army's smallest tactical unit, the *syntagma*, of 256 men. The first five ranks (rows) could lower their weapons (only the first three could do so in a hoplite phalanx), creating an impenetrable wall. The other 11 ranks held their spears high, blocking missiles from falling onto the phalanx. Better protected, the *pezhetairoi* needed less armor,

◁ **King Philip's armor**
This iron cuirass, decorated in gold, belonged to Philip II of Macedonia and was buried with him in his tomb at Aigai in 336 BCE.

often wearing just leg protectors (greaves) and a helmet, making them more mobile. Supplementing the *pezhetairoi* were the *hypaspistai* (or hypaspists), infantry with shorter thrusting spears and swords, and the unarmored peltasts, who carried javelins. These and other units such as archers and slingers made up a diverse force able to adapt to most battle situations.

In battles during his invasion of the Persian Empire, Alexander deployed the *pezhetairoi* in the center of his line, with the *hetairoi* to the right, and lighter infantry (including the hypaspists) and cavalry to the left. Generally, the Macedonians' main attack came from this stronger right: the left wing acted as a holding force while the stronger units enveloped the Persians. The force of the *pezhetairoi* could crush the enemy, or as at Chaeronea in 338 BCE, impale them on their sarissas. Better trained than their foes, and with the *syntagma* allowing enormous flexibility, the Macedonians could carry out complex maneuvers.

These changes would have had less impact without the leadership of Philip and the military genius of Alexander, who adapted his tactics brilliantly to local terrain and ruthlessly exploited his enemies' weak points. In eight years of campaigning, Alexander's army killed 200,000 men in pitched battles; this was something that perhaps no other general or army could have achieved.

A file of 16 hoplites; with 16 files of 16 men, the basic phalanx had 256 men

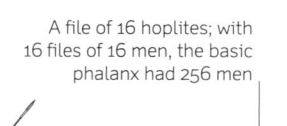

◁ **Macedonian phalanx**
Armed with sarissas that were up to 18 ft (5.5 m) long, the *pezhetairoi* of the phalanx formed a highly effective unit.

This Macedonian hypaspist (shield-bearer) once carried a short sword as well as his shield

This Persian archer, wearing the distinctive floppy Phrygian hat, takes aim with a traditional bow and arrow

"That **terrible sight** frightens the very **souls** of the **enemy**."

GREEK PHILOSOPHER ONASANDER, *STRATEGIKOS*

△ **Macedonian and Persian soldiers**
This detail, depicting Macedonians fighting the Persians at the Battle of Issus (333 BCE), is from a 4th-century BCE marble tomb, known as the Alexander Sarcophagus, from Sidon in modern-day Lebanon.

Long trousers tucked into footwear and clothes covering the rest of his body identify this warrior as Persian

This bare-legged Macedonian soldier may once have held a sword or spear in his right hand

Alexander's Conquests

A Macedonian empire

Alexander's expansion into Asia was delivered through shrewd political maneuvering, the exploitation of existing political loyalties and mechanisms of state, marriage alliance, military strategy, and the use of extreme violence.

On Philip II's death (see p.223), Alexander immediately took steps to secure his position, purging those who represented a threat. These included Alexander's half-brother from Philip's marriage to Cleopatra Eurydice; Cleopatra's uncle, Attalus; and Alexander's cousin, Amyntas. Farther afield, the states of the Panhellenic League of Corinth (organized under Philip's leadership in 337 BCE) revolted. Alexander swiftly suppressed the uprising, and became the league's hegemon. Campaigns against Macedonia's neighbors, the Illyrians and the Triballi, and the brutal quelling of a Theban revolt, which left 6,000 dead and 30,000 imprisoned, brought stability at home. Bolstered by the authority of the League of Corinth, Alexander was finally able to move on Asia. In early 334 BCE, he crossed the Hellespont with 160 triremes, around 30,000 infantry and 5,000 cavalry, among them mercenaries, Macedonians, and allies. On disembarking in Asia, he planted his spear in the ground and proclaimed it

◁ **Record of the conquest**
This Babylonian clay tablet with records in cuneiform of astronomical observations from 331–330 BCE mentions Alexander's defeat of Darius.

"spear-won land." Within weeks, he had secured his first victory, when his army defeated a smaller Persian force at the Battle of the Granicus in northwestern Anatolia.

Moving southward, Alexander arrived at Sardis, the wealthy capital of the satrapy of Lydia, which surrendered peacefully. He then took Ephesus and received further surrenders from Magnesia and Tralles. Refusing to accept Miletus's desire to remain welcoming to both Persians and Greeks, Alexander besieged and took the city. At Halicarnassus in Caria, he exploited existing rivalries to his own end, backing the rightful queen of Caria, Ada, against her usurper nephew. Ada in turn adopted Alexander and was reinstated as queen.

After advancing through Lycia and Pamphilia, Alexander moved into central Anatolia. In the old palace of King Midas at Gordian, Alexander is said to have cut the Gordian Knot, thereby fulfilling a prophecy holding that whoever did so would control Asia. However, sickness slowed his progress and gave the Persian Great King, Darius III, the opportunity to raise a huge army—which the Greek historian Arrian estimated to be an unlikely 600,000 strong.

◁ **Gilded youth**
This Roman gilt bronze, from the 2nd century CE, depicts Alexander as a young man.

"The **king** of the **world** [**Alexander**] erected his **standard** and **attacked**."

BABYLONIAN ASTRONOMICAL DIARIES

In late 333 BCE, the armies of Darius and Alexander faced each other across the Pinarus River near Issus in southern Anatolia. The Persians exacted heavy losses before Alexander's cavalry collapsed the Persian ranks and forced Darius to flee. The slaughter was obscene, with Arrian recording 100,000 Persian deaths.

From the Levant and Egypt to India

Alexander's next serious challenge came at the Phoenician port of Tyre in 332 BCE. For six months Alexander besieged the city, deploying engines, rams, artillery, and a fleet of Persian defectors. When Tyre fell, Alexander's retribution was terrible: 8,000 Tyrians were killed, including 2,000 who were crucified, and 30,000 were enslaved. His brutality prompted the other Levantine centers, with the exception of Gaza, to surrender. A siege at Gaza saw Alexander badly wounded. Its citizens would pay for his suffering when the city fell: according to Arrian, the men were all slaughtered in the fighting; the women and children were enslaved. In Egypt, Alexander was embraced as a liberator, and was crowned pharaoh at Memphis in late 332 BCE. He founded Alexandria (see pp.242–243), the most successful of his eponymous cities, before returning to the war.

Toward the end of 331 BCE, Alexander faced Darius and an overwhelming Persian army at Gaugamela, near Arbela (now Irbil in Iraq). Again the Persian king fled, and again Alexander pursued. His chase took him to Persepolis, where he plundered the city and, while drunk and allegedly at the insistence of an Athenian *hetaira*, razed it. Motivated by vengeance, perhaps swelled by an encounter at Persepolis with a group of elderly Greek artisans who had been long imprisoned and mutilated, it was an act he would later regret.

In 330 BCE, before Alexander could catch up with him, Darius was murdered by a disgruntled Bactrian satrap named Bessus. Bessus then proclaimed himself heir to Darius's empire. Angered by this, Alexander set off in pursuit of this new enemy. »

△ **Boeotian helmet**
Perhaps once belonging to one of Alexander's cavalrymen, this bronze helmet was found in the Tigris River in Anatolia.

▽ **Military companions**
Alexander the Great (left) is depicted with his companion and general Hephaestion—Patroclus to Alexander's Achilles—hunting a lion in this late 4th-century BCE mosaic from the House of Dionysus in Pella.

Alexander caught up with Bessus in the region of Sogdiana (now part of modern Uzbekistan and Tajikistan) in 329 BCE, where he had been arrested by the local satrap, Spitamenes, and was offered to Alexander as an apparent signal of submission. Bessus was mutilated and executed, while Spitamenes went on to lead an uprising against Alexander. With the quelling of the revolt, and the death of Spitamenes at the hands of his own allies, Alexander saw the Achaemenid Empire brought under his control.

Rather than return home and consolidate, in 327 BCE Alexander chose to drive his forces onward, over the Hindu Kush and into the Indian subcontinent. The surviving Greek accounts of the campaign, all from later, are more or less problematic, and there are no contemporary sources that give voice to the experience of the indigenous peoples. Indeed, Alexander is named explicitly

△ **Alexander in Babylon**
Alexander is depicted entering Babylon in an elephant-drawn chariot in *The Triumph of Alexander*, a 17th-century artwork by French painter Charles Le Brun.

only once within Sanskrit literature, in a passing comment in the 9th-century CE *Harshacharita*. The motivation for his Indian campaign is therefore a matter of debate. In the Greek mind, and particularly that of Alexander's teacher Aristotle, the limit of the world lay just beyond the Indus River. Alexander thus had the chance to become, in effect, ruler of the world as it was then understood; such dominance would also cement his victory over the Achaemenid Empire, which had historically extended to the Punjab. The historian Pliny, however, identified in Alexander's actions a curiosity, a longing (*pothos*) for experience and understanding. Certainly, his retinue included writers, philosophers, and historians, and he was said to have expressed a deep interest in the ascetic philosophers of the Punjabi city of Taxila.

▽ **The Porus Medallion**
Representing Alexander's victory at the Hydaspes, this silver tetradrachm shows a Macedonian cavalryman charging an elephant; the reverse shows Alexander.

Though India was unfamiliar, Alexander's strategy was the same as ever, variously deploying diplomacy and brutal violence to achieve his ends. Arrian's account of the siege of Massaga offers a case in point. There, the Macedonians mounted a relentless attack, against which the city's staunch defenders stood little chance. After breaching the walls, Alexander ordered the massacre of the defenders, but he allowed Queen Cleophis to retain her throne—a tactic that, alongside the foundation of new cities, helped Alexander secure his rear as he continued forward.

Rebellion and return

The most significant battle of the Indian campaign was fought in monsoon rain and mud against King Porus at the Hydaspes River (the modern Jhelum) in 326 BCE. Porus would surrender, although not before two of his sons and his brother lay dead, alongside 20,000 infantry and 3,000 cavalry, killed in the chaos of a battle in which Porus's elephants ran amok. Among the Greek losses was Alexander's horse, Bucephalus, which was subsequently honored by the foundation of the eponymous city of Bucephala. Porus, like Cleophis, was restored as a vassal ruler.

In the battle's aftermath, and following a further engagement at Sangala that left thousands more dead, Alexander could no longer ignore the growing dissent in his ranks. At the Hyphasis River (the modern Beas), his wet, ragged, and exhausted men refused to go on. Alexander reluctantly began the journey home.

The army's return to Babylon was brutal. After making its way along the Indus to Patala, the army split into three: Alexander's general Craterus led part of it overland; another of his generals, Nearchus, navigated up the Hydaspes and on to Babylon in boats; and

THE LEGEND OF ALEXANDER

The Alexander Romance is a mixture of history, legend, and biography concerning Alexander that evolved over centuries but whose earliest-known version was compiled in Greek around the 3rd century BCE. Offering a fictionalized account of Alexander's life, the Romance framed him as a larger-than-life hero, interweaving real events with the fantastical: identifying him as the son of the pharaoh Nectanebo; sending him on epic quests to the Land of Darkness and the Fountain of Life; pitching him against distant enemies; and having him meet mythical creatures. The Romance was hugely popular, and it was translated and adapted across Europe and Asia. The oldest Persian version, the *Iskandarnameh* (an illustrated page from which is shown here), dates perhaps from the 11th century and depicts Alexander as a Muslim Iranian leader.

ALEXANDER AND DARIUS IN BATTLE

Alexander led his battalion on a 60-day trek across the Makran desert during which many of them died. Pressing on through Pasargadae and Persepolis, the army reached Susa, where Alexander gave his blessing to the marriages of about 10,000 of his men to Asian women, so they might form a new Perso-Macedonian ruling class. Alexander reached Babylon, which was to be his empire's capital, in 323 BCE. He began planning a new campaign in the Arabian peninsula. However, he developed a fever and died before he could execute his plans. Rumors circulated of poisoning, although drinking, malaria, or some other illness may have been the true cause. According to the account of Diodorus Siculus, when asked who should succeed him, Alexander replied "the strongest" ("*ho krateristos*"), although he may have actually nominated Craterus. Either way, a struggle for supremacy in the vast empire followed.

▷ **Tomb of Cyrus**
In 345 BCE, Alexander found that Cyrus's tomb at Pasargadae had been desecrated. Distressed at the sight, Alexander ordered the tomb's restoration and tried to find the culprits.

"The **elephants** veered and **turned upon** their **own** ranks."

The Alexander Mosaic
This Roman mosaic, measuring around 194 sq ft (18 sq m), uses around 1.5 million tesserae to create a dynamic scene of Alexander the Great (left, riding Bucephalus) fighting the Persian king Darius III (right, in a chariot) at the Battle of Issus (333 BCE). It once decorated a floor in the House of the Faun, a Hellenistic palace in Pompeii, Italy, buried by ash from Mount Vesuvius in 79 CE and rediscovered in 1831. The mosaic dates to 120–100 BCE and is thought to be a copy of a Hellenistic painting from the late 4th century BCE. It reflects the Romans' fascination with both Greek art and Alexander.

The Natural Sciences

Laying the foundations of scientific inquiry

In the 6th century BCE, thinkers in Ionia radically changed the way the ancient Greeks understood the world around them. Instead of ascribing the workings of the universe to the gods, they sought rational explanations of natural phenomena.

The Greeks had a good understanding of practical astronomy, useful for calculating calendars, and mathematics, essential in architecture, civil engineering, and commerce. However, in the 6th century BCE, the thinkers based at Miletus in Ionia moved away from seeing mathematics and astronomy as purely practical subjects and began approaching them as theoretical subjects that could be examined through philosophical inquiry. Rather than just describing the universe as they saw it, the Milesians, led by Thales, began to seek explanations of its workings that would be based on reason rather than mythological or religious beliefs. Their method was simple but revolutionary: observation, followed by reasoned inquiry.

Thales of Miletus is thought to have been the first to apply this method in his attempt to determine what the universe was made of and find the basic element of nature. From his observations—according to Aristotle—"that the nurture of all creatures is moist," Thales reasoned that the "first cause" of everything in the world was water. Using the same method, his followers Anaximander and Anaximenes came to

different conclusions, believing the first cause to be "the infinite" and air respectively, but together they firmly established the idea that the universe was governed by natural laws that could be deduced by observation and inquiry. This laid the foundations for systematic inquiry into what we now call the natural sciences: Earth science, astronomy, physics, chemistry, and biology.

Toward a scientific method

The approach spread rapidly across the ancient Greek world. For example, at his commune in Croton in the 6th century BCE, Pythagoras argued that the laws ruling the cosmos could be deduced by mathematical reasoning. In the 5th century BCE, a more influential idea came from Empedocles, who proposed that everything in nature was made up of four roots, or elements: air, water, earth, and fire. Alongside these were two basic principles or forces: love and strife. Empedocles' concept of four elements persisted until the 17th century CE. Even more radically, Leucippus and his pupil Democritus (see pp.96–97) developed the theory that the world consisted of indivisible particles called "atoms" that were in constant motion in empty space.

Not all Classical Athenian thinkers embraced the idea of systematic rational inquiry. Socrates and his protégé Plato dismissed the importance of observation in their investigations. Plato in particular argued that knowledge of the world came from reasoning alone rather than from observation. His pupil Aristotle, however, rejected this approach, arguing for an empirical process, and drawing his conclusions from observation, methodical examination, and inductive reasoning. He conducted a systematic study of a wide range of topics in the natural world, most notably classifying all known living things according to their characteristics. Aristotle's empirical system paved the way for the development of a truly scientific method and inspired the "scientists" of the Hellenistic Age.

△ **Anaximander**
Pictured with a sundial in this 3rd-century CE Roman mosaic, Anaximander was a pre-Socratic Greek philosopher and student of Thales who lived in Miletus.

THEOPHRASTUS, THE **FATHER OF BOTANY**

The philosopher Theophrastus is credited with establishing botany as a distinct field of study. After documenting the wildlife of the Eastern Mediterranean with his mentor, Aristotle, Theophrastus wrote the first systematic examinations of plant life. He produced two important botanical treatises, *Inquiry into Plants* (shown right is a medieval illustration from this text) and *On the Causes of Plants*, which became foundational texts in the study of botany.

▽ **The Four Elements**
A philosopher holds the world—divided into the four elements identified by Empedocles, and the sky—in this ink and tempera illustration from a 15th-century French manuscript of Aristotle's *Physics*.

Fire, shown with darker orange flames

Air, identifiable by the darker blue curls of "wind"

Water, distinguished by wavelike marks

Earth, here shown with plants and a hare

"The **first principles** of the **universe** are **atoms** and **empty space**; everything else is merely **thought** to **exist**."

DEMOCRITUS, AS QUOTED BY DIOGENES LAËRTIUS IN *DEMOCRITUS*

6

Hellenistic Greece

323–31 BCE

The Successors of Alexander

The Hellenistic period that followed the sudden death of Alexander the Great in Babylon in 323 BCE was characterized by a flowering of Greek culture that saw the pastoral poetry championed by Theocritus and the exquisite realism of statues such as the *Boxer at Rest* (see pp.266–267), as well as the emergence of mathematics as a separate subject. However, this was set against a background of continual conflict between Alexander's successors, the Diadochi.

Wars of the Diadochi

The turmoil began almost immediately, as Alexander had failed to explicitly nominate a successor. To manage the empire, Alexander's friend and bodyguard Perdiccas was appointed regent for Alexander's unborn child. The Partition of Babylon divided the empire into satrapies, governed by the Diadochi, most of whom were ambitious Macedonian army officers. Inevitably, the empire was plunged into a complex series of conflicts between Alexander's successors known as the Wars of the Diadochi (322–301 BCE).

After Perdiccas was assassinated in 321 BCE, the empire broke down as four of the Diadochi claimed kingship for themselves, establishing rival kingdoms. Seleucus commanded the largest of these, stretching from the east of Anatolia across Mesopotamia and into parts of India; in 312 BCE, he declared himself King Seleucus I Nicator (the Victorious), the founder of the Seleucid dynasty. Likewise, in 306–305 BCE, the ruler of most of Anatolia, Antigonus, founded the Antigonid dynasty as King Antigonus I, and Ptolemy claimed pharaonic status in Egypt. In 302 BCE,

Cassander, son of the regent Antipater, made himself king of Macedonia, having executed any of Alexander's family with a claim to the throne. He also dethroned the young king of Epirus, Pyrrhus, who would go on to reclaim his kingdom in 297 BCE.

The final War of the Diadochi ended in 301 BCE at the Battle of Ipsus in Phrygia, where Antigonus I was killed and his son Demetrius driven out of Anatolia by Seleucus I, in alliance with Cassander and Lysimachus, the ruler of Thrace. With their territory severely diminished, the Antigonids looked to Greece for opportunities, and in 294 BCE took revenge on Cassander's family by overthrowing his short-lived Antipatrid dynasty and taking control of Macedonia.

New threats

The three remaining great Hellenistic dynasties, the Seleucids, the Antigonids, and the Ptolemies, had largely established the bounds of their respective kingdoms in the wars, but their rivalry continued. Now, however, they faced threats from elsewhere too. With a geographically huge region under their rule, the Seleucids were overstretched, and were forced to cede some territory to the South Asian Maurya Empire, to Persia, and to other Asian powers.

Meanwhile, through a series of wars, often in alliance with the Greek Aetolian and Achaean leagues, Rome gained control of Macedonia by 197 BCE, forced the Seleucids from Anatolia by 188 BCE, and secured control of all mainland Greece after sacking Corinth in 146 BCE. The end of the Hellenistic period, and Greek independence with it, came with Egypt's defeat at the Battle of Actium in 31 BCE.

◁ **Lynx rhyton, Eastern Seleucid Empire, 51–50 BCE**

323 BCE The Partition of Babylon divides Alexander's empire

322 BCE The Wars of the Diadochi begin; they end in 301 BCE

305 BCE Ptolemy takes the role of pharaoh in Egypt as Ptolemy I Soter

312 BCE Seleucus I Nicator founds the Seleucid dynasty

306 BCE Antigonus I founds the Antigonid dynasty

302 BCE Cassander declares himself king of Macedonia

1 Alexander was first buried in Memphis c. 322 BCE

2 Petra, attacked by the Antigonids in 312 BCE

3 Demetrias, founded by the Antigonids in 294 BCE

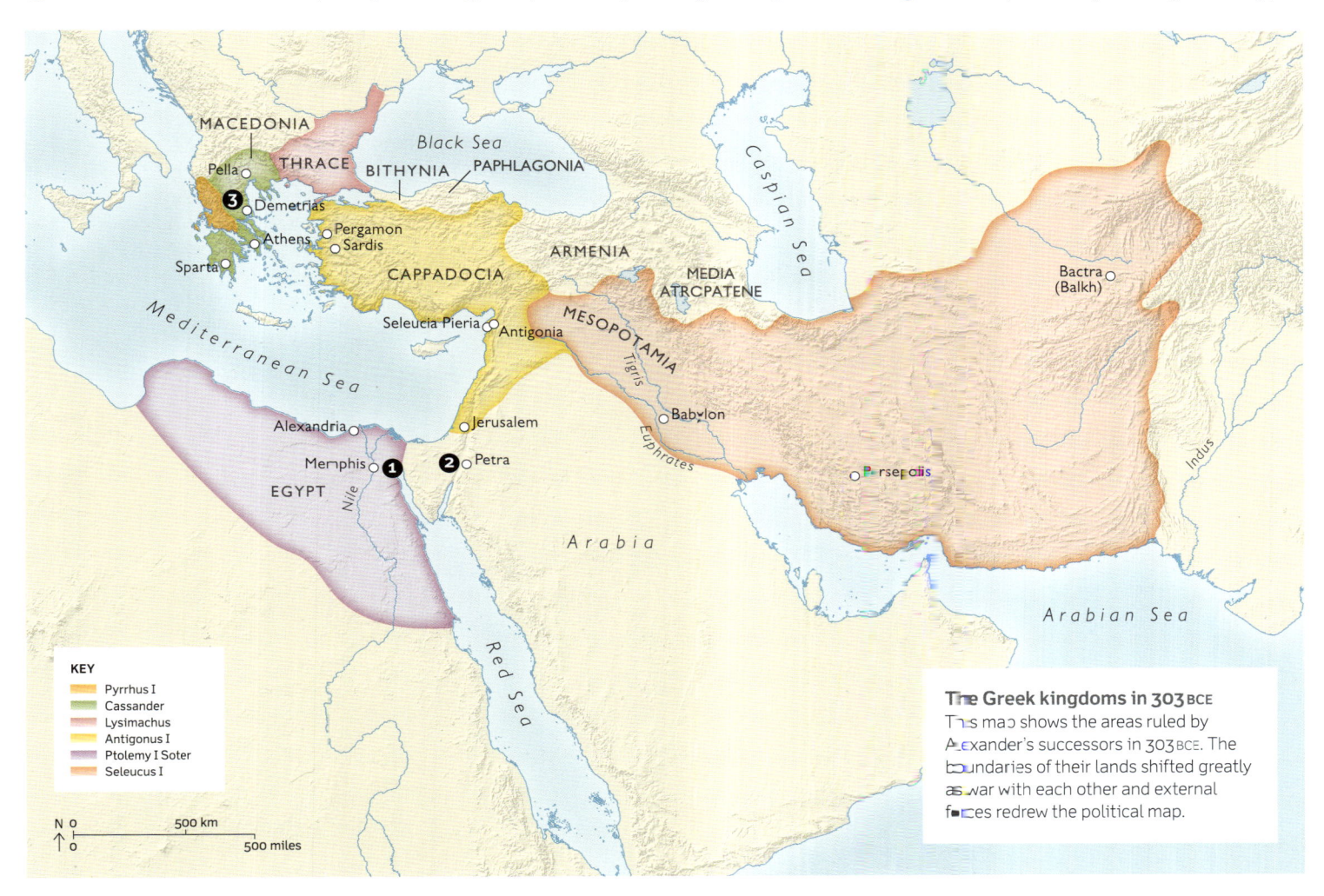

The Greek kingdoms in 303 BCE
This map shows the areas ruled by Alexander's successors in 303 BCE. The boundaries of their lands shifted greatly as war with each other and external forces redrew the political map.

KEY
- Pyrrhus I
- Cassander
- Lysimachus
- Antigonus I
- Ptolemy I Soter
- Seleucus I

N
0   500 km
0   500 miles

301 BCE Antigonus I defeated and killed at the Battle of Ipsus

c. 280 BCE The Achaean League is founded in the Peloponnese

188 BCE Rome and its allies take the Seleucids' territory in Anatolia

146 BCE The Romans sack Corinth and become rulers of all mainland Greece

294 BCE The Antigonid Demetrius I becomes ruler of Macedonia

214–196 BCE Rome defeats Philip V in the first two wars with Macedonia

171–168 BCE Perseus of Macedonia attempts to regain control from the Romans

31 BCE Ptolemaic Egypt falls to the Roman Empire

The Ptolemaic Kingdom

Egypt under the Greeks

For almost 300 years after the death of Alexander the Great, Egypt was ruled by the Greek Ptolemaic dynasty. It became a leading center of Hellenistic culture and trade, thriving as an independent kingdom until it fell to the Roman Empire.

From 343 to 332 BCE, Egypt had been under Persian control, but Alexander's conquest of the country marked the beginning of a long period of Greek rule. When Alexander's empire was divided up following his sudden death in 323 BCE, his right-hand man, the Macedonian general Ptolemy, was appointed satrap (governor) of Egypt. There, he established what would be Egypt's last pharaonic dynasty.

In the first years of Ptolemy's reign, wars between the Diadochi, and in particular with the neighboring Seleucid Empire, occupied his attention, but as the situation stabilized he began to establish a distinctive presence in Egypt. In 305 BCE, he declared himself pharaoh, adopting the title Ptolemy I Soter (Savior), marking the beginning of a dynasty with a tradition of naming each male ruler Ptolemy with a descriptive epithet. Despite taking on the title of pharaoh as a nod to Egyptian tradition, Ptolemy I Soter was anxious to preserve his Greek identity, and to emphasize that he was a Greek monarch as well as a pharaoh. He spoke only Greek and saw that the business of government was conducted in Greek. To lend

△ **Ptolemy the Greek**
Issued by Ptolemy I, this stater reflects a Greek tradition of coin portraiture, confirming Egypt's status as a Hellenistic kingdom.

▷ **Greek pharaoh**
Ptolemy I is presented in the guise of an Egyptian pharaoh, wearing the striped cloth headdress known as a nemes and the sacred snake symbol, the uraeus, of the pharaohs, in this statue from 305–283 BCE.

legitimacy to his claim on Egypt, Ptolemy I Soter made frequent official reference to Alexander the Great: he used Alexander's image on coins, made the newly established Hellenistic city of Alexandria (see pp.242–243) his capital, and even snatched Alexander's body from the funeral cortege carrying it to Macedonia, and took it to Memphis.

Ptolemy also moved the center of government from Memphis to Alexandria, where he commissioned the building of a great library dedicated to Greek culture and learning. In this way, local people could access bureaucracy and education only by becoming Hellenized. This set a precedent: under the Ptolemies, rather than a blend of cultures, there was to be a Hellenization of Egyptian culture, and the Greeks would only superficially assimilate Egyptian culture.

Ptolemy did, however, make some concessions to Egyptian culture. He was tolerant of the local religion, and also encouraged a cult that worshipped the Greco-Egyptian god Serapis, hoping to promote unity among the population.

The successors of Ptolemy

Ptolemy II Philadelphus (Sister-Loving) continued his father's ostensible adoption of local customs. He adopted the pharaonic tradition of marriage between siblings—which was derived from the myth of Osiris, who married his sister Isis—and married his sister Arsinoe II. The practice continued throughout the Ptolemaic era: Ptolemy IV Philopator (Father-Loving) was even depicted on coins with his sister and wife Arsinoe III in a double portrait with the inscription "siblings."

With Alexandria established as the intellectual center of the Greek world, and as a major trading city in the Mediterranean, Egypt continued to flourish under Ptolemy II Philadelphus (r. 284–246 BCE) and his successor Ptolemy III Euergetes (Benefactor) (r. 246–221 BCE). In the 2nd century BCE, however, Egypt became involved in a succession of foreign wars which, although not ending in defeat, considerably

◁ **Alexander's imitator**
Ptolemy IV, shown with Arsinoe, is portrayed as a powerful commander in this 3rd-century BCE cameo, which also includes motifs linked to Alexander the Great

weakened the country and opened the door to Roman interference. During the reign of Ptolemy VI Philometor (Mother-Loving) (r. 186–145 BCE), Egypt was invaded twice by the Seleucid king Antiochus IV between 169 BCE and 164 BCE, and the pharaoh was only able to retain control with Roman help. After Ptolemy VI's death, discipline all but collapsed as various members of the family vied to take over the throne, and the country descended into civil war. There followed a succession of six short-lived Ptolemaic rulers, all increasingly reliant on the support of Rome to hold power. By the beginning of the 1st century BCE, the dynasty was effectively a puppet regime under Roman control.

The last of the Ptolemies came to the throne in 51 BCE. Not for the first time, the pharaoh was a woman—Cleopatra VII. Her involvement with the leaders of the civil war in Rome, immortalized by William Shakespeare, has become legendary. After her suicide in 30 BCE and the death of Caesarion, her son by Julius Caesar, the Ptolemaic dynasty, and with it dynastic rule in Egypt, came to an end. However, by that time, Hellenistic civilization had become so deeply entrenched in Egypt that Greek culture and the Greek language continued to thrive there until Egypt was conquered by Muslim armies in 641 BCE.

△ **Greco-Egyptian god**
This 2nd-century CE painting shows the god Serapis, who combined elements of the Egyptian gods Osiris and Apis in a human form acceptable to the Greeks.

CLEOPATRA, QUEEN OF EGYPT

Cleopatra VII Thea Philopator (Father-Loving Goddess) was born in 69 BCE. Highly educated, a capable administrator, proficient in several languages, and a skilled politician, she became coruler with her brother and husband Ptolemy XIII on their father Ptolemy XII's death. Around 48/47 BCE, Cleopatra became the lover of Roman general Julius Caesar. When Ptolemy XIII drowned, she married her young brother Ptolemy XIV. On his death in 44 BCE, she installed Caesarion, her son by Caesar, as coruler. She went on to marry Caesar's heir, Mark Antony, enraging his rival Octavian (later Emperor Augustus), who declared war on the couple, and defeated their forces at the Battle of Actium. Cleopatra died by suicide, ending the Ptolemaic dynasty.

"Je tiens l'affaire!" ("I've got it!)"

JEAN-FRANÇOIS CHAMPOLLION

The top register of Egyptian hieroglyphs includes the pharaoh Ptolemy V's name, which is enclosed in a cartouche

△ **Reconstruction**
Over time, the top 19 in (49 cm) of the Rosetta Stone broke off and was lost. Scholars have been able to reconstruct it (as shown above) using the decoration and hieroglyphic inscriptions from similar stelae as models.

The middle register comprises 32 lines of Demotic script

The surface is smooth gray granodiorite, with pinkish veins in some areas

The bottom register has 53 lines of the ancient Greek version of the decree

◁ **The Rosetta Stone**
Written from right to left, the Rosetta Stone contains a decree of the 13-year-old pharaoh Ptolemy V issued in 196 BCE, one year after his coronation. It is more than 44 in (112 cm) tall and weighs some 1,675 lb (760 kg).

The Ptolemaic Decrees

Inscriptions from Hellenistic Egypt

Inscribed decrees found on the Rosetta Stone and other stone stelae demonstrate the links between the Greek and Egyptian cultures under Egypt's Hellenistic rulers, and provided the key to unlocking Egyptian hieroglyphs.

In 1798, a French force under Napoleon Bonaparte occupied Egypt with the aim of defending French trade interests, in part by blocking Britain's trade route to India. The following year, a group of French engineers working at the fortress at el-Rashid (Rosetta) in the Nile Delta found several blocks of stone that had been taken from ancient Egyptian monuments. Among them was a broken slab of granodiorite (a type of granite) inscribed with three blocks of text, each written in a different script. Scholars quickly realized that the bottom section was written in Greek, which had become Egypt's official language when the Ptolemaic dynasty took control of the country following the breakup of Alexander the Great's empire (see pp.238–239). They identified the topmost script as hieroglyphs, which had once been used by Egyptian priests but had largely fallen out of use by the 4th century CE. The text of the middle section was identified as Demotic, the everyday cursive script of the Egyptian people.

Decoding the inscriptions

The stele was taken to England as part of a peace treaty between Britain and France in 1801. By 1802, scholars working on Demotic script had identified several names from the Greek section in the Demotic section of the Rosetta Stone, confirming the suspicion that the same message was recorded in all three texts. Thus, with the Greek text as the key, linguists took up the task of deciphering the lost language of ancient Egypt. A breakthrough came with the realization that most of the hieroglyphs did not have some strange symbolic meaning, but represented sounds. By 1822, French scholar Jean-François Champollion had cracked the hieroglyphic code.

Intriguingly, the Rosetta Stone text, now identified as the Decree of Memphis from 196 BCE, referred to an uprising among the Egyptian population against their Greek rulers. It detailed tax cuts, gifts to Egyptian temples, and other measures taken by Ptolemy V to pacify his discontented subjects.

Since the Rosetta Stone was found, more multi-script stelae featuring Ptolemaic decrees have been uncovered. These include further examples of the Decree of Memphis, and texts of the Decree of Canopus, which commemorates an assembly of priests held at Canopus to honor Ptolemy III Euergetes in 238 BCE. It records the king's donations to the temples and his support for the Egyptian Apis and Mnevis bull cults. The Raphia Decree, found on several stelae, records Ptolemy IV's victory over the Syrians in 217 BCE, describing the king in terms reminiscent of the conquering pharaohs of the past. Both decrees provide an interesting insight into Ptolemaic power in Egypt, showing how the kings leveraged Egypt's religion and history to cement their own authority.

△ **Canopus Decree**
Found in 1881 by French Egyptologist Gaston Maspero at the site of Kom el-Hisn in Egypt's Nile Delta, this is one of two near complete examples of the Canopus Decree.

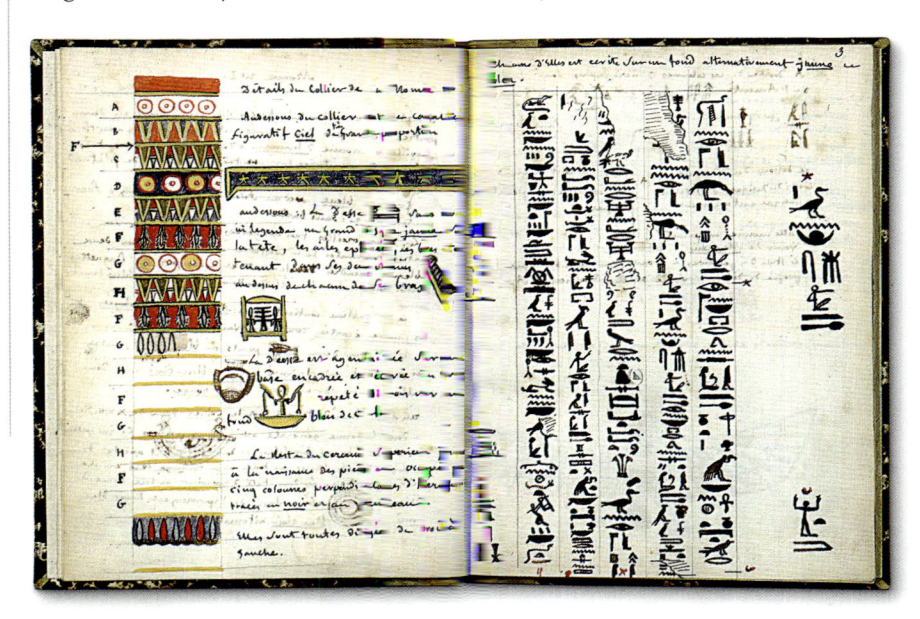

▷ **Philologist's notebook**
Belonging to Jean-François Champollion (1790–1832), this notebook records the French Egyptologist's work on inscriptions, including those from mummies' tombs.

Alexandria

The great city of Alexander

Founded by Alexander the Great in the 4th century BCE, Alexandria grew to a city of half a million people, with lavish monuments including the Pharos, one of the Seven Wonders of the Ancient World.

Alexandria, the largest Greek city in the Eastern Mediterranean, owed its origins to a dream. In 331 BCE, Alexander the Great had a vision of the poet Homer directing him to go to Pharos, an island "on the Egyptian shore." There, he found a sleepy fishing settlement called Rakhotis on marshy ground on the mainland facing the island. Recognizing the place's strategic location at the intersection of routes linking Europe and Africa, and with easy access to the Nile, Mediterranean, and Red Sea, Alexander is said to have used grains of barley to sketch a plan for the new city he proposed to found. He ordered the construction of the Heptastadion, a 4,300-ft- (1,300-m-) long causeway linking the island with the mainland, left the architect Deinokrates of Rhodes to implement his plan for a new city, and returned to his campaign in Asia.

Deinokrates did justice to his master's plan, laying out the city's grid with a 115-ft- (35-m-) wide central avenue, the Canopic Way, and an equally grand road running north to south from the Heptastadion to the Gate of the Sun. Alexandria became filled with merchants, scholars, and artisans from all over the Hellenistic world. It was home to a large Jewish community of more than 50,000 people at its height, whose members produced the Septuagint, a translation of the Torah into Greek, in the 3rd century BCE.

On Alexander's death in 323 BCE, rule over Alexandria passed to his general Ptolemy (see pp.238–239), who commissioned several lavish monuments in the city. Among them was the Soma, a tomb created for Alexander, whose corpse Ptolemy had hijacked as it was being taken to Macedonia and buried initially in Memphis. The Soma was built near the Canopic Way and attracted famous visitors, including Julius Caesar in 48 BCE and Octavian (later the Roman emperor Augustus)—who, according to the Roman historian Cassius Dio, broke Alexander's nose when he leaned down to kiss his mummified body—in 30 BCE. The location of the tomb was subsequently lost.

> "The **city** founded by him would be … a **nursing mother** for **men** of **every nation**."
>
> PROPHECY REGARDING ALEXANDRIA IN PLUTARCH, *PARALLEL LIVES*

◁ **Triumphal column**
This giant Corinthian pillar was built near the Serapeum in Alexandria around 297 CE to honor the Roman emperor Diocletian, after he defeated a rival who had usurped power in Egypt.

△ **Catacombs of Kom el Shoqafa**
Created in the 2nd century CE, the catacombs under Alexandria house several painted tomb chambers, including one (shown here) depicting the goddess Isis assisting with an embalming.

Work had already begun on the Pharos lighthouse when Ptolemy II Philadelphus (r. 284–246 BCE) became pharaoh. The Pharos guided ships into the city's two harbors—of which the Portus Magnus could hold 1,200 vessels. Construction of the Great Library, whose location is uncertain, also began in Ptolemy II's reign. Housing around 500,000 scrolls, it was the largest library in the ancient world. The research institute attached to it, the Mouseion, attracted noted scholars, including the engineer Heron, the mathematician Euclid, and the physician Erasistratus of Ceos (who pioneered the use of the pulse for diagnosis). Its librarians were of the caliber of Eratosthenes.

The Mouseion continued to operate even after the library was partially destroyed when Julius Caesar besieged Alexandria in 48 BCE. There was also an offshoot of the Mouseion at the Serapeum, the temple built in the reign of Ptolemy III Euergetes and dedicated to the Greco-Egyptian god Serapis. By the early 5th century CE, however, the city was already much diminished. Damage caused during the Jewish uprising in 115 CE; destruction ordered by Emperor Caracalla in 215, after the city's inhabitants mocked him; a tsunami caused by an earthquake near Crete in 365; and a reduction in trade as the Roman Empire declined had all taken their toll. By the time the armies of the Rashidun Caliphate took the city in 641, it was a pale shadow of what it had once been. But over the centuries, Alexandria would rise again to become Egypt's second-largest city.

LIBRARIANS OF **THE MOUSEION**

The wealth of the Library of Alexandria's collection attracted the Greek world's leading scholars. The first librarian, Demetrius of Phaleron (c. 350–280 BCE) was a renowned orator, a student of Theophrastus (see p.232), and an Aristotelian philosopher. The poet Callimachus (c. 310–240 BCE), a pioneer of aesthetics, created the library's first catalog, the Pinakes, during his tenure from the 280s BCE. He was followed by Apollonius of Rhodes, the author of the *Argonautica*, an epic poem on Jason and the Argonauts' quest for the Golden Fleece. Apollonius's successor was Eratosthenes (c. 276–194 BCE), a geographer and astronomer credited with the invention of the armillary sphere, a model of the celestial sphere.

ERATOSTHENES

◁ **Alexandrian drachm**
Ancient coins carrying representations of the Pharos, such as this Alexandrian drachm from the 2nd century CE, provide clues about its appearance in the Roman era: a square tower with windows, and figures on top.

" … this tower, in a straight and upright line, **appears to cleave the sky** … a great fire **blazing from its summit.**"

POSIDIPPUS OF PELLA

The Pharos of Alexandria

Ptolemaic wonder of the world

In the early 3rd century BCE, when Alexandria was establishing itself as a cultural and commercial capital, Ptolemy I Soter (305–284 BCE) embarked on the construction of a great lighthouse at the mouth of the city's harbor. Located off the island of Pharos, from which it took its name, this massive stone tower was a beacon of safety for seafarers along a treacherous coastline. It was completed during the reign of Ptolemy II Philadelphus (r. 284–246 BCE), when the Greek poet Posidippus of Pella, resident in Alexandria, wrote an epigram to mark the event.

Exactly what the original lighthouse looked like remains uncertain, as the earliest descriptions of any detail date to the 10th century CE, by which time it had already evolved. Posidippus's words, however, indicate that it inspired awe from the start. Becoming the symbol of Alexandria, the Pharos stood tall for more than 1,500 years, withstanding numerous earthquakes before it finally collapsed in the 14th century.

The face is worn after centuries under water

◁ **Colossal pharaoh**
This statue of a pharaoh, once some 33 ft (10 m) tall, was recovered from Alexandria's harbor. Thought to depict Ptolemy II Philadelphus, it may have stood inside the Pharos, at its base.

The Greek ruler is shown wearing Egyptian dress

UNDERWATER **ARCHAEOLOGY**

In 1994, the Center for Alexandrian Studies began underwater excavations in Alexandria's harbor. Archaeologists have identified more than 3,000 architectural fragments, among them immense masonry blocks weighing up to 75 metric tons each, which, they concluded, belonged to the legendary Pharos. Other finds included colossal statues and a red granite lintel nearly 42 ft (13 m) tall, part of a monumental doorway.

GRANITE DOORWAY LINTEL

▷ **Guiding light**
This reconstruction depicts the Pharos as it may have appeared when first built: an imposing landmark visible from far out to sea. Open fires guided ships to safety when visibility was poor.

Some ancient representations depict tritons at the corners

A statue of Zeus Soter (Savior) topped the tower

Red granite from Aswan was used for detailing

Signal fires could be seen from afar

Fuel for the fires was probably carried by pack animals

A spiral ramp wound around a cylindrical core

Rooms with windows surrounded the internal ramp

The walls were made of granite and limestone

▽ **Evolution of the tower**

The Pharos underwent numerous changes and repairs in its long history. Accounts from the Islamic period, when it reached its greatest height, describe a tower with three tiers.

Mirrors magnified the fires for visibility

Second tier added in brick

Domed mosque added c. 865 CE

Brick cylindrical tier

Brick octagonal tier

The tower stood more than 330 ft (100 m) tall

ROMAN PHAROS
c. 50 CE

ISLAMIC PHAROS
c. 1165 CE

KEY

▭ Seleucid territory 281 BCE

▭ Seleucid territory 188 BCE

— Territory boundaries 188 BCE

The Seleucid Empire

A new power rises

At its height, the Seleucid Empire was the largest of the Hellenistic power blocs created after the death of Alexander the Great, stretching across western Asia from Anatolia to the Indus.

As one of the Diadochi, the successors to Alexander the Great's empire (see p.236), the Macedonian general Seleucus was appointed satrap of Babylon in 321 BCE. In 316 BCE, he fled Babylon after Antigonus (see pp.248–249) demanded he hand over the satrapy's income. Returning in 312 BCE, Seleucus defeated Antigonus's son Demetrius at the Battle of Gaza.

As Seleucus I Nicator (Victor), he then established an empire that would spread across the lands conquered by Alexander and survive for nearly 250 years. His campaigns took him to the borders of the Maurya Empire in India, where after two years of fighting, he negotiated an alliance in 303 BCE. Sealing the deal by giving his daughter in marriage to Chandragupta Maurya, Seleucus received 500 war elephants. These proved invaluable to the Seleucids in defeating Antigonus at the Battle of Ipsus (301 BCE) to take control of Mesopotamia and Central Asia.

Like Alexander, Seleucus respected local religious and cultural traditions. However, at the same time, he ensured the political dominance of a Greek elite by integrating this ruling class into the existing social structures to promote a unified population, and by encouraging an amalgamation of western and eastern cultures rather than imposing Greek customs. This strategy inspired a wealth of Hellenistic-influenced art and architecture throughout the empire.

THE **GRECO-BACTRIAN KINGDOM**

While the Seleucid Empire was engaged in repeated wars to hold its western territories, the satrap of Bactria, in the east, took the opportunity to secede from the empire. Declaring himself King Diodotus I Soter, he established the Greco–Bactrian Kingdom in about 250 BCE. The kingdom endured until it was conquered by the nomadic Yuezhi in 120 BCE. Known as the "land of a thousand cities," the Greco–Bactrian Kingdom was a prosperous state that at its height stretched from Sogdiana in the north to the Indus Valley, and from the Himalayas to the Caspian Sea.

BACTRIAN PLATE WITH GODDESSES CYBELE AND NIKE

Under Seleucus's rule, the empire prospered, because it was ideally placed for trade between Central and East Asia and the Mediterranean. With a steady influx of Greek settlers, Hellenistic culture also flourished. Seleucus founded the city of Antioch on the Orontes River to be his capital, the center of government for the western end of the empire, and a major trading city, second only to Alexandria in size and importance in the Hellenistic world. To administer the eastern part of his empire, he founded the city of Seleucia on the Tigris River, where he installed his son Antiochus I Soter (Savior) as coruler in 291 BCE.

Seleucus's successors

In 281 BCE, Seleucus was assassinated by Ptolemy Keraunos—who hoped to take control of his Seleucid territories—and was succeeded by his son Antiochus. Throughout the 3rd century BCE, Antiochus and his successors faced revolts across the empire. There were uprisings in Anatolia and Armenia; around 250 BCE, Sogdiana and Bactria declared independence under their ruler Diodatus, and Parthia broke away. On its western borders, meanwhile, the Seleucid Empire was in conflict with Ptolemaic Egypt for control of Syria.

The empire had been drastically reduced by the time Antiochus III came to the throne in 223 BCE, and the cost of the conflicts had severely damaged its prosperity. The new ruler embarked on a campaign to recapture lost territories. He reconquered most of the breakaway states, including Bactria and Anatolia, and forced Egypt out of Syria and Judea. For restoring Seleucid pride and reestablishing an empire that once again stretched from Anatolia to India, the king became known as Antiochus the Great, an epithet echoing that of Alexander.

With the Roman Empire an increasing threat Antiochus decided to make a preemptive strike, staging an invasion of Greece. His strategy turned out to be disastrous: he was heavily defeated in battles at Thermopylae in 191 BCE and at Magnesia in 190 BCE. Forced to acknowledge that the Romans had the upper hand, he signed the Treaty of Apamea in 188 BCE. This limited the extent of the empire, and the Seleucids were forced to give up their elephants and most of their ships, and to pay an indemnity of 15,000 talents. The Seleucid Empire rapidly declined and began to fragment into autonomous breakaway states, leaving the once great empire open to conquest by Rome, which was achieved by Pompey in 63 BCE.

△ **Clay records**
This cuneiform tablet is an astronomical calendar from Seleucid-era Babylon, around 178 BCE.

◁ **Seleucus I Nicator**
This 1st-century BCE Roman bust of the founder and ruler of the Seleucid Empire comes from the Villa of the Papyri at Herculaneum in southern Italy.

> "**Seleucus** became the **greatest king**, was the most kingly in **mind**, and ruled over the **greatest** extent of **land** after **Alexander** himself."
>
> GREEK HISTORIAN ARRIAN,
> *THE ANABASIS OF ALEXANDER*

The Antigonids

Dynastic power in Greece's heartland

Losing out to the Seleucids in the battle for Alexander's wider empire, the Antigonids captured Athens and Macedonia to carve out a powerful kingdom in mainland Greece that saw off threats from the Ptolemaic dynasty and the Celts.

△ **Demetrius Poliorcetes**
Minted in Amphipolis, in ancient Macedonia, this silver stater features a portrait of Demetrius, who gained the nickname Poliorcetes (the Besieger) after he besieged Rhodes in 305 BCE. Demetrius was Macedonia's king from 294 to 288 BCE.

Founded when Antigonus Monophthalmus (the One-Eyed), one of Alexander the Great's generals, made himself king in 306 BCE, the Antigonid dynasty played a significant role in shaping the Hellenistic world after Alexander's death. After decades of conflict, the Antigonid kingdom was secured in 276 BCE and endured for several generations as a powerful presence in mainland Greece.

Antigonus I rose to prominence as satrap (governor) of Greater Phrygia under Philip II and then Alexander. A phenomenal military leader and strategist, by 316 BCE he had defeated Perdiccas (regent of the empire, who was based in Babylon) and Eumenes (satrap of Cappadocia, in central Anatolia) to take control of an area that stretched from modern-day Iran to the Aegean. Alarmed by Antigonus's ambition, Ptolemy (ruler of Egypt), Cassander (regent for the Macedonian king, Alexander IV), and Lysimachus (satrap of Thrace) demanded that he give up his conquests. In response, Antigonus invaded Syria, which was under Ptolemy's control, beginning the Third War of the Diadochi in 315 BCE. By 311 BCE, however, it was clear Antigonus could not beat the coalition ranged against him, and he made peace.

△ **Scene from Demetrias**
A funerary stele featuring a painting of a family, this was found at Demetrias, the Antigonid capital in Thessaly founded by Demetrius Poliorcetes in 294 BCE.

The peace did not last long. In 310–309 BCE, Antigonus engaged in a brief, unsuccessful war in Babylon, where the Greek general Seleucus had seized control in 311 BCE. With Seleucus consolidating his power in the east and Ptolemy asserting himself in the Aegean, Antigonus and his son Demetrius Poliorcetes turned their attention to Greece.

The battle for Greece

In 307 BCE, Demetrius invaded Greece and expelled Cassander's governor from Athens. He then defeated Ptolemy's fleet at the Battle of Salamis, after which his army proclaimed him king, and took Cyprus from Egypt in 306 BCE. By 303 BCE, Demetrius had driven Cassander's forces from central Greece, occupied much of the Peloponnese, allied with Achaea, Elis, and most of Arcadia, and was threatening Macedonia. To relieve pressure on Cassander, Lysimachus invaded Anatolia. Demetrius returned to Asia Minor to help his father, but the Antigonid forces were crushed and Antigonus killed at the Battle of Ipsus in 301 BCE.

THE CELTIC INVASION

In 279 BCE, a Celtic army commanded by Brennus, Bolgios, and Acichorius marched into northern Greece. The Macedonian king, Ptolemy Keraunos, was swiftly decapitated in a battle with Bolgios's forces. In central Greece, Brennus met a combined force drawn from the Aetolian League and Athens at Thermopylae, suffering huge losses before finding a way through the pass. He sacked Delphi but was then forced to retreat. Some of the Celts settled in Thrace after their defeat by Antigonus II in 277 BCE; others established Galatia in Asia Minor, and plundered the region, until their defeat by Attalus of Pergamon (see p.260) around 240 BCE.

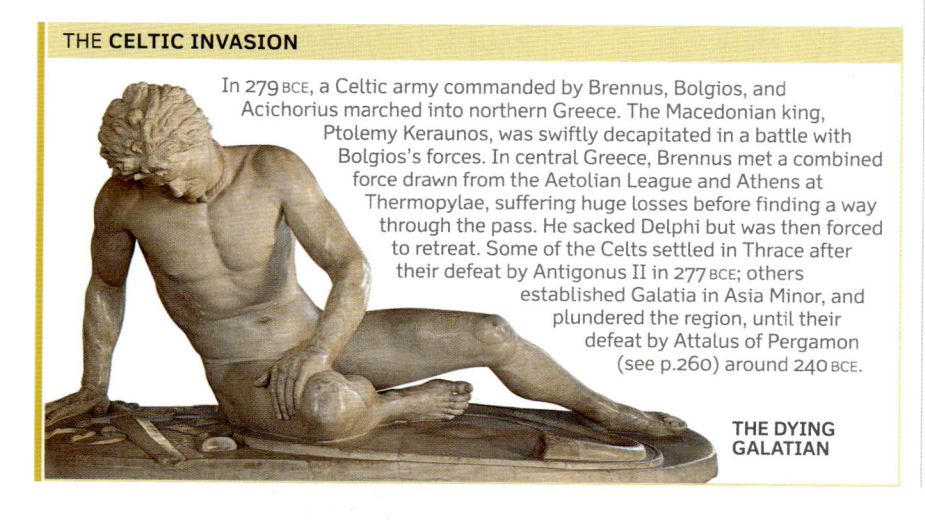

THE DYING GALATIAN

All was not lost, however, and Demetrius began to rebuild his fortunes. He allied himself to Seleucus, who married his daughter, Stratonice. He captured Athens in 295 BCE and defeated the Spartans in battle at Mantinea the following year. Sparta itself was saved only because Demetrius became embroiled in Macedonia, where Cassander had died in 298 BCE, and the kingdom had been divided between his sons, Antipater I and Alexander V. Demetrius happily obliged when Alexander invited him to intervene in his struggles with Antipater. He entered Macedonia and overthrew Antipater before having Alexander killed and making himself king in 294 BCE.

Demetrius continued to extend his power across Greece, until he was overthrown by Lysimachus and Pyrrhus (see pp.254–255), with the support of Seleucus and Ptolemy, in 288 BCE. Demetrius then decided to attack Lysimachus in Asia, where his power was centered, but his campaign quickly foundered and he died as a prisoner of Seleucus in 283 BCE.

In 279 BCE, Celts swept south into Greece and killed the Macedonian king, Ptolemy Ceraunos (Ptolemy's son, who had seized control in 281 BCE) leaving a power vacuum. Demetrius's son, Antigonus II Gonatas, led the fight against the Celts and, after his victory at the Battle of Lysimachia in 277 BCE, was able to claim Macedonia for himself and his successors.

△ **Hellenistic court**
This detail from a Roman fresco from c. 40 BCE found in Boscoreale, Italy, is thought to show a scene from a Hellenistic court, perhaps Macedonian, given the shield's star symbol.

"The **power of Antigonus** was a **danger** to them all."

PAUSANIAS, *DESCRIPTION OF GREECE*

Disability and Difference

Ableism and acceptance in the Greek world

Recent work on disability and physical and mental health conditions in ancient Greece has revealed new, and sometimes unexpected, aspects of its society, mythology, and culture, and of the lived experience of its inhabitants.

The majority of ancient Greek people would have had some experience of disabilities, whether directly themselves or among their families and communities, and whether from birth or caused by disease, trauma, or war injuries. While ancient Greece was relatively forward-looking with respect to disability and other conditions, it could also be a precarious place for disabled people to live.

Care and cruelty

Evidence points to the care that could be extended to disabled people. For example, medical treatises and archaeological findings indicate the treatments that might be offered to disabled babies, including those born with club feet and cleft palates. As for physically disabled adults, those unable to earn a living in Athens owing to physical impairments could apply for a state benefit, subject to an annual review. Meanwhile, participation in ancient Greek society appears to have been enabled by mobility aids such as prostheses (often used because of limb loss in war) and crutches, while ramps improved access to public spaces such as sanctuaries.

◁ **Man with kyphosis**
This Hellenistic bronze statue from 2nd–1st-century BCE Egypt depicts a man with a curved spine. The Greeks viewed such "humps" as a sign of good luck.

However, there is also evidence to suggest that the ancient Greeks could treat disabled people cruelly. For example, disabled babies born in Sparta were reportedly thrown into a chasm at the foot of Mount Taygetus, although this tradition might reflect the othering of Sparta by non-Spartans rather than any actual ancient practice. Plato and Aristotle both opposed euthanasia, apart from for disabled people. The Greeks also disparaged and misrepresented those with dwarfism. Aristotle associated their stature with intellectual inferiority. Artists often depicted dwarves in comic or unusual poses, suggesting they viewed them as figures of mocking. Some viewed them as bringers of good luck, adding to their othering.

While work continues on understanding Greek attitudes to disabled people, recent research into neurodivergence, learning differences, and mental illness is opening up new ways to interpret a range of conditions in ancient Greece. For instance, the behavior of warriors—including Achilles and Epizelos, an Athenian combatant who became blind during the Battle of Marathon—has been read in relation to PTSD. Meanwhile, research into autism may offer fresh perspectives on the intense interests pursued by each of the Olympian gods.

◁ **Blinded king**
Antigone leads her self-blinded father, Oedipus, into exile in this 1843 painting by French artist Ernest Hillemacher.

Dionysus, cloaked in a panther skin and holding a cup of wine

Hephaestus depicted
as a young man, his disability
(club feet) clearly visible

A maenad holding a snake
follows Hephaestus; behind
her is a satyr

"Concerning the **rearing** or **exposure** of **newborns**, let there be **a law** that no **incapacitated child** shall be **raised**"

ARISTOTLE, *POLITICS*

△ **A disabled god**
The master blacksmith and god of fire and artisans Hephaestus is depicted riding a donkey in this painting of his return to Olympus on a vase from c. 525 BCE. According to myth, Hera cast Hephaestus out of Olympus. This may have been due to his disability, or may have caused it.

Pastoral Poetry

The birth of bucolic idylls

In the Hellenistic period, nostalgia for a utopian rural "Golden Age" prompted the emergence of a new genre of poetry, presenting an idealized pastoral setting in which shepherds sang and wooed nymphs and shepherdesses.

Depictions of rural life in ancient poetry were not new, but the romanticized portrayal of country life found in the pastoral poetry that emerged in Greece in the 3rd century BCE was in marked contrast to the more true-to-life descriptions of previous poets, such as in Hesiod's *Works and Days* (see p.56).

The poet credited with originating this pastoral genre was Theocritus, believed to have been born in the early 3rd century BCE in Syracuse, Sicily. Little is known of his life, but it is likely he spent time in Alexandria, which was then home to a flourishing Hellenistic school of poetry. Unlike his contemporaries, however, Theocritus largely avoided writing historical or heroic poems, and chose more intimate, everyday subjects. His most characteristic poems are bucolic (from *boukolos*, the Greek word for "cowherd") in nature, and set in a countryside inhabited by shepherds and nymphs.

Known as idylls (little poems), Theocritus's pastoral poems laid the foundations of a form of poetry that became popular with a newly urbanized public hankering for the simplicity of a bygone rural age. To appeal to this sophisticated audience, while maintaining a rustic atmosphere, he adopted the meter of the Greek epic poems, dactylic hexameter, but wrote in the less high-flown Doric dialect. This juxtaposition of stylistic elements created a poetic world that was neither a sentimental imagining nor a realistic description of country life. It made it credible for his simple peasant characters to express poetic thoughts in a manner and language that would not have come naturally to them.

Theocritus was most innovative, however, in his handling of his subject matter. His idylls include familiar characters from mythology, but he puts them with herdsmen not heroes, and

△ **The honey thief**
This 15th-century plaque illustrates *Idyll* XIX, showing Eros (right) running to Aphrodite after a bee stings him. The idyll is now thought to have been by a later writer and not Theocritus.

◁ **Father of pastoral poetry**
Theocritus is shown here in an 18th-century engraving wearing a laurel wreath, used since ancient times to honor poets and heroes.

sets his stories in the pasture, not on the battlefield. Also, rather than describing the gods' sexual conquests of humans, he depicts shepherds and cowherds in amorous pursuit of nymphs.

Theocritus even transports himself into his idyllic world. In *Idyll* VII, he writes in the first person, presenting thinly disguised caricatures of his friends and fellow poets as peasants celebrating a festival on the island of Cos. Not all the idylls are light-hearted: *Idyll* I relates the sad tale of Daphnis, a cowherd who chooses death rather than the curse of love inflicted on him by Cypris, another name for Aphrodite.

The pastoral genre established by Theocritus remained popular, influencing Greek poets such as Moschus of Syracuse and Bion of Smyrna, Roman poets including Virgil and Horace, and later writers.

▽ **Theocritus fragment**
This papyrus from the 2nd century BCE includes lines from Theocritus's *Idyll* XIII, which tells the story of the rape of Hylas, Heracles' lover, by a group of water nymphs.

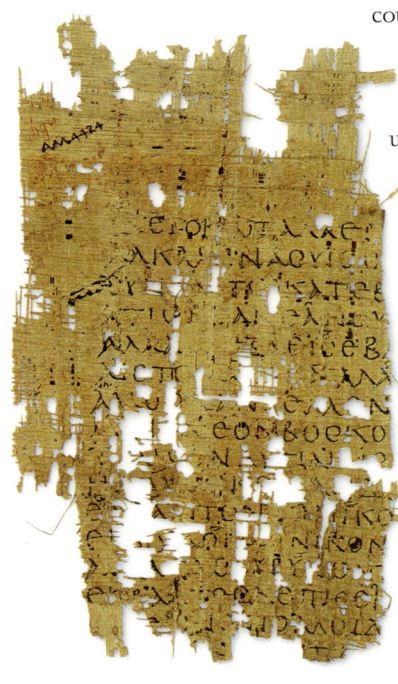

Cypris's attendant waits, ready to hand the goddess her clothes and a mirror

Cypris hides her anger at Daphnis's claim that he would never succumb to temptation

An orange grove forms the backdrop to the confrontation

The cowherd Daphnis, who claims that he can master love and remain faithful to his beloved

"Something **sweet** is the **whisper** of the **pine**, O goatherd, that makes her **music** by yonder **springs**."

THEOCRITUS, *IDYLL* I

△ **Shepherd and goddess**
Twentieth-century Scottish artist William Russell Flint painted several watercolors of Theocritus's idylls, including the one shown above of *Idyll* I, depicting Daphnis's meeting with Cypris.

▷ **Bust of Pyrrhus**
This Roman marble bust shows Pyrrhus in martial garb, with a laurel-wreathed helmet indicating his military success. The bust is a copy of a 3rd-century BCE Greek original and dates to 50–25 BCE. It was found at the Villa of the Papyri at Herculaneum, buried in the Vesuvius eruption of 79 CE, along with almost 100 other sculptures, many of them of Greek.

Attic-type helmet with peaked front and cheek protectors

"If we are **victorious** in one more **battle** with the Romans, we shall be **utterly ruined**."

PYRRHUS, AFTER THE BATTLE OF ASCULUM

Italian marble probably copied from a plaster model of the original shipped from Greece

Pyrrhus of Epirus

Rome's fiercest Greek enemy

A highly effective general who raised his kingdom of Epirus to the rank of a major power, Pyrrhus was a king whose reputation has been overshadowed by the terrible cost of his victories against the Roman Republic.

Pyrrhus's life and career was shaped by the vicious civil wars fought by Alexander the Great's generals to gain control of Alexander's legacy following his death in 323 BCE. Born in 319 BCE in Epirus, on Greece's western margins, Pyrrhus was brought up in Taulantii, at the court of the Illyrian king Glaucias (r. 335–302 BCE), after nearly being killed at the age of three by rebels. The Illyrian ruler managed to return Pyrrhus to Epirus as king eight years later, only for him to be deposed by his cousin Neoptolemus in 302 BCE. Pyrrhus then went into exile, joining the Macedonian generals Demetrius Poliorcetes and Antigonus Monophthalmus in the Wars of the Diadochi (see p.236), and taking part in the crucial Battle of Ipsus (301 BCE).

After marrying Ptolemy I's stepdaughter, Antigone, Pyrrhus was able to return to Epirus with the backing of his father-in-law's soldiers in 297 BCE. To avoid civil war, he agreed to share power with Neoptolemus. Pyrrhus became sole king when Neoptolemus was murdered, possibly on Pyrrhus's orders.

Imperial ambitions

Pyrrhus successfully took most of Thessaly and western Macedonia, only to lose them to Demetrius's successor Lysimachus by 284 BCE. Thwarted in Greece, in 281 BCE, Pyrrhus responded to an appeal for help from the southern Italian city of Tarentum, then in dispute with the Romans. He crossed into Italy with an army of 25,000 men and 20 war elephants and secured victories at Heraclea and Asculum, but his losses were exceedingly high.

In 278 BCE, the Greek cities in Sicily asked him to drive the Carthaginians from the island, and he accepted, wanting respite from fighting Rome. Pyrrhus captured most of Sicily and returned to mainland Italy in 275 BCE. The same year, a defeat at Beneventum drove him back to Greece. There, he engaged in a new series of wars: first against Antigonus Gonatas, the king of Macedonia, then in Sparta, and finally in Argos. As he entered Argos, his troops hemmed in among the narrow streets, Pyrrhus was killed by a tile hurled from a rooftop. With his death Epirus's bid for regional dominance ended. The memory of Pyrrhus as a talented military commander endured, but his name is forever linked with the idea of a "Pyrrhic victory"—a victory almost more costly than a defeat.

△ **Fighting the Romans**
Pyrrhus's forces, including war elephants, are shown fighting the Romans in this Flemish painting from the 17th century.

◁ **Gold stater**
The reverse (shown here) of this stater issued by Pyrrhus shows Nike, goddess of victory. The obverse depicts the goddess of war, Athena.

The Age of Leagues

Seeking strength in inter-state alliances

A feature of Greek politics from at least the 7th century BCE, leagues were increasingly important in the Hellenistic era, as city-states struggled to maintain a degree of independence from Macedonian control.

Federations and alliances such as the Ionian (see pp.80–81) and Delian (see pp.158–159) leagues had been part of Greece's political landscape for centuries. However, the need to create alliances became more acute with the growth and breakup of the Macedonian Empire in the second half of the 4th century BCE. Stretching across the north of the Greek peninsula, Macedonia dominated the city-states to the south. It made sense for them to seek safety in numbers.

The Aetolian and Achaean leagues

Greece's two longest-lasting federations were the Aetolian and Achaean leagues, based respectively in central Greece and the Peloponnese. To manage the intricate politics of the time, the leagues relied on regular assemblies of free citizens. Although ostensibly democratic, they were dominated for the most part by

◁ **Symbol of unity**
Coins issued by *poleis* in the Achaean League, like this mid-2nd-century BCE example from Elis, carried a monogram of the word "Achaean" (the cross motif in the center).

a political elite, who kept close control over the appointment of the *strategoi* (generals) who were responsible for governing the leagues and managing their wars. The leagues' activities extended to economic matters, for example, with the introduction of a shared currency.

The Aetolian League came together formally in the 4th century BCE, although Aetolia, north of the Gulf of Corinth, had long enjoyed a marked regional identity. In the years after Alexander's empire broke up, the league extended its embrace to Athens and the island of Rhodes; it even linked up with Pergamon in Asia Minor. The sacred city of Delphi fell within its territory, and the league gained extra prestige when, in 279 BCE, it helped repel invading Celts who were threatening the sanctuary (see p.248).

The Achaean League came together rather later, in 280 BCE. Over the next century, the league benefited from the leadership of two exceptional generals. The first, Aratus of Sicyon, successfully combated Macedonian influence to free Athens in 229 BCE and bring Argos into the Achaean League. His success aroused the hostility of the Spartan king, Cleomenes III, and Aratus was forced to call on Macedonia to help secure control of the Peloponnese, except for Sparta, in the Cleomenean War (c. 229–222 BCE). In 220 BCE, the Achaean and Aetolian leagues came into direct conflict in the so-called Social War,

▽ **Inter-league conflict**
This 18th-century engraving depicts the Battle of Caphyae, part of the Social War (220–217 BCE) between the Aetolian and Achaean leagues; the Aetolians won the battle but not the war.

▷ **Philopoemen**
Carved in marble by 19th-century French sculptor David d'Angers, Philopoemen led the Achaean League as *strategos* eight times from 209 BCE.

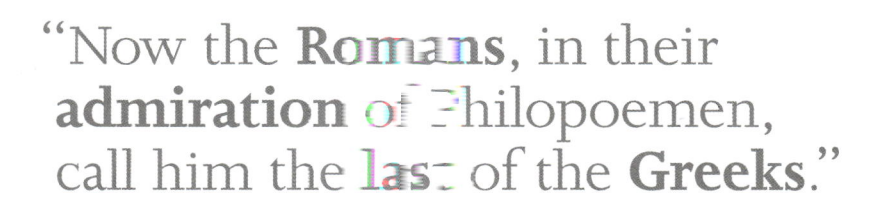

> "Now the **Romans**, in their **admiration** of Philopoemen, call him the **last** of the **Greeks**."

PLUTARCH, *PARALLEL LIVES*

with the Achaeans again relying on Macedonian support to emerge victorious. Having supported Macedonia against Rome and the Aetolian League in the First Macedonian War, the Achaeans switched sides in the Second (see pp.276–277) and allied with Rome. In 188 BCE, with Rome's support, the Achaeans—led by their other great general, Philopoemen—defeated Sparta and took control of the entire Peloponnese.

The end of the leagues

Eventually the leagues' search for outside help proved their undoing. Robbed of its ally the Seleucid Empire by the Treaty of Apamea in 188 BCE, which made Rome the predominant power in Anatolia, the Aetolian League could not withstand Rome, which annexed the League's territory around 146 BCE. Rome's defeat of the Achaean League (see pp.280–281) at the same time brought an end to the political independence of the *poleis*, and there would be no more Greek leagues.

△ **Greece divided**
This map shows the Aetolian and Achaean leagues in the 3rd century BCE, illustrating how much of Greece they controlled between them.

Magic and Witchcraft

Spells and superstition

Magic (*mageia*) was practiced widely at every level of ancient Greek society, sometimes overlapping with more official religious and philosophical beliefs. It continued well into the Roman period in Greece. The original scholars of magic, the *magoi*, were the wise men of Anatolia and Persia, who studied subjects including astrology and alchemy. To many ancient Greeks, however, the *magoi*'s esoteric knowledge seemed alien, even malevolent, despite the fact that the Greeks themselves used magic in their daily lives, for protection and revenge, to overcome obstacles and opponents, or to manage loss and uncertainty.

The practice of magic took various different forms. *Epoidai* (spells), for example, were essentially prayers to the spirits of death and darkness to bring pain or misfortune on enemies. Those who cast spells often inscribed them on stone, metal, or ceramic *katadesmoi* (curse tablets), which were sometimes placed in graves in the hope that the dead would take them with them to the Underworld.

Magic and curses were sometimes activated simply by the act of looking or seeing: for example, by casting a malevolent gaze, the "evil eye," toward a victim. Similarly, the legendary snake-haired Medusa was said to have had the power to turn any man who looked upon her face to stone. The hero Perseus had to use her reflection in a shield to get close enough to kill her. People wore charms and amulets, referred to as *periapta* (literally, things "hung around" the neck or wrist), to repel spells or the evil eye.

△ **The cult of Dionysus, c. 1400 BCE**
Already active in Mycenaean Greece, the cult of Dionysus (above right) was associated with intoxication and riotous behavior, which is said to have had a similar function to the shamanistic practice of trance in other early religious traditions.

△ **Circe in the Odyssey, c. 800 BCE**
The *Odyssey* tells of how Circe (above left), Greek myth's most notorious witch, turned Odysseus's crew into pigs, as well as drugging them with a potion made of barley, cheese, honey, wine, and herbs to make them forget their homes. Odysseus was helped by Hermes, who showed him an herb that would protect him from Circe's spells.

△ **The cult of Hecate, c. 750 BCE**
Goddess of night, the moon, and witchcraft, Hecate faced three ways at once (as shown in this Hellenistic statue). She is first mentioned in Hesiod's *Theogony*, and her cult became well established in Eleusis, Samothrace, and Athens.

"[Circe] added **malignant drugs** to make them **forgetful** of their **own country**."

HOMER, *ODYSSEY*

Magic was deeply embedded in Greek myth and literature. Dionysus, for example, was god of altered states, magic, and mysticism, while the magical powers of the hero Orpheus were linked to music, with which he charmed all creatures. His journey to the Underworld inspired cults of darkness.

Witchcraft and misogyny

Women with magical powers also played key roles in myth, where they were cast as transgressive and fearsome, as in the case of Medusa. Other prominent female figures include Hecate—the goddess of witchcraft, associated with ghosts and malevolent magic—and the mighty witch and sorceress Circe, renowned for her knowledge of potions and herbs,

with which she transformed humans into animals, such as lions and pigs. Similarly, in Euripides' tragedy *Hippolytus*, c. 428 BCE, a nurse claims she can concoct a medicine that will cause Hippolytus to fall in love with Phaedra. Potions that could alter behavior and feelings were known as *philtra*. Numerous other medicines and potions (some benign, others deadly poisons) were categorized as *pharmaka*.

The historical links between women and witchcraft are well documented and have persisted to the present day in many cultures. Modern scholars increasingly views these representations as an effect of deep-rooted misogyny and an attempt to undermine and discredit women who wield power or do not conform to accepted conventions and stereotypes.

△ **Orphic amulet**
Most likely used as a magic charm, this carnelian gem from the 3rd century CE is carved with symbols (bottom) and lines of Greek characters (top) that refer to Orpheus (bottom).

△ **Curse tablet from c. 600 BCE**
While some curse tablets focused on general hostilities, others were specific and were used, for example, to influence the outcome of legal disputes (as above). A few were in *voces magicae* (magical language), which, it was assumed, only the spirits could read.

△ **Medea's evil eye, 3rd century BCE**
In his epic poem, *Argonautica*, the 3rd-century BCE writer Apollonius of Rhodes describes the sorceress Medea subduing a monster by the sheer power of her glare. He was reflecting the belief, widespread across the Mediterranean, in the "evil eye," which could be averted by motifs such as the eyes on this Etruscan pot.

△ **Greco-Roman spells, 2nd century BCE**
Numerous spells, hymns, and rituals were written down in Greco-Roman Egypt from the 2nd century BCE to the 4th century CE. Later collated as "The Greek Magical Papyri" (see detail above), these spells provide evidence for the use of magic in the late Hellenistic period.

DIE AKROPOLI
VON
PERGAMON
RECONSTRUIRT NACH
DEN BISHERIGEN AUSGRABUN
VON F. THIERSCH. FEBR. 1882

Pergamon and Pontus

Hellenistic outposts in Asia Minor

△ **Pergamon's acropolis**
This 1882 painting by German architect Friedrich Thiersch was based on the first published findings from excavations at Pergamon's acropolis, when many details were not yet known.

In the 3rd century BCE, the focus of Greek culture shifted eastward, notably to the powerful realm of Pergamon in western Anatolia and to the kingdom of Pontus on the shores of the Black Sea, in which Greek and Persian cultures merged.

In the chaos that followed the division of Alexander the Great's empire, local leaders took advantage of the lack of a single central authority to carve out two kingdoms. In northwest Anatolia, a former army officer, Philetaerus, established the Attalid dynasty, which ruled Pergamon from 282 BCE to 129 BCE. In 281 BCE, in northeast Anatolia, a Persian nobleman called Mithradates declared himself king of Pontus, a dominion that he had carved out for himself from a base in Paphlagonia,

◁ **Hero of Pergamon**
Attalus I (shown here) took the name Soter, meaning "savior," after the Battle of Caecus River against the Galatians in the 230s BCE.

on the south coast of the Black Sea. He was the first of six kings named Mithradates to rule Pontus. Although their roots lay in different cultures, Philetaerus, Mithradates, and their successors embraced their status as the inheritors of Alexander's empire and kept the flame of "Greekness" alive in Asia Minor, albeit in different ways.

The rise of Pergamon

Philetaerus was serving Lysimachus—who ruled Asia Minor from 306 BCE—as governor of Pergamon when he switched allegiance in 282 BCE. With the help of Seleucus (see pp.246–247), he shook off Lysimachus's control and established himself as Pergamon's ruler, albeit under Seleucid suzerainty. In 262 BCE, Philetaerus's

"Attalus … was **the first** to be proclaimed **king**, after conquering the **Galatians** in a **great battle**."

STRABO, *GEOGRAPHIES*

successor, his nephew Eumenes I, revolted against the Seleucid king Antiochus I to secure Pergamon's independence. Eumenes' successor, Attalus I (r. 241–197 BCE), then proclaimed himself *basileus* (king) after defeating the neighboring Celtic settlers in Anatolia, the Galatians, and consolidating Pergamon's territories through a mixture of war and negotiation with the Seleucids.

Attalus also strengthened his ties with Athens, and financed several forts in Aetolia, securing its friendship. This drew Pergamon into an alliance with Rome and the Aetolian League during the First Macedonian War. Attalus's successor, Eumenes II (r. 197–159 BCE), maintained Pergamon's alliance with Rome in Rome's subsequent wars with Macedonia and the Seleucid Empire (see p.276–277). Rome rewarded Pergamon for its loyalty with land, and by the early 2nd century BCE, Pergamon's territory extended over much of what is now central Türkiye.

Throughout the kingdom's history, Pergamon's rulers maintained their cultural connections with the Greek cities to the west, frequently sending gifts to

△ **Royal tombs**
The ancient tombs carved out of the rock at Amasya, in northern Türkiye, were the burial places of Pontus's royals, including Mithradates I.

Delphi and Athens. They brought something of Athens to their capital city, also called Pergamon, built on a massif above the Caicus Plain. They enriched it with magnificent buildings and artwork, including the Pergamon altar (see pp.262–263), a royal palace (Palace V) filled with extraordinary mosaics, and libraries that turned Pergamon into an intellectual center second only to Alexandria (see pp.242–243).

A Greco-Persian kingdom

The kingdom of Pontus always served as a cultural bridge linking different traditions. Its rulers chose Persian names for their sons, and followed Persian tradition in maintaining harems and eunuchs. Yet it was home to several cities that had been Greek colonies since the 8th century BCE. From the 3rd century BCE onward, its official language was Greek, and in religious affairs, it coupled veneration of the Greek gods with elements of Persian and local Anatolian religion.

Pontus survived through the usual mix of dynastic alliances (particularly with the Seleucids), diplomacy, and conflict. For example, it was rewarded with Phrygia after helping Rome against Carthage in 149–146 BCE, and against Aristonicus, who claimed to be king of Pergamon, in 133–129 BCE. However, the kingdom only really thrived under Mithradates VI (see p.283), who extended his control eastward around the Black Sea coast to the Crimean peninsula, and into Cappadocia. His 25-year struggle (88–63 BCE) to break Roman domination over Asia Minor and the Hellenistic kingdoms was the work of a man determined to reclaim the empire of Alexander. His attempt failed, and Pontus was split in two in 63 BCE; the western half was incorporated into the Roman Empire; the eastern half became a client kingdom of Rome.

▽ **Pergamon mosaic**
This mid-2nd-century BCE mosaic, which includes birds and other motifs, was part of a floor found in the "altar room" at Palace V on Pergamon's acropolis.

Hellenistic battle scene

Shown here is a detail from the east section of the Gigantomachy frieze on the Pergamon Altar, in Asia Minor. Built for Attalid ruler Eumenes II Soter in the early 2nd century BCE at the city's acropolis, the altar was huge, measuring around 118 ft (36 m) by 108 ft (33 m). The east frieze showcases the Hellenistic Baroque style of the time, characterized by contorted body poses and intense facial expressions. Here, Athena, the city goddess of Pergamon, grasps the Giant Alcyoneus by the hair while his mother, Gaia, rises from the ground to help him and Nike waits to crown the victor. The Turkish government has asked the Pergamon Museum in Berlin to return the altar.

A drill has been used to achieve depth in Laocoön's hair and beard, producing effects difficult to obtain with a chisel

◁ **Pergamene Baroque**
This near life-sized sculpture depicts the Trojan priest of Neptune, Laocoön, and his sons, Antiphantes and Thymbraeus, in a fatal struggle with the sea serpents of Athena immediately before the sack of Troy. It is probably a Roman copy of a Hellenistic bronze.

The son on the left seems to have abandoned hope and looks up in anguish at his father

The serpents do their deadly business through biting as well as crushing. One is about to sink its fangs into Laocoön's side

This figure appears to have almost broken free from the serpent's coils, but both sons died according to the myth

Hellenistic Art

Diversity, drama, and realism

In the new cultural milieu that had arisen in the wake of Alexander's conquest of Asia, Hellenistic art took inspiration from, and appealed to, a multicultural market that was highly receptive to a fusion of the novel and the familiar.

As new Hellenistic kingdoms emerged after Alexander's death, a process of hybridization spread Greek culture across his former empire. This exposed the artists of these kingdoms to a host of new influences that began to change what it meant to be Greek, and how that identity was reflected in art.

In pottery production, as the manufacture of red-figure pottery declined, potters and painters in regional centers embraced both the simple and the complex. For example, the relatively simple designs of Athenian West Slope ware contrast with the realism of styles such as Gnathian ware, which incorporates an increased use of color, shade, and highlight over black glaze. As a Persian-inspired fashion for affluence and luxury (*tryphe*) took hold, mold-made pottery also became popular, offering relief decoration that imitated that of more expensive metal vessels. Though rare, metal vessels such as those of the richly decorated Panagyurishte Treasure from late 4th–3rd-century BCE Thrace can also be seen to embody the hybrid nature of many items from the time, incorporating Persian, Greek, and Thracian artistic influences, and perhaps manufactured in Anatolia.

Technique and realism

Glassware, though manufactured during the Classical period, experienced a dramatic increase in popularity and a development of form and technique following eastern inspiration. Advances included the use of polychromy (many colors), and the creation of so-called sandwich-gold glass, perhaps at Alexandria, which incorporated motifs of gold leaf between glass layers. Specialized workshops, many in the Eastern Mediterranean, manufactured complete dining sets in glass, which were popular with elites at sites such as Canosa in Italy. Jewelery and personal adornment also embraced eastern fashions and motifs (see p.278)

◁ **Goat rhyton**
This gold drinking cup from the treasure found at Panagyurishte in Bulgaria in 1949 dates to around 300 BCE and reflects Persian, Greek, and Anatolian influences. It may have been a diplomatic gift to a local Thracian ruler.

and made use of the wealth of new materials circulating throughout the Hellenistic kingdoms.

In sculpture, the period witnessed an important shift from naturalism, which adopted a conventional approach to elements such as hair, musculature, and eyes to present an idealized Greekness, to realism, which sought instead to faithfully depict individual traits or personal quirks. For example, Polyeuktos's statue from c. 280 BCE, of the middle-aged Athenian statesman Demosthenes captured in the moment before he commences an address, depicts a powerful blend of intellectual intensity and facial and corporeal realism. The Baroque style, which was exemplified by works such as the *Laocoön Group* (see opposite) and the Pergamon Altar (see pp.262–263), was designed to evoke a "swaying of the soul" (psychagogia), and incorporated a dramatic intensity of expression and dynamism of pose.

Women in the eastern kingdoms enjoyed greater public freedom than those in Greece itself, and there was no cultural taboo against the naked female form. This influence prompted the appearance of the first Greek life-sized female nudes, of which the earliest was Praxiteles' statue of Aphrodite. Others soon followed, including the Aphrodite of Melos (or Venus de Milo).

△ **Aphrodite**
This is a Roman copy of Praxiteles' lost late-4th-century BCE *Aphrodite* (known as the Aphrodite of Cnidus). The original statue was rejected by the scandalized people of Cos in favor of a clothed version.

▽ **Equestrian drama**
Recovered in pieces from the sea near Cape Artemision, this bronze statue of a horse and young jockey captures a moment of drama as the horse leaps forward, ears back, tail flying out behind.

> "**Lifting** their **mighty hands** on high one against the other, [**they**] **fell to**, and their hands **clashed together** in **heavy blows**."

DESCRIPTION OF THE BOXING MATCH AT PATROCLUS'S FUNERAL GAMES, HOMER'S *ILIAD*

Boxer at Rest

Blood and bruises in a Hellenistic bronze

A highly evocative bronze statue, the *Boxer at Rest* dates from the Hellenistic period, that is, sometime between 323 and 31 BCE. The statue was found in 1885 during excavations near the Baths of Constantine on the Quirinal Hill in Rome, where it may have been displayed. The statue may have survived as the result of being deliberately buried, perhaps to save it from the Germanic invasions of the 5th century CE, thus protecting its precious metal from being melted down and reused.

Visceral drama

Cast in several sections, which were then joined together, the bronze statue is a great technical achievement. It is approximately life-size, allowing every detail to be seen, from the tendons and muscles that are depicted beneath the surface of the skin to the blood, scars, and bruises that mark it.

Powerful shoulders bent forward, forearms resting lightly on his legs, the boxer raises his head to the right, perhaps looking at his adversary. The ordered curls of his hair and beard are at odds with his battered appearance—a bashed and swollen face, misshapen ear, and broken nose—while his strongly muscled body rests for a moment. Inlaid copper, with a reddish sheen, is used to highlight wounds to his forehead and cheeks, and spatters his gloves, legs, and shoulders. His sunken lips suggest damage to his teeth. This gritty realism adds to the statue's drama. However, it offers more than just a study of the human physique, vividly depicting the boxer's emotions as well as the impact of the fight. It evokes a sense of weariness and suffering, but also determination: the tension shown in his muscles suggests the boxer is ready to fight again.

Boxing was an important albeit brutal sport in the ancient Greek world. Unlike in modern boxing, two combatants would have exchanged blows to the head without a time limit, ending only when one of them could no longer go on; the victor would then face another opponent. The statue wears key elements of a boxer's equipment: protective forearm bindings, gloves, and a *kynodèsme* (a type of athletic support designed for modesty).

Whether it was made to commemorate a famous boxer or to evoke the human cost of boxing, the statue is a complex and moving example of the sculptor's art.

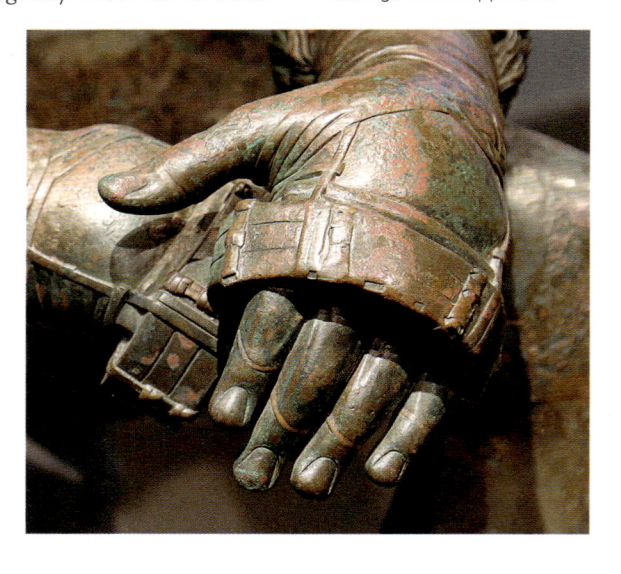

▽ **Boxing gloves**
The boxer's gloves would have been made with wool padding and strips of hard leather to protect his hands and allow him to inflict more damage on his opponent.

A different alloy is used to create a bruised color under his right eye

Misshapen "cauliflower" ear—a common condition among boxers

Cast bronze captures the fine detail of the musculature

The bones of and around the knee are shown in detail

△ **Front view**
Leaning forward, the boxer looks very lifelike. He radiates power, from his broad feet through his large hands to his well-muscled shoulders.

◁ **Turning to talk**
Naked but for his boxing gloves and *kynodèsme*, the boxer sits with his head turned to the right as if he is looking at someone, perhaps his opponent or trainer, standing nearby.

TETRAHEDRON (FIRE)   **CUBE (EARTH)**   **OCTAHEDRON (AIR)**

Greek Mathematics

The development of a discipline

The mathematicians of ancient Greece played an important part in the early history of mathematics, elevating it from its utilitarian role in engineering, astronomy, and commerce, and eventually establishing it as a distinct subject.

It is a common misconception that the ancient Greeks somehow "invented" mathematics. The Babylonian and Egyptian civilizations had used mathematical operations in arithmetic, algebra, and geometry for financial and commercial calculations, building and construction, and astronomy since around 3000 BCE. However, the Greeks did develop mathematics as a subject in its own right, subjecting it to more rigorous analytical reasoning. This process accompanied the development of philosophy in Ionia (see pp.96–97) in the 6th century BCE. Thales of Miletus, the earliest-known philosopher, was also a very accomplished mathematician, having probably learned the subject in Egypt. He stressed that both reason and observation, rather than just observation alone, were important, and applied this approach to mathematics, suggesting

elementary theorems in geometry and introducing the notion of deductive proof. Mathematics, for Thales, was not just practical, but was an integral part of an understanding of the world based on rational thought.

That connection with philosophy continued to be a characteristic of Greek mathematics, most notably in the work of Pythagoras (see p.115), who found a philosophical significance in mathematical relationships, linking geometry and number with the movements of the heavenly bodies, music, and

▷ **Portrait of Euclid**
Euclid is shown holding a pair of compasses, an important mathematical instrument, in this 16th-century portrait by Italian artist Girolamo Mocetto.

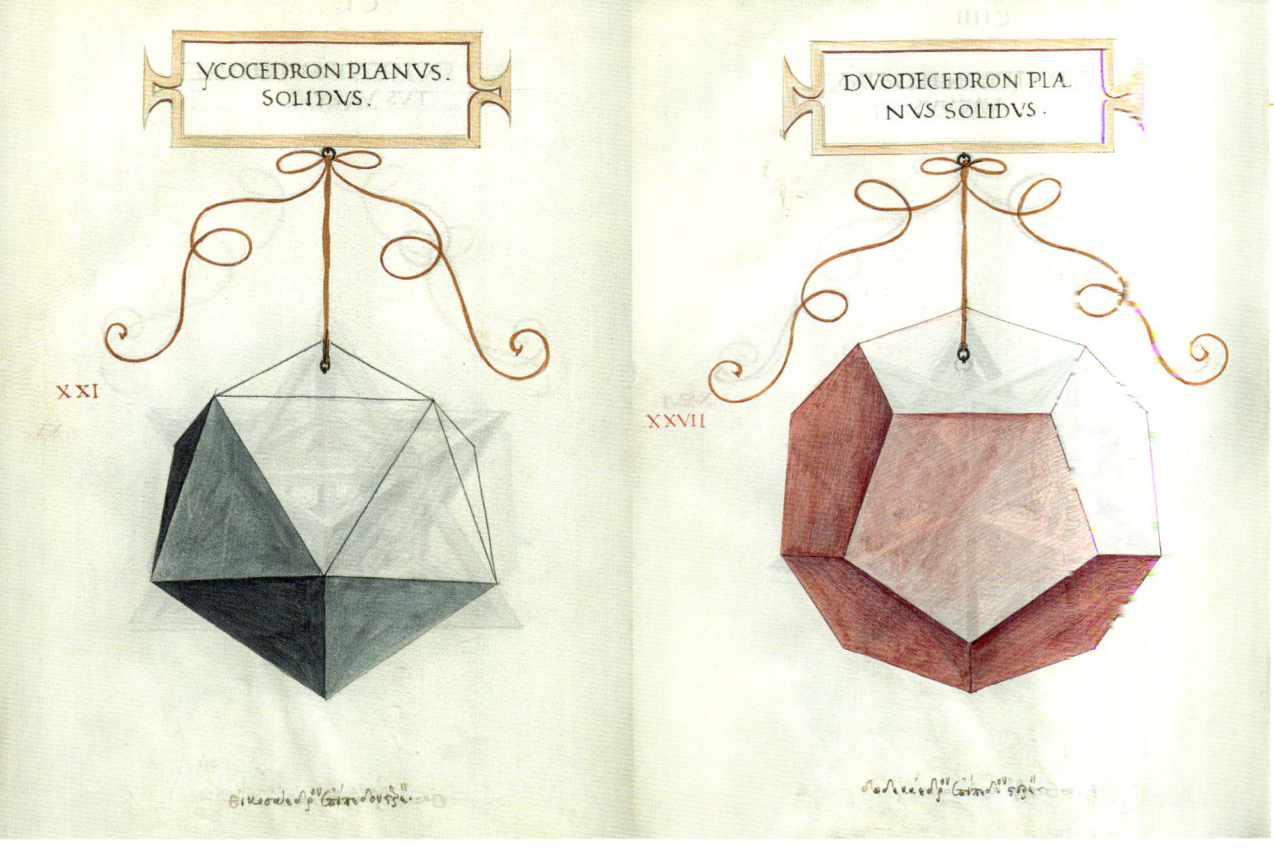

YCOCEDRON PLANVS. SOLIDVS.

XXI

DVODECEDRON PLANVS SOLIDVS·

XXVII

DODECAHEDRON (ETHER)

ICOSAHEDRON (WATER)

◁ **Platonic solids**
The influence of Plato was still strong in the 15th century, when Italian artist Leonardo da Vinci made these drawings of the Platonic solids, which were five highly regular three-dimensional shapes with identical faces, edges, and angles. Plato believed that each shape represented an element of the universe.

▽ **Alexandrian maths**
Shown here is a page from a 10th-century manuscript of the 4th-century CE Greek mathematician Pappus of Alexandria's commentary on the *Almagest*, a treatise on astronomy by Alexandrian mathematician Claudius Ptolemy (c. 100–170 CE).

even the immortality of the soul. Despite this apparent mysticism, Pythagoras advocated a rational approach to the study of mathematics, inspiring followers at his school in Croton, including Hippasus (c. 530–450 BCE) and Philolaus (c. 470–385 BCE).

The Athenian philosophers Plato and Aristotle took up Pythagoras's idea of finding truth through mathematics. In his *Dialogues*, Plato frequently made reference to mathematics to illustrate a philosophical point and considered certain geometric solids (three-dimensional shapes) to represent the elements and the model for the cosmos. Aristotle used mathematics in his explanations of both natural phenomena and concepts of morality.

Beyond philosophy

Greek mathematics came of age in the Hellenistic period, as it became more separated from its philosophical roots and developed as a distinct discipline. However, it did maintain its connection with astronomy in the work of Eratosthenes (c. 276–194 BCE), Apollonius (c. 240–190 BCE), Hipparchus (c. 190–120 BCE), and Ptolemy (c. 100–170 CE).

The first, and undoubtedly the most influential, of the great Hellenistic mathematicians was Euclid, whose *Elements* established the foundations of geometry and remained a standard text on the subject until the 19th century. In it, Euclid set out his method of deductive reasoning, progressing from a set of postulates, or axioms, to the proof of a theorem,

stressing the importance of mathematical rigor and giving numerous proofs as examples. Euclid is said to have inspired Egypt's ruler Ptolemy I Soter to found the Library of Alexandria, which under his successor, Ptolemy II Philadelphus became the major center for mathematical scholarship. Among those attracted to Alexandria was Archimedes (see p.271), who kept up a lengthy correspondence with the scholars at the library from his base in Syracuse. His numerous contributions to mathematics included work that anticipated the notion of calculus, the calculation of pi, and several geometric theorems.

Greek mathematicians of the Roman imperial period, such as Pappus (c. 290–350 CE), Theon (c. 335–405), and Hypatia (see p.299), tended to be less original than previous generations, producing mainly commentaries on earlier works. Diophantus, in the 3rd century, was the exception, demonstrating the use of algebraic equations, and becoming the first person to use a symbol for an unknown quantity.

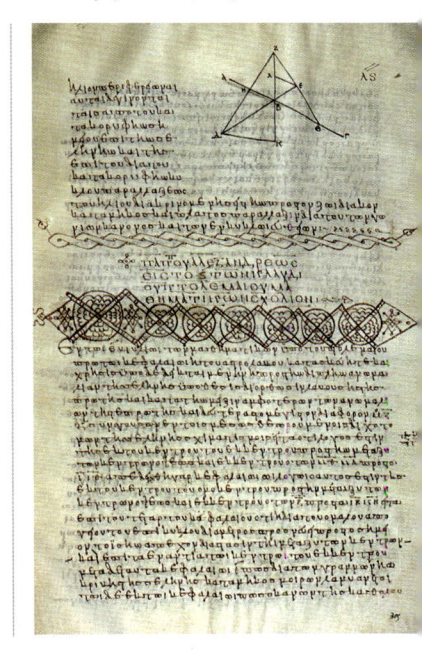

> "**Number** is the **ruler** of **forms** and **ideas**, and the **cause** of **gods** and **daemons**."

PYTHAGORAS, QUOTED BY IAMBLICHUS, *LIFE OF PYTHAGORAS*

Archimedes

Greece's greatest scientific thinker

With insights and discoveries often centuries ahead of his time, Archimedes developed a deep understanding of the principles of mathematics and physics that he put into practice in numerous engineering projects.

Archimedes was born in the Greek colony of Syracuse, Sicily, in around 287 BCE. His father, Phidias, was an astronomer and possibly related to Hiero II, ruler of Syracuse from 275 BCE. It is likely that the young Archimedes spent time studying in the North African city of Alexandria. While there, he befriended the astronomer and mathematician Conon of Samos—with whom he conducted a lifelong correspondence after his return to Syracuse—and the librarian Eratosthenes. Beyond that, little is known with certainty about his life, although anecdotes from later writers give some insight into the man and his achievements.

Inventions and discoveries

In Syracuse, Archimedes was probably employed by Hiero as an advisor and was well known for his skill as an engineer. There, he developed practical applications for devices such as levers, compound pulleys, and the screw pump (see p.272). He is regarded as the preeminent scientist of antiquity for his perceptive and innovative work in physics and mathematics, understood by only a few at the time. Among his writings are rigorous proofs of numerous geometric theorems and treatises on the principles of the lever and buoyancy, and on the more abstract ideas of pure mathematics, including calculus. Archimedes is perhaps most famous for his discovery that the volume of an object could be measured by the

◁ **The Fields Medal**
Awarded for mathematics, this medal depicts Archimedes; the words mean "To transcend one's human limitations and master the universe."

amount of water it displaced. The Roman author Vitruvius tells of how Archimedes made the discovery in his bath and ran naked into the street shouting "Eureka!" ("I've found it!").

During the Second Punic War (218–201 BCE), when the Romans laid siege to Syracuse, Archimedes' inventions—among them an array of mirrors to focus the sun's rays onto incoming ships and the Archimedes claw to sink them—helped hold off the invasion for several months. When the Romans eventually took the city, they were given instructions to spare the life of Archimedes. However, a Roman soldier found Archimedes engrossed in his work and not wanting to be disturbed. Either for frustration at being made to wait or in revenge for Roman deaths, the soldier killed him on the spot.

△ **Archimedes found**
The *Archimedes Palimpsest* is a Byzantine prayer book found to have been written using parchment from two of Archimedes' lost works: *Method of Mechanical Theorems* and *Ostomachion*.

> "Give me but **one firm spot** on which to **stand**, and I will **move** the **Earth**."

ARCHIMEDES, QUOTED IN PAPPUS OF ALEXANDRIA'S *SYNAGOGE*

c.**287** BCE Archimedes is born in Syracuse, Sicily

c.**262–240** BCE Hiero II employs Archimedes as an advisor

c.**240** BCE Designs a massive cargo ship, *Syracusia*, using his principle of buoyancy

213 BCE Archimedes' war machines help defend Syracuse during the Roman siege

c.**267–262** BCE Travels to Alexandria to study astronomy and mathematics

c.**262–240** BCE Correspondence with scholars at Alexandria brings Archimedes wider recognition

215 BCE Syracuse's alliance with Rome collapses after the death of Hiero II

c.**212** BCE Archimedes dies at the hands of a Roman soldier

Technology
Progress and invention

Driven by necessity in the Classical period, technical innovation stepped up a gear in the 3rd century BCE, as Greek thinkers began turning theory into practice, using their mathematical and engineering knowledge for novel inventions.

Although they were skilled in construction and military technology, the ancient Greeks were not generally known for their innovation. Life in the *poleis* in the Classical period was comfortable, and the Greeks felt no pressing need for new technology. Instead, engineers of the period focused on perfecting existing technology: increasing the efficiency of construction and the aesthetic appeal of their buildings, improving metalworking methods to provide better military hardware, and making some advances in boat-building (see pp.132–133). The most important technological advances were often to do with water. To supply water to the *poleis*, engineers built watercourses using aqueducts and tunnels, such as Eupalinos's on Samos, and developed sophisticated plumbing systems.

The Hellenistic revolution and beyond

With the advent of the Hellenistic period, there was a change in attitudes toward technological progress. In Syracuse, Archimedes (see p.271) continued the practice of improving existing technology with, for example, the "Archimedes screw," a pipe fitted with a screw surface inside that could lift water. However, in addition, his explanations of the physical and mathematical principles behind devices such as pulleys and levers opened the way for their use in more complex machines, and inspired the idea of seeking practical applications for theoretical principles.

The most striking advances of the period were made in Alexandria from the 3rd century BCE. In his nine-volume *Mechanike syntaxis* (*Compendium of Mechanics*), Philo, nicknamed Mechanicus (the Engineer), describes several ingenious devices, including a gimbal for a non-spill ink well

△ **Eupalinos's tunnel**
Built by Eupalinos in the 6th century BCE, this 0.6-mile- (1-km-) long aqueduct carried water through Mount Kasto to the capital city of Samos for many centuries.

and an early version of a thermometer. Although these may or may not have been his own inventions, Philo gave the first detailed description of the mechanisms. Philo's contemporary Ctesibius of Alexandria wrote an influential treatise that detailed his discoveries in the science of compressed air, and also wrote descriptions of inventions based on his experiments. Among these were the hydraulis, an organ played by compressed air blown through pipes; and a water-powered clock (a clepsydra) with an alarm function that was capable of sounding a gong or blowing air through a horn at a preset time.

The Hellenistic spirit of invention endured into Roman times with Heron of Alexandria (c. 60 CE), credited with inventing a coin-operated vending machine, a wind-powered organ, and a rudimentary steam turbine, the aeolipile. However, perhaps the most impressive of all ancient Greek inventions dates back to the 2nd or 1st centuries BCE. The Antikythera mechanism, a complex system of gears housed in a wooden case, was a calculating device specifically for determining astronomical events, and has been described as an early analog computer.

▽ **Ancient calculator**
This rather unsightly piece of metal is one of more than 80 fragments of the Antikythera mechanism, discovered in the sea off the island of Antikythera in 1901. Modern scientists have scanned the pieces, using its inscriptions to help reconstruct it and understand its function.

Upper bronze container supplied with water from a spring

Spigot controls the flow to the smaller container below

Small figure of a man pointing to the time

Rotating drum marked with the hours of day and night

Bronze container in which the pointer floated, rising as the water rose

△ **Hydraulic clock**
The artist of this engraving from a 17th-century French edition of The Ten Books of Vitruvian Architecture, edited by architect Claude Perrault, visualizes what Ctesibius's clepsydra may have looked like.

"The mechanicians of **Heron's school** say that **mechanics** can be divided into a **theoretical** and a **manual part.**"

PAPPUS, *MATHEMATICAL COLLECTION*

◁ **Ctesibius's clepsydra**
Shown here is a reconstruction of Ctesibius's water clock. A marvel of automation, the clock could continuously operate without human intervention and remained the most accurate means for telling the time until mechanical clocks replaced hydraulic clocks in the 14th century.

Music

The sounds of Greek society

Ancient Greek music played an important role as entertainment and in poetry, drama, and religious ceremonies. While few examples of it remain, knowledge of the instruments played provides some insight into the sounds of ancient Greece.

△ **Kithara and song**
A young man sings and plays the kithara on this amphora from c. 490 BCE. The swaying cloth suggests that he is moving along to the music.

Associated with the Muses, who sang, danced, and played music for the gods' amusement, music had a revered status in ancient Greek society. Playing a role in religious ceremonies and rites of passage, it was also considered an essential subject in Classical Greek education. By the 6th century BCE, the Greeks had developed a sophisticated system of musical notation that used a combination of letter names and symbols, but only fragments of this have survived.

Likewise, very few of the instruments played in ancient Greece have survived intact, but from written descriptions and paintings, we know that there was a variety of stringed, wind, and percussion instruments.

Making music
The stringed instruments were designed to be strummed or plucked, not bowed, and almost invariably acted as accompanying instruments to singing or recitation. The most common of these was the lyre. Originally a folk instrument, it consisted of a number of stretched strings attached to a sound box, which was traditionally fashioned from a tortoise shell (see p.99). The lyre was considered to be a beginner's instrument. The kithara was a more sophisticated stringed instrument played by more experienced musicians, as was the barbiton, a bass instrument.

◁ **The Song of Seikilos**
Inscribed with a poem and signs representing the pitches of the accompanying melody, this 2nd-century CE column is the oldest example of musical notation.

There were also various kinds of harp, based on Egyptian models, and occasionally a lute-like instrument called the pandura, with three strings stretched along a fretted neck attached to a sound box, was played.

Of the wind instruments, the aulos and syrinx were among the most common. The aulos was a reeded instrument similar to a modern oboe. It was generally, but not always, built as a double instrument, with two pipes played simultaneously to create a rich, and often eerie, mix of sounds. The syrinx, or panpipes, consisted of a series of hollow tubes bound together in a row, which the player blew across. The most complex instrument was the hydraulis, a sort of pipe organ invented by Ctesibius of Alexandria in the 3rd century BCE. Its sound was produced by compressed air blown through the pipes from a reservoir of air in a cistern of water. Whether played together or apart, these instruments contributed much to the cultural life of ancient Greece.

▷ **Musical challenge**
Apollo (left) and the satyr Marsyas (right) compete in a musical contest in this 4th-century BCE marble relief. In the myth, Marsyas lost and was tied to a tree and flayed.

"Let me **not live** without **music**!"

EURIPIDES, *HERACLES MAINOMENOS*

▽ **An aulos player**
Carved on a large block of marble
known as the Ludovisi Throne, from
Locri in southern Italy, this relief of
a musician playing a double aulos
is thought to have been created
around 460 BCE, although it may
date to much later.

The right-hand
and left-hand pipes
were tuned slightly
differently from each
other to provide a
larger range of notes

Single mouthpiece for the
two pipes; many auloi had
mouthpieces for each pipe

Left-hand pipe with four
or five holes; single auloi
could have many more

Greece under Threat

The Macedonian and Seleucid wars

As the 3rd century BCE drew to a close, Macedonia and the Seleucid Empire were drawn into a series of wars with Rome that spanned more than 60 years and ended with Macedonia and a large part of Asia Minor under Roman control.

The Macedonian Wars began in 215 BCE with Philip V of Macedonia invading Roman territory, and ended with his son, Perseus, losing Macedonia to Rome. Amid its three main wars with Macedonia—in 215–205 BCE, 200–197 BCE, and 171–168 BCE—Rome also went to war with the Seleucids (192–188 BCE), forcing them to eventually cede control of western Asia Minor to Rome's allies.

In 217 BCE, a conference was held at Naupactus (now Lepanto), in western Greece, to try to bring an end to the wars that were continuing to blight Greece in the second half of the 3rd century BCE. Agelaus, a leading official in the Aetolian League (see p.256), pointed to the threat presented by the Second Punic War (218–201 BCE) between Rome and Carthage as a reason for the Greek states to draw closer together. However, the young king of Macedonia, Philip V, viewed things differently, seeing instead a chance to expand Macedonian authority into both Roman-controlled areas and Greece. Believing that Rome was doomed after the Carthaginian victory at the Battle of Cannae in 216 BCE, the following year Philip invaded Rome's client states in Illyria, on Macedonia's northwest border. He also agreed to support the Carthaginian leader Hannibal in Italy, if Hannibal would support him in subjugating Greece.

Rome fights back

In 214 BCE, Rome responded to the provocation in Illyria, sending an expedition across the Adriatic to keep Philip occupied and prevent Macedonia sending help to Hannibal. Rome also encouraged its Greek allies—the Aetolian League and the kingdom of Pergamon—to engage Macedonia and its ally, the Achaean League. However, Philip inflicted heavy losses on the Aetolian forces at Lamia and ravaged their base in Elis in 209 BCE. When Attalus I returned with his forces to Pergamon, which was under threat from the Bithynians, the Aetolians made peace. In 205 BCE, Rome and Macedonia called an uneasy truce.

Philip turned his attention to Egypt, which had been in a state of civil war since it was left in the hands of the child king Ptolemy V in 204 BCE. In 202 BCE, Philip

▷ **Philip V**
This 3rd-century BCE bronze head of a man wearing a *kausia*, a hat worn only by Macedonian royalty, is believed to represent King Philip V.

> **"A mighty cloud** from the west … will **overshadow Macedonia** first."
>
> ACARNANIAN DIPLOMAT LYCISCUS, IN POLYBIUS, *HISTORIES*

◁ **Macedonia humbled**
The Macedonian king Perseus is shown kneeling before the Roman general Aemilius Paulus, who conquered Macedonia in the Third Macedonian War, in this 19th-century painting by French artist Jean-François-Pierre Peyron.

and the Seleucid king, Antiochus III, agreed to divide Egypt's possessions between them. Antiochus moved into southern Syria, while Philip besieged Samos and captured Miletus, both of which had been under Egyptian control. The combined fleet of Rhodes, Pergamon, Byzantium, and Cyzicus defeated the Macedonian fleet at the Battle of Chios in 201 BCE, but the allies were unable to hold Philip in check in Asia Minor and called on Rome for help.

Rome takes control

After three years of campaigning across Greece, the Aegean, and Asia Minor, a Roman force led by Titus Quinctius Flamininus finally defeated the Macedonians at the Battle of Cynoscephalae, in Thessaly, in 197 BCE. By the terms of the peace, Philip had to give up most of his navy and all of his territories outside Macedonia.

With Philip contained in Macedonia, the way was clear for the Seleucid Empire to expand. Antiochus had already restored Seleucid authority over the east, won Syria from Egypt, and regained control over western Asia Minor. The prospect of the Seleucid Empire expanding into the Eastern Mediterranean worried Rome. When Antiochus sent a small force to support the Aetolian League in its attempt to break free of Roman influence, Rome's reaction was swift. It sent the Roman general Scipio Africanus to lead a Greco-Roman army against Antiochus. The Romans defeated his forces at Thermopylae in 191 BCE, and destroyed his fleet at Mysonessus in 190 BCE. At the end of the year, a Roman force, supported by soldiers from Pergamon, routed Antiochus's army at Magnesia. In the subsequent Treaty of Apamea (188 BCE), the

Seleucid Empire was made to abandon Europe and give up its territories in Asia Minor west of the Taurus Mountains. These were then divided between Pergamon and Rhodes.

In Macedonia, Philip V's death in 179 BCE brought his son Perseus to the throne. Resolved to succeed where his father had failed, Perseus invaded Thessaly in 171 BCE, triggering the Third Macedonian War. That year, the Macedonians defeated the Romans at the Battle of Callinicus. Over the next two years, the Romans campaigned across Thessaly and Illyria, securing a decisive victory against Perseus at Pydna in 168 BCE. Perseus was taken in chains to Rome, and Macedonia was split into four republics known as *merides*, with capitals at Pelagonia, Pella, Amphipolis, and Thessalonica. These rebelled in 150–145 BCE, prompting Rome to take total control and turn Macedonia into a Roman province.

△ **Roman general**
This gold stater was issued in 196 BCE in the name of Titus Quinctius Flamininus, the general who began Rome's conquest of Greece.

THE **PHALANX FAILS**

Philip V's disastrous defeat at Cynoscephalae highlighted the weakness of Macedonia's phalanxes. The phalanxes (see right) were hard to break, but also unwieldy and slow. They were unsuited both to the hilly, broken ground of the battlefield at Cynoscephalae and to the more nimble Roman forces. These were divided into maniples (handfuls) of 100–120 men, loosely grouped at the front to serve as skirmishers, and more tightly packed behind for solidity. Once engaged, the inflexible phalanxes proved an easy target.

Jewelery

Beauty and artistry

Ancient Greek jewelery was crafted from gold, silver, gemstones, and other materials, using a range of techniques. It often featured intricate designs—inspired by nature, mythology, and cultural connections, with motifs including plants, animals, and deities—that reflected a wealth of knowledge and skill.

Male triton holding a winged Eros

Female triton

Snake scales chased into the gold

△ **Gold armbands**
Beautiful and practical, these heavy gold armbands from c. 200 BCE could be clipped to clothing to hold them in place using the hoops behind the figures' heads.

Carnelian stone with intaglio carving of Cassandra

Female figurines hang among the pendants

▽ **Minoan bracelet**
Gold, lapis lazuli, and carnelian beads in the shape of a right hand holding a woman's breast form this bracelet from 1700–1500 BCE. It is unclear if it is meant to be erotic or maternal.

Carved carnelian bead

△ **Trojan heroine**
This oval gem from the late 1st century BCE depicts the Trojan priestess and daughter of King Priam, Cassandra, fated to utter true prophecies that were never believed.

△ **Elaborate earrings**
Tiny figures of Nike (the personification of victory) driving two horses nestle amid the floral elements above the boat-shaped forms on these gold earrings from c. 300 BCE.

Gold wire stems attach the leaves and acorns to the branch

A large seedpod embellishes the necklace's chain

Atef crown set with stones and glass

Oak leaves cut from delicate sheets of gold

△ **Fertility necklace**
Seedpods, such as those shown as pendants on this 4th-century BCE gold necklace from Italy, were linked to the goddess Demeter and represented fertility.

△ **Egyptian fashion**
Egyptian motifs were popular in Greece in the Ptolemaic period. Made in the 3rd–2nd century BCE, these earrings feature the Atef crown of Osiris.

△ **Gold oak wreath**
Oak was a symbol of Zeus and represented wisdom. Gold wreaths like this example from the 4th century BCE were too fragile to wear except on special occasions, but could adorn tombs or be dedicated to gods.

The net is made with gold spool beads linked by filigree chains

△ Hellenistic hairnet
This gold hairnet was likely made in Alexandria around 225–175 BCE. The central bust of Aphrodite has a hairstyle and the features seen in depictions of the Ptolemaic queen Arsinoe.

Relief bust of Aphrodite with her son Eros on her left shoulder

▽ Minoan necklace
Twenty-six gold beads, which have small collars at each end, adorn this necklace created in 1700–1500 BCE in Crete and found in Aegina. At the clasp are six round gold beads.

One of 25 gold ovoid pendants that hang from small chains between each bead

Gold granulation on the cabochon garnet's setting

A tassel made from garnets, gold beads, and a type of cable chain

△ Lucky charm
At the center of this gold armband from the 3rd–2nd century BCE is a Heracles knot design, inlaid with garnets, emeralds, and enamel. The knot was said to cure wounds, and may have been thought to have the power to avert the evil eye.

Small traces of the enamel that once decorated the band

Cabochon emerald, cut and polished but not faceted

△ Egyptian gem
Emeralds, such as the one in this ring from 330–300 BCE, most often came from Egypt. From c. 500 BCE, the stones were mined at Sikait in the Eastern Desert.

△ Amphora earrings
Decorative symbols of wealth, the amphorae on this pair of earrings from the 2nd century BCE are made with twisted gold wire and cabochon (shaped and polished) garnets.

Empty eye socket that probably once held a gem

▽ Bi-metal bracelet
Made in the 5th–4th centuries BCE, this silver torque bangle has gold finials in the shape of lions' heads. Bone finds show that lions once roamed Greece, perhaps into the 5th century BCE.

The Roman Conquest

Greece overcome

The final subjugation of the Greek city-states and the Hellenistic kingdoms in Asia as independent political powers was a gradual process, stretching over many decades from the 2nd century BCE to near the end of the 1st century BCE.

By the start of the 2nd century BCE, the Greek heartland was diminished culturally and politically. The spread of Hellenistic civilization in the wake of Alexander the Great's conquests had created new centers in distant lands: Alexandria in Egypt and Antioch in Syria. Fresh powers—notably Macedonia—threatened central Greece's borders, giving added importance to the two major leagues, Aetolian and Achaean (see pp.256–257), into which many city-states had banded to seek protection in numbers. Yet the struggle for power within Greece itself continued unchecked, and by calling on Rome to intervene in this struggle, the Greeks opened the door to conquest.

In 200 BCE, the Achaeans and Aetolians had come together to seek Rome's support against Philip V of Macedonia, and had benefited from his defeat in the Second Macedonian War (see pp.276–277). At the war's end in 197 BCE, the Roman general Flaminius was invited to the Panhellenic Isthmian Games. There, according to the historian Appian, he proclaimed that, spared from Macedonian hegemony, "Greece shall be free from foreign garrisons, not subject to tribute, and shall live under her own customs and laws."

A slippery slope

The harmony did not last long. Roman forces played a crucial part in the final destruction of Sparta, whose last independent king, Nabis, was assassinated in 192 BCE. In the same year, the Aetolian League tried to eradicate Rome's abiding influence by allying itself with the Seleucid ruler Antiochus III in the Roman–Seleucid War. The result was a total defeat that saw the league's territory reduced to the status of a client state, committed to maintaining "the empire and majesty of the people of Rome."

The rival Achaeans temporarily benefited by adopting a less hostile attitude to Rome, seen as a potential counterweight to the more immediate threat from Macedonia. But as the Macedonian threat receded and Rome's influence continued to grow, the Achaeans' loyalties began to waver. On the outbreak of the Third Macedonian War in 171 BCE, one faction supported Macedonia against Rome, with the result that, after the war ended in total Macedonian defeat, 1,000 people accused of pro-Macedonian sympathies were sent as hostages to Rome. Thereafter, Roman policymakers kept careful watch over Achaean ambitions. Matters came to a head in 148 BCE, when the league launched a successful assault on Sparta at the same time that the conquered Macedonians, led by a pretender to the Macedonian throne named Andriscus, rebelled unsuccessfully

▽ **Roman warship**
Biremes such as the one depicted on this Roman relief from the 1st century CE were used at the Battle of Actium, which ended Egypt's independence.

against Roman rule. Having put down the revolt and turned Macedonia into a Roman province, the Romans turned on the Aetolian and Achaean leagues.

In 146 BCE, Roman soldiers sacked Corinth; the city's men were massacred, its women and children sold into slavery, and the entire city razed to the ground. The sack of Corinth effectively marked the end of Greek independence. Subsequently the leagues were abolished, all of Greece was placed under the supervision of the Roman governor of Macedonia, and oligarchy replaced democracy.

Over the next century, Rome gained control of the Hellenistic kingdoms in Asia. In 133 BCE, Pergamon's last king, Attalus III, bequeathed the kingdom to Rome. In 66 BCE, the Roman general Pompey took command of the Roman forces in the region. Within three years, he had

driven Mithradates VI—who had been a thorn in Rome's side since 88 BCE (see p.283)—out of Pontus; abolished the empire of Mithradates' ally, Tigranes of Armenia, who had captured what was left of the Seleucid Empire in 83 BCE; and made Syria, where the last independent Seleucid king (Antiochus XIII) ruled a small domain, a Roman province.

By 50 BCE, only Egypt remained an independent kingdom, but it soon became embroiled in Rome's civil wars. These held out the prospect of Egypt's queen, Cleopatra, carving out substantial power for herself and her lover Mark Antony, who controlled Rome's eastern territories by 42 BCE. However, Antony was defeated at the Battle of Actium in 31 BCE. Cleopatra died by suicide the following year, and power in the Roman Empire, along with Egypt, went to Antony's rival, Octavian

▷ **Roman general**
Known commonly as Sulla, Lucius Cornelius Sulla (138–78 BCE) was the Roman general and statesman who led the war against Mithradates VI of Pontus from 88 to 85 BCE.

"The Greek **world** was **split asunder.**"

CASSIUS DIO, *ROMAN HISTORY*

Heir of Heracles
Mithradates is depicted wearing a lion-skin headdress like that worn by the Greek hero Heracles, from whom Mithradates claimed descent, in this 1st-century CE Roman marble bust.

Mithradates VI

Rome's most dangerous enemy

A talented general and skilled diplomat who claimed descent from the mighty Achaemenid emperors and the Seleucid kings, Mithradates had the potential to rebuild the eastern empire of Alexander and challenge the power of Rome.

Mithradates was the eldest son of Laodice VI, who ruled the kingdom of Pontus as regent after her husband died in 120 BCE. The manner of his father's passing—sudden, poisoned at a banquet—haunted Mithradates VI. He subsequently tried to immunize himself with a sort of homeopathy, taking tiny doses of known poisons regularly (a process still known as "mithradatism"), and was said to have created a universal antidote.

Building an empire

Around 113 BCE, Mithradates emerged from hiding to seize power and imprison his mother and brother. He then invaded Colchis (now coastal Georgia) and, after defeating the Scythians threatening it from the north, became protector of the Greek settlements on the north coast of the Black Sea.

Mithradates turned his upbringing as a Persian prince, schooled in diplomacy and in a dozen of the region's languages, to good use. He married his daughter Cleopatra to Tigranes, king of Pontus's neighbor Armenia. Tigranes then supported Mithradates' seizure of Bithynia (on the death of its king) and the Roman-controlled region of Cappadocia.

Turning westward from 89 BCE, Mithradates found the Greek colonies in Asia Minor eager for assistance against the advancing Romans. His forces swept across western Anatolia. In a massacre known as the "Asiatic Vespers," they killed up to 80,000 Roman soldiers and Latin-speaking civilians in western centers such as Pergamon and Tralles. After crossing the Bosporus, Mithradates pushed into Greece, where several cities, including Athens, welcomed him.

The Romans fought back in 88 BCE, beginning the first of a series of three wars. It took them four years to drive Mithradates from Greece, and a further three years to send him back to Pontus. In 63 BCE, Mithradates' son Pharnaces II led a revolt against him. With the Romans closing in, Mithradates tried to poison himself. With little poison left after sharing the dose with his daughters, the attempt failed, and Mithradates instead ordered a servant to kill him.

△ **A mithradatum**
This elaborate gilded jar, made in Italy in the 16th century, was designed to store mithradate—the semi-mythical antidote for all poisons said to have been created by Mithradates.

> "Few **men** desire **freedom**. Most merely want **just masters**."

MITHRADATES VI, CITED IN *EPISTULA MITHRIDATIS*

◁ **Comet coin**
The obverse of this coin from Pontus shows a portrait of Mithradates VI, obscured by punched countermarks; its reverse features a comet. According to legend, an unusually large comet appeared in the sky when Mithradates was born.

281 BCE Mithradates I Ktistes founds the Mithradatic dynasty in Pontus

133 BCE Mithradates VI is born, the eldest son of Mithradates V

C. 113 BCE Mithradates takes power in his own right. He marries his sister Laodice

95 BCE Rome backs Mithradates' rival, Nicomedes III of Bithynia

88–84 BCE Mithradates threatens Roman rule in Greece in the First Mithradatic War

83–81 BCE A bitterly fought Second Mithradatic War ends with Mithradates pushed back to Pontus

83 BCE Mithradates puts down a major rebellion in Colchis

63 BCE Rome triumphs over Pontus and Mithradates dies

ΦΑΤΟ ΤΟΝ ΔΕ ΠΑΤΗΡ ΟΛΟΦΥΓΑΤΟ ΔΑΚΡΥ ΧΕΩ
ΥССЕ ΔΕ ΘΟΙ ΛΑΩΝ СΟΟΝ ЕΜΜЕΝΑΙ ΟΥ Δ ΑΠΟΛΕ
ΤΙ ΚΑΛΛΙ СΤΟΝ Η ΚΕ ΤΕ ΛΕΙΟΤΑΤΟΝ ΠЕΤЕ Η Ν
ΟΝ ΕΧΟΝ ΤΟΝ ΥΧΕС СΙ ΤΕΚΟС ΕΛΑΦ ΟΙ Ο ΤΑΧ
ΑΙΟС Β ΘΦ ΙС Ω ΠЕΡΙ ΚΑΛΛΑ СΙ ΚΑΒ ΒΑΛЕ Ν
ΤΑΝ ΟΜ ΦΑΙС Ω ΖΗ Ν Ι ΡЕΖЕС ΚΟΝ ΑΧΑΙ ΟΙ
СΟΥ Ν Ι Λ ΟΝ Θ Ο ΟΤΑ ΓЕ ΚΑΙ ΟС Η ΑΥ ΟС Ν ΟΡ Ν Ι
Λ ΟΝ ЕΠΙ ΤΡЕ Ψ ЕС СΙ Ο Θ ΟΤΟΝ ΜΝ Η С ΑΝ ΤΟ ΔЕ Χ
Ν ЕС ЕΠΙ ΤΟ Ρ ЕΟС СΑ ΛΛ Α Ν Α Θ Ο Ν ΠН С ΑΝ ΛΑ ΩΝ Η С Π

7

The Afterlife of a Culture

31 BCE—

Greece Re-formed

Greece remained under the rule of Rome and its successor state, the Greek-speaking Byzantine Empire, for more than 1,500 years. It witnessed the advent of Christianity, the division of the Roman Empire into two in 395 CE and the collapse of its Western half around 476, and the spread of Islam and the new powers that emerged with it, until it was subsumed by the Ottoman Empire, which—like the ancient Achaemenid Empire before it—had sprung from West Asia.

From Roman to Christian

Greece was fully absorbed into the Roman system after the accession of Augustus, the first emperor, in 27 BCE. It was divided into provinces, Roman governors replaced the governments of previously independent city-states and monarchies, and eventually the Greek elites began to take part in the administration of the wider empire.

For a time, Greek culture flourished under Roman rule. However, the strength of the classical and pagan tradition waned after Emperor Constantine legalized Christianity in 313 CE. Within decades, Christianity had become the dominant, and official, religion of the empire. Pre-Christian beliefs and philosophy did survive, particularly in Athens, where Plato's Academy was not closed down until 529. However, Greek temples were replaced with churches, and the chief cities of the Hellenistic world, Antioch, Alexandria, and Constantinople (the name for Byzantium from 330), became the bases for Christianity's leaders—the patriarchs.

The fall of the Western Roman Empire in the late 5th century left the Greek-speaking East as the standard-bearer of the Roman political heritage. Under Emperor Justinian (r. 527–565), this Byzantine Empire expanded, conquering some of the lost Western Roman provinces. But wars with Persia in the 7th century left Rome vulnerable to the advancing armies of the Islamic caliphate that was growing rapidly from its heartland in the Arabian peninsula. By 650, the Byzantine Empire had lost its territories in North Africa and the Levant to the caliphate, and Slavic peoples had also invaded Byzantine territory to the west, reaching the Peloponnese.

The Byzantine Empire survived and underwent a military revival in the 10th and early 11th centuries. However, it was never able to restore its territories in Syria and Palestine, including Jerusalem. In 1096, Western European Christian rulers launched the Crusades to retake Jerusalem from the powerful Seljuk Empire, which then ruled a large part of West Asia. However, the Crusaders attacked Constantinople itself in 1204 and divided much of the Byzantine Empire between themselves and the powerful city of Venice.

End and legacy

By the 14th century, most of the former Greek-speaking areas in West Asia were under the rule of Arab or Turkish dynasties, principally the Ottoman Turks. In 1453, the Ottoman sultan Mehmed II conquered Constantinople, and the last Byzantine emperor, Constantine XI, died. Slivers of the empire resisted until 1460, but a long chain of political and cultural continuity stretching back nearly 2,500 years was broken. Yet, although ancient Greece's kings, oligarchs, philosophers, and city-states are long gone, its legacy lives on in politics, science, literature, architecture, and art.

◁ **Byzantine Christian medallion, c. 1100 CE**

27 BCE The Roman Empire is founded, with Augustus as emperor

66–67 CE Nero visits Greece and takes part in the Olympic Games

330 Constantine makes Constantinople (Byzantium) his eastern capital

391 Theodosius I orders the closure of all pagan temples

395 The Roman Empire is divided into Western and Eastern halves

476 The Western Roman Empire falls to Germanic peoples

1 Roman sculpture from Eleusis, c. 100 CE

2 The Library of Celsus at Ephesus, c. 130 CE

3 The Arch of Hadrian in Athens, c. 131 CE

Roman provinces, 31 BCE

The Greek territories were divided into public (or senatorial) provinces, governed by an annually appointed proconsul, or imperial provinces, governed by the emperor's representative indefinitely.

KEY

- Imperial provinces
- Public provinces
- Provinces added after 14 CE, with date
- Later subdivisions of provinces, with date

529 Justinian expels teachers of pagan philosophy from Athens

532 The church of Hagia Sophia is completed in Constantinople

634–640 Arab Muslim armies conquer Egypt, Syria, and Palestine

867 Basil I establishes the Macedonian dynasty as rulers of the Byzantine Empire

1071 Seljuk Turks take much of Anatolia from the Byzantine Empire

1204 The army of the Fourth Crusade sacks Constantinople

1354 Ottoman Turks capture Gallipoli, their first European possession

1453 Constantinople falls to the Ottoman Turks; the Byzantine Empire ends

Under Roman Rule

Peace and prosperity in the Greek provinces

The Roman occupation of Greece from the mid-2nd century BCE had profound consequences for the Greek cities that were incorporated into the Roman Empire as provinces, but it also changed Rome itself.

△ **Nero the athlete**
Issued in Egypt, this bronze coin shows the Roman emperor Nero wearing a victor's crown, marking his participation in the Nemean Games in 67 CE. The games honored Zeus, who is shown on the coin's reverse.

The Hellenistic Age ended with Egypt's defeat at the Battle of Actium in 31 BCE, which left the whole Greek world west of the Euphrates River in West Asia under direct or indirect Roman control. Rome's emperors were intrigued by the achievements of the Greek *poleis*, exerting a soft power that drew the Greeks into the administration of the empire and encouraged a productive cultural interchange that helped secure the Pax Romana—a 200-year period of peace and prosperity in the empire.

Made emperor in 27 BCE, Augustus (previously Octavian) spent two years reestablishing the imperial administration in the eastern half of the Roman Empire. He organized Macedonia and Achaea as senatorial provinces, governed by proconsuls (civil governors). Rome based several legions in Macedonia, where they could defend the province from the peoples to the north, and the Via Egnatia—a 680-mile- (1,100-km-) long road from Illyria to Byzantium—provided a conduit for trade and a highway for its legions to the Greek provinces of Thrace (annexed by Rome in 46 CE) and Asia.

The close interest the emperors took in Greece also served to draw the Greeks closer into the orbit of the Roman world. Augustus visited Athens three times and provided funds for the building of the Roman Agora in the city. Nero visited Greece in 66–67, gathering the Greeks at Corinth (the capital of Achaea) and declaring the province of Achaea free from taxation. He also participated in the Isthmian, Pythian, Nemean, and Olympic games, and went on to establish the Neronia in Rome—a Greek-style festival with games. However, it was perhaps Emperor Hadrian (see opposite) who loved Greece the most.

Under Hadrian, the Greeks became the Romans' social and political equals and were given positions in the administration of the empire. The Athenian

> "**Conquered Greece** took **captive** her savage **conqueror** and brought her **arts** into rustic **Latium**."
>
> HORACE, *EPISTLES*

▷ **Via Egnatia**
Constructed in the 2nd century BCE, the Via Egnatia ran from Dyrrachium—where it was connected by a short sea journey to Brindisi and the Via Appia on the Italian mainland—through northern Greece to Byzantium on the Bosporus.

Map labels: Adriatic Sea, ITALIA, Brindisi, ALBANIA, Dyrrachium, Mansio Scampa, Lychnidos, MACEDONIA, Edessa, Pella, Thessalonica, EPIRUS, THESSALY, CHALCIDICE, Amphipolis, Philippi, Serdica, Philippopolis, Adrianople, THRACE, Heraclea, Byzantium, Sea of Marmara, Develtos, Black Sea, Aegean Sea, ASIA

KEY — Via Egnatia

N 0 — 100 km / 0 — 100 miles

rhetorician Herodes Atticus, for example, became a consul (civil and military magistrate) in 131, and also served as tutor to the future emperor and philosopher Marcus Aurelius (r. 161–180). Meanwhile, the historian Plutarch became procurator (treasury officer) of Achaea.

Greco-Roman synthesis

Bilingualism became a sign of refinement for elite Romans, though few were as adept as P. Crassus Mucianus, consul in 131 BCE, who was reputedly able to converse in five different Greek dialects. Greek art came to Rome, partly through pieces looted by armies from Syracuse, Corinth, and other captured cities. Greek cults, such as that of Dionysus, became integrated into the Roman religious tradition as Greek deities became identified with their Roman equivalents, for example, Zeus with Jupiter. Schools of Greek philosophy such as Stoicism, with its rejection of worldly concerns, also became part of the mainstream of Roman thought. Marcus Aurelius even wrote a book in Greek, *Meditations*, in which he set down his reflections on Stoicism.

In almost every field of endeavor Greece, though politically helpless, exerted a disproportionate influence on the empire. The Roman armies adopted the tactical formation of the phalanx, adapting it to be more flexible. Greek temples provided a model for new Roman sanctuaries, such as the Temple of Venus and Roma constructed in Rome by Emperor Hadrian. Ideologically, the Greeks' willingness to venerate their rulers helped promote an imperial cult that began with the senate's deification of Julius Caesar in 42 BCE and within decades led to the appearance of temples of the imperial cult throughout the empire, such as that of Augustus and Livia in Vienne, France. In the end, with the survival of the Greek-speaking eastern provinces as the Byzantine Empire, Greece would become the protector of Rome's legacy.

△ **Roman Agora**
Completed around 50 BCE, the octagonal clock tower called the Tower of the Winds still stands in the Roman Agora in Athens.

A ROMAN EMPEROR IN GREECE

Hadrian, emperor from 117 to 138 CE, was a lover of Greek culture, and a Greek-style beard, which earned him the derogatory nickname *graeculus* (little Greek). He visited Greece three times, in 124–125, 128–129, and 131/132 CE. In an attempt to restore it to its former glory, he gave the city of Athens—which had previously been given honorary citizenship on him—a large grant of money and grain. On his first visit, Hadrian was initiated into the Eleusinian Mysteries (see p.210) and presided over the Greater Dionysia festival, while the city named an additional tribe (deme) in his honor. Among the many buildings he commissioned in Athens were a gymnasium and a library; he also presided over the completion of the Temple of Olympian Zeus, begun 600 years earlier.

Mapping the World

The evolution of Greek cartography

As understanding of the shape of the world grew from the 4th century BCE, new disciplines and techniques emerged for representing Earth on flat surfaces. These laid the foundations for cartography and remain in use today.

The first known attempt to map the world was made by Anaximander (c. 610–546 BCE), a student of Thales of Miletus, in the 6th century BCE. Anaximander suggested that Earth was an independent entity, floating at the center of an infinite universe. He proposed that it was a cylinder at the top of which was a disk on which sat the world as he knew it, with Greece at its center. Anaximander's conception of the world—added to and improved by scholars such as Hecataeus of Miletus (c. 550–476 BCE) and the explorer Scylax of Caryanda—was largely accepted until the idea that Earth was a globe took hold. In the 6th century BCE, Pythagoras had speculated that Earth might be a sphere, and Empedocles and Anaxagoras added their support to the claim in the 5th century BCE. It was a widely held view by the 4th century BCE, when Aristotle confirmed its validity, unlocking vital new knowledge.

Eratosthenes (c. 276–194 BCE), the head librarian at the Library of Alexandria, used his understanding of mathematics and astronomy in the study of the world, for which he coined the term "geography."

◁ **Anaximander's map**
This map depicts the lands known to the Greeks in Anaximander's lifetime, which excluded northern Europe and most of Africa and Asia.

In his master work, *Geography*, he explained for the first time his method for calculating Earth's circumference and its axial tilt, achieving a remarkable degree of accuracy for both. He also mapped the world as he knew it in great detail, naming and locating cities and features, and suggested that there might be different climate zones. However, Eratosthenes' most significant contribution to mapmaking was to superimpose a grid of lines, analogous to lines of latitude and longitude, on his maps of the world, to aid in specifying locations and calculating distances.

Toward mapmaking today

In his 17-volume treatise *Geography*, the traveler and geographer Strabo (c. 64 BCE–24 CE) set out to define the scope and purpose of the discipline. His contribution to cartography was confined to a critique of the shortcomings of existing maps, but he did make a reference to the first globe representing Earth, created by Crates of Mallus in the 2nd century BCE.

The Alexandrian scholar Claudius Ptolemy significantly improved mapmaking around 150 CE. He devised a way of inscribing the lines of latitude and longitude on a two-dimensional map to help represent the curvature of Earth and preserve the proportionality of distances. This anticipated the conventions adopted by later mapmakers that are still in use today.

◁ **Crates' sphere**
This 19th-century engraving imagines what the globe described by Strabo and created by Crates, head of the library of Pergamon, might have looked like.

The cities and geographical features of the lands around the Mediterranean are shown in detail

Lines of latitude and longitude are curved to indicate Earth's spherical shape

The Gulf of the Ganges, now known as the Bay of Bengal

The sources and branches of the Nile River are shown, reflecting its importance as a major artery

The southern Indian Ocean was known as the Mare Prasodum (Green Sea) in antiquity

△ **Ptolemy's map**

German cartographer Nicolaus Germanus used the positions of around 8,000 locations recorded by Ptolemy to create this map, published in a 1482 edition of Ptolemy's *Geography*.

The Madaba Mosaic

Found in the Byzantine church of Saint George in Madaba, Jordan, which was dedicated in 542 CE, the Madaba Mosaic is the world's earliest mosaic floor map and the oldest map of the Holy Land. The work shows an area stretching from Lebanon to the Nile Delta and from the Mediterranean Sea to the Eastern Desert. At its center is the walled city of Jerusalem (below center), the heart of Christianity and a Byzantine metropolis in the 4th–7th centuries CE. The mosaic originally measured 69 ft (21 m) by 23 ft (7 m), but large portions have been lost.

The Spread of Christianity

From sect to state religion

Christianity was born in the Hellenistic world, and over four centuries it survived persecutions and splits to grow from a tiny sect in Palestine to the dominant religion in the Greek East and the state religion of the Roman Empire.

Few could have predicted Christianity's ultimate success. It began in the mid-1st century CE in Palestine as a sect within Judaism, its founder executed, its numbers tiny. The new religion's appeal was hugely widened by its flexibility in responding to the Hellenistic culture that surrounded it and its willingness to accept converts from among the ranks of those it defined as pagans (people who practiced polytheism), many of them Greek speakers. This created a powerful and appealing fusion of Greek philosophical thought and religious practice rooted in Judaism that would transform the Greco-Roman world.

Christianity's first Church council, held in Jerusalem around 50 CE, affirmed that conversion to Judaism was not a prerequisite for becoming a Christian. The Church's leaders began to send missionaries out to secure converts. Chief among

◁ **Pagan emperor**
This cameo from the 4th century shows a Roman emperor (right), probably Julian, performing a pagan sacrifice.

them was St. Paul, a convert and former pagan himself. Traveling through Syria, Asia Minor, and Greece, he visited Athens, Philippi, Corinth, and Thessalonica. His letters to the infant *ecclesiae*, or communities, in the last three of these later formed part of the New Testament.

Important early centers of Christianity appeared in Antioch, Ephesus, and Alexandria, but by 100 CE there were still probably fewer than 10,000 Christians in the Roman Empire—many from marginalized groups, such as women and enslaved people.

Persecution and acceptance

As the number of converts to Christianity slowly grew, pagan polemicists began to attack the religion. In the late 2nd century, the Greek philosopher Celsus refuted Christian ideas, such as the Virgin Birth, and claimed that the Christian God was not as powerful as the Greek gods. In response, Christian writers, such as Origen of Alexandria, defended Christianity; Origen saw it as a kind of divine philosophy, which surpassed Greek philosophy but was not incompatible with it.

The state also attempted to destroy Christianity. Christians who refused to participate in public pagan worship were sporadically persecuted, as when Emperor Decius made pagan sacrifice compulsory in 250, and those who failed to conform were often killed. Emperor Diocletian began the last major persecution of Christians in 303.

Everything changed for Christianity under the emperor Constantine, who believed that the Christian God had helped him win control of the empire at the Battle of the Milvian Bridge in 312

EARLY CHRISTIAN CHURCHES

The earliest Christians gathered in places of safety, such as the underground catacombs in Rome, or in house churches—rooms in the homes of believers—such as the mid-3rd century church in Dura-Europos. After Christianity became legal in 313, Christians were able to build formal churches. The larger ones adapted the form of the Roman basilica, or law court, with a long central nave; others, especially in the Greek East, were built in the form of a cross superimposed on a circle.

DURA-EUROPOS CHURCH, SYRIA

(see p.296). The following year, he issued the Edict of Milan, legalizing Christian worship. From then on, Christianity had active imperial backing, except for a short-lived period when the emperor Julian (r. 355–360) tried to revive paganism.

Legitimacy

Once it was legal, Christianity tried to give uniformity to its previously diverse beliefs. The Council of Nicaea in 325 laid down a single creed that encapsulated approved dogma, leading those who dissented to be labeled as heretics. Members of the elite began converting in larger numbers. In 366, Constantius II outlawed pagan sacrifice, and in 380 Theodosius I effectively made Christianity the official religion of the Roman Empire. This led to the frequently violent repression of pagan religion and thought that often exceeded the bounds of the law. The historian Libanius wrote of "a black-robed tribe" of monks that ravaged the temples of Syria. In 391, Theodosius sanctioned the demolition of temples in Alexandria. The Serapeum and its library, containing part of the Great Library's collection, were destroyed. Violence against non-Christians even led to murder in the case of Hypatia (see p.299). Yet stamping out paganism was a slow, and incomplete, process: temples were still being converted into churches in the 5th century, and the Academy in Athens was closed only in 529.

By the mid-5th century, Christians had become a majority in most urban centers. Yet Christianity's success contained the seeds of division. Quarrels over doctrine and which patriarch—the primary bishops of Constantinople, Alexandria, Rome, Jerusalem, and Antioch—had primacy created bitterness and schisms in the Church.

△ **St. Paul in Athens**
One of several tapestries made in Belgium to designs drawn by the Italian artist Raphael in the 16th century, this tapestry once hung in the Sistine Chapel in the Papal Palace in Vatican City.

"**Moses** is more **ancient** than all **Greek writers** and everything the **poets** and **philosophers** have said."

2ND-CENTURY CHRISTIAN THEOLOGIAN JUSTIN, *FIRST APOLOGY*

Byzantine Greece

A thousand-year empire

The Greek-speaking Eastern Roman Empire survived the fall of Rome by a thousand years through its ability to adapt to, and sometimes overcome, multiple military, political, and religious crises and a succession of foreign invasions.

△ **The Byzantine Empire**
This map shows the Byzantine Empire at its greatest extent, following Justinian's conquests in the 6th century. By 565, it stretched around 3.4 million sq miles (5.5 million sq km) across the Mediterranean and into the Balkans, West Asia, and North Africa.

The foundations of the Byzantine Empire (or Eastern Roman Empire) lay in the late 3rd century CE, when Emperor Diocletian established the Tetrarchy in 293. This divided the administration of the vast Roman Empire between two emperors and their junior colleagues and successors, the *caesares*. The system was short-lived: at the Battle of the Milvian Bridge in 312, the emperor Constantine I (r. 306–337) defeated a rival, Maxentius, to secure his control of the western portion of the empire. Following a civil war with his co-emperor, Licinius, in 326 Constantine became emperor of the entire Roman Empire. He chose the old city of Byzantium as his imperial base in the east in 330. The city, which was renamed Constantinople, would become the heart of the Byzantine Empire—born out of the collapse of the Roman Empire.

In the 4th and 5th centuries, both western and eastern halves of the Roman Empire suffered devastating incursions from peoples including the Goths, Huns, and Vandals. The West lost province after province; the East, however, consolidated under Theodosius I (r. 379–395). Upon his death, the empire was officially divided in two. In 476, a Germanic military leader called Odoacer deposed the last Western emperor, and Roman power in the west collapsed. However, the eastern empire, also known as the Byzantine Empire, survived and thrived.

Expansion and contraction

Under Justinian (r. 527–565), the Byzantine Empire expanded to its greatest extent, as his armies retook the former Roman province of Africa from the Vandals from 533, and Italy from the Ostrogoths between 535 and 554. Yet like the earlier Greek city-states and kingdoms, the Byzantine Empire came under near constant pressure from external forces. The Persian ruler Khosrow I sacked Antioch in 540, beginning a period of chronic warfare in the east that, along with a devastating plague outbreak in 541–542, sapped the empire's strength. It was also troubled by Slavic incursions in the Balkans.

The Byzantine Empire recovered under Maurice (r. 582–602), but the peace he made with Persia was dramatically disrupted when Khosrow II invaded in 602. He took Jerusalem in 614, and besieged Constantinople in 626. Although Heraclius (r. 610–641) recovered the lost territories, the empire was threatened by the emergence of the Rashidun Caliphate, which inherited the territories conquered by the Prophet Muhammad, and

◁ **Emperor Constantine**
A remnant of a monumental sculpture of Constantine that once stood in the Basilica of Maxentius on the Via Sacra in Rome, this head is more than 8 ft (2.5 m) high.

which took Antioch in 637, Jerusalem in 638, and Egypt four years later. After the loss of Carthage in North Africa to the Umayyad Caliphate in 698, the Byzantine Empire began to retract.

Disputes over iconoclasm (the banning of religious images) wracked the empire for almost 90 years from 754. By then, it had also lost Ravenna, its last northern Italian outpost, to the Lombards. In 811, the Bulgars, who had invaded the Balkans, killed Emperor Nikephoros I. Crete was lost to the Abbasid Caliphate in 826, and most of Sicily was lost by 843.

Only the accession of Basil I—the first emperor of the Macedonian dynasty—in 867 stemmed the losses. Claiming descent from Alexander the Great, as well as from Constantine, the Macedonian rulers oversaw a period of Hellenization that was marked by a cultural, linguistic, and literary revival, with a renewed interest in the ancient Greek heritage of the empire.

In the 10th century, the Byzantine Empire recovered some territory, reconquering Antioch in 969 after three centuries of Arab rule. Basil II's (r. 976–1025) victory at the Battle of Kleidion in 1014 also removed the Bulgar threat to the empire. However, Basil was

followed by short-lived emperors who were poorly prepared to face the threat from the Seljuk Turks infiltrating Anatolia from their empire to its east. In 1071, Romanos IV Diogenes marched eastward to face them. At the Battle of Manzikert, his forces were defeated, and he was captured. The conflict left the Byzantine Empire reliant on foreign mercenaries and support from the European kingdoms to the west.

△ **Emperor Justinian**
Marked by a nimbus around his head, Justinian stands in the center of this 6th-century mosaic from the Basilica of San Vitale in Italy.

THE MACEDONIAN RENAISSANCE

The arrival of the Macedonian dynasty in 867 heralded a cultural and artistic flowering inspired by Classical antiquity. It was epitomized by the Byzantine monk Michael Psellos (c. 1018–1096), who attempted to integrate Plato's philosophy with Christian doctrine. Likewise Anna Komnene (1083–1153) styled her *Alexiad*, a biography of her father, the emperor Alexios, on earlier Greek historians, including Thucydides. The illustrations in the Paris Psalter, meanwhile, combined biblical subjects, notably David with classical art—in one (right), he is depicted as Orpheus, surrounded by personifications of "Melody" and "Echo."

Renaissance revival
This figure in *The School of Athens* by Italian painter Raphael is believed to be Hypatia. She was largely overlooked until Raphael helped revive her reputation in the 16th century.

Hypatia

Neoplatonist philosopher, mathematician, and astronomer

One of antiquity's few prominent female thinkers and mathematicians, Hypatia headed a school of philosophy in Alexandria, but her involvement in bitter quarrels between pagans and Christians led to her murder in 415 CE.

Born around 350 CE, Hypatia was the daughter of Theon, a mathematician and founder of a school in Alexandria. She succeeded her father as the school's head, and continued his work preserving Greece's mathematical and astronomical heritage. We know of three works by Hypatia, all now lost: a discourse on Diophantus's (c. 200–284 CE) work on algebraic equations, *Arithmetica*; a commentary on Apollonius of Perga's (240–190 BCE) treatise on conic sections; and an astronomical table. We know a little more of her work from the letters of her student Synesius of Cyrene, later bishop of Ptolemais, who writes that she taught him how to construct a plane astrolabe and that he asked her to make a hydrometer for measuring the density of liquids. Otherwise, we know only of later writers' views on her as a trusted and admired teacher.

Pagan philosophy

Hypatia's drive for knowledge came from her Neoplatonist beliefs, which held that the material world was a poor shadow of the spiritual world, and that mathematics was key to accessing this higher level. It was a dangerous time to have such "pagan" beliefs, as Christian leaders were growing intolerant.

Hypatia became a victim of the tensions that flared up in Alexandria after 412, when Cyril, a hard-line opponent of paganism, became bishop. In 415, she was caught up in a dispute between Cyril and the Roman prefect, Orestes. A mob, its passions inflamed by Christian leaders, dragged her to the Caesareum, where they murdered her.

△ **Astrolabe**
Working on astrolabes, like this later Arabic example, Hypatia was part of a Greek tradition that went back to Apollonius of Perga in the 2nd century BCE.

△ **Hypatia in Alexandria**
In this painting from the 19th century, British artist Robert Trewick Bone shows Hypatia (center) teaching at her school in Alexandria and surrounded by students.

> "A person so **renowned**, her **reputation** seemed literally **incredible.**"
>
> SYNESIUS, *LETTER TO HERCULIANUS*

c. 350 CE Suggested date for Hypatia's birth in Alexandria

391 The authorities outlaw pagan worship in Alexandria

414 Riots break out after Alexandria's synagogues are closed

c. 850 Photios, patriarch of Constantinople, includes accounts of Hypatia in his *Bibliotheka*

c. 380 Hypatia succeeds Theon as head of the school he founded

c. 393 Hypatia begins her correspondence with Synesius of Cyrene

415 Hypatia is murdered by a Christian mob led by a man called Peter the lector

1853 Charles Kingsley's novel *Hypatia* popularizes her image as the last pagan philosopher

Late Byzantine Empire

The long twilight

Weakened by dynastic civil wars, the impact of the Crusades, and the rise of new powers in the Balkans and Anatolia, the Byzantine Empire showed surprising resilience in surviving the disaster at Manzikert for almost four centuries.

Thrown into chaos following the Battle of Manzikert (see pp.296–297), the Byzantine Empire could easily have fallen in 1071. Yet it struggled on, growing weaker as internal and external challenges took their toll, until it was overwhelmed by the Ottoman Empire.

In the ten years after the Battle of Manzikert, various factions sought to gain control of the empire, deposing first Romanos IV Diogenes and then Michael VII Doukas (r. 1071–1078). At the same time, the Seljuk Turks were spreading westward. The Byzantine Empire sought the help of a group of Normans, who then revolted; taxes soared, and rebellions broke out in Thrace and Anatolia. Order was restored only by Alexios I Komnenos (r. 1081–1118), who strengthened the empire and ruled over a period of relative stability. Although he lost Epirus to a Norman invasion, he defeated an incursion by the Turkic Pecheneg people on the Danube in 1092, and recovered ground against the Seljuks in northwestern Anatolia.

◁ **Byzantine currency**
Pierced with a link so it could be used as jewelery, this hyperpyron (a coin introduced in the 11th century) was issued by Emperor Isaac II Angelos.

In 1095, Alexios sent a deputation to Pope Urban II appealing for help from western Christendom in his war against the Seljuks, and stressing the oppression allegedly experienced by Christian pilgrims to Jerusalem (then in the hands of the Seljuks). His appeal sparked the First Crusade, and set in motion 350 years of often damaging, and at times disastrous, western interference in the Byzantine Empire. While the armies of the First Crusade did restore Nicaea (lost to the Seljuks in 1081) to the Byzantine Empire in 1097, they did not hand over their conquests in Syria or Palestine as Alexios had hoped, and instead set up their own Crusader kingdoms.

An empire in decline

The stability of the Byzantine Empire endured through the reigns of John II Komnenos and Manuel I Komnenos, but under Manuel I (r. 1143–1180), it began to crumble once more. Manuel's decision to confiscate the property of all the Venetians in the empire in 1171 fatefully damaged its relations with Venice. A catastrophic defeat against the Turks at Myriokephalon in 1176 unleashed another wave of Seljuk expansion in Anatolia. Meanwhile Serbia broke away in 1180, beginning a similar dissolution of Byzantine control in the Balkans.

As the empire shrank, tax revenues diminished, and this was exacerbated by the decision to grant land to aristocrats who then established semi-independent fiefdoms, such as that created by David Komnenos in Trebizond, on the Black Sea coast. The empire's increasing tendency toward dynastic squabbling

EMPEROR **BASIL II**

Basil II Porphyrogenitus (Born in the Purple) was the Byzantine Empire's longest-reigning emperor, ruling for 49 years 11 months from 976 to 1025. A vigorous general, he gained land from the Fatimid Caliphate in Syria and the Khazars (a nomadic Turkic people) in southern Crimea, as well as territory in Georgia and Armenia. He is best known for the conquest of Bulgaria, which culminated in a crushing defeat of the Bulgars at the Battle of Kleidion in 1014 (see p.297). His brutal treatment of the captives from the battle gained him the nickname "Bulgar-Slayer." He died in 1025 while about to embark on an expedition to recover Sicily for the empire. The emperors that followed were weak by comparison, and the empire steadily declined.

proved catastrophic when Alexios IV Angelos sought western aid after his father Isaac II (r. 1185–1195) was deposed. As a result, the Venetians sent the armies of the Fourth Crusade to Constantinople in 1203–1204. Rather than restore Isaac, the Crusaders sacked the city and divided the empire between themselves.

A constellation of successor states, both Crusader and Greek, emerged. Only in 1261 was Michael VIII Palaiologos able to recover Constantinople from the Latin Empire (a Crusader state) and reinstate the Byzantine Empire. However, his son, Andronikos II (r. 1282–1328), then reduced the size of the Byzantine army and lost territory in the Balkans to the Serbs.

The final decades

Tranches of Anatolia were lost to the Ottoman Empire, an emerging power that gradually captured the territory of other Turkish emirates, and went on to take Bursa and Nicaea from the Byzantine Empire by 1331, and crossed into Europe at Gallipoli in 1355. Civil wars in 1321–1328 and 1341–1347 left the empire helpless to respond, and the outbreak of the Black Death in 1347 further frayed Byzantine strength. By 1372, Emperor John V was a vassal of the Ottoman

> ## "And the **cannon**, on being **brought up** to the wall, **shook it** to **pieces** and **toppled** it down."
>
> MICHAEL KRITOBOULOS, *HISTORY OF MEHMED THE CONQUEROR*

sultan Murad I. Manuel II (r. 1391–1420) roused western interest in a new Crusade, but it was crushed at Nicopolis (in modern-day Bulgaria) in 1396. Only the defeat of the Ottomans by Timur's Mongols in 1402 saved the Byzantine Empire.

When the dynamic Mehmed II became sultan in 1451, he wasted little time in launching an attack on Constantinople. Blasted by cannon—whose designer the last Byzantine emperor, Constantine XI (r. 1449–1453), had spurned—the city's walls weakened. On May 29, 1453, Mehmed's armies swarmed into Constantinople. Although a few territories resisted the Ottomans for a while—the Peloponnese falling in 1460 and Trebizond in 1461—the more than 1,100-year history of the Byzantine Empire was at an end.

▽ **Constantinople falls**
So shocking was the capture of Constantinople by the Ottomans in 1453 that it was a popular subject for artists for centuries after. Shown here is a 16th-century fresco of the event from Moldovita Monastery in Romania.

"He was **guided** to the **saint's cell** and … **embellished** it with **slabs** of the **local stone**."

LIFE OF SAINT LUKE, 11TH CENTURY

Hosios Loukas Mosaics

Sacred art from Byzantium's Golden Age

△ **Golden king**
This mosaic from the narthex of the Katholikon shows Christ Pantocrator (Ruler of All) bestowing a blessing and holding a Gospel book.

Situated on the western slopes of Mount Helikon in Boeotia, south of Delphi, is Hosios Loukas, a monastic complex dedicated to the 10th-century CE hermit-saint Luke of Steiris. There, the church known as the Katholikon is home to one of the most spectacular examples of Middle Byzantine Art. Saint Luke's death in 953 CE was followed by the building of a small church dedicated to the Theotokos (Mother of God), where the saint was initially buried. Around 1010, at the height of the Macedonian Renaissance (see p.297), the Katholikon was built to provide a much larger home for the saint's relics. It was the earliest example of a Byzantine domed, octagonal church; the eight-sided shape symbolized Christ's Resurrection, on the third day after his Crucifixion.

The Katholikon's interior was decorated with a cycle of mosaics representing the life of Christ and episodes from the Old and New Testaments. The mosaics were placed according to a strict iconographic program. Twelve key moments from Christ's story, including the Annunciation, Nativity, and Crucifixion, were represented in the narthex (the portico at the west end of a church). Other biblical scenes and figures were placed in the sanctuary's side chapels and the four curved vaults supporting the central dome. The dome originally had a mosaic of Christ seated on a throne, which was destroyed by an earthquake in 1593 and replaced by a fresco. The dome of the apse at the east end of the church was decorated with the mosaics shown (opposite).

Creating a masterpiece

The mosaics were created by two separate master artisans and their assistants. Working from wooden scaffolds, the mosaicists applied three layers of lime plaster. The final one, mixed with marble dust, was to affix the glass tesserae, which were colored by adding cobalt, copper, manganese, and iron during firing or backed with gold leaf. Each tessera was placed on the wall in situ, with a preliminary painting underneath to guide the mosaicists as they worked. The artisans used smaller tesserae to create the fine details of the hands, hair, and faces; larger glass cubes were used for the plain gold background that surrounds the images. Despite all the gold, the style of the mosaics is austere, featuring a relatively narrow color palette and a restricted set of gestures. Yet the Hosios Loukas cycle, awarded the status of UNESCO World Heritage site in 1990, is one of the finest near-complete sets of Byzantine mosaics to have survived.

◁ **Biblical scenes**
The mosaics in the dome above the Katholikon's apse show the Virgin with Christ as a child and Pentecost, when the apostles were inspired by the Holy Spirit after Christ's Ascension. These scenes symbolically mark the beginning and end of Christ's earthly life.

Each apostle is shown seated, a ray containing a flame of divine inspiration touching his head

Mosaic portraits of saints and benefactors of the Byzantine Church

Decorative border provides a frame for the portrait of the Virgin Mary and Christ

The Virgin Mary, halo indicating her sanctity, sits on an elaborate throne

The infant Christ, dressed in a lavish gold robe and holding a scroll, sits in his mother's lap

The Legacy of Greece

Inspiration from the ancient world

Long after ancient Greece was eclipsed by later empires, its influence has remained strong, visible in buildings and artwork that draw on Greek style, in the prevalence of democracy, and in the continuing appeal of the Greek myths.

△ **Forever Free**
Created by American artist Edmonia Lewis, this 1867 neoclassical sculpture co-opts Greek art and ideas of freedom to celebrate the emancipation of enslaved people in 1865.

Pediment inspired by buildings such as the Temple of Athena Polias in Priene

Ionic columns

Ancient Greek culture, politics, philosophy, art, science, and literature remain profoundly important today, forming the bedrock of many contemporary practices and ideals. Greek philosophy established the foundational ideas of Western thought, and Greek scientific method underpins the sciences. The principles of democracy formulated in Greece remain a cornerstone of much modern governance. The Greeks set enduring standards of beauty, exemplified by structures such as the Parthenon and the sculpture of the Hellenistic period. Greek literature, including Homer's epic tales, continues to captivate and educate.

A perennial fascination

The Romans were among the first to pick up the baton of Greek culture. Many Greek texts and famous ancient statues are known today only because the Romans made copies of them. They also adapted Greek beliefs, preserving equivalents of the Greek gods in their own pantheon of deities, and debated the significance of Greek philosophy and history. A revival of interest in its Greek past helped ancient culture survive the dominance of Christianity in the Byzantine Empire, and Islamic scholars preserved and

△ **Socrates reimagined**
This illustration from a 13th-century manuscript of Arab philosopher Al-Mubashshir ibn Fatik's collection of sayings of the ancient sages shows Socrates with his pupils.

built upon ancient Greek science, mathematics, and philosophy. Stories about the adventures of Alexander the Great circulated across Europe, Africa, and Asia throughout the Middle Ages.

The Greek diaspora that spread westward after Constantinople fell to the Ottoman Empire in 1453, along with new discoveries of ancient objects, helped fuel the Renaissance's fascination with classical culture in the 15th and 16th centuries. During this period, the Academy was founded in Florence in 1462 for students of literature and philosophy, and artists began echoing the style and subjects of ancient artwork. The Italian artist Botticelli's *Birth of Venus*, for example,

◁ **Neoclassical style**
The architecture of the British Museum mimics that of a Greek temple. Built in the 19th century, it houses hundreds of artifacts taken from Greece.

presents the myth of Aphrodite's beginnings, but also an allegory of the Greek Neoplatonist belief in the divine origin of beauty and love.

An influential heritage

In the late 18th and 19th centuries, wealthy Europeans returned from touring Greece and Italy with images of statues and ruins that had a profound influence on architecture, art, and even fashion, as seen in the Regency English vogue for simple Grecian-style gowns. The rediscovery of the Rosetta Stone (see pp.240–241) and the controversial removal of the Parthenon Marbles to Britain by Lord Elgin in the early 19th century prompted a neoclassical revival, clearly seen in such buildings as the British Museum.

In the 20th century, German philosopher Martin Heidegger drew on the pre-Socratic philosophers, while artists such as Italian painter Amedeo Modigliani and Japanese conceptual artist Yayoi Kusama were inspired by Cycladic sculpture and Greek myth. Such was the hold of ancient Greece on the Western imagination that both sides in World War II claimed to be its true heirs: the Nazis tried to assert that the achievements of ancient Greece were made by Aryan invaders; the Allies focused on their inheritance of ideas of democracy and a culture of freedom. Just as ancient Greece's long history saw many changes, disagreements, and debates, so each generation explores and debates its ongoing legacy.

△ **Renaissance revival**
Painted by the 16th-century Italian artist Titian, *Bacchus and Ariadne* tells the tale of Dionysus (Bacchus) finding Ariadne on the island where Theseus had abandoned her.

"Someone will **remember us**, I say, even in **another time**."

SAPPHO, FRAGMENT 147

◁ **Libation bowl**
The exterior of this gold phiale (libation bowl), which dates from the 4th–3rd centuries BCE, is decorated with an intricate pattern of bees, acorns, and beechnuts that was hammered through from the inside. It was perhaps once left as a gift at a sanctuary, and the inscription, in Greek and Punic characters, gives an indication of the weight of the vessel.

Directory

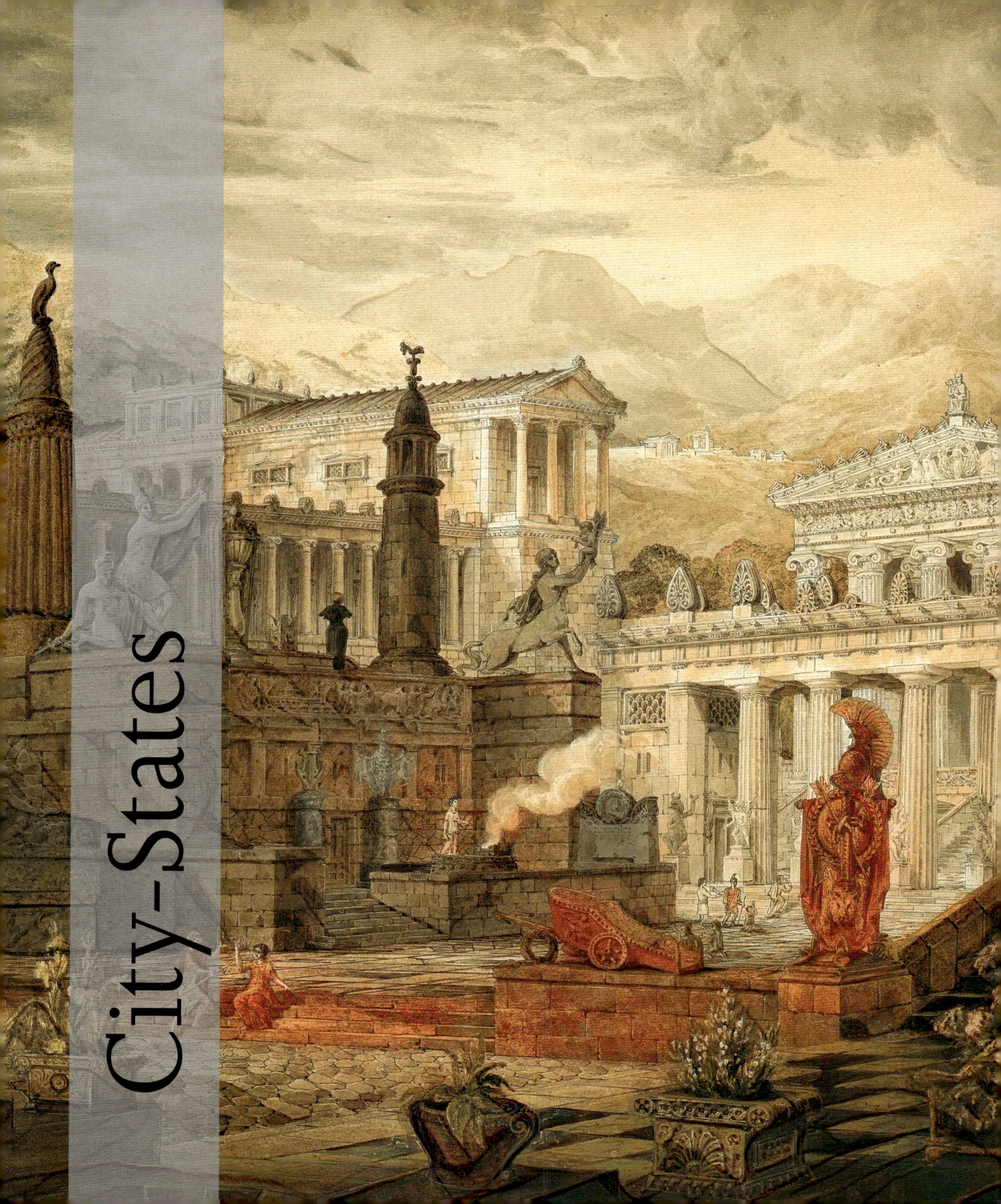

City-States

Mainland Greece

Today, mainland Greece is part of a single modern national state, but in ancient times it was the location of hundreds of independent, often isolated city-states. Rivalries and conflicts between these sites were endemic, although they also shared a sense of cultural identity.

Pylos

As well as being the capital of Homer's legendary King Nestor, Pylos was the site of a major Bronze Age palace complex. It occupied a large area and included a port and acropolis that were most likely situated on the Koryphasion promontory, adjacent to the northern end of the island of Sphacteria across the bay from the modern city of Pylos. The palace, the best preserved of any in Greece, was destroyed at the time of the fall of the Mycenaean palace culture c. 1200/1190 BCE. The site became important again in Classical times, when the Koryphasion promontory was fortified by Athens in the Peloponnesian War (431–404 BCE).

Messene

The foundation dates of Peloponnesian cities can rarely be determined with any certainty. In the case of Messene, however, the date of its rebuilding is precisely known: the city was newly founded in 369 BCE by the Greek general and statesman Epaminondas, two years after

◁ Painting depicting monuments in Sparta (Joseph Gandy, 19th century)

the Battle of Leuctra put an end to the Spartan domination of Messenia. It was established on the southern slope of the mountain of Ithome. This was a well-defensible location that had formerly served as the Bronze Age settlement of Ithome. A large city by ancient standards, with impressive city walls and public buildings, Messene flourished in Hellenistic and Roman times and in late antiquity. (See also p.378.)

Sparta

During the great period of Greek expansion beginning in the 8th century BCE, the Laconian city of Sparta began expanding too, but within the Peloponnese rather than by founding overseas colonies. This took place with the annexation of the neighboring region of Messenia and the reduction of its people to serf status as helots. To keep control of this territory and the serf population, Sparta devised a system that involved a militarized life for the Spartiates who, with a population of serfs to work the land, could serve as full-time warriors. A distinctive constitution was developed too, combining monarchical, oligarchic, and democratic features. It was geared toward

maintaining the city's prized condition of eunomia (good order). Following its conquest of Messenia around 720 BCE, Sparta became a dominant force, in both the Peloponnese and the wider Greek world, and went on to lead Greece's defense against the Persians in 490–479 BCE. In the aftermath of the victory, however, while Athens emerged as the main imperial power of the Greek world, Sparta had to deal with a major helot revolt, following an earthquake in about 465 BCE. The decades after this saw a series of conflicts with Athens that culminated in the Peloponnesian War of 431–404 BCE, which ended with Sparta's victory at the Battle of Aegospotami. Now the leading power of the Greek world, Sparta spent the years after its victory pursuing imperialistic ambitions until, following the King's Peace of 387 BCE (see p.159), it turned its focus to becoming the supreme force of mainland Greece. This domination lasted

until Sparta's defeat by Thebes at the Battle of Leuctra in 371 BCE and the resulting liberation of Messenia. Sparta never regained its earlier supremacy. (See also pp.106–109; p.378.)

Megalopolis

The Arcadian city of Megalopolis (Great City) was founded by Epaminondas of Thebes around 370 BCE, after Spartan domination of the Peloponnese ended with the Battle of Leuctra (see left) and Epaminondas invaded the region. Like the city of Messene (see left), which Epaminondas also founded, Megalopolis was especially notable for its extensive circuit walls. Its population was drawn from existing communities, who maintained their distinctive identities. The city remained important until the 2nd century BCE, then declined in Roman times, although it continued to be inhabited into late antiquity.

△ View of Tiryns, in Argolis in the Peloponnese, with the archaeological site in the foreground

Tegea

Like numerous *poleis*, most famously Athens, the Arcadian city of Tegea was formed from the unification of a number of once-independent communities. Until the Battle of Leuctra in 371 BCE, Tegea was an ally of Sparta. After the battle, it was instrumental, with Mantinea (see below), in the formation of the Arcadian League (see p.192), which split owing to disputes between the two cities. Tegea remained a key political power in the region until the 2nd century BCE, after which it declined in importance.

Mantinea

In the 6th or 5th century BCE, several *poleis* were united to form the new city of Mantinea,

situated in an upland plain in eastern Arcadia, which became the site of three important battles (in 418 BCE, 362 BCE, and 207 BCE). From at least 420 BCE, the city was run as a democracy. Following a period of significant decline, Mantinea went on to prosper—most notably under the reign (117–138 CE) of Hadrian. He revived its public buildings in honor of his lover, Antinous, whose birthplace, Bithynium, was thought to have been founded by the people of Mantinea.

Argos

In the *Iliad*, the king of Argos, Diomedes, acknowledges the overlordship of the king of Mycenae, Menelaus. This probably suggests that Argos was relatively subordinate to its neighbor in the Bronze Age.

By the Archaic period, Argos had become the main power in the Argolis region, with an extensive territory that included the major sanctuary of Hera, located around 5 miles (8 km) from the urban center. Under its 7th-century BCE king, Pheidon, Argos rose to prominence in Greece. After Sparta succeeded it as the leading force in the Peloponnese, it tended to ally itself with Athens. Argos retained its independence following the rise of Macedonia and went on to prosper in Roman times. (See also pp.64–65; pp.376–377.)

Tiryns

The Mycenaean city of Tiryns, which was said to have been used as a base by Heracles during his Twelve Labors (see pp.368–369), was located on a low rocky hill in Argolis in the Peloponnese.

It was notable for its huge city walls and its impressive palace complex, which flourished in the Bronze Age, but was destroyed in c. 1200 BCE. Afterward, the city became the main settlement of the Argive Plain, eventually dividing into a number of small communities. For centuries, Tiryns was dominated by its neighbor, Argos (see left), which destroyed the city in c. 470 BCE. (See also p.376.)

Mycenae

Mycenae, on the Argive Plain, was, according to the *Iliad*, "rich in gold." It was also the site of a huge Bronze Age palace complex, destroyed around 1200 BCE at the time of the fall of palace culture across the Greek world. The site remained occupied in the post-palatial period, and by around 600 BCE it had risen to prosperity. Mycenae was dominated by the nearby city of Argos (see left), which destroyed it in c. 468 BCE, but then refounded it in the 3rd century BCE. (See also p.376.)

Corinth

Known proverbially as "wealthy Corinth" in antiquity, Corinth was a major power in ancient Greece from the 8th century BCE onward. Situated in an excellent location near the Isthmus joining the Peloponnese and the rest of mainland Greece, it benefited from many springs and a rich coastal plain. A major trading and maritime power, Corinth founded Corcyra (see p.313) as a port of call between Greece and Italy; and then, with Corcyra, went on to found other colonies, most notably Epidamnus, as a stopover point on the Illyrian coast. Corinth was renowned for its architecture and crafts, including pottery. Its original rulers, the Bacchiad clan, were overthrown by the tyrant Cypselus, who was succeeded by its most illustrious leader, Periander. The city's history was marked by uneasy relations with Corcyra. It allied with Sparta in the Peloponnesian War. Conversely, it allied with other powers against Sparta in the Corinthian War of the early 4th century BCE. Rome destroyed Corinth in 146 BCE and rebuilt it in 44 BCE. Corinth became a flourishing city that had a cosmopolitan population of Greeks, Jews, Romans, and, later, Christians. (See also p.377.)

Sicyon

Sicyon was a prosperous city situated on a fertile plain close to the Gulf of Corinth. In the 6th century BCE, a contest was held in the city for the hand in marriage of Agariste, daughter of Cleisthenes, the tyrant of Sicyon. The event reportedly attracted suitors from across the Greek world—the magnitude of this contest is evidence of the immense wealth and power of archaic Sicyon. Cleisthenes was one of the Orthagorid dynasty of tyrants who ruled the city for around a hundred years before being overthrown, like other archaic tyrannies, by Sparta, which instituted an oligarchy.

In the 360s BCE, Sicyon's leading citizen, Euphron, introduced a form of democracy. While his opponents called him a tyrant, his many supporters honored Euphron by burying his body in the Agora after he was murdered by his enemies. Around 300 BCE, the Macedonians conquered Sicyon. The city subsequently changed hands between a succession of major powers but declined under Roman rule, when it was eclipsed by Corinth.

Megara

Despite the observation of the geographer and traveler Pausanias in the 2nd century CE that the Megarians were the only Greeks that "not even the emperor Hadrian could make prosper," Megara played a key role at several points in Greek history. It was a significant colonizing power of the Archaic period, possibly motivated by limited availability of good land at home. Situated between Athens and Corinth, the city tended to be dominated by its neighbors. One of the causes of the outbreak of the Peloponnesian War was Megara's cultivation of sacred land on the borderlands between its territory and that of Athens. After the war, possibly reflecting a diminished status, it appears to have played no part in the various power struggles between the major Greek cities.

△ Painting showing the invasion and destruction of Corinth by the Romans in 146 BCE (Tony Robert-Fleury, c. 1870)

Athens

Often hailed as the epitome of an ancient Greek *polis*, Athens was in many ways unusual. The *polis* was created from the unification of once-independent communities of Attica into a single political unit dominated by Athens. With this unification, the *polis* came to possess a huge territory. It did not play a part in the early phase of overseas colonization in the 8th century BCE. The Archaic period saw civil strife, but tyranny came late, with the usurpation of power by Pisistratus (see pp.116–117). Under him, and then his sons Hippias and Hipparchus, Athens rose to become a major political and cultural center of the Greek world. Decades of stability were followed by social unrest, sparked by the assassination of Hipparchus in 514 BCE. Hippias was ousted by the Spartans in 510 BCE, and out of the civil strife that followed, Cleisthenes emerged as the key democratic leader. The budding democracy gained a boost in 490 BCE when, having failed to secure Spartan assistance against the invading Persians, the Athenians defeated a far greater Persian force at the Battle of Marathon. When the Persians invaded again ten years later, Athens was one of the powers leading the defense of Greece and emerged after 479 BCE as a major force in the Delian League (see pp.158–159), set up to fund the continuation of the war with Persia. After the war, around the mid-5th century BCE, Athens began using its wealth to fund a building plan run by Pericles (see pp.172–173). Under him, Athens became a thriving and cosmopolitan cultural center. With Athens' hegemony over the Delian League becoming a concern to its key rival, Sparta, the Peloponnesian War broke out in 431 BCE. The conflict came to an end in 404 BCE, when the Athenian fleet was destroyed at the Battle of Aegospotami. Following years of Spartan-imposed oligarchy, democracy was restored in Athens, and the 4th century BCE saw its return to hegemonic status within Greece for several decades. After the rise of Macedonia, Athens continued to thrive as a cultural center and went on to prosper as a city that was loved by many Romans.

Chalcis

Located on the island of Euboea, barely separated from mainland Greece, Chalcis was one of the most important Greek trading and manufacturing centers of the early Archaic period. It played a significant role, along with Eretria, another Euboean city, in Greece's expansion into southern Italy and Sicily and then into the northern Aegean. During the 8th century BCE, it fought a long-running war against Eretria for control of the fertile Lelantine Plain, located between the two cities. Chalcis is thought to have won the war, but the protracted conflict broke the power of the city, after which it became relatively unimportant.

△ Painting depicting the Acropolis in Athens (Leo von Klenze, 1846)

Thebes

As well as being the city of key mythological figures, such as Oedipus, Tiresias, Cadmus, and Dionysus, Thebes was, from ancient times, a major power of Boeotia and the wider Mediterranean world and instrumental in the establishment of the Boeotian League. During peacetime, its attack on nearby Plataea helped spark the Peloponnesian War. It allied with the eventual victor, Sparta, during the war, but later joined with other powers against its former ally. When Sparta was defeated by the Boeotians in 371 BCE, thanks largely to the skill of the Theban general Epaminondas, Thebes became the dominant power of the Greek world. It declined in importance in Hellenistic times, but thrived under Rome. (See pp.204–205.)

Orchomenos

According to the poet Pindar's ode *Olympian XIV*, Orchomenos was a "Town of beautiful horses … [a] splendid city." The poem honors a young man from the city who won the boys' foot race, possibly in the Games of 488 BCE. Orchomenos sat between Mount Akrontion and the plain of Lake Copais, in the northwest of the region. It was a leading power in the Boeotian League (see p.204), and the most promising city of the region, after Thebes, and its history is dominated by its rivalry with that city. In the 4th century BCE, it was destroyed by Thebes in the aftermath of the Battle of Leuctra. It went on to be rebuilt but never regained its former status and by Roman times was insignificant.

△ Painting showing the Theban general and statesman Epaminondas on his deathbed (Isaac Walraven, 1726)

Corcyra

In the age of expansion in the 8th century BCE, the trading city of Corinth established Corcyra (now Corfu), on the east of the island of the same name, which is separated from mainland Greece by the narrow Corfu Straits. With three fine harbors and on the trading route between Greece, the Adriatic, Italy, and the Western Mediterranean, the city flourished, becoming one of the three key naval powers of the Greek world, along with Athens and Corinth. Also with Corinth, it founded other colonies on the mainland, notably Epidamnus, but its history was often marked by an uneasy relationship with Corinth, including in the second half of the 5th century BCE, when disputes over Epidamnus helped spark the Peloponnesian War. From the 4th century BCE, the city was occupied by a succession of powers, culminating in its subjugation to Rome in the 2nd century CE.

Thessalonica

After its foundation around 315 BCE in the northwest Aegean, Thessalonica became the dominant city of Macedonia. It was founded by Cassander of Macedonia (see pp 236 and 248–249), who named it after his wife, Thessalonike, daughter of Philip of Macedonia. The city continued to flourish in Roman and Byzantine times, aided greatly by its location on the north–south trade route between the Adriatic and the Balkans.

Abdera

The key Thracian trading center of Abdera was located on major trade routes, both land and sea. Its settlement is thought to have begun with the Phoenicians. The Ionian city of Clazomenae then tried to settle the site in the 7th century BCE, around 654 BCE. It was finally settled in 544 BCE by the coastal city of Teos, in the wake of the Persian invasion of Ionia. Abdera flourished for centuries, but by Roman times it had become a byword for foolishness—its citizens were rumored to be unintelligent.

Aegean Islands and Asia Minor

The ancient Greeks, a maritime people, established numerous settlements on the islands that dot the Aegean Sea. Many cities also were situated on the fertile coastlands of western Asia Minor, whose monuments were often counted among the Seven Wonders of the Ancient World.

Thasos

Thasos was a wealthy and prosperous city on the island of the same name in the far north of the Aegean Sea. It was settled by Paros (see right) at the beginning of the 7th century BCE. As Thasos flourished, it established a number of major mining outposts on the nearby Thracian mainland. A bitter dispute with Athens over the rich and highly profitable mining and trading rights of these mainland outposts led Thasos to rebel against Athenian control and the Delian League—an alliance of more than 150 Greek cities—around 465 BCE (see pp.158–159). Following a two-year siege by the Athenians, the rebellion was finally quashed and Thasos lost its mining and trading rights. The Delian League became the Athenian Empire—according to the historian Thucydides, this transition was influenced by the earlier siege. Thasos regained its trading and mining rights and continued to flourish. When mining revenues fell, it remained wealthy thanks to the production of, and trade in, the fine wines for which the island of Thasos had become renowned.

Mytilene, Lesbos

Mytilene is perhaps best known today as the city of the lyric poet Alcaeus (see p.321) and his rival the tyrant and sage Pittacus, one of the so-called Seven Sages of ancient Greece. Mytilene was the most important city on the island of Lesbos in the North Aegean, with a territory that included land across the straits of Mytilene on the coast of Asia Minor. After falling under Persian domination, it became an ally of Athens, until it revolted in 428 BCE and was then settled by Athenian citizens. The city prospered in Hellenistic, Roman, and Late Roman times and was part of the Ottoman Empire until it was captured by Greece in 1912 CE.

Samos

Samos was the wealthiest and most powerful *polis* on the island of Samos in the Aegean, close to the coast of Asia Minor. The site may originally have been settled by Carians before the arrival of Ionian Greeks in the early Iron Age. Samos's best known ruler was the tyrant Polycrates (see p.72), under whom it flourished as a military, commercial, and cultural center. Following the death of Polycrates, under the control of the Persians the city continued to be ruled by tyrants, now Persian appointees. After the Greco-Persian Wars in the 5th century BCE, Samos became an important member of the Delian League (see pp.158–159) until, following a revolt of eight months, it was settled by Athenians as a cleruchy— a colony that was a dependency of Athens and where the settlers retained their original Athenian citizenship. Samos continued to thrive in Hellenistic times and under Rome, as a part of the province of Asia.

Naxos

The city of Naxos, on the Cycladean island of the same name, was established by early colonists around 1025 BCE on the site of a once-flourishing Bronze Age settlement. The city prospered in Archaic times as a major craft center. After the tyrant Lygdamis was overthrown around 525 BCE, it came to dominate the Cyclades. The Persians attempted, and failed, to take the city in 499 BCE, but succeeded some ten years later. After the Greek victories over Persia of 480–479 BCE, the city joined the Delian League (see pp.158–159), but was the first to revolt in 470 BCE. Naxos's independence ended in the mid-5th century BCE, when, like Samos (see left), it was settled by the Athenians as a cleruchy.

Paros

Famed in particular for its pure-white marble, Paros was a prosperous city on the site of a Bronze Age settlement on the island of Paros. Like its ally Miletus (see p.316), it fought on the side of the Persians in the Greco-Persian Wars, then joined the Delian League (see pp.158–159), paying a large tribute to match its wealth and prosperity.

Thera, Santorini

The best-known achievement of the Cycladean city of Thera was the foundation of the major North African colony of Cyrene around 631 BCE (see p.319). It was a relatively minor power during Archaic and Classical times, but went on to prosper in the Hellenistic era, when it was the base for the Ptolemies' Aegean fleet. It declined in the Roman period and was finally abandoned in the 8th century CE, following a volcanic eruption.

Knossos, Crete

Knossos is famous as the site of a huge Bronze Age temple complex on Crete (see p.380), but from Archaic times it was the location of a thriving Greek city. This was followed by a period of decline, but after the 4th century BCE, it flourished once again.

Lindos, Rhodes

Known today for its impressive archaeological remains (see p.380), Lindos is situated on a headland in the southeast of the island of Rhodes. The site had good harbors, and was already inhabited in prehistoric and Bronze Age times, rising to become the most important of the three cities on Rhodes. The 6th-century BCE tyrant Cleobulus, the city's most notable ruler, was one of the Seven Sages of ancient Greece. In the late 5th century BCE, the city lost independence, when it joined with Ialysos and Camirus to form the federated city of Rhodes.

Halicarnassus, Türkiye

Halicarnassus was a Greek city of southwest Caria in Asia Minor and was founded around 500 BCE by Ionian Greek settlers from Troezen. By the time of one of its best-known inhabitants, the historian Herodotus, in the 5th century BCE, it had become a cosmopolitan city allied with the Persian Empire. Among its notable rulers was Artemisia, who led the Halicarnassan unit that fought the Greeks at the battles of Artemisium and Salamis in 480 BCE. The city was beautified in the following century by another woman called Artemisia, and her husband and brother, Mausolus, who ruled as Persian satraps. The tomb built for Mausolus after his death in 353 BCE (see pp.208–209) was one of the Seven Wonders of the Ancient World. Later that century, following its siege and capture by Alexander the Great, the city began to decline in importance.

△ View of the remains of the ancient tiered theater of Halicarnassus

Miletus, Türkiye

According to the *Iliad*, the people of Miletus fought with the Carians against the Greeks at Troy. By the Archaic period, however, Miletus was a major Greek city, established when Ionian settlers took it from the Carians. A key maritime power, it founded many colonies in the Black Sea region in the 7th and 6th centuries BCE, including Sinope. It was also central to the movement of Greeks into Egypt in the Archaic period. Home to the philosophers Anaximenes and Thales, it was a significant intellectual center of the period. Like other Greek cities of Asia Minor, it was ruled by tyrants: first by local Miletans, then, with the Persian takeover of Miletus and other Ionian cities in the mid-6th century BCE, by Persian appointees. Miletus was instrumental in leading the revolt of the Ionian cities in 499 BCE, resulting in the Persian victory at the Battle of Lade and the capture of Miletus (see pp.142–143). The city remained under Persian control until 479 BCE, when the Persians were defeated at the Battle of Mycale by the Ionian Greeks, aided by Sparta and Athens. It then became a member of the Delian League until it fell under Athenian control. Miletus revolted against the Athenians in 412 BCE, during the Peloponnesian War, when it became the maritime base for Sparta in Ionia. Like the other Ionian cities, it came under Persian rule with the King's Peace of 387 BCE (see p.195). After Alexander the Great's capture of the city, it enjoyed good relations with the Hellenistic kings and then prospered under Roman rule and in Byzantine times; its maritime importance was weakened with the silting up of the harbor, which today is some 9 miles (14 km) from the sea. (See pp.82–83.)

Ephesus, Türkiye

Today, Ephesus is among the best-known Greek cities of Asia Minor, thanks largely to its Temple of Artemis, one of the Seven Wonders of the Ancient World, which, according to Antipater of Sidon, "mounted to the clouds," eclipsing all the other marvels. Ephesus was an independent city until its capture by King Croesus of Lydia in the 6th century BCE. Like other Ionian cities, it came under Persian control later in the same century. Eventually succeeding Miletus (see left) as the foremost Ionian city, it flourished as a regional administrative and religious center of the Roman Empire and thrived until it was captured by the Turks in 1304 CE.

Smyrna, Türkiye

Smyrna was a Greek city on the west coast of Asia Minor, established in a well-defensible location at the head of the Gulf of Izmir, initially in the northeastern corner of the gulf. In the 3rd century BCE, unable to sustain its population, the city was relocated to the slopes of nearby Mount Pagus, where it thrived as an intellectual center in Hellenistic, Roman, and Byzantine times.

Phocaea, Türkiye

Phocaea, the most northerly of the Greek cities of Asia Minor, is a prime example of an ancient city with poor land that founded colonies on sites rich in natural resources. The Phocaeans, described by Herodotus as "the first of the Greeks to make long sea voyages," were responsible for opening up the Mediterranean to Greek influence in the great colonizing period between the 8th and 6th centuries BCE, establishing cities in Spain and France, including Emporion (Empúries) and Massalia (Marseille). When other Greek cities of Asia Minor came under Persian control, many Phocaeans left the site, eventually founding the colony of Elea, southern Italy, in c. 540 BCE. After this, Phocaea declined, but the site remained occupied until late antiquity.

△ View of Smyrna's Agora; the original 4th-century BCE structure was rebuilt in the 2nd century CE following an earthquake.

Magna Graecia and North Africa

Today, anyone asked to name an ancient Greek city would probably say Athens, Sparta, or one of the other major Greek mainland *poleis*. Yet some of the largest, most densely populated, and most flourishing cities were situated far from there, in Sicily, southern Italy, and North Africa.

Pithecusae, Italy

Pithecusae was a multicultural trading and staging post on Ischia in the Bay of Naples. It flourished for several decades in the 8th century BCE until the foundation of Cumae (see below), on the nearby mainland, by Pithecusae itself and its own founders, Chalcis and Eretria.

Cumae, Italy

As Greek people began to spread westward during the 8th century BCE, settlers from Pithecusae (above), Chalcis, and Eretria left the trading post of Pithecusae, suppressed the local population, and then, around 740 BCE, founded Cumae on the nearby mainland. This location benefited from excellent landing places as well as proximity to the fertile Campanian Plain. After a brief period of tyranny under the charismatic former general Aristodemus, Cumae was ruled by an elite until its fall in 421 BCE during the conquest of Campania by the Oscans (Italic people from southern Italy). As Roman influence spread into southern Italy, the city enjoyed good relations with Rome, gaining notable prominence with the incorporation of the Cumaean Sibyl (a priestess and prophet of Apollo's Oracle at Cumae) into Augustan mythology.

Neapolis, Italy

When Cumae—the founder of Neapolis (modern Naples) c. 600 BCE—fell to the Oscans (see left), Neapolis became the main city of Campania in southern Italy, and enjoyed good relations with the Oscans. It was besieged by Rome in the Samnite Wars (343–290 BCE), before becoming a Roman ally, gaining municipal status in 89 BCE. In 82 BCE, it was besieged then brutally sacked by the Roman general Sulla. Thereafter, Neapolis's rich Greek culture made it attractive to the Roman ruling class and it thrived as a resort, retaining its magistracies until the 3rd century CE.

Paestum, Italy

Paestum, formerly Poseidonia, is a city in southern Italy that is most likely best known today for three magnificent temples (two to Hera, one to Athena), which are considered among the best preserved of any from antiquity (see p.384). Founded around 600 BCE by Sybaris (see right), it became a major cultural and economic power, benefiting from rich agricultural resources. After being conquered by the nearby Lucanians in 410 BCE, its culture was gradually assimilated into theirs. In 273 BCE Paestum was colonized by the Romans. Following centuries of prosperity, the city was abandoned in late antiquity, probably as a result of malarial conditions arising from changes in land drainage systems.

Tarentum, Italy

Tarentum (modern Taranto) was a Spartan colony in southern Italy, founded at the beginning of the 8th century BCE by the Partheniae (Sons of Maidens), an expelled population who were said to be the offspring of Helots and Spartiate women. The city expanded in the first half of the 5th century BCE after securing victories over southern Italy's Messapians and Peucetians. Tarentum emerged as one of the largest of the Greek cities, as well as a significant economic, political, cultural, and military center. Its rule by an aristocratic elite was supplanted by a democracy, whose most distinguished leader, in the first half of the 4th century BCE, was Archytas. After falling to Rome in 270 BCE, the city of Tarentum remained an important, culturally Greek, center for wool and textile production.

Sybaris, Italy

Sybaris was an important Greek city on the Tyrrhenian coast of southern Italy. Its reputation for opulence and hedonism gave rise to the English word "sybaritic" (see p.125). Founded by Achaea and Troezen around 720 BCE, it swiftly established its own colonies, including Poseidonia (Paestum, see left). The city flourished until it was eventually sacked in 510 BCE by the neighboring city of Croton, after which the population relocated to Paestum and Laos.

△ View of the Temple of Hera in the Valley of the Temples, Agrigento

Rhegium, Italy

One of the earliest and most important Greek cities in southern Italy, Rhegium was founded by Chalcis in c. 734 or 730 BCE and refounded by Messene in c. 600 BCE. It was sacked by the Syracusan tyrant Diogenes I in the 4th century BCE, and remained under Syracusan influence. Roman expansion into southern Italy fostered good relations with Rome as it was a key location en route to Sicily.

Selinus, Sicily

Selinus was a prosperous, well-populated and, by ancient standards, huge city on the southwest coast of Sicily. It is known in modern times for its rich archaeological discoveries and remains, including the sanctuaries of Demeter, Zeus, and Persephone. The city was founded in the 7th century BCE by Megara Hyblaea, on the east coast of Sicily, and by Megara Hyblaea's own metropolis, the city of Megara, on mainland Greece. Selinus's oligarchic elite were overthrown by a tyranny that was itself displaced early in the 5th century BCE with the help of Euryleon of Sparta—one of the companions of Dorieus, a Spartan prince from the Agiad royal house. Euryleon went on to rule before himself being overthrown. The history of the city was characterized by periods of conflict with the local neighboring population, the Segestans. Selinus was the farthest west of the Greek cities in Sicily, so it was also in contact with Phoenician cities, including Carthage. In 409 BCE, the city was sacked by Carthage, and its walls were destroyed soon afterward. Selinus then remained under Carthaginian control until it was abandoned in 250 BCE.

Agrigento, Sicily

A major Greek city in southern Sicily, Agrigento (known to the Greeks as Akragas) became the blueprint for the Sicilian model of militaristic and imperialistic tyranny. Like many colonies, it had been chosen by its founder (the city of Gela, around 580 BCE) for its location—in this case, well-defensible terrain between the acropolis to the north and a ridge to the south. The expulsion of the ruling aristocracy by the tyrant Phalaris from Agrigento c. 570 BCE began a long period of tyranny, under which the city flourished as a wealthy cultural center with magnificent temples and a large necropolis. Akragas remained wealthy under Roman dominance. The area occupied by the ancient city was significantly larger than the extent of the modern city. (See also p.385.)

Syracuse, Sicily

Syracuse was the foremost city of Magna Graecia, and one of the greatest Greek cities anywhere in the ancient Mediterranean. It was founded by settlers from Tenea, a town outside Corinth, around 734 BCE, initially on the island of Ortygia, off the east coast of Sicily, which benefited from two natural harbors and a freshwater spring. Soon after, the settlement moved to the mainland, which was linked to Ortygia via an artificial causeway. The city was ruled by a Greek elite, the *gamoroi*, who dominated the local population, the *killyroi*, until the *killyroi* expelled them in the early 5th century BCE. In the aftermath of this, Gelon emerged as the first of its tyrants. Syracuse flourished under him and also under the reign of his brother, Hieron (r. 478–466 BCE), as a major military and cultural center. The city came to be distinguished for its extensive fortifications and temples—most famously, the Temple of Athena, which was dedicated after Gelon's triumph over Carthage at the Battle of Himera in 480 BCE. The temple's exterior was—and remains—incorporated into the walls of the 7th-century CE Cathedral of Syracuse. In the 4th century BCE (and following the wars with Athens in 427–424 BCE and 415–413 BCE), Syracuse became the major power in Magna Graecia. It continued to dominate the region until it was sacked by the Romans in 211 BCE, after a lengthy siege. Syracuse returned to prosperity until its conquest by Arabs in 878 CE. (See also pp.128–129.)

Cyrene, Libya

Cyrene, founded around 631 BCE, was the most significant of the Greek colonies of North Africa. Agriculturally rich and in a fertile location in the Cyrenaica region, it was a key trading center. It was also culturally rich, and home to the geographer Eratosthenes and the poet Callimachus. Cyrene remained a major city until it was devastated by earthquakes in the 3rd and 4th centuries CE.

Naucratis, Egypt

Naucratis was a culturally diverse, bustling city and trading post in the Nile Delta in ancient Egypt and was populated by Greek people originating from a wide range of cities, such as Phocaea, Miletus, Rhodes, Halicarnassus, Clazomenae, Mytilene, Aegina, and Samos. Naucratis was the earliest permanent Greek settlement in Egypt and was established on a site that had previously been occupied by, among others, Egyptians, Greeks, and possibly Phoenicians. It flourished as a trading post between Egypt and Greece and was instrumental in bringing Egyptian art and ideas to Greece. Naucratis declined with the shifting of the Nile and the rise of Alexander the Great in the 4th century BCE, but remained a gateway for Mediterranean trade until the 7th century CE.

△ Painting showing Gelon's triumphal entry into Syracuse after the Battle of Himera in 480 BCE (Giuseppe Carta, 1850)

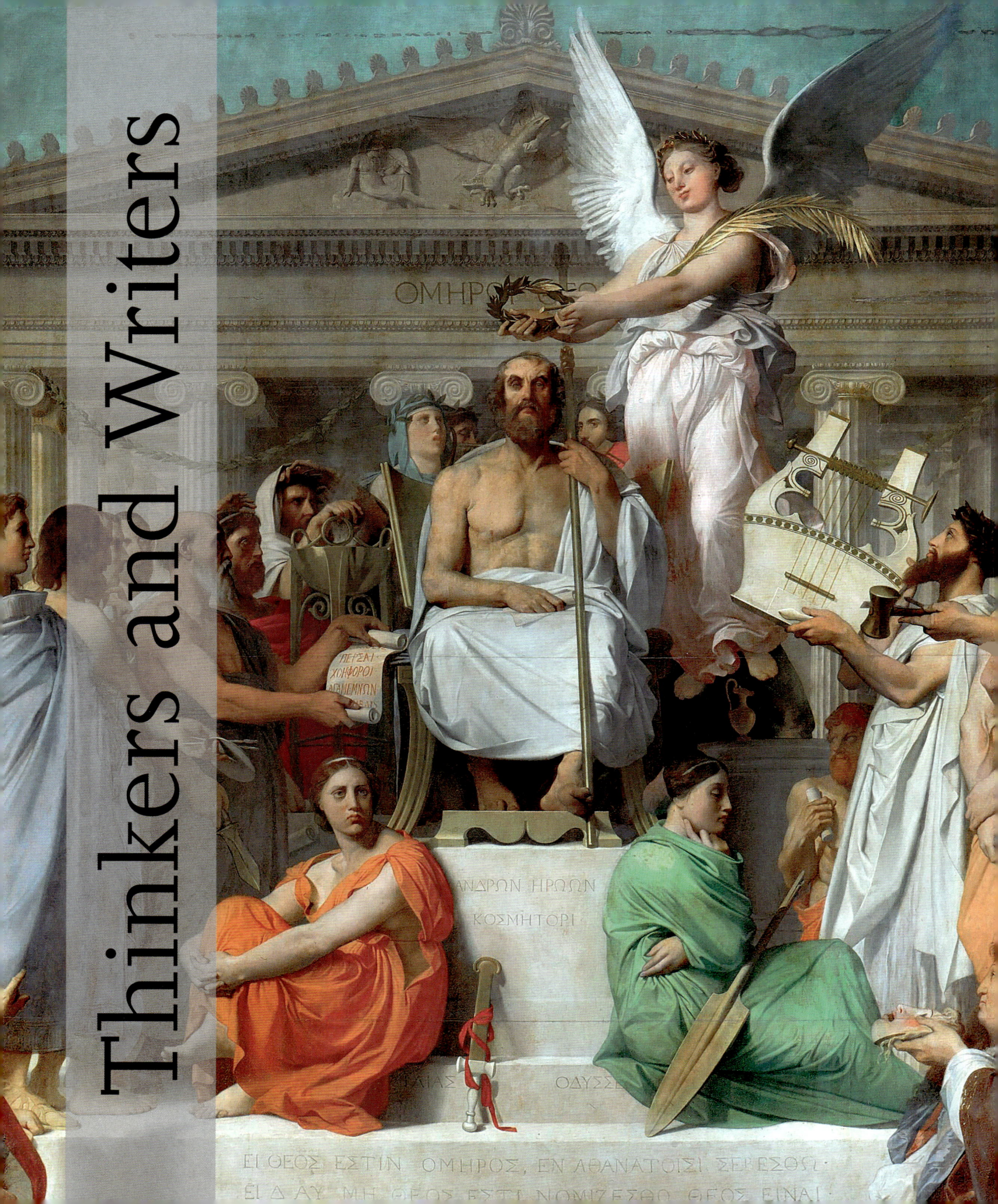

Thinkers and Writers

Poets and Dramatists

Building on a rich oral tradition of storytelling, literature in ancient Greece began with the epic poems of Homer and Hesiod, developing into poetry of all kinds, from pastoral and love poems to ribald drinking songs. A new genre also emerged—drama, with actors staging public performances.

Aeschylus
Tragedian

c. 525–456 BCE

Widely regarded as the "father of Greek tragedy," Aeschylus is believed to have written more than 70 plays, of which seven have survived, including *The Persians* (472 BCE), *Seven Against Thebes* (467 BCE), *The Suppliants* (463 BCE), and the *Oresteia* trilogy (458 BCE). His principal innovations were introducing a second actor in drama and establishing a formal basis for the genre of tragedy. Born in Eleusis, Attica, Aeschylus was said to have worked at a local vineyard until 499 BCE, when he began writing tragedies. His first victory was at a literary competition at the Dionysia festival in Athens in 484 BCE; in subsequent annual competitions, he was almost invariably awarded first prize. As well as his writing, Aeschylus distinguished himself as a soldier, serving in the Athenian army against Persia at the battles of Marathon (490 BCE) and Salamis (480 BCE). According to legend, Aeschylus was killed during a visit to Sicily, when an eagle dropped a tortoise onto his head, mistaking it for a rock.

◁ Painting of Homer being crowned (Jean-Auguste-Dominique Ingres, 1827)

Alcaeus
Lyric poet

c. 620–580 BCE

The lyric poet Alcaeus was born in Mytilene, the major city of the island of Lesbos, during a period of political turmoil. A member of the ruling aristocratic class, he became deeply involved in various conflicts in the region as rival factions vied for power, opposing the rule of a succession of tyrants. As a result of his political activities, Alcaeus was forced into exile for a number of years, probably fleeing to Egypt. He was eventually pardoned by the tyrant Pittacus and allowed to return to Lesbos. Alcaeus was a contemporary of the poet Sappho (see p.101), also thought to be a native of Lesbos. His poetry ranges from political and drinking songs to hymns and love poems—these were later collected into ten books and included in the canonical list of nine lyric poets compiled by Hellenistic Alexandrian scholars.

Alcman
Lyric poet

7th century BCE

Of the six books of choral lyric poetry that were written by Alcman, only fragments of

papyrus and quotations by other writers have survived to the present. However, his inclusion in the Alexandrian list of the nine major lyric poets attests to the esteem in which he was held in ancient Greece. Little is known of Alcman's life, and even his nationality is uncertain: it is likely he was active in Sparta in the late 7th century BCE, although he may not have been born there—according to one legend, he originally came from Lydia, but was later enslaved and taken to Sparta.

Anyte
Poet

fl. c. 300 BCE

Born in Tegea, Arcadia, Anyte was active in the early Hellenistic period, contributing a number of epigrams, about 20 of which have been confirmed as authentic. One of the most respected female poets of the time, she is credited with introducing rustic themes to the genre, possibly providing the inspiration for Theocritus's pastoral poetry (see p.252).

△ Painting of Alcaeus playing the cithara (Lawrence Alma-Tadema, 1881)

Apollonius of Rhodes
Epic poet

3rd century BCE

Despite his epithet *Rhodios* (of Rhodes), the epic poet Apollonius was born in Ptolemaic Egypt, probably in Alexandria or Naucratis. He studied with the scholar and poet Callimachus at Alexandria before becoming the head of the library there himself. It was only much later that he moved to Rhodes, where it is likely that he died in the late 3rd century BCE. His most celebrated work was the *Argonautica*, an epic telling of the quest by Jason and the Argonauts for the Golden Fleece.

Archilochus
Lyric poet

c. 680–640 BCE

Regarded as a rather iconoclastic character, Archilochus broke with the Greek poetic tradition of his time by writing poems that were largely based on personal experience. His often ribald accounts of life as a warrior and sailor, although ostensibly autobiographical, offer an unreliable narrative of his existence. All that is known for certain is that he was born

◁ Statue of the comic playwright Aristophanes

into an aristocratic family on the island of Paros, where he also probably died. Despite the sometimes flippant or angry opinions in his poems, he was praised for his stylistic skill, and achieved hero status and a cult following, especially among devotees of the god Dionysus. They dedicated a sanctuary, the Archilocheion, on Paros in his honor in the 3rd century BCE.

Aristophanes
Comic playwright

c. 450–388 BCE

The genre of comic drama known as Old Attic Comedy or Old Comedy was dominated by Aristophanes, whose biting satires and parodies lampooned almost every aspect of the social and political life of Athens in the 5th century BCE. He wrote about 40 plays, of which 11 have survived virtually intact, including *The Clouds* (423 BCE), *The Wasps* (422 BCE), *The Birds* (414 BCE), and *The Frogs* (405 BCE). Aristophanes was a frequent prizewinner at festivals, and a controversial but well-liked character in Athenian society. However, almost nothing is known of his life outside the theater. Plato, who suggests that Aristophanes' caricature of Socrates in *The Clouds* damaged the latter's reputation, nevertheless portrays the writer in his *Symposium* as an amiable bon vivant. Other targets of Aristophanes' wit, notably the politician Cleon, were less kind about him. In addition to his ridiculing of the hypocrisy and corruption of the establishment, Aristophanes promoted positive values in his plays, including peace and community spirit, and—surprisingly for the time—

presented a sympathetic view of the role of women in society in works such as *Thesmophoriazusae* (411 BCE), *Lysistrata* (411 BCE), and *Ecclesiazusae* (c. 392 BCE).

Cratinus
Comic playwright

c. 520–423 BCE

Along with Eupolis (see opposite) and Aristophanes (left), Cratinus was acknowledged as one of the three masters of Old Comedy, regularly winning competitions at the Dionysia and the Lenaea festivals. His 21 comedies survive in fragments, but contemporary accounts describe them as savage satires, in a direct style that was influenced by Aeschylus (see p.321). Born in Athens, Cratinus served as an officer in the Athenian army, but earned a reputation as a drunkard; the theme of drunkenness appears in his best-known comedy, *Pytine* (Bottle). He continued writing prizewinning plays until shortly before his death, aged about 97.

Diphilus
Comic playwright

4th–3rd centuries BCE

It is generally believed that Diphilus wrote more than 100 plays. With their frequent mythological themes, combined with innovative versification, these works bridged the transition from Middle to New Comedy. Originally from Sinope, an Ionian colony on the Black Sea, Diphilus made his name— alongside the giants of New Comedy, Menander and Philemon (see p.324)— in Athens, which is where his remains were buried after his death in Smyrna.

Erinna
Poet

4th century BCE

Little is known of the life of Erinna. Some ancient sources claim she was a contemporary of Sappho (see p.101), but it is more likely that she lived in the early 4th century BCE, and was a native of Tilos. She is known for *The Distaff*—a 300-line poem of lament written in memory of her friend Baucis—and also for epigrams, a handful of which have survived to the present day.

Eupolis
Comic playwright

C.446–411 BCE

One of the Old Comedy writers, with Aristophanes and Cratinus (see opposite), Eupolis is credited with writing 19 comedies in his comparatively short career, including *Flatterers*, which won the Dionysia festival in 421 BCE. His rivalry with Aristophanes became increasingly bitter, culminating in the latter accusing him of plagiarism. Eupolis's death is the subject of legends: some say he was drowned by the politician Alcibiades in retaliation for his satirical portrayal of him, others that he was killed in a naval battle in the Peloponnesian War.

Euripides
Tragedian

C.485–406 BCE

Euripides was the youngest of the three great Greek tragedians of the 5th century BCE, the others being Aeschylus (see p.321) and Sophocles (see p.325). He presented his first play at a competition at the Dionysia

△ Marble relief showing Euripides holding a tragic mask (1st century BCE–1st century CE)

festival in 455 BCE, soon after the death of Aeschylus. In a career spanning nearly 50 years, he wrote about 90 plays but, with competition from Sophocles, was awarded a first prize only five times. Much of his output is now lost, but extant plays include *Medea* (431 BCE), *The Trojan Women* (415 BCE), and *Iphigenia in Aulis*, for which he won a posthumous first prize in 405 BCE. Euripides was a native of Salamis and, according to legend, lived a reclusive life in

a cave on the island after two unsuccessful marriages. He spent his final years in Macedon as a the guest of King Archelaus.

Hesiod
Epic poet

8th–7th centuries BCE

The poet Hesiod is thought to have lived some time between 750 and 650 BCE and was a near-contemporary of Homer

(see pp.60–61), with whom he is often compared and contrasted. The little that is known of Hesiod's life has been gleaned from personal references within various of his own poems, where he describes himself as being born in Cyme, Aeolian Anatolia, the son of a merchant, and later, when the sea trade dwindled, moving to the small rural settlement of Ascra, next to Mount Helicon in Boeotia. In his *Theogony*, Hesiod writes that while working in the fields he was visited by the Muses (inspirational goddesses), which ignited his poetic career. His two surviving works, *Theogony* and *Works and Days*, are long poems composed in the same hexameter style as the Homeric epics—but they are epic in language rather than scope or subject matter, describing the genealogy of the gods and the rural calendar respectively. Another body of poems, the "Hesiodic corpus," has also been attributed to him, including the epic *Shield of Heracles*, and *Catalogue of Women*.

Homer
Epic poet

c. 750–700 BCE

The two great epic poems of ancient Greece, the *Iliad* and the *Odyssey*, are attributed to Homer, even though he may never have existed. The *Iliad* tells the story of the Trojan War via the perspective of Achilles, one of its characters; the *Odyssey* continues the story. (See main entry pp.60–61.)

Menander
Comic playwright

c. 342–292 BCE

Reputed to be the finest of the playwrights of the New Comedy, Menander wrote more than 100 comedies, although during his lifetime he was often eclipsed by his older rival Philemon (see right), whose broader humor seems to have appealed more to contemporary audiences. Only one of Menander's works, *Dyskolos*, has survived almost intact; the rest have been lost or exist only in fragments, or in later versions by Latin writers. However, many of his one-line

maxims, such as "Old men are children for the second time," have achieved proverbial status. Menander was an Athenian and a member of a highly respected family. He counted among his circle of friends prominent statesmen as well as philosophers, intellectuals, and fellow dramatists. Ptolemy I Soter of Egypt was a patron of his works. Menander is believed to have died as a result of a bathing accident, aged about 51.

Philemon
Comic playwright

c. 361–263 BCE

Philemon was active in Athens from some time before 330 BCE, and by 306 BCE had been granted Athenian citizenship. He was born in either Syracuse in Sicily, or Soli in Cilicia, on the south coast of Asia Minor. It appears that apart from a brief spell in Egypt at the court of Ptolemy II Philadelphus, Philemon lived and worked in Athens for most of his life. He was popular with audiences in Athens, writing 97 comedies in his very long career, and seldom losing competitions to his younger rival Menander (see left). According to legend, he died, aged almost 100, while he was being crowned on stage for his lifetime achievements. Philemon's style of comedy fell out of favor after his death, and only fragments of his work have survived to the present.

Phrynichus
Tragedian

5th–4th centuries BCE

One of the earliest tragedians of ancient Greece, Phrynichus is credited with establishing many

△ Painting of Pindar wearing a laurel crown (Jean-Auguste-Dominique Ingres, 1827)

of the conventions of the genre. For example, he introduced the idea of an actor separate from the chorus, making dramatic dialogue possible, and may also have added female characters to the action, albeit played by men. Phrynichus's plays include many tragedies on mythological themes and contemporary issues. His play *The Capture of Miletus* from 492 BCE—which recounts the Persian capture of the Greek city of Miletus in 494 BCE (see p.180)—was banned because its subject matter apparently brought audiences to tears.

Pindar
Lyric poet

c. 518–439 BCE

The Theban poet Pindar was regarded by scholars as the greatest of the canonical nine lyric poets, praised for his distinctive and sometimes enigmatic style. His poems were collected into 17 books by the scholars of Alexandria and, because of the reverence in which he was held, more of his work has survived than that of others of the period. Legend has it that when he was a child, bees built their comb in his mouth, bestowing on him the ability to write honeyed verse. His talent earned him numerous commissions, most notably for victory odes celebrating the triumphs of competitors at Panhellenic festivals. During the Greco-Persian Wars, he took refuge in Aegina, where he became a respected citizen, composing victory odes for the ruling families there. He died, aged about 80, on a visit to a festival in Argos, and his ashes were taken to his home city of Thebes for burial.

Sappho
Lyric poet

c. 610–570 BCE

Sappho is considered by many scholars to be one of the finest poets of Greek antiquity, but little is known of her life. The only poem of hers to survive intact is a hymn to Aphrodite. (See main entry p.101)

Simonides
Lyric poet

c. 556–468 BCE

Alexandrian scholars listed Simonides as one of the canonical nine lyric poets in recognition of his talent as a writer of charming lyric poetry. However, his fame rests almost as much on his reputation as a miser, an acrimonious rival of Pindar (see opposite), an inventor of some of the letters of the Greek alphabet, and a creator of a memorization system. Aged about 30, he moved from his native Ceos to the court of the tyrant Hipparchus in Athens, in search of recognition and reward

for his poetry. Hipparchus was assassinated in 514 BCE, and Simonides, having made his name internationally, departed to Thessaly and later settled in Sicily, ingratiating himself with the tyrant Hiero I of Syracuse.

Sophocles
Tragedian

c. 496–406 BCE

One of the three great tragedians of the Greek Classical period, with Aeschylus (see p.321) and Euripides (p.323), Sophocles is best known for his so-called Theban plays (*Oedipus Rex*, *Oedipus at Colonus*, and *Antigone*). These are among the 7 surviving of the more than 120 plays he wrote in a career spanning almost 50 years. He dominated the competitions of the Lenaea and Dionysia festivals, winning more victories than any of his rivals, and is credited with introducing a third actor into his dramas, giving more opportunity for plot development. As well as being a respected playwright, Sophocles was elected as an official in the government of Athens under Pericles, and saw active service in the war with Samos. Several anecdotes surround his death, including the myth that he died while attempting to read a particularly long passage from one of his plays in a single breath. Whatever the truth, he continued to write in his old

▷ Marble statue of Sophocles (1st century CE)

age, and finished his final play *Oedipus at Colonus*, only just before his death, aged 90 or 91.

Stesichorus
Lyric poet

c. 630–555 BCE

Although Stesichorus is listed as one of the nine lyric poets of the Alexandrian canon, only a few fragments of his work survive. However, he was prolific, producing 26 books of poems, including epics in lyric meters. He is said to have earned the name Stesichorus (he was originally named Tisias) by introducing the use of a chorus with a kithara accompaniment.

Theocritus
Pastoral poet

c. 300–260 BCE

Despite achieving fame as the founder of pastoral poetry, Theocritus also wrote hymns, mimes, and erotic poems in his later life. There is little reliable information about him, although he is thought to have been born in Syracuse and to have spent some time in Alexandria, Egypt. (See main entry pp.252.)

Tyrtaeus
Elegiac poet

7th century BCE

The Spartan elegiac poet Tyrtaeus is known today only from fragments of his work and spurious accounts of his life by later biographers, who described him as "lame," and even "insane." He was, however, highly regarded in Sparta, and at a time of turmoil in the region his stirring poetry provided great inspiration and comfort.

△ Painting of Eratosthenes teaching in Alexandria (Bernardo Strozzi, 1635)

Historians and Geographers

In the Classical period, writers broke with the tradition of poetic renditions of legends. Some presented a more factual account of historical events, laying the foundations of Western history. At the same time, others described and mapped the lands and seas of the world that they knew.

Artemidorus of Ephesus
Geographer

fl. 100 BCE

Artemidorus wrote an 11-volume treatise on geography, using information gleaned from his travels around the Mediterranean and the Black Sea, as well as the works of previous authors. His treatise was well known in antiquity, and was referred to by Strabo and Pliny in the 1st century CE, but it is now lost.

Diodorus Siculus
Historian

1st century BCE

Born in Agyrium, Diodorus Siculus (Diodorus of Sicily) was the author of a comprehensive history of the world, the *Bibliotheca historica*, written in the middle decades of the 1st century BCE. The work runs to a monumental 40 books in total, of which only 15 have survived, along with some fragments of the lost books. Diodorus drew on information from numerous sources to create a description of the mythology, geography, and history of the world known to him.

Diogenes Laertius
Biographer

3rd century CE

Little is known for certain of the life of Diogenes Laertius, except as the author of the *Lives and Opinions of Eminent Philosophers*. Believed to have been written in the early 3rd century CE, the biographies in the *Lives* are notoriously unreliable and have significant omissions, yet the book is a valuable source of information on philosophical writings for which the primary sources have been lost.

Eratosthenes
Geographer

c. 276–194 BCE

Widely regarded as the founder of the study of geography, Eratosthenes was a polymath who became the Head Librarian at the Library of Alexandria, the intellectual center of the Greek world at the time. He was born in Cyrene, in present-day Libya, but moved to Athens to study philosophy, earning a reputation as a scholar. In around 245 BCE, he moved to Alexandria, where he remained for the rest of his life.

Broadening his studies into astronomy and mathematics, he became the first to calculate the circumference of the Earth and its axial tilt, and produced an influential global projection of the world.

Hecataeus of Miletus
Historian, geographer

c. 550–476 BCE

Best known today for revising and improving the map of the world devised by the philosopher Anaximander, Hecataeus was also the author of geographical and historical treatises, including *Periodos Ges* (*Journey Around the Earth*), an account of his extensive travels, and the *Historia*.

Herodotus
Historian

c. 484–425 BCE

A native of the Greek city of Halicarnassus in Asia Minor, Herodotus is known for his account of the Greco-Persian Wars in his *Histories*. (See main entry p.149.)

Hippodamus of Miletus
Urban planner, philosopher

fl. c. 500–440 BCE

Regarded as the founder of European urban planning, Hippodamus was responsible for designing several Greek city centers—including that of his native city, Miletus—with a rectangular grid plan. While such designs had been used since the 8th century BCE, he applied the concept methodically, intending to create an ordered environment that might promote social and political harmony.

Plutarch

Biographer, historian

c. 46–after 119 CE

A prolific writer, Plutarch was best known for *Parallel Lives*, his anthology of biographies of prominent Greek and Roman figures, and for his collection of historical and philosophical essays, *Moralia*. He was born into an aristocratic Greek family in Chaeronea, Boeotia. As a young man, he spent several years in Athens studying philosophy and mathematics, before returning to Chaeronea to take up an official position as a magistrate. He also represented Chaeronea on diplomatic missions to various foreign countries. For these services, he was granted Roman citizenship. Some sources suggest he was also imperial procurator (treasurer) in Achaea under the Roman emperor Hadrian. In addition, Plutarch was a priest at the Temple of Apollo in Delphi, and played a significant role in the revival of the shrine in the time of Trajan and Hadrian.

Polybius

Historian

c. 200–118 BCE

A native of Megalopolis, in Arcadia, Polybius was born into an influential Greek family, and later became a statesman himself. As such, he gained a valuable insight into the political and military machinations involved in the advent of Roman control over the Mediterranean region. These he documented in *Historiai* (*Histories*), a detailed account of the years from 264 BCE to 146 BCE, including Rome's wars with the Carthaginians and the Macedonians. As a young man, Polybius accompanied his father on diplomatic missions. He later served as a cavalry officer until he was captured by the Romans and taken to Rome in 167 BCE. There, he became a trusted tutor to Scipio Aemilianus, who would later lead the Roman forces against Carthage. Polybius was allowed to return to Greece in 150 BCE, but maintained his relationship with Scipio as a counselor, accompanying him on his campaigns and returning with him to Rome, where he worked on the *Histories*. It is thought that he later returned to Greece, and died there.

Strabo

Geographer, historian

c. 64 BCE–24 CE

Born in Amaseia in Pontus, the geographer and historian Strabo spent his early life in what is today Cappadocia. After a period studying and writing in Rome from 44 BCE, he embarked upon a lifetime of traveling around Asia Minor and the Mediterranean, and into Africa, following the Nile down as far as Ethiopia. Originally considering himself a historian, he wrote his *Historical Sketches* in about 20 BCE, but his great work was the *Geographica* (*Geography*), his comprehensive description of the people and places around the world that he visited on his travels, which he continued to update and revise until his death.

Thucydides

Historian

c. 460–400 BCE

Often contrasted with Herodotus, a historian of the previous generation, Thucydides took a more analytical and scientific approach to writing history. As a general in the Athenian army during the Peloponnesian War (431–404 BCE) against Sparta, Thucydides was well qualified to give a firsthand description of the conflict, and he also took pains to find other eyewitness accounts. Breaking away from traditional historiography, he avoided mentioning divine influence or giving irrelevant background, and instead attempted to present a factual report of events, in a strict chronological order. As well as detailing the military tactics of the two sides, he examined the role of politics, and the motives of individual leaders, in shaping the war, often quoting speeches, such as the famous funeral oration by Pericles, to illustrate the personalities of the major figures. This revolutionary approach made his *History of the Peloponnesian War* an early example of political realism.

◁ A statue probably representing the philosopher Plutarch

△ Portrait of Thucydides from the Jerash Mosaic in Jordan

Timaeus

Historian

C. 345–250 BCE

A prolific writer of history in copious detail, Timaeus was the son of the ruling tyrant of the city of Tauromenium (present-day Taormina), in Sicily. Forced to leave his home town by the tyrant of Syracuse, Agathocles, Timaeus fled to Athens. Initially intending to study there, he settled in the city and began working on his huge 38-volume *Histories*, which covered Greece's history from its earliest days to around 360 BCE. It also explored the histories of Sicily and Italy. Timaeus is believed to have returned to Sicily when he was in his nineties, and to have died there shortly after.

Xenophon of Athens

Historian, philosopher

C. 430–354 BCE

As a young man, the Athenian Xenophon and his contemporary Plato were protégés of Socrates, and both wrote philosophical works influenced by him. But Xenophon went on to follow a military career. He became a commander of the Ten Thousand mercenaries employed by Cyrus the Younger in his unsuccessful attempt to take control of the Achaemenid Empire in 401 BCE. His account of the campaign, *Anabasis* (also known as *Up Country*, *The Expedition of Cyrus*, or *March of the Ten Thousand*), secured Xenophon's reputation as an authoritative historian and a distinguished military leader and philosopher.

Philosophers and Scientists

Renowned as the birthplace of philosophy, ancient Greece was home to successive generations of thinkers whose ideas, based on reason rather than superstition and mythology, revolutionized our understanding of the world and formed the basis for modern science.

Anaxagoras
Philosopher

c.500–428 BCE

As part of the early Greek philosophical quest for the basic substance and ordering principle of the universe, the pre-Socratic philosopher Anaxagoras suggested the concept of *Nous* (Mind). Anaxagoras was born in the Ionian city of Clazomenae, Anatolia, which was at that time part of the Achaemenid Empire. Some time after the Greco-Persian War, he moved to Athens, where he befriended the statesman Pericles. Charges of impiety, possibly motivated by his association with Pericles, forced him to flee from Athens to Lampsacus in about 434 BCE, where he stayed until his death.

Anaximander
Philosopher

c.610–546 BCE

The pre-Socratic philosopher Anaximander was a follower, and likely a student, of Thales in Miletus (see pp.82–83) in the earliest days of Greek philosophy, and succeeded him to become the second head of the Milesian school of philosophy. In his response to his mentor's idea that the fundamental substance of the universe, known as the *arche*, is water, Anaximander suggested an abstract concept, *apeiron* (the Infinite), as the governing principle. He is also known for devising a map of the world he knew, later improved upon by Hecataeus of Miletus. He was a well-traveled man and was said to have helped found Apollonia on the Black Sea coast.

△ Painting of Anaxagoras (Jusepe de Ribera, 17th century)

◁ Roman marble bust of Antisthenes from the 2nd century CE

Anaximenes
Philosopher

fl.546–525 BCE

The last of the three masters of the Milesian school of philosophy, Anaximenes was a student of Anaximander. Like his teacher, and like Thales before him, Anaximenes sought the essential substance of the universe. He argued that this was air, and went on to develop the idea that Earth, which he believed to be a flat disk, was floating on air, with the sun and other heavenly bodies revolving around it.

Antisthenes
Philosopher

c.446–366 BCE

Born in Athens, Antisthenes initially studied with the rhetorician Gorgias, but after encountering Socrates (see p.187) became a follower of his, enthusiastically adopting his ethics-based philosophy. As one of Socrates' closest protégés, he was present at his death, for which he never forgave the Athenian authorities. Like Plato, a fellow disciple of Socrates, Antisthenes went on to found his own school, in the Cynosarges, a gymnasium just outside Athens, where he taught the Socratic values of a simple, virtuous, and inquisitive life.

Apollonius of Perga
Mathematician, astronomer

c. 240–190 BCE

Despite ranking alongside Euclid and Archimedes (see p.271) as one of ancient Greece's greatest mathematicians, very little is known about Apollonius of Perga's life. From his epithet, we can assume he was a native of Perga, on Anatolia's southern coast. However, he also had connections with the Library of Pergamon, and it is probable that he also studied and worked in Alexandria, the intellectual center of Hellenistic Greece. Only one of his numerous works, the eight-volume *Conics*, has survived (some volumes in their original Greek, others in their Arabic translation), and what is known of his other writings is from references by other authors. In addition to breaking new ground in geometry, Apollonius was also a highly accomplished and respected astronomer.

Archimedes
Philosopher, mathematician

c. 287–212 BCE

A native of the Greek city of Syracuse in Sicily, Archimedes made significant contributions to geometry, mechanics, and calculus, as well as inventing innovative machines, including several war machines. (See main entry p.271).

Aristarchus of Samos
Astronomer, mathematician

c. 310–230 BCE

One of the foremost astronomers of the Hellenistic period, Aristarchus of Samos proposed the earliest-known model of a heliocentric universe, with Earth and other planets orbiting the sun, correctly placing them at different distances from it. He also deduced that it takes a year for Earth to circle the sun, and that Earth rotates around an axis each day. Only one of his many works is known to have survived: *On the Sizes and Distances of the Sun and Moon*. Aristarchus left his home of Samos to study in Athens at the Lyceum founded by Aristotle, and later lived and worked in Alexandria, where he died.

Aristotle
Philosopher

384–322 BCE

The third of the three great philosophers of Classical Athens, with Socrates and Plato, Aristotle was a teacher and prolific writer on a wide range of subjects that included the natural sciences, the arts, philosophy, and politics. He was born in Stagira, Chalcidice, where his father was a physician to the king of Macedonia. Aged about 17, he moved to Athens to study with Plato at his Academy, staying there until Plato's death some 20 years later. He then spent time researching plant and animal life on Lesbos and in Anatolia, and briefly returned to Macedonia as a tutor to the young Alexander the Great. In 335 BCE, he went back to Athens, where he set up the Peripatetic school at the Lyceum, and produced a huge number of treatises and teaching materials.

Amid a rise in anti-Macedonian feeling in Athens following the death of Alexander the Great, he retired to his family estate in Chalcis, Euboea, in 322 BCE and died there later that year.

Chrysippus
Philosopher

c. 279–206 BCE

The success of the Stoic school of philosophy in Hellenistic Greece (see p.97) is largely due to the influence of Chrysippus, whose prolific writings provided a extensive analysis of Stoicism. He came from Soli in Asia Minor, but studied in Athens with Cleanthes, successor to Zeno of Citium, founder of the Stoic school. Chrysippus headed the Stoic school after Cleanthes' death.

◁ Hellenistic bust of Aristotle by the Greek sculptor Lysippos (4th century BCE)

△ Diogenes Searching for an Honest Man (Jacob Jordaens, c.1642)

Cleanthes
Philosopher

c.330–230 BCE

An advocate of the virtue of hard work, Cleanthes was the natural successor to Zeno of Citium as head of the Stoic school of philosophy. As a young man in Assos, in northwestern Anatolia, he had been a professional boxer, but he moved to Athens to study with Zeno, paying for his keep in true Stoic fashion by working as a water-carrier. He continued to do both manual and teaching jobs when he became head of the school, and lived to a great age.

Democritus
Philosopher

c.460–370 BCE

Together with his mentor, Leucippus, Democritus developed the theory of Atomism—the concept that everything in the universe consists of minute, indivisible particles surrounded by empty space. He was probably born in Abdera, in Thrace, but although apocryphal stories abound about the "laughing philosopher"—named for his emphasis on cheerfulness—very little is known for certain about his life. None of his writings has survived, but numerous references by other writers, including Aristotle, provide a good overview of Democritus's materialist philosophy.

Diogenes of Sinope
Philosopher

c.412/404–324/321 BCE

Known in Athens as Diogenes the Cynic, from the Greek *kynikos* (doglike), Diogenes famously lived on the streets of the city, sleeping in a large ceramic jar in the Agora, and extolling the virtues of simplicity and poverty. To show his disdain for the conventions of urban life, he carried a lamp with him during the daytime, explaining that he was looking for an honest man. He was born in Sinope (modern-day Türkiye), where his father was in charge of the mint. Following a scandal involving adulteration or debasement of the currency, Diogenes lost his citizenship and was exiled. He fled to Athens, where he became a follower of Socrates' student Antisthenes, developing his austere philosophy. At some point he was kidnapped by pirates and enslaved. He ended up in Corinth, where he spent the rest of his life.

Empedocles
Philosopher

c. 494–434 BCE

The pre-Socratic philosopher Empedocles was one of the first of the early Greek thinkers to break with monism, the belief that the universe consists of a single fundamental substance. Instead, he developed a theory of four elements—water, air, earth, and fire—from combinations of which everything is derived. He claimed that the opposing forces of Love (attraction) and Strife (repulsion) governed the mixing and separating of these elements. While we know that he was born in Akragas, Sicily, details of his life are clouded by unreliable anecdotes, in particular the story that he threw himself into the volcano Mount Etna to prove that he could become a god.

▷ Roman marble bust of Epicurus (c. 270 BCE)

Epictetus
Philosopher

c. 50–135 CE

Born to enslaved parents in Hierapolis, in Roman-occupied Phrygia, the Stoic philosopher Epictetus was later taken to Rome, where he was allowed to study and eventually gained his freedom. He worked for a while as a teacher, but along with other philosophers was banished in 89 CE by Emperor Domitian, who thought them a source of dissent, and settled in Nicopolis, Greece. He apparently wrote nothing himself, but instead his teachings were taken down by his student Arrian and published as the *Discourses* and *Enchiridion*.

Epicurus
Philosopher

341–270 BCE

Influenced by the materialist theories of Democritus, Epicurus developed his own humanist and essentially practical philosophy, Epicureanism. Although born on the island of Samos, he was an Athenian citizen. After moving around the cities of Colophon, Mytilene, and Lampsacus, he settled in Athens. There he founded a school of philosophy, The Garden, where he and his pupils lived in seclusion. He was also said to have written more than 300 works. Central to his philosophy was the attainment of eudaemonia, the good or happy life, which he believed came from tranquility, peace, and the absence of pain. He argued that the main obstacle to this was fear, specifically the fear of death. This, he said, could be overcome by the realization that death was simply the end of body and soul, and nothing to fear. His own death, from kidney stones, was long and painful.

Euclid
Mathematician

fl. 300 BCE

In his 13-volume mathematical treatise *Elements*, Euclid set out a framework that formed the basis for the study of geometry until the 19th century. Euclid used earlier Greek mathematicians' ideas as his starting point to develop his own theories, and most notably proposed the method of deducing theorems from a set of assumptions, or axioms. Many of his treatises are now lost, but he is known to have contributed important texts on optics, number theory, and various aspects of geometry. There is almost no reliable information about Euclid's life, although it is possible that he studied at the Academy in Athens before taking up a post at the Mouseion in Alexandria, where he became one of the first great Alexandrian mathematicians.

Eudoxus of Cnidus
Astronomer, mathematician

c. 390–340 BCE

Best known for his study of the motion of the planets in celestial spheres with the Earth at their center, Eudoxus was born in Cnidus, Anatolia. After studying in Athens and Egypt, he settled once again in Cnidus. He devoted the rest of his life to teaching, setting up an observatory, and writing, although none of his works has survived.

Galen
Physician, philosopher

129–216 CE

Born into a wealthy and cultured Greek family in Pergamon, then an intellectual center rivaling Alexandria, Galen had the advantage of both financial and educational privilege, allowing him to travel widely and study a broad range of scientific and philosophical subjects. He ended his studies at the medical school in Alexandria, and returned to Pergamon to work as a physician. There, he gained practical experience as well as medical knowledge, which he took with him to Rome in 162 CE, where he became a physician to several emperors, including Commodus and Septimius Severus. While in Rome he is thought to have written about 500 treatises on medical science and philosophy, of which about one third have survived. His theories of disease were derived from Hippocrates' idea of the four humors, and combined philosophy with his knowledge of human anatomy, gained from the dissection of animals. It is possible that, after a long career Galen retired to Sicily, where according to some sources he died aged 87.

△ Heraclitus (Hendrick ter Brugghen, 1628)

Heraclitus of Ephesus
Philosopher

fl. c. 500 BCE

Sometimes referred to as "the weeping philosopher" for his melancholic and short-tempered disposition, Heraclitus developed an idiosyncratic philosophy that was in stark contrast to the ideas of Parmenides and his other pre-Socratic contemporaries. They saw reality as static, but Heraclitus argued instead that "everything flows" ("*panta rhei*"): that the universe is characterized by change and the unity of opposites. Heraclitus wrote only one work, composed of cryptic, sometimes paradoxical epigrams. This survives only in fragments, but his ideas remain influential.

Heron of Alexandria
Engineer, mathematician

fl. 60 CE

Continuing the scientific advances of the Hellenistic period into Roman times, Heron was born in Alexandria, where it is thought he spent most of his life, teaching and studying at the prestigious Mouseion. He is now best known for his ingenious inventions, which included the steam-powered aeolipile (a type of turbine), a wind-driven organ, and a water basin with metal birds that sang. Heron also worked on physics, mechanics, pneumatics, and mathematics, and wrote about the making of automatons, particularly the "miracle-working" devices used in temples.

△ Hipparchus Refusing the Gifts of Artaxerxes (Anne-Louis Girodet Trioson, 1792)

Hipparchia of Maroneia

Philosopher

c. 350–280 BCE

Born in Maroneia, Thrace, Hipparchia became a staunch advocate of Cynic philosophy after her family moved to Athens. There she met Crates of Thebes, the successor to Diogenes of Sinope as head of the Cynic school. Rejecting suitors her family deemed more appropriate, Hipparchia married Crates, and the couple came to exemplify Cynic teachings, living a frugal and unconventional life.

Hipparchus

Astronomer, mathematician

c. 190–120 BCE

The mathematician and astronomer Hipparchus was born in Nicaea, on the Black Sea coast of Anatolia, but little is known about his life. None of the dozen or so books he is said to have written has survived, but his contributions to astronomy were recorded by later writers. These include a comprehensive star catalog, which was the first of its kind, and a description and measurement of the precession of the equinoxes—the periodic change in the orientation of the Earth's rotational axis. He has also been credited with the invention of the astrolabe and an armillary sphere.

Hippocrates

Physician

c. 460–375 BCE

Widely considered the "Father of Medicine," Hippocrates pioneered the study of medical sciences as a distinct discipline, providing its practitioners with professional status. Yet almost nothing is known for certain of Hippocrates' life, and surviving biographies were written long after his death. He was born on the island of Cos, and probably traveled around Greece as a teacher and physician, ending his life in Larissa, Thessaly. He broke with Greek medical tradition by dismissing supernatural causes for disease, which he thought resulted from environment and lifestyle. He also used observation rather than divination in his prognoses, although this rational approach was tempered by a reliance on the theory of the four humors (see p.212) and an inadequate knowledge of human anatomy and physiology.

Hypatia
Astronomer, mathematician

c. 350–415 CE

A renowned mathematician, philosopher, and astronomer in Alexandria, Hypatia was known for her work on mathematics and Neoplatonism. Her murder symbolized the conflict between science and philosophy on one side and Christianity on the other in the late 4th century CE. (See main entry p.299).

Leucippus
Philosopher

5th century BCE

So little is known about the pre-Socratic philosopher Leucippus—and references to him by contemporaries are so contradictory—that scholars have even doubted his existence. However, it is now generally accepted that he, along with his protégé Democritus, came up with the theory of Atomism.

Pappus of Alexandria
Mathematician

c. 290–350 CE

Working as a teacher in his home city of Alexandria, Pappus was almost a lone figure in the field of mathematics in late Roman Greece. Many of his writings are now lost, but almost all of his eight-volume *Synagoge* (*Collection*) has survived, giving an insight into the scope of his work. In the form of a textbook, it covers a number of topics, including astronomy, physics, geometry, and engineering. Pappus presents the principal theories known at that time, along with his own comments and additions.

△ Leucippus (Luca Giordano, c. 1562)

Parmenides
Philosopher

6th–5th centuries BCE

The pre-Socratic philosopher Parmenides lived in the late 6th and early 5th centuries BCE, bridging the period between the early Greek Milesian school and the Classical philosophers who followed Socrates. He was born and worked in Elea, in the Greek colony of Magna Graecia in southern Italy, where he founded the Eleatic school of philosophy, attracting followers including Zeno of Elea and the philosopher and naval commander Melissus of Samos. Despite writing only one known work (later referred to, like many pre-Socratic texts, as *On Nature*), Parmenides had a profound influence on later thinkers, including Plato. The essence of his philosophy is that there are two ways of viewing reality: truth and opinion. The truth is that reality is a single entity, unchanging and eternal, whereas opinion is the false perception that we take from our unreliable senses of a world of apparent change and variety. Thus, he argued, change and plurality are illusions.

△ Parmenides, detail from *The School of Athens* (Raphael, 1509–1511)

Plato
Philosopher

c.427–348 BCE

Nicknamed *Platon* (Broad) for his stocky build, Plato was born in Athens or on the nearby island of Aegina, and named Aristocles by his aristocratic family. As a young man, Plato was one of a group of followers of Socrates, and his most talented disciple. After Socrates' death, Plato spent some time traveling, before founding a school of philosophy at the Academy in Athens. Other than a couple of disastrous visits to Syracuse—on one of which he was enslaved after becoming entangled in the rivalry between tyrants, then bought and freed by the philosopher Anniceris—Plato remained in Athens for the rest of his life. In a series of texts written in the form of dialogues between well-known figures, he presented his philosophy, which included his theory of Forms, from which much of his thinking on epistemology, metaphysics, and ethics is derived. Plato's teaching was inspirational, and the Academy attracted the brightest Greek thinkers, most notably Aristotle. His ideas also informed the philosophical basis of both Christianity and Islam, and largely set the agenda for all subsequent Western philosophy.

Plotinus
Philosopher

c.205–270 CE

Regarded as the originator of the philosophy today known as Neoplatonism, Plotinus was born in Egypt, which was then under Roman control. He studied Platonic philosophy in Alexandria for about 11 years, and then set off to broaden his education in Persia and India, but his ambition was thwarted by the defeat of the Roman army, and he made his way to Rome, where he lived until his retirement in Sicily. In his reinterpretation of Plato's metaphysics, he proposed the three fundamental principles of being—the One, the Intellect, and the Soul—which became a cornerstone of Neoplatonism.

Protagoras
Philosopher

c.490–420 BCE

With his famous statement "Man is the measure of all things," Protagoras challenged the notion of objective truth, suggesting that judgments are colored by personal experience and expectations. Protagoras was one of the class of professional teachers of rhetoric and ethics in Athens known as Sophists, who schooled their clients in presenting their case in disputes, and so recognized that there was often more than one side in an argument. His ideas were derided by philosophers such as Socrates and Plato and, as a basis for the concept of moral relativism, remain controversial today.

Ptolemy
Astronomer, mathematician, geographer

c.100–170 CE

Often referred to simply as Ptolemy, Claudius Ptolemy was arguably the most influential of the astronomers who worked in Alexandria in the Hellenistic and Roman periods. His writings were preserved as standard texts for more than a millennium. *Almagest*, his astronomical treatise,

△ Urania, the Muse of Astronomy, Reveals to Thales the Secrets of the Skies (Antonio Canova, c.1788)

presented a detailed study of the universe, which, because of his chosen geocentric model, necessitated complex calculations to explain the apparent motion of the heavenly bodies. He was also renowned for *Geography*, his study of the people and places of the world as known to him. With his knowledge of astronomy, he also wrote a treatise on astrology, the *Tetrabiblos*.

Pyrrho of Elis
Philosopher

c.360–270 BCE

One of the earliest philosophical skeptics, who questioned the possibility of knowledge, Pyrrho of Elis formulated his ideas in the 4th century BCE. However, the school of thought named after him, Pyrrhonism, was not founded until some 300 years later. Pyrrho himself produced no written texts, and founded no formal school, but his ideas were recorded for posterity by a disciple called Timon of Phlius. Central to Pyrrho's thinking was the attainment of *ataraxia*, peace of mind, which he argued could be achieved by the avoidance of dogmatic thinking and the suspension of judgment of ideas and beliefs, for example by examining arguments both for and against a particular issue. According to the biographer Diogenes Laertius, Pyrrho was a painter before he became interested in philosophy.

Pythagoras
Philosopher, mathematician

c.570–495 BCE

Born on Samos, the polymath Pythagoras was best known for his geometric theorem. Around 530 BCE, he settled with some followers in Croton, Italy. There he taught music, mathematics, and mysticism. (See main entry p.115.)

Socrates
Philosopher

c.470–399 BCE

Known for his contributions to ethics and epistemology, Socrates created a method of seeking truth through questioning that was to have a profound influence on later philosophers across Europe and Asia. (See main entry p.187.)

Sosipatra
Philosopher

4th century CE

Highly regarded as a philosopher by her contemporaries, Sosipatra combined mysticism with Neoplatonism in her teaching. She was born into a wealthy family in Ephesus. Well educated and intelligent, she married a fellow philosopher, Eustathius of Cappadocia. Moving to Pergamon after his death, she established a school of philosophy there. Although none of her writings survives, the Greek historian Eunapius, writing in the 4th–5th centuries, presents Sosipatra as an accomplished theurgist (wonder-worker) and as a holy woman with expertise in divination and ritual.

Thales of Miletus
Philosopher, mathematician

c.626–548 BCE

Considered to be the first of the early Greek philosophers, and founder of the Milesian school of philosophy, Thales of Miletus challenged the conventional mythological explanations of natural phenomena, instead advocating the use of rational thought and deduction, and encouraging discussion. He was an accomplished mathematician, astronomer, and engineer, and applied his methodical reasoning to the quest to discover the *arche*, the fundamental substance and governing force from which he believed everything in the universe derived. He concluded that this substance was water.

Theaetetus of Athens
Mathematician

c.417–369 BCE

Perhaps best known as the title character of one of Plato's dialogues, Theaetetus of Athens was a prominent mathematician, whose work on irrational numbers and the geometry of regular polyhedrons earned his inclusion in Euclid's *Elements*. Through his studies with the mathematician Theodorus of Cyrene, Theaetetus came into contact with both Socrates and Plato, who held him in high regard as both a mathematician and a friend. In 369 BCE, he died shortly after being wounded in battle against Corinth in the Theban–Spartan War (see pp.204–205).

Theophrastus
Philosopher

c. 371–287 BCE

The philosopher and natural scientist Theophrastus moved from his native Lesbos to Athens to study with Plato at his Academy, where he met Aristotle. After Plato's death, Theophrastus left the Academy to study with Aristotle, and the two became lifelong friends. Theophrastus shared his mentor's interest in the natural sciences, and accompanied him on a trip to explore the wildlife of Lesbos. He also succeeded Aristotle as head of the Peripatetic school at the Lyceum in Athens. He wrote on a broad range of philosophical and scientific subjects, and his treatises *On the Causes of Plants* and *Inquiry into Plants* helped establish the discipline of botany.

Xenophanes
Philosopher, poet

c. 570–478 BCE

Born in the Ionian city of Colophon, Xenophanes was among the second generation of early Greek philosophers, and was also a respected poet. He was known as a ferocious critic of conventional Greek values and beliefs, and scholars have even debated whether he rejected polytheism. More than any other pre-Socratic philosopher perhaps, Xenophanes sought to distance explanations of the natural world from mythology and superstition,

emphasizing the distinction between knowledge—which was the basis for the philosophical field of epistemology—and mere belief.

Zeno of Citium
Philosopher

c. 334–262 BCE

The Stoic school of philosophy, founded by Zeno of Citium, takes its name from the colonnade in Athens, the *Stoa Poikile*, where he gave his first lessons. Zeno came from the Phoenician colony of Citium in Cyprus, and when he moved to Athens he was introduced to philosophy by Crates, at that time the leading Cynic philosopher. Influenced by Crates' ideas of austerity and virtue, Zeno developed his own philosophy, Stoicism, which became the predominant philosophical approach in the Hellenistic period and during the later Roman Empire.

Zeno of Elea
Philosopher

c. 490–430 BCE

Born in Elea, in Magna Graecia, Zeno became a leading light in the Eleatic school of philosophy. He was famous for devising a series of paradoxes to illustrate his mentor Parmenides' ideas on the impossibility of motion, and even of time and space. Although none of his writings has survived, Zeno's paradoxes were well known in ancient Greece. Their seemingly insoluble problems, including "Achilles and the Tortoise" and "The Flying Arrow," were retold by numerous philosophers and continue to be discussed by logicians and mathematicians.

▷ Statue of Theophrastus from the Villa Giulia, Palermo, Sicily

Gods and Goddesses

Olympians

The Olympians—the most powerful gods and goddesses—and their closest divine entourage, were worshipped widely in the Greek world, often acting as the patrons of city-states, their temples the focus of public festivals. Each had their own attributes and symbols, which were frequently depicted in art.

Aphrodite
Olympian: Love

There are conflicting accounts of the conception and origins of the goddess of love, Aphrodite (see p.360). What is certain, however, is that Cyprus—in particular, Paphos—was recognized as the center of her cult. Her dominion over love was absolute, and only the virgin goddesses Artemis, Athena, and Hestia were immune to her power. Aphrodite married Hephaestus (see p.344) but they had no children. She took Ares (see right) as her lover, and had children with him, including Harmonia, goddess of peace, and the warrior gods Deimos (terror) and Phobos (fear). Eros (see p.347) is sometimes said to be her child; others say he was a primal force present at her birth. Zeus made Aphrodite fall in love with Anchises, a member of the Trojan royal family, so she could experience the pain of loving a mortal; their child was the hero Aeneas (see p.352). Among her other children was Hermaphroditus (who had male and female sexual characteristics), born to Hermes (see p.345). The most common artistic depiction of Aphrodite is of her birth, but

◁ Painting of Poseidon and his wife, Amphitrite (Jacob Jordaens, 1644)

she is also the subject of statues, including the Aphrodite of Melos (known later as the Venus de Milo). In Athens, the Aphrodisia festival, associated with fertility, was held in her honor. She was also the patron of sex workers and, as Aphrodite Euploia or Pontica, of seafarers.

Apollo
Olympian: Prophecy, music, poetry

Son of Zeus and Leto and twin brother of Artemis, Apollo was born on Delos, where he long had a shrine. He established an oracle at Delphi, which became the center of his worship as the deity that was most associated with divination. Music and poetry were also his domain, and he is often portrayed as a beautiful naked youth, carrying a lyre. Among his epithets was Musagetes, leader of the muses, and he had a special song, the paean, sung after sacrifices to him. Apollo also cared for youths newly initiated as citizens, who dedicated a lock of their hair to the god. He was known from Homer onward as Phoebus Apollo (the Shining One) and in later times he was associated with the sun. Quick to anger, he could bring plague on his enemies with arrows, and he was ruthless to those who

slighted him, such as the satyr Marsyas, whom he flayed alive for challenging him to a lyre contest (see p.365). His children by mortal women included the healer god Asclepius (see p.342). He pursued Daphne, daughter of a river god, who escaped him by turning into a laurel tree, which became another of Apollo's symbols. His chief festivals included the Pythian Games held every fourth year in Delphi.

Ares
Olympian: War

Ares was the son of Zeus and Hera. His name appears in Linear B tablets (see p.58); in the Iliad, he is depicted as delighting in blood, terror, and the frenzy of war—he was, however, strangely unsuccessful in battle. Unmarried, he had an affair and children with Aphrodite (see left), who persuaded him aside

▷ Roman copy of a Greek statue of Ares (2nd century CE)

with the Trojans in the war. His other children included the bandit Cycnus (who murdered passersby, then stole their offerings intended for Ares) and an Amazon queen, Penthesilea. He was an unpopular god; his few temples included shrines at Knossos, Argos, and Troezen; he also had a temple in Athens with Athena Areia, in their role as protectors of young soldiers. Ares is rarely depicted in art as a central figure, except for the scene in which Hephaestus finds him with his wife, Aphrodite, and binds him in a net.

Artemis
Olympian: Animals, the hunt, women

The virgin goddess Artemis was the daughter of Zeus and Leto and the twin sister of Apollo. From ancient times, she was given the epithet Potnia Theron, "mistress of the animals," but she also presided over transitions in women's lives: from girl to woman to mother. Another of her epithets, as goddess of the hunt, is Elaphebolos, "shooter of deer." She was conceived of as roaming the mountains and forests with a band of nymphs, punishing anyone who violated their company, such as Actaeon, whom she transformed into a stag, which was torn apart by his own dogs. She had important cults in Attica, and at Munichia, where young men sailed to the harbor in sacred ships and a festival with torches was held in honor of Artemis Phosphoros, "the light-bearer." At Brauron, she was served by young girls, known as *arktoi* (bears), who performed a special bear dance. However, her most famous temple was at Ephesus, which was thought to be one of the Ancient World's Seven Wonders. Worshippers occasionally made sacrifices of deer and wild boar, not normally offered at

▷ Marble sculpture of a bronze original of Artemis with a doe (2nd century BCE)

Greek temples; the Athenians also sacrificed 500 goats to her every year in thanks for her help at the Battle of Marathon. In art, Artemis is shown as a young woman with a bow and arrow, and often accompanied by a deer.

Asclepius
Olympian: Healing, medicine

Asclepius was the son of Apollo (see p.341) and a Thessalian woman, Coronis. Apollo killed Coronis after discovering she had been unfaithful. Asclepius was then raised by the centaur Chiron, from whom he learned the medical arts. He was struck down by Zeus after raising the dead, but later, at Apollo's request, he was made immortal. His sanctuaries, Asclepieia, were places of healing, where devotees practiced incubation— sleeping in the temple to receive dreams that gave an indication of cures. Asclepius's most ancient sanctuary was at Tricca in Thessaly, but the cult spread quickly from the late 6th century BCE, often carried by physicians from the medical school at Epidaurus and, later, Cos. It reached Athens around 420 BCE, where there was a large Asclepieion on the west slope of the Acropolis. In art, Asclepius is shown as a mature, bearded figure, holding a staff with a snake coiled around it; his sanctuaries often held sacred snakes and dogs and were also centers of worship for his daughter, Hygieia (see p.213).

Athena
Olympian: War, crafts, wisdom

A goddess with many aspects, Athena presided over the rational features of warfare (in contrast to Ares), and as Athena Ergane was the patroness of the crafts: those traditionally associated with women, such as spinning and weaving, as well as those perceived to be male-dominated, including carpentry, metalwork, and pottery. As Athena Polias, she was the protector of Athens, the city with which she was most closely identified (and whose guardian she became by giving its citizens the first olive tree, beating Poseidon's offer of a well). Athena was born when Hephaestus split her father Zeus's head with an ax after he swallowed her mother, Metis, following a prophecy she would bear a son who would depose him. She remained an unmarried virgin and was worshipped widely, especially at Athens, where her great sanctuary was the Parthenon, in which stood a massive gold and ivory statue of her by the sculptor Phidias. Her special festival was the annual Panathenaea, when Athenian maidens would present the statue with a new robe. In art, she is generally shown fully armed with a helmet, spear, aegis (a cape decorated with snakes), and a shield made from the flayed skin of the Titan Pallas; she is often accompanied by an owl, symbol of wisdom, for which she is also revered. (See also p.360.)

Demeter
Olympian: Agricultural fertility

Venerated as the giver of life through the fertility of crops, Demeter was one of the children of the Titans Cronus and Rhea. She is best known for her search for her daughter Persephone, who had been abducted by Hades (see p.359). The places associated with her search (after she left Olympus, enraged by Zeus's compliance with the kidnapping) had important cults in her honor. She spent time at Eleusis, whose queen, Metaneira, built her a temple, where she lived for a year. In return, Demeter taught Metaneira the rites of the Eleusinian Mysteries (see p.374), which were performed until the sanctuary's abolition in 395 CE. Demeter was also said to have given the first fig tree to Phytalus, an Athenian who showed her great hospitality. Her main festival, the Thesmophoria, was open only to women and took place during the fall, in the sowing season. Another of her festivals was held annually at Cyane and marked the location where Persephone's abduction is said to have occurred. Her other children included Plutus (wealth), who symbolized good fortune and the Earth's bounty, and Philomelus, who invented the plow. In artworks, Demeter is often represented carrying a scepter, ears of corn, and a poppy or torches.

△ Painting showing Demeter (left) being reunited with her daughter, Persephone (Frederic Leighton, c.1891)

Dionysus
Olympian: Wine, drunkenness

Dionysus was god of wine, intoxication, religious ecstasy, and ritual madness. The key feature of all his roles was subversion of the normal order of things. He was also patron of the theater, with actors' masks functioning as symbols of transformation. Son of a mortal being, Semele, and the god Zeus, Dionysus was twice-born: first when his mother was burned to death by his father's lightning bolt, and then from Zeus's thigh. Driven mad by Zeus's jealous wife Hera (after she discovered her husband had slept with Semele), Dionysus roamed the Earth, introducing men to wine and drunkenness. His followers were the satyrs (half-man, half-goat) and the maenads, women who killed animals and ate their raw flesh. Those who angered Dionysus suffered terrible fates, including Pentheus, king of Thebes, torn apart by his own mother. Dionysus married Ariadne after Theseus left her on Naxos (see p.368); in winter, he lived in Delphi. A popular god, he had temples all over the Greek world and many festivals, with seven in Athens, including the City Dionysia. In art, he is shown as mature, bearded, wreathed in ivy, and with a cup; in later works he is a beardless youth.

△ Painting depicting the abduction of Ganymede (Antonio da Correggio, c. 1532)

Ganymede
Cupbearer of the Olympian gods

Ganymede was a Trojan prince, son of Callirhoe (daughter of the river god Scamander) and Tros. His great beauty provoked the interest of Zeus, who kidnapped him by disguising himself as an eagle (some versions of the myth say it was a whirlwind). He was carried up to Olympus, where he was made immortal and became cupbearer of the gods. In recompense for losing his son, Tros received a gift of golden vines wrought by Hephaestus, or marvelous horses. Ganymede became a symbol of same-sex love. His abduction was a popular scene on vases from the 5th century BCE and, much later, in Renaissance works, including by Correggio, Michelangelo, Rubens, and Rembrandt.

Hades
Olympian: Death

King of the Underworld (also called Hades), Hades was the son of Cronus and Rhea. When he split up the universe with his brothers, Poseidon and Zeus, he took the land of the dead. Although grim and foreboding, he was not seen as inherently evil, and his epithets included Polyxeinos (Host of Many), since he eventually received all mortals into the Underworld. His consort was Persephone, who stayed six months a year in his domain, due to the pomegranate seeds she ate (see p.359). Hades had an affair with Minthe, who turned into a mint plant after the jealous Persephone trampled her to death. Hades was also called Plouton (the Rich One) for the bounty that came from the Earth (in food, and mineral wealth). He received worship in this form jointly with Persephone at Eleusis, Ephesus, Cnidus, and Mytilene. Worship in his aspect as Hades was rare; his temple at Elis was open for just one day a year and could be entered only by a priest. He is rarely depicted in art—when he is, it is usually as an old man holding a scepter and a pomegranate or vase.

Hebe
Olympian: Cupbearer of the gods; youth

The goddess Hebe—"youth" personified—was the daughter of Hera and Zeus, though a later myth related that she was the daughter of Hera alone, who became pregnant after eating lettuce. She was, like Ganymede (left), a cupbearer of the gods, and became Heracles' wife after he was made immortal. She sometimes appears in cults linked with her husband, as at Aixone in Attica. In art, she is often shown in a scene in which Heracles arrives on Mount Olympus.

Hephaestus
Olympian: Fire, blacksmiths

The god of fire, metalworking, and artisans, Hephaestus was the son of Zeus and Hera. Myth tells that he was hurled from Olympus by Hera (see p.251), but saved by the sea goddess Thetis. He was a talented blacksmith: among his creations were invisible fetters that bound his mother in revenge, gold-wheeled tripods that moved unaided, and Achilles' armor. In some accounts, he is described as a huge, hairy man with spindly legs, and in others as a raging fire that scorches and boils rivers. He had his forges beneath volcanoes such as Sicily's Mount Etna (where the Cyclopes worked alongside him). His wife was Aphrodite, who was unfaithful to him with Ares (see p.341). When Hephaestus was hurled from Olympus a second time (on that occasion, by Zeus), he landed on Lemnos, the location of his main sanctuary. He had a large temple in Athens, above the Agora, where the Hephaesteia festival was held every five years; and in the Chalkeia festival, also devoted to Hephaestus, artisans walked through the town in his honor. In art, he is shown with a blacksmith's ax and tongs, and a brimless workman's hat.

Hera
Olympian: Queen of the gods

The sister and wife of Zeus, Hera was queen of the gods and goddess of marriage and childbirth. One of the children of the Titans Cronus and Rhea, she was swallowed at birth by Cronus, but saved when Zeus gave him a drug to regurgitate her and four of her siblings (see p.359). Hera and Zeus had four children: Eileithyia, goddess of childbirth; Hebe; Ares; and Hephaestus (see left). Honored throughout the Greek world, her favored cities were Sparta, Mycenae, and Argos (where one of her most ancient sanctuaries was). Other important Hera temples were at Tiryns, Olympia, the island of Samos, and, in the wider Greek world, Croton and Paestum. Hera is often shown in art carrying a scepter, wearing a crown, and accompanied by a peacock, a symbol of vanity. As protector of marriage, she was faithful to Zeus: when Endymion tried to seduce her, Zeus cast him into Hades. Vindictive to those who angered her, she sent the Sphinx (see p.70) against the city of Thebes when its inhabitants dishonored her.

Hermes
Olympian: Travelers

The herald and messenger of the gods, Hermes was closely associated with travelers. Son of Zeus and Maia, daughter of Atlas (see p.347), he was born in a cave on Mount Cyllene in Arcadia. As a baby, he invented the lyre using a tortoise shell and sheep-gut strings, which he gave to Apollo in apology for stealing the god's cattle (see p.99). Hermes also became god of flocks and herds, and—via his reputation for sharp dealing—god of merchants and thieves. Owing to his role in ensuring success, he was also patron of athletes. He acted as guide to both gods and mortals, leading Athena, Hera, and Aphrodite to the Judgment of Paris (see p.369), and the souls of the dead to Hades. His cult was widespread in the Peloponnese, including in Megalopolis, Corinth, and Argos; and in Athens, the Hermaea festival for young boys was held in his honor. In art, Hermes is shown as a young man, carrying a herald's staff and wearing a wide-brimmed hat and winged sandals. He was unmarried; his children include the goat-god Pan and the thief Autolycus.

Hestia
Olympian: The hearth

Daughter of Cronus and Rhea—and, like four of her siblings, initially swallowed by her father (see p.359)—Hestia rejected the advances of the gods Apollo and Poseidon and swore herself to eternal virginity. Zeus then decreed she would receive offerings before all other gods, and at sacrifices a portion would be offered to her at the start of the ceremony. She presided over the hearth, the center of all Greek households, where daily offerings were made, and newborns and brides initiated. Each city-state had a *prytaneion*, a public hearth, where a fire was kept constantly burning (though there was only one for all of Attica—in Athens). Rarely appearing in myths because she remained secluded on Olympus, Hestia is shown in art as a heavily veiled young woman.

△ Fresco showing Hera (center) with her messenger, Iris (Pompeii, 2nd century CE)

△ Floor mosaic depicting Poseidon in a chariot pulled by hippocampi (near Sousse, Tunisia, 3rd century CE)

Persephone
Olympian: Queen of the Underworld

Persephone was the daughter of Demeter by Zeus. Her main myth is of her abduction by Hades (see p.359), as a result of which she was forced to spend part of the year in the Underworld and part in the upper world. This meant she was feared for her rule over the dead, and revered for the hope that spring brings each year. Generally worshipped together with her mother, as at Eleusis, she had her own cult at Locris, where she was seen as protector of marriage, and at Hipponium, where a ritual remembering her picking of flowers before her kidnapping

was conducted. Her main festival, also shared with Demeter, was the Thesmophoria, a women's festival celebrated throughout the Greek world. Also known as Kore (the Maiden), she sometimes allowed mortals to leave the Underworld—including Eurydice, the wife of Orpheus, after she heard Orpheus's enchanting lyre-playing. In art, Persephone was shown as a young woman, often with a torch, a stalk of grain, or a scepter.

Poseidon
Olympian: Seas, rivers, horses

Poseidon, son of Cronus and Rhea, was given control of the sea in the division of the cosmos

between him and his brothers, Hades and Zeus. His rage was said to bring on storms and earthquakes. Poseidon had an ancient cult at Pylos in Messenia; his sanctuaries were generally on coastal sites such as Sounion in Attica—where boat races were held in his honor every four years—and at cult sites close to inland pools, streams, and springs. He lost a contest with Athena to be patron of Athens (see p.360), but became patron of Corinth. Linked with horses, Poseidon is often shown in a chariot drawn by them or hippocampi (part-horse, part-fish), carrying a trident, which causes earth tremors when it strikes the ground. He lived in a golden underwater palace

with his wife, Amphitrite, who bore him Triton, the sea god, but he had many lovers, including Aethra and Medusa, who bore him Theseus and the winged horse Pegasus respectively. Some of his offspring, such as the Cyclopes, were monsters.

Zeus
Olympian: King of the gods

The name Zeus means "father of the day," and from Mycenaean times, this king of the gods was associated with weather and the sky. At birth, Zeus—the son of Cronus and Rhea—was hidden in a cave by his mother so his father would not swallow him (see p.39 and p.359). Raised on Mount Dicte in Crete, he long had a cult there. Elsewhere, as a Panhellenic deity, he had few city temples or festivals, but in Athens the Diisoteria featured sacrifices to Zeus Soter (the Savior) and Athena Soteira, while the Dipolieia saw a sacrifice to Zeus on the Acropolis. Worshipped mainly on mountains, especially on Mount Olympus, he had one main oracle, Greece's oldest, at Dodona. In art, he is often depicted as a bearded man, with a thunderbolt and an eagle. Zeus swallowed his first wife, Metis, after it was foretold that a son of his born to her would overthrow him and a daughter would be wiser than her mother; his queen was his second wife, Hera (see p.345). He had children with many other deities, including Hermes with Maia, and Persephone with Demeter. But Zeus had children by mortal women too, sometimes appearing to them (as he did with nymphs and deities) in disguise—for example, when he came to Leda in the form of a swan (see p.362).

Primal Deities, Titans, and Personifications

The primal deities and Titans were older generations of gods, worshipped in ancient times, but later supplanted by the Olympians. They were often sinister and terrifying forces, though a wider range of divine personifications was added over time to represent natural phenomena, such as the dawn.

Atlas

Titan: The world-bearer

Atlas was the son of the Titan Iapetus and the Oceanid (sea nymph) Clymene, and the brother of Prometheus (see pp.350–351). For his part in the revolt of the Titans against Zeus (see p.359), he was condemned to hold up the sky for eternity in the Garden of the Hesperides (nymphs of the evening). Only when Heracles offered to hold it instead in exchange for the golden apples from the garden was Atlas relieved briefly—a scene that is frequently depicted in art. He became identified with the Atlas Mountains of North Africa because Perseus was said to have turned him to stone with the head of the Gorgon, and he gave his name to the "atlas" as a collection of maps.

Cronus

Primal deity: Former king of the gods

The youngest of the Titans, Cronus was born of Gaia (see p.348) and Uranus (see p.351), whom he deposed to become supreme ruler of the gods. Cronus's rule was brutal and he imprisoned his brothers, the Cyclopes, in Tartarus, the Underworld, where souls were judged after death and the wicked were punished. Cronus had five children by his sister, Rhea: Hestia, Demeter, Hera, Hades, and Poseidon. However, upon hearing a prophecy that a son would overthrow him, he swallowed his offspring. His last-born child, Zeus, was rescued by Rhea, who gave Cronus a rock disguised as a baby to swallow (see p.39). Another tradition describes Cronus's reign as a Golden Age free of toil. After his overthrow, he became the ruler of Elysium, the destination for the souls of heroes. Cults to him are rare—however, there was one at Olympia and a Cronia festival in Athens, following the harvest, where both enslaved people and their enslavers feasted together.

Eos

Personification: Dawn

Daughter of Theia, goddess of sight, and Hyperion, god of watchfulness, Eos is described by Homer as "rosy-fingered" and "saffron-robed." She brings dawn each morning in a chariot that is drawn by two horses, Lampos (the Shining One) and Phaethon (the Blazing One). She carried off the hunter Orion and the Trojan prince Tithonus to be her lovers. When he begged the gods for immortality for Tithonus, she forgot also to ask for eternal youth and he shriveled away. With Tithonus she had the warrior Memnon, and in art she is often shown weeping over her son's corpse after he was killed by Achilles during the Trojan War.

Erebus

Personification: Darkness

Erebus and his sister, Nyx (see p.350), were born out of the primeval, shapeless Chaos at the beginning of time. With his sister, he produced Aether (brightness) and Hemera (day). Erebus, the embodiment of darkness, had no particular cult places or worship; his name was mostly used as an alternative term for the Underworld.

Eros

Primal deity: Love

A primeval god, symbolizing the passion that seizes those in love, Eros existed, according to some traditions, just after Chaos at the beginning of time (see p.38). In Homer, he was depicted simply as a powerful force that possesses the lovestruck. By Archaic times, he had become personified, smiting his victims with a whip that caused them to fall in love. Eros was shown as a beautiful young male carrying a lyre or hare, and a bow and arrows, which, when sharp, would lead to love, but, if blunt, caused repulsion. The companion of Aphrodite, he shared a cult with her on the north slope of the Acropolis. His worship was also widespread elsewhere: among individuals, at sanctuaries such as Thespiae in Boeotia (where he was associated with fertility), at gymnasia, and among the elite army unit known as the Sacred Band of Thebes (see p.204).

△ Painting showing Eos (left) and Tithonus (Jean-Baptiste Marie Pierre, 1747)

Gaia
Primal deity; personification: Earth

The primordial goddess of Earth, Gaia was preceded only by Chaos (see p.38). She had many children by her own son, Uranus, including the Titans and the Cyclopes. By Tartarus, the primordial god of the abyss, she gave birth to the monster Typhon, and by her own son, Pontus, she was the mother of the sea god Nereus. As Gaia Kourotrophos (Child Nurturer), she had a cult at the Acropolis in Athens and was widely worshipped at fertility shrines throughout the Greek world. Most often shown in art handing the infant hero Erichthonius to Athena, she was seen as an ambiguous deity—on the one hand nurturing, on the other, dangerous.

Helios
Titan; personification: The sun

Known to the Romans as Sol, Helios was the son of the Titans Hyperion and Theia and brother of Selene (the moon) and Eos (the dawn, see p.347). He drove his four-horse sun chariot each day across the sky to bring light to the world, returning to his home each evening across the ocean in a golden bowl. When Zeus apportioned the world between the gods, Helios was away in his chariot and therefore received nothing. But he fell in love with Rhodes and claimed it as his own: one of his few sanctuaries was on the island, which held a Halieia festival, when the islanders hurled a chariot and four horses into the sea in his honor each year. He was also associated with the Acrocorinth fortress at Corinth. His wife, the Oceanid Perse, bore him children, including Pasiphaë, mother of the Minotaur; the sorceress Circe; and Augeas, whose stables Heracles cleaned for one of his labors (see p.369). If angered, Helios refused to drive his chariot—for example, when some of his sacred cattle were stolen by Odysseus's crew.

△ Detail of a fresco depicting Ariadne asleep at Hypnos's side (Pompeii, 1st century CE)

Hypnos
Personification: Sleep

Hypnos was the son of Nyx (night, see p.350) and the twin brother of Thanatos (death). He rarely appears as a person in myths, except in the *Iliad*, when Hera persuades him to send Zeus to sleep so Poseidon can help the Trojans—he agrees to this, in exchange for marriage to Pasithea, goddess of relaxation. Hypnos is shown in vase paintings carrying the body of the hero Sarpedon back to Lycia, together with Thanatos. In some accounts, he lives in a dark cavern through which Lethe, the Underworld river of Oblivion, flows; in others, he lives on Lemnos. He is often depicted as a winged youth with a branch that induces sleep. His only major cult center was at Troezen, in the Peloponnese.

Iris
Personification: Rainbow

Iris was the daughter of the Titan Thaumas and the Oceanid Electra. Goddess of the rainbow, she was seen as a link between heaven and Earth, and thus the messenger of the gods. Homer gave her the epithet "storm-footed" and her appearance portended storms. She was the sister of the Harpies (half-bird, half-human) and sometimes said to be married to Zephyrus, the west wind. In Archaic art, she is depicted with winged boots and a short chiton, but is later shown with actual wings and carrying a herald's staff. She is also depicted as the messenger or servant of Zeus, or escorting the gods.

Leto
Titan: Motherhood

Daughter of the Titans Coeus and Phoebe, Leto became mother of Apollo and Artemis by Zeus. The island of Delos, then floating in the Aegean, allowed her to give birth there on the condition that it would become fixed and a principal sanctuary of Apollo. At the birth, Hera refused to allow Eileithyia, the childbirth goddess, to attend to her, so Leto's labor lasted nine days. She was also said to have given birth in Ephesus, where she had an important sanctuary, which she shared with Apollo (they also shared a shrine at Didyma). As well as caring for mothers, she looked after young people, and at Chios she was given dedications by parents hoping

▷ Alabaster statue of Leto with her children (1742)

for victories for girl athletes in the Chian games. In art, she is generally shown alongside Apollo and Artemis.

Metis
Titan; personification: Intelligence

The daughter of Oceanus (see p.350) and Tethys (see p.351), Metis is the personification of cunning and intelligence. She gave Zeus the emetic that caused Cronus to regurgitate his other children, whom he had swallowed (see p.359). After this event, despite her protests, Zeus married Metis. On hearing a prophecy that a son of his born to her would depose him and become ruler of the universe, Zeus swallowed her. However, Hephaestus (see p.344) split open Zeus's skull with an ax, allowing Athena to be born from his head.

Nemesis
Personification: Retribution

In the *Iliad*, Homer employed the concept of *nemesis* to indicate righteous indignation; for later Greeks, the word came to mean divine retribution, personified as the goddess Nemesis. She was the daughter of Nyx (see p.350) and, according to one tradition, Oceanus was her father. Nemesis symbolized the punishment for those who violated the natural order of things or who had an excess of pride or wealth. She is sometimes shown in art with a measuring rod to warn against excess, and a bridle to signify the curbing of arrogant speech. Zeus pursued her in various animal shapes, including as a swan. In one account, Nemesis, then in the form of a goose, laid an egg that was taken to Leda (see p.362) and hatched into Helen of Troy. The oldest cults of Nemesis were at Rhamnous in Attica, and at Smyrna in Ionia.

Nereus
Titan: The Old Man of the Sea

An ancient sea god (sometimes referred to as the "Old Man of the Sea"), Nereus was the son of Pontus and the Oceanid (sea nymph) Doris. He lived with his daughters deep in the Aegean Sea and his power of prophecy led Heracles to attempt to capture him so he could discover the whereabouts of the golden apples in the Garden of the Hesperides (see p.369). Nereus was a shape-changer, and his battle with Heracles, as he mutates from fish to snake to lion to fire, is often depicted in vase paintings.

△ Detail from a Roman mosaic depicting Oceanus with his sister and wife, Tethys (Türkiye, c. 2nd/3rd centuries CE)

Nyx
Primal deity; personification: Night

Nyx was said to have been born from Chaos, the great void of emptiness, at the same time as Erebus (darkness). From their union came Aether (brightness) and Hemera (day). Alone, Nyx produced many children, including Keres (violent death), Thanatos (death), Hypnos (sleep), Nemesis (retribution), the Moirae (Fates), and Eris (strife). She was said to be the only being that Zeus feared. Nyx had no formal cults, but was in general connected to oracles, and was sometimes thought of as giving prophecies from inside a cave. She played a key role in the Orphic mystery cult (see pp.43 and 259). Orphic texts perceived her as the original ruler of the universe, eventually handing over her scepter to Uranus.

Oceanus
Titan; personification: The ocean

Eldest of the Titans, Oceanus was the son of Uranus and Gaia. In early belief, he was thought of as more a force than a person, the spirit of the great river that was believed to surround the world. Beyond this lay the domain of monsters (such as the Gorgons), as well as the Garden of the Hesperides and the entrance to Hades, or the Underworld. The sun god Helios lived on the river bank. Oceanus married his sister Tethys (see opposite): their 3,000 sons were Earth's rivers and their 3,000 daughters were Oceanid nymphs. He was sometimes shown on Greek vases—bearded, with a fish-tail—but more often on Roman sarcophagi.

Phaethon
Titan: Son of the sun

The son of Helios, the sun god, by his lover the Oceanid Clymene, Phaethon was granted any wish by his father when he first visited Helios's palace. He asked to drive the sun chariot for just one day, but the horses veered out of control, scorching the earth, creating deserts, and then setting the sky ablaze, forming the Milky Way. Zeus put an end to the chaos by hurling a thunderbolt, which killed Phaethon. His corpse plummeted into the Eridanus River, where his sisters, the Heliades, wept so copiously that they were turned into poplar trees and their tears transmuted into amber.

Prometheus
Titan: Bringer of fire

Son of the Titan Iapetus and the Oceanid Clymene, Prometheus (forethought) was a great benefactor of humankind, smuggling fire to Earth from Olympus in a fennel stalk. Zeus punished him by chaining him to a rock, where an eagle pecked at his liver each day, only for it to regenerate every night. In some versions of the myth, Heracles eventually shot the bird (see also p.360). Prometheus's chaining and release are often depicted in vase paintings, and were the subject of a trilogy of plays by Aeschylus (see p.321). He was worshipped by potters in Athens (where a torch race was held in his honor) and at a sanctuary at Opus, north of Boeotia. Prometheus's son Deucalion was said to have been the progenitor of all humankind as he and his wife, Pyrrha, were the sole survivors of a catastrophic flood.

Psyche
Personification: The soul

Psyche was originally a term for the aspect of the soul that left the body after death for Hades, or the Underworld. After Greek and Roman times, however, it came to be regarded as the seat of consciousness. By the time of Apuleius in the 2nd century CE (see p.362), it had become personified as a mortal woman, a princess who excited the jealousy of Venus, but with whom Eros fell in love. After Psyche was abandoned by him when she ignored his warning not to look upon his true appearance (and after her extensive wanderings in search of her lost lover), the gods gave her various

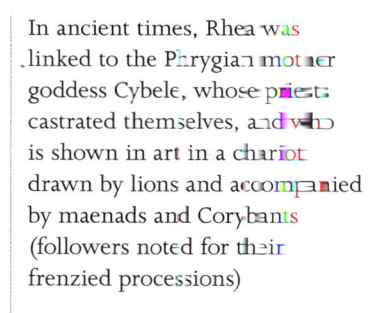

▷ Marble statue of Psyche (Pietro Tenerani, c.1819)

arduous tasks. But eventually, they took pity on her and made her immortal and she and Eros were reunited. The couple had a daughter, Hedone (pleasure).

Rhea
Primal deity: Mother goddess

The daughter of Uranus and Gaia, Rhea bore Cronus, her husband, six children; he swallowed all of them, except Zeus (see p.359).

In ancient times, Rhea was linked to the Phrygian mother goddess Cybele, whose priests castrated themselves, and who is shown in art in a chariot drawn by lions and accompanied by maenads and Corybants (followers noted for their frenzied processions)

Tethys
Titan: Ocean goddess

The daughter of Gaia, Tethys was both sister and wife of Oceanus; their offspring were the 3,000 Rivers and 3,000 Oceanics (see opposite). Their eldest daughter was the Oceanid Styx, the river of the Underworld. Tethys cared for Hera during Zeus's war with the Titans; and when Zeus transformed his lover Callisto into the Great Bear constellation, Tethys, out of deference to Hera, would not allow it to descend into the Ocean—which explains why the constellation never sets.

Themis
Titan: Justice, order, prophecy

The daughter of Gaia and Uranus, Themis was identified with justice and presided over the assemblies of the gods on Mount Olympus. She also had prophetic powers and, with Gaia (see p.348), was seen as the founder of the Oracle at Delphi. In art she is sometimes shown delivering prophecies seated on a tripod and with a laurel branch. Hesiod related that Themis was the second wife of Zeus and bore him the Horai

(hours), Dike (justice), Eunomia (lawfulness), Eirene (peace), and the Moirae (Fates).

Tyche
Personification: Fortune

The daughter of Tethys and Oceanus, Tyche was the only deity who concerned herself with human affairs directly, determining the destiny of men and women at birth and also guiding it thereafter. She was sometimes seen as one of the Moirae (Fates). In Hellenistic times, her worship expanded, with shrines established at Thebes, Athens, Megara, and Sicyon, and an altar at Olympia. Tyche was increasingly seen not as fair and just, but as dangerous and in need of appeasement. She is frequently represented in art carrying a rudder or cornucopia and standing on top of a sphere.

Uranus
Primal deity; personification: The sky

One of the most ancient of all the gods, Uranus personified the sky. He was born from Gaia (Earth), and had several children with her, including the Titans—the last-born of which was Cronus (see p.347)—and various monsters such as the Cyclopes. When Uranus attempted to push his offspring back into Gaia's womb, Cronus hacked off his genitals with a sickle and from these were born, according to some accounts, the Giants; the Meliades, nymphs of the ash-tree; the Furies; and—arising out of the sea-foam—Aphrodite. Uranus had no major cult sites and was rarely depicted in art.

Heroes

Despite the immense power of the gods, a select band of heroes played a key role in Greek religious tradition, often going against the gods' will, frequently with tragic results. Only a few had their own cults, but their stories were told and retold in plays, poetry, and vase paintings.

Achilles
Hero of the Trojan War

Achilles was the son of Thetis (a sea goddess and Nereid, or sea nymph) and King Peleus of Phthia. When he was a baby, his mother dipped him in the River Styx in an attempt to make him immortal—but she held him by the heel, and ever after he was vulnerable in that spot. Achilles was brought up by the centaur Chiron. When in Phthia, Achilles befriended Patroclus—the pair are believed to have become lovers. When the Greeks set out for Troy, Thetis, knowing Achilles would die there, tried to conceal him by dressing him as a woman, but his masculine bearing gave him away. On the voyage to Troy, Achilles killed King Tenes of Tenedos (an island in the northeast of the Aegean Sea), angering Apollo. For nine years, Achilles was the leading Greek warrior, slaying many Trojan heroes. But in a quarrel with Agamemnon, leader of the Greek army, over the spoils of war, he was forced to give up his concubine Chryseis, and in a fit of anger retired to his tent. He ignored his comrades' pleas to come out and fight, and the Greeks suffered mounting losses. Eventually, Patroclus put on Achilles' armor, causing the Trojans to flee—all except Hector, who slayed him. Enraged, Achilles returned to the fray, killing Hector and dragging his corpse around the walls of Troy behind his chariot. Not long after, he was killed by Paris, who shot an arrow, which, guided by Apollo, hit his vulnerable heel.

Aeneas
Hero of the Trojan War

Regarded as the ancestor of the Romans, Aeneas was the son of Anchises and the goddess Aphrodite (see p.341), who protected him throughout the war with the Greeks. He fought a notable duel with Achilles (see left) and was wounded, almost mortally, until Poseidon transported him to safety. After Troy's fall, he fled, carrying his father on his back, and leading his son Ascanius to safety. He led a fleet of Trojan exiles, which landed in Thrace, on Delos, and then on Crete, where a settlement failed. Aeneas sailed to Italy and endured many trials, including attacks by the Harpies (half-bird, half-human) and the twin perils of the whirlpool Charybdis and the monster Scylla off Sicily. In North Africa, Aeneas had a love affair with Dido, queen of Carthage, but when he abandoned her, she died by suicide, thereby explaining the ancient enmity between her city and Rome. After landing in Italy, Aeneas went to the Underworld to consult with the ghost of Anchises (who had died in Sicily). Arriving in Latium, central Italy, he saw the sign of a white sow with 30 piglets that a seer had foretold would mark the spot where the Trojans should settle. After becoming involved in warfare between the Latins, he married Lavinia, daughter of the king of Latium, and established a city there. His descendant, Romulus, founded the city of Rome.

Agamemnon
Hero of the Trojan War

Son of Atreus and Aerope, king and queen of Mycenae, Agamemnon and his brother, Menelaus, were expelled from the city after their father's death. Agamemnon's wife, Clytemnestra, daughter of Tyndareus of Sparta, helped the brothers reclaim the throne of Mycenae. He had a son, Orestes, and three daughters by Clytemnestra. Agamemnon led a Greek force to Troy to rescue the kidnapped Helen, and on the

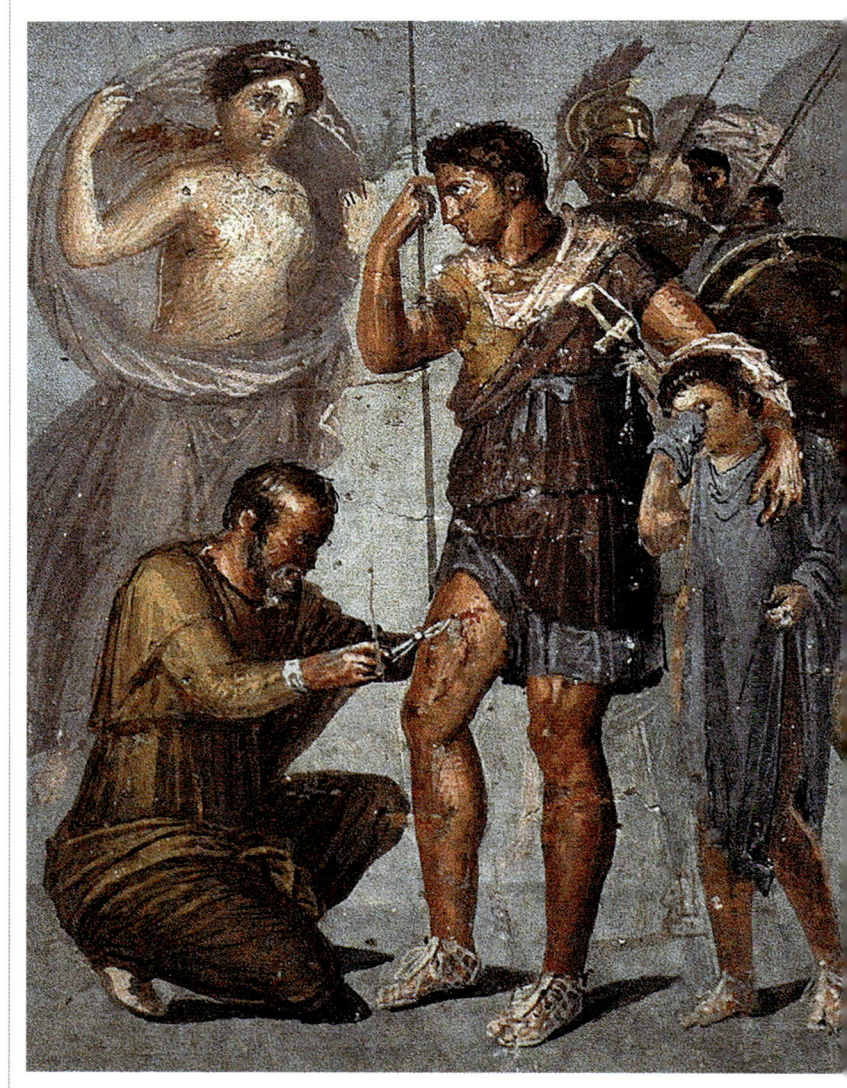

△ Fresco showing Aeneas being treated for a wound (Pompeii, 1st century CE)

△ Vase painting depicting Achilles (left) and Ajax playing dice during the Trojan War (Exekias, mid-6th century BCE)

way, sacrificed his daughter Iphigenia at Aulis to ensure the venture's success (see p.369). However, he proved to be an uncertain, irresolute leader; his quarrel with Achilles over the spoils of war and Chryseis almost cost the Greeks the Trojan War (see opposite). On his return to Mycenae, Agamemnon was murdered by Clytemnestra and her lover, Aegisthus, in revenge for Iphigenia's death. His story was retold in plays by Aeschylus, Sophocles, and Euripides (see pp.180–181), and he had cults in Laconia, Tarentum, and Mycenae.

Ajax
Hero of the Trojan War

Son of Telamon, king of Salamis, and half-brother of Teucer, Ajax was the foremost Greek warrior after Achilles and led 12 ships of warriors to Troy. It is said that Heracles wrapped the infant Ajax in the skin of the Nemean lion, rendering him invulnerable, except for a spot on his left side. Hugely strong, Ajax bore a shield that was seven ox-hides in thickness. He fought a prolonged duel with the Trojan Hector, almost killing him; but the fight ended in an exchange of gifts between the evenly matched heroes. Ajax led the last-ditch defense of the Greek camp when Hector almost took it, but after Achilles' death, he argued with Odysseus about who should get his armor. Losing the argument, Ajax resolved to kill Odysseus, but Athena intervened by causing Ajax's insanity, and he ended up killing a flock of sheep instead. Regaining his senses, a disgusted Ajax died by suicide. In Homer's *Odyssey*, Odysseus meets Ajax's ghost and begs him to end their argument, but the ghost refuses. According to Ovid, where Ajax's blood fell, the first hyacinth grew. Ajax was an eponymous hero of one of the ten *phylai* of Athens (see pp.116–117); he had a cult there, at Salamis, and in the Troad, the region around Troy.

Atalanta
Hero: Hunter and athlete

Daughter of King Schoeneus of Boeotia, Atalanta was abandoned at birth by her father, but raised by a bear. She was a companion of Artemis and a hunter, and took part in the Calydonian Boar Hunt (see p.368). She also participated in the funeral games held in honor of King Pelias of Iolcus, where she defeated the

hero Peleus in a wrestling match. Her father promised her hand in marriage to anyone who could defeat her in a running race, but Atalanta outpaced all of her suitors, who were then put to death. But with the help of Aphrodite, the prince Melanion finally married her (see p.368). According to some traditions, the couple made love in a sanctuary of Zeus and were transformed into lions, which drew the chariot of the goddess Cybele.

Bellerophon
Hero: Monster slayer; tamer of Pegasus

Bellerophon was the son of the sea god Glaucus, and Eurymede, a mortal woman. Exiled from Corinth for killing a man, he traveled to Tiryns. There, Anteia, wife of King Proetus, accused him of seducing her. Rather than kill a guest, Proetus sent him to Iobates, king of Lycia, with a letter requesting his execution. But Iobates, also unwilling to murder a guest, set Bellerophon three tasks: to kill the Chimaera (see p.371); to overcome the Solymi, fearsome fighters living on Lycia's border; and to defeat the Amazons in battle. Before going, Bellerophon secured the help of Athena and the winged horse Pegasus (see p.371), which enabled him to defeat all three foes. He then returned to Lycia, where Proetus gave him half his kingdom and his daughter Philonoe in marriage. They had three children: Hippolochus, who led the Lycians in the Trojan War, Isander, and Laodamia. In *Bellerophon* by Euripides, the hero tries to ride Pegasus to Mount Olympus, but Zeus causes him to fall back to Earth.

△ Painting depicting Cadmus and Athena (both left), soon after Cadmus has slain the dragon (Jacob Jordaens, 1636–1638)

Cadmus

Hero: Founder of Thebes; monster slayer

Legendary founder of Thebes, Cadmus was the son of the Phoenician king Agenor. While searching for his sister Europa, kidnapped by Zeus (see p.361), Cadmus consulted the Delphic Oracle, which told him to give up his search and to found a city where he saw a cow lie down. He located the spot and established Thebes. When he was attacked by a dragon, which he killed, Athena advised him to sow its teeth into the ground; but these became warriors who assaulted him. He slayed most of them, but five became the ancestors of the Theban people. Cadmus married Harmonia, daughter of Ares and Aphrodite, and had five children: Semele (whom Zeus inadvertently burned to death), Polydorus, Ino, Autonoë, and Agave. According to the historian Herodotus, Cadmus brought the Phoenician alphabet (see pp.58–59) to Greece.

Daedalus

Hero: Inventor; architect of the Cretan Labyrinth

Grandson of King Erechtheus of Athens, and a talented inventor, Daedalus was forced to leave Athens after murdering his nephew. Exiled in Crete, he built a hollow wooden cow to enable King Minos's wife, Pasiphaë, to hide when she mated with a sacred bull. The result of the union was the Minotaur, half-man, half-bull. Daedalus built the Labyrinth to house the Minotaur. He also provided Ariadne with the ball of thread that allowed Theseus to escape after killing the Minotaur, so Minos held him prisoner in the Labyrinth with his son, Icarus. They escaped after Daedalus made wings from wax and feathers, but Icarus's wings melted, and he drowned (see p.368). Daedalus escaped, but Minos found him on Sicily. However, the daughters of the Sicilian ruler Cocalus saved him by scalding Minos to death.

Hector

Hero of the Trojan War

Eldest son of Priam and Hecuba, king and queen of Troy, husband of Andromache, and father of Astyanax, Hector was the greatest Trojan hero. He killed Protesilaus, the first Greek to disembark on Trojan soil, and he remained the bulwark of Troy's defense for ten years. When Achilles withdrew from the fight (see p.352), Hector led an attack on the Greek camp, almost taking it, and setting fire to the Greek ships. After Achilles returned to the fray and killed Polydorus (Hector's brother), Hector went out to find him. They pursued each other three times around the city walls, until Achilles thrust a spear into Hector's throat, mortally wounding him. At first, Achilles refused to return Hector's corpse, but when King Priam went to the Greek camp at night, Achilles finally released it. Hector's body was, according to some sources, ultimately buried at Thebes, where there was a hero cult to him. His death at the hands of Achilles was often depicted in art.

Helen

Hero: Spark of the Trojan War

Born from an egg after her mother, Leda (the wife of Tyndareus, king of Sparta), was raped by Zeus disguised as a swan (see p.362), the beautiful Helen attracted suitors who came from all over Greece to seek her hand. To avoid bloodshed,

Tyndareus made them swear that whoever succeeded would be defended by the other suitors in any future conflicts. Menelaus (see right) won Helen's hand. When Paris later abducted Helen (see p.369), Menelaus reminded the other suitors of their oath, so together they attacked Troy and eventually won Helen back. She finally returned to Sparta and lived with her husband. Following their death, the couple were buried at Therapne, where a shrine was constructed for them. Zeus then made Helen immortal; she was worshipped at Rhodes and Sparta.

△ Fresco showing Helen after her abduction by Paris (Pompeii, 1st century CE)

Heracles
Hero: Completed immense labors

The greatest of Greek heroes, Heracles was the son of Zeus and Alcmene, the granddaughter of Perseus (see p.357). As a child, he showed his strength by strangling two snakes that crawled into his bed; as a youth, he slayed a lion. Heracles killed his wife, Megara, and his children after Hera drove him insane. As a penalty, he was told by the Delphic Oracle to serve King Eurystheus of Mycenae for 12 years. The king set him 12 tasks (see pp.368–369). After completing them, he endured three years enslaved by Queen Omphale of Libya, possibly as punishment for the murder of Iphitus, one of the Argonauts. Heracles finally died when his new wife, Deianeira, jealous of his affairs, smeared poisonous blood from the dying centaur Nessus on a cloak she gave him. He was then granted immortality by the gods. His many children included the Heraclid ancestors of the Spartan kings.

Hippolyte
Hero: Amazon queen, warrior

Hippolyte, the Amazon queen, possessed a girdle given to her by Ares; one of Heracles' 12 tasks was to seize it (see p.369). The queen was about to give it to him freely—but Hera, not wanting him to achieve his task so easily, spread a rumor that Heracles had abducted Hippolyte. The mighty Amazons then charged his ship, and Heracles, thinking he was being betrayed, killed Hippolyte, took her belt, and then defeated the Amazons.

Jason
Hero: Secured the Golden Fleece

Jason was the son of Aeson of Iolcus and Alcimede, daughter of King Phylacus, founder of the city of Phylace. He was sent into hiding by his parents, fearing that Aeson's brother, King Pelias (who overthrew Aeson), would kill him. Returning years later to Iolcus, Jason met his uncle Pelias, who saw he had just one sandal: according to an oracle this was the sign of the man who was to kill him. Pelias challenged Jason to fetch the Golden Fleece from the land of Colchis, a quest he felt sure would be fatal. Jason gathered a team of heroes and demigods and sailed in the *Argo* to Colchis. There, with the help of Medea, daughter of King Aeetes of Colchis, he seized the fleece. On returning to Iolcus, Medea killed Pelias by persuading his daughters he would regain his youth if they boiled him. Medea and Jason then fled Iolcus to Corinth, where Jason joined other heroes in the hunt for the Calydonian Boar (see p.368), returning to Iolcus years later to claim the kingship. In Euripides' play, Jason abandons Medea who, in revenge, kills his new wife, Glauce (see p.181), and two of her own sons by Jason, who is then killed by a beam that falls from the rotting *Argo*.

Menelaus
Hero of the Trojan War

Son of Atreus, king of Mycenae, Menelaus became king of Sparta after Tyndareus, who had helped restore his brother Agamemnon to the throne of Mycenae. He married Helen but found, after a journey to Crete, that the Trojan prince Paris had abducted her (see left). He and Agamemnon assembled an army of Greeks to go to Troy to win her back. During the war, he fought a duel with Paris over Helen until Aphrodite intervened, causing a thick mist to descend on the battlefield. At the fall of Troy, he almost killed Helen, but spared her when he saw her beauty. Their journey home took eight years, and they made it back to Sparta only with the help of Proteus, a sea god. Menelaus appears in plays by Euripides and Sophocles, and he and Helen had a joint shrine at Therapne, southeast of Sparta.

Narcissus
Tragic hero

Narcissus was the son of the river god Cephissus and the nymph Liriope. This handsome young man was loved by many, but he rejected all his suitors. The goddess Nemesis punished him by making him fall in love with his own reflection in a clear pool in the woods—he gazed endlessly at the image, trying to grasp it, but finding it always dissolved. Eventually, he was transformed into the flower that bears his name, the narcissus. (See also p.365.)

Odysseus
Hero of the Trojan War

King of Ithaca, and son of Laertes and Anticlea, Odysseus was the husband of Penelope. He was renowned for his cunning: when the Greeks were recruiting for the Trojan War, he at first pretended to be mad, knowing an oracle had foretold that if he went, he would not return for 20 years. Odysseus captured the Trojan prophet Helenus, who told him they could seize Troy if they built a wooden horse (see p.370). His voyage home, recounted in Homer's *Odyssey*, was prolonged, and included encounters with a Cyclops, Scylla and Charybdis (see p.370), and the Sirens, whom he escaped by tying himself to his ship's mast so he could not jump into the sea. On the island of Aeaea, the sorceress Circe turned his men into pigs, but Odysseus was immune because the god Hermes had given him a magical plant. His ships were wrecked, and Odysseus was the only person to reach Ithaca. There, he found Penelope (who had believed him to be dead), surrounded by suitors. She had resisted them by saying she would marry only when she had completed a shroud, which each night she unpicked. Disguising himself as a beggar, Odysseus slayed the suitors at a feast, before revealing his identity to Penelope. He was said to have been killed by Telegonus, the son he had with Circe. Odysseus's adventures were a popular subject in art.

Oedipus
Tragic hero

Oedipus is the subject of plays by Aeschylus and Sophocles, and he is mentioned in Homer's *Odyssey*; the details of his story vary in each version. The son of Laius, king of Thebes, Oedipus was abandoned by his father as a baby, after the Delphic Oracle warned that Laius would be killed by his son. But the infant was saved by a shepherd and raised in Corinth. Later, Oedipus unwittingly killed his father, Laius, in a quarrel and married his mother, Jocasta (see p.371). On learning the truth, he blinded himself and fled to Colonus, a city near Athens. He cursed the sons of his incestuous union, who fought a ruinous civil war for the Theban throne. There were cults of Oedipus at Colonus, Attica, and Athens.

Orpheus
Hero; Musician; traveler to the Underworld

A brilliant musician, Orpheus was the son of Apollo and Calliope, the Muse. He took part in the Golden Fleece expedition (see p.355), calming the waves with his singing and saving the *Argo*'s crew by drowning out the songs of the Sirens. When his wife Eurydice died, he went to the Underworld to bring her back. His music charmed Hades (see p.344), king of the Underworld, who agreed to release Eurydice as long as Orpheus did not look at her before reaching the upper world. But he turned to glimpse her and she was sucked back into Hades. (See also pp.360–361.) Founder of the Orphic mystery cult, Orpheus is said to have been buried at his shrine in Pieria, Macedonia.

Paris
Hero of the Trojan War

Paris was the son of King Priam and Queen Hecuba of Troy. Before he was born, his mother dreamed she gave birth instead to a firebrand, which burned down the city—because of this omen, his parents left the baby to die on Mount Ida. However, he was

△ Roman mosaic showing Odysseus tied to the mast of his ship to save him from the Sirens (Tunis, 3rd century CE)

△ Fresco of the Judgment of Paris, depicting Paris (seated) as a shepherd (Pompeii, 1st century CE)

rescued by a herdsman, who adopted him. When he was older, Paris returned to Troy, where he was recognized by his sister, Cassandra, and readmitted into the family. While tending his flocks one day on Mount Ida, Paris was selected by Zeus to judge a beauty contest between the goddesses Hera, Athena, and Aphrodite. This contest (see p.369) ultimately led to Paris's abduction of Helen, Menelaus's wife, which, in turn, sparked the Trojan War (see p.355). An able archer, Paris was the person who slayed Achilles by wounding him in his vulnerable heel (see p.352). Afterward, Paris himself was fatally wounded by an arrow shot by the hero Philoctetes. Dying, Paris went up Mount Ida to find his first wife, Oenone, a nymph, who had pledged to cure him of any wound. However, angered by his affair with Helen, she refused, and Paris died.

Perseus
Hero: Gorgon slayer

Son of Zeus and the mortal Danaë, Perseus was revered as a slayer of monsters. His grandfather, Acrisius, king of Argos, had locked his daughter, Danaë, in a bronze chamber because of a prophecy that her future son (Perseus) would kill him. Perseus was conceived when Zeus entered Danaë's prison as a golden rain shower. When Perseus was born, he and his mother were cast adrift by Acrisius in a chest, and were later rescued by the fisherman Dictys, brother of King Polydectes of Seriphos. As an adult, Perseus agreed to bring back the head of the monstrous Gorgon Medusa as a trophy for Polydectes who, against Perseus's wishes, wanted to marry his mother (see p.366). With help from the gods, Perseus decapitated the sleeping Medusa. Escaping Medusa's two Gorgon sisters, he then passed through Ethiopia, where he rescued Princess Andromeda—daughter of King Cepheus of Ethiopia—from a sea monster (see p.366). Perseus used Medusa's head to turn to stone those who were attempting to prevent his marriage to Andromeda. Later, he took part in funeral games at Larissa, where he accidentally killed Acrisius, thus fulfilling the original prophecy. Perseus and Andromeda's son was Perses, an ancestor of the Persian royal house.

Theseus
Hero: Founder of Athens; Minotaur slayer

The greatest Athenian hero, Theseus was the son of King Aegeus (or, in some accounts, of Poseidon) and Aethra, daughter of the Troezenian king Pittheus. He was brought up in Troezen, but later traveled to Athens. Theseus killed various opponents on the way, including Procrustes, who hosted travelers and was known to chop off his visitors' legs if they were too tall to fit the bed or to stretch them if they were too short (see p.367). Dispatched as one of the 14 Athenian youths offered each year to King Minos of Crete, Theseus was sent into the Cretan Labyrinth to face the Minotaur, half-bull, half-human (see p.367). Helped by Minos's daughter, Ariadne, he slayed the beast and escaped from the Labyrinth. He abandoned Ariadne on the island of Naxos on the return journey (see p.368). On reaching Athens, he forgot to change his ship's sails from black to white—so Aegeus, fearing his son was dead, threw himself into the sea in despair. Theseus then became king of Athens. His later exploits included joining the voyage of the Argonauts (see p.366) and the Calydonian Boar Hunt (p.368). He eventually lost popularity in Athens, where rebel factions forced his abdication. Theseus then sailed to Skyros, where he was pushed off a cliff by Lycomedes, king of the island, and fell into the sea and died.

Myths

Creation and the Gods

Greek myth recognized a First Family of gods, ruling from Mount Olympus, who won power by dethroning earlier supreme beings and fending off rebellions. Many lesser deities also vied for influence, fighting over matters of prestige and seeking to satisfy their lusts, much like mortal rulers.

Clash of the Titans

Cronus—son of Uranus and Gaia and youngest of the 12 Titans—was warned that one of his children would overthrow him as ruler of the universe. His son Zeus soon set out to fulfill this prophecy. Zeus gave Cronus a drug that made him regurgitate the five offspring (Zeus's brothers and sisters) he had previously swallowed (see p.39)—who then flocked to Zeus's aid. Zeus also recruited help from the one-eyed Cyclopes, whom he had freed from imprisonment, and from the three giants known as the Hundred-Handed Ones. Most Titans took the side of Cronus, their brother, but under the leadership of his nephew, Atlas (see p.347), because Cronus was growing old. A terrible ten-year war ensued before an assault on the Titans' headquarters on Mount Othrys forced their total surrender. Many of the Titans were hurled into Tartarus, in the Underworld, but Atlas received special punishment: he was forced to hold up the heavens on his shoulders for all eternity.

◁ Fresco of Perseus and Andromeda (House of the Dioscuri, Pompeii)

Battle of the Gods and Giants

The Earth goddess, Gaia, had supported Zeus in his struggle with her son Cronus (see left), but growing impatient with his high-handedness, she spawned the litter of Giants that went on to contest his supremacy. They attacked Mount Olympus, the abode of the gods, with rocks and burning trees, and for a time seemed likely to prevail. The tide turned only after Zeus's wife, Hera, realized in a vision that, while the gods could wound Giants, only a human could actually kill them. So Athena, Zeus's daughter, immediately enlisted Heracles, who was semidivine but also semi-mortal, and with his aid the tide of battle began to change. One by one, the Giants were struck down until the revolt was vanquished. It was claimed that one gigantic corpse became the island of Sicily.

Typhon Challenges Zeus

Infuriated by the Giants' defeat by the gods (see above), Gaia produced a new and terrible offspring: the monstrous Typhon, who had legs that were formed from serpents' bodies and snake heads in place of hands. When spread wide, his arms stretched for a hundred leagues and his head touched the stars. On seeing fire flashing from his eyes and flaming rocks issuing from his mouth, the gods of Olympus fled in terror to Egypt, assuming animal disguises for safety. Only Athena, goddess of wisdom, held her ground; her example shamed Zeus, king of the gods, into returning to confront the horror. At first, Typhon had the upper hand, paralyzing Zeus by cutting the sinews from his hands and feet, but when Hermes restored his mobility he returned to the fray, refreshed. Gradually, Zeus's thunderbolts turned the tide of battle, driving Typhon to Sicily, where Zeus finally disposed of him by burying him beneath the volcanic Mount Etna, which still belches fire to this day.

Demeter and Persephone

Hades, god of the Underworld fell in love with Persephone and carried her off to his domain. Her mother, Demeter, was distraught and wandered the Earth in search of Persephone, abandoning her regular duties as goddess of agricultural fertility. This negligence caused crops to fail and trees to stop bearing fruit. Faced with the threat of famine, Zeus intervened, telling Hades he must release his bride, assuming she had not broken the taboo on eating food derived from the Underworld. But it emerged that Persephone had swallowed seven pomegranate seeds, so a compromise had to be reached: each year, Persephone should stay in Hades during the winter months but return to Earth in the spring, bringing renewed growth with her. Eleusis, near Athens, where Demeter ended her mourning, was to become one of ancient Greece's most celebrated cult centers.

▷ Marble sculpture showing Atlas holding a celestial globe (2nd century CE, Roman)

△ Painting showing Prometheus bringing fire to humans (Heinrich Füger, c. 1817)

The Birth of Aphrodite

Aphrodite entered the world fully formed and riding naked on a scallop shell that bore her to the shores of the island of Cythera; other accounts claim it was a beach near Paphos in Cyprus, which would later become the center of her cult. There was also disagreement as to how she was conceived: some claimed she was born of the mingling of sperm from the castrated genitals of her father, Uranus, with the foam of the sea; others held that she was a daughter of Zeus, born of the nymph Dione. Either way, she was the goddess of love in both its sacred and its profane forms, and her festival, the Aphrodisia, was celebrated across Greece.

The Naming of Athens

Athens always had a special relationship with Athena, the goddess who is said to have given the city its name. Her temple, the Parthenon, stood on the Acropolis (see pp.374–375), and another, smaller shrine arose nearby. Later generations told how the gods watched jealously as Attica's ruler, Cecrops, began building a capital they knew would be one of the world's great hubs. Athena and Poseidon competed to be its patron, and the other gods decided the prize should go to the one who devised an invention that would be of the most benefit to humankind. Poseidon struck the ground with his trident, and a spring welled up (though others say he created the first horse). However, Athena won the day by introducing the first olive tree. She pointed out to her audience that the tree would provide not only food for humans but also oil for sacrifices to the gods. In historical terms, her gift became the staple growth of Attica's rugged terrain.

Prometheus Steals Fire

Prometheus, whose name means "forethought," made a wise choice in the war between the gods and Titans (see p.359), choosing to support the former rather than his own Titanic kin. In reward, Zeus, king of the gods, gave him the task of creating life on Earth, making him for ever a champion of his own creation: humankind. But Zeus became jealous, and when Prometheus committed the sin of stealing fire from Heaven to give to mortals, Zeus enacted a cruel revenge. Prometheus was condemned to be bound to a rock where, each day, an eagle came to peck away at his liver— an endlessly repeated torment because every night the organ grew back again. According to some versions of this myth, Prometheus was eventually freed through the action of the hero Heracles, who shot the eagle with an arrow and broke his chains.

Pandora's Box

Not satisfied with the revenge he had taken on Prometheus (see left), Zeus decided to punish his creation, the human race, for the gift of fire. He told Hephaestus, the blacksmith god, to create a charming but rash woman called Pandora. Zeus subsequently sent her down to Earth with a box—but she was given strict instructions never to open it. However, curiosity got the better of Pandora, and she could not resist lifting the lid, whereupon all the ills afflicting humanity immediately flew out: sorrow, sickness, vice, death, and labor pains among them. Only hope, included in the box at the secret urging of Prometheus, stopped its victims from seeking relief in mass self-destruction.

Orpheus and Eurydice

Orpheus was the finest musician that ever lived. His songs were so sweet that wild beasts and even rocks and trees followed him when he played. He married Eurydice, but she died soon after the wedding from a snake bite. Undaunted, he followed her to Tartarus (the Underworld), where he played so beautifully that Hades, the Underworld god, agreed to release her on condition that Orpheus did not look at her until both of them had left the Underworld. But his love was intense and he could not resist turning to catch a glimpse of his wife as they approached the light. Immediately, she sank back into the world of shade, leaving him to wander the world, shunning the company of women. His contempt infuriated the maenads, followers of the god

Dionysus, so they tore him limb from limb. But his head went on singing as it floated down a river to the sea, finally finding rest on the island of Lesbos.

Europa and the Bull

The supreme, all-seeing god Zeus, who rarely missed a mortal beauty, was entranced by Europa, a daughter of the king of Phoenicia on the Mediterranean's eastern shore. One day, as Europa and her friends were enjoying the sunshine, they noticed a new bull had joined the cows that regularly grazed in the nearby coastal meadows. Although larger than any bull they had ever seen, it proved gentle and playful, so Europa climbed on its back. Immediately, it charged to the water's edge and swam all the way to Crete. Here, Zeus revealed that he had disguised himself as the bull. Unable to escape him, Europa went on to bear Zeus three sons. Meanwhile, Europa's brother, Cadmus, set out to find what had happened to his abducted sister. He reached mainland Greece without success, but decided he could not return to his distraught family empty-handed—so he stayed to found a new settlement, which grew into the great city of Thebes.

Midas's Golden Touch

The ancient kingdom of Phrygia, in central Anatolia, was known for its wealth. Mythmakers later devised a story that reflected this reputation: Phrygia's ruler, King Midas, won the favor of Dionysus by helping the god's friend and teacher Silenus, a satyr (half-man, half-goat), when he found him drunk and asleep in a garden one day. In repayment, Dionysus offered Midas whatever he wished. Midas asked that in future everything he touched should turn to gold. However, the gift soon turned into a curse, as the king realized he could no longer eat, because food turned to metal in his hands and mouth. Desperate, he begged Dionysus to reverse the wish. The god agreed, telling him to bathe in the Pactolus River—and ever since that day, its waters have carried sediments of gold.

△ Painting depicting Europa being abducted by Zeus, disguised as a bull (Rembrandt, 1632)

Aphrodite and Adonis

Myrrha, daughter of the Assyrian king Cinyras, was so vain that she refused to pay due respect to Aphrodite, goddess of love. The goddess took revenge by making Myrrha fall in love with her own father. When a son, Adonis, was born from their incestuous union, the guilt-stricken deity decided to protect him by putting him in a chest and giving him to the goddess Persephone, wife of Hades (see p.359), but with strict instructions never to peek inside. However, curiosity got the better of Persephone—when she raised the lid, she was amazed by Adonis's beauty and refused to return the chest to Aphrodite.

The two goddesses were equally smitten by Adonis, so looked to Zeus, king of the gods, for guidance on who should care for him. Zeus determined that the boy should spend eight months of each year with Aphrodite and four months with Persephone. This arrangement continued until Adonis was gored to death by a boar. In mourning, Aphrodite transformed Adonis's spilled blood into red anemones. Over time, a resurrection cult grew up around him, celebrating his rebirth in the growth of beautiful spring flowers.

Eros and Psyche

As recounted in *The Golden Ass* by the Roman writer Apuleius, the young princess Psyche (from the Greek for "soul") was, on instructions from the Delphic Oracle, abandoned by her parents on the top of a mountain, but was later carried off to a magnificent palace by an unseen force. There, every night, an unknown lover came to her in the darkness, only to disappear before break of day. Psyche's jealous sisters persuaded her that, despite the instructions she had received, she must find out the identity of her lover. One night, Psyche duly produced a lamp that illuminated the beautiful body of Eros, god of sensual love. Furious at her indiscretion, Eros took flight, leaving her broken-hearted and alone. It was only after surviving a succession of seemingly impossible trials—imposed on her by Eros's mother—that Psyche was finally able to win back her lost love. Eventually, Zeus welcomed her to Olympus to live among the gods as Eros's heavenly bride.

◁ Marble statue of Zeus, in the guise of a swan, seducing Leda (1st century CE)

Asclepius, God of Healing

The son of Apollo by a mortal woman, Asclepius was sent for his education to Chiron, the wise centaur (half-man, half-horse), and emerged as the world's finest healer, serving as physician to the Argonauts on their search for the Golden Fleece (see p.366). But Asclepius went too far in restoring life to dead people. Hades, god of the Underworld, complained to Zeus, who struck Asclepius with a thunderbolt. Zeus later relented and restored Asclepius to life, this time as an immortal; thereafter, he had divine status as god of healing, worshipped at Epidaurus and at other sanctuaries of healing around the Greek world.

Leda and the Swan

The lustful god Zeus took many forms in his pursuit of women, one being his transformation into a swan. He chose this disguise to seduce and rape Leda, wife of King Tyndareus of Sparta, who, some said, was already pregnant after sleeping with her husband the same night. In due course, she laid two eggs, from one of which Helen of Troy and her brother Polydeuces (in Latin, Pollux) hatched. The other produced Castor (see below) and Clytemnestra, both conceived of her husband and hence mortal.

Castor and Pollux

Jointly known as the Dioscuri, the half-brothers Castor and Pollux (Polydeuces in Greek) were inseparable (see above). At their home in Sparta, Castor won

△ Painting showing (from left to right) Zeus and Hermes with Philemon and Baucis (Peter Paul Rubens, c. 1620–1622)

fame as a horse-breaker, Pollux as a boxer. Both were involved in the quest for the Golden Fleece (see p.366) and in hunting the Calydonian Boar (see p.368), before engaging in a bitter feud with the twin brothers Lynceus and Idas, after trying to abduct their fiancées. This proved fatal when Idas murdered the mortal Castor. Zeus intervened to kill Idas as he turned on Pollux, who begged his divine father to bestow on his half-brother the

immortality that he, the son of a god, possessed. Zeus responded by making the two the brightest stars in the heavenly constellation of Gemini (the Twins). They became patrons of sailors, who looked to them for good winds.

Baucis and Philemon

When the gods Zeus and Hermes decided to travel among mortals disguised as peasants, they found

every door closed to them until they arrived at the humble dwelling of the elderly married couple Baucis and Philemon. In stark contrast to their neighbors, this couple lavished hospitality on their guests, giving them all the food and wine they had. It was only when Baucis noticed that the pitcher from which she had replenished the visitors' cups remained full that she began to suspect they might be gods. Touched by the couple's

kindness, Zeus told them to follow him up a nearby hill. From its summit they saw that a flood had swept away their ungenerous neighbors, but that their cottage had been transformed into a temple. The couple asked if they themselves could tend it, and their wish was granted, as was a second request: that when the time came for one of them to die, the other should go too, so that they would never have to face life alone.

△ Roman fresco depicting Pentheus being torn apart by devotees of Dionysus (House of the Vettii, Pompeii)

ability to remove and replace her eyes at will, which made her appear monstrous. Later myth identified her with the Empusae, shape-shifting female phantoms who seduced young men, then sucked their blood as they slept.

Pentheus and the Bacchantes

Mortals always angered gods at their peril, and few suffered a worse fate in return than Pentheus, king of Thebes. When he tried to ban the Bacchantes' orgiastic rites in honor of the god Dionysus—his own cousin but, unlike him, an immortal— the celebrants left the city to carry out their rituals in the surrounding hills. Fatally tempted to spy on their activities, Pentheus hid up a tree to keep watch. However, directed by Dionysus, the revelers found him and, driven mad by the excesses of their revels, tore him limb from limb. As recounted in Euripides' play *The Bacchae*, those who led the slaughter were his aunts and his own mother.

The Punishment of Tantalus

Tantalus, a mortal being who had been befriended by Zeus, one day invited the gods to a banquet. However, on finding that he lacked sufficient provisions (or, according to other sources, to test his guests' omniscience), Tantalus killed his own son, Pelops, cut him into pieces, and served him up as food. His guests recognized the enormity of what he had done— all, that is, except Demeter, who was so distraught at the loss of her daughter, Persephone

Deucalion's Flood

Greek myth told the story of a devastating flood, sent by the god Zeus to wipe out the wicked human race. However, one couple, Deucalion and his wife, Pyrrha, were warned by Deucalion's father, Prometheus (see p.360), of the impending catastrophe, and survived it in a boat that, after nine days, struck land on the peak of Mount Parnassus. Recognizing

their virtue, Zeus allowed the couple to live, but life had little to offer in the empty world that emerged as the floodwaters subsided. So they consulted the Oracle at Delphi, which told them to cast their mothers' bones over their shoulders. The advice seemed shocking, until Deucalion realized what was meant—the Earth was their mother, and they were able to repopulate it by throwing stones that, on touching the ground, turned into men and women.

The Misery of Lamia

According to myth, parents often terrified youngsters with tales of the child-eating Lamia, a Libyan queen who was seduced by Zeus, the promiscuous king of the gods, and had an affair with him. His jealous wife, Hera, killed the offspring of their union and, in her grief, Lamia took to devouring any other women's children that fell within her grasp. Zeus had given her the (see p.359), that unthinkingly she ate part of the victim's shoulder. Zeus had the boy made whole and restored to life again, but condemned Tantalus to a terrible fate: to spend eternity bound beneath a fruit tree without ever being able to reach the fruit, and up to his waist in water that he could never bend over to drink.

Sisyphus's Task

The rogue and trickster Sisyphus, who had usurped the throne of Corinth from his brother and had betrayed Zeus's secrets, faced a terrible fate: to push a huge boulder up a hill toward the summit but never to reach it; before he could do so, the stone rolled back all the way to the bottom and he had to start again. His name became proverbially attached to impossible tasks that can never be fulfilled.

The Flaying of Marsyas

Having chanced upon a twin-reeded flute that the goddess Athena had once thrown away (she thought it made her look unsightly when she puffed up her cheeks to play it), the satyr Marsyas, half-man and half-goat, discovered he could produce music that, according to listeners, rivaled that of the gods. This praise reached the ears of Apollo, deity of music, who challenged the upstart to a contest in which the loser would suffer whatever penalty the winner chose to inflict. Unwisely, Marsyas accepted the challenge: when, inevitably, he lost, Apollo took merciless revenge by flaying Marsyas alive and nailing his skin to the bark of a tree.

The Fate of Narcissus

Narcissus was so beautiful that many men and women fell in love with him, but his egotism was so great he never responded to their advances. To punish this, the goddess Nemesis made him glance into a pool of still water: in his reflection he found a being worthy of his love. But he could not tear himself away from his own image. The gods took pity on him, transforming him into the flower that bears his name, whose head hangs down, often on the edge of ponds or streams.

△ Painting showing Narcissus transfixed by his own reflection in a pool of water (John William Waterhouse, 1903)

Realm of Humans and Animals

Perhaps because of their exalted view of human potential, the Greeks had more hero myths than any other culture. Yet the heroes they celebrated remained fallible, experiencing setbacks as well as triumphs. This gave them an relatable quality that has kept their names familiar to the present day.

Perseus and Medusa

In an attempt to save his mother, Danaë, from an unwanted marriage to King Polydectes of Seriphos, the hero Perseus offered her suitor any trophy he desired. Polydectes responded by demanding the head of the Gorgon Medusa—a monster with serpents for hair and an aspect so terrible that anyone who looked upon her face was turned to stone. The task seemed impossible, but Perseus was given help. Athena gave him a polished shield and instructed him to look at Medusa's reflection in it in order to kill her. From Hermes, he received a sickle, and the nymphs gave him three other essential pieces of equipment: winged sandals, a satchel to place Medusa's head in, and a helmet that made him invisible. Suitably armed, Perseus traveled to the Gorgons' lair and, taking care not to disturb her two sleeping sisters, crept up on Medusa. Using the shield as a mirror, he severed her head with a single blow of the sickle. Her sisters awoke, but with the aid of the sandals and the helmet, the hero made his escape, carrying the severed head with him.

Andromeda, the Bride of Perseus

Flying in his winged sandals one day, after having killed Medusa, Perseus saw a naked princess, Andromeda, chained to a cliff by the sea. On descending, he learned the reason for her plight: her mother had rashly boasted that she and her daughter were more beautiful than the Nereids (sea nymphs; see p.70). Poseidon, their patron, had sent a sea monster to ravage the coast to avenge the insult, and had made it known that the parents could appease his wrath only by sacrificing their daughter to the beast. Struck by the girl's beauty, Perseus offered to rescue her in return for her hand in marriage. When the monster appeared, he duly slayed it with his sickle, only to find that the parents had reneged on their promise by summoning a suitor to whom she was already promised, who came with a host of supporters to claim her. But Perseus had a powerful magic weapon: Medusa's head (see left), which he held aloft, turning the warriors and Andromeda's parents to stone, thereby enabling him to claim his bride.

Jason and the Argonauts

Raised by the wise centaur Chiron in the ways of a hero, Jason claimed the throne of the city-state of Iolcus, stolen from his father by Pelias, Jason's uncle. Pelias agreed to step down on one condition: Jason must return the fleece of a magical golden ram, a gift from the god Hermes, from Colchis on the eastern shore of the Black Sea. Accepting the challenge, Jason assembled a team of heroes and demigods, among them Orpheus (see p.360) and, for a time, Heracles (see p.368), to sail with him on a specially prepared ship, the *Argo*. The 56 Argonauts endured many challenges before reaching Colchis, and even there the local ruler sought to thwart their purpose. It was only with the help of the king's daughter, Medea, who fell in love with Jason, that the hero was able to distract the dragon guarding the treasure and to escape with it back to his ship, in time for an equally perilous journey home.

Jason and Medea

Jason had sworn himself to Medea forever (see above) but, according to some versions of the myth, he soon came to fear his bride's ruthlessness and her magical powers, even though they could be used to his advantage—for example, in retrieving the Golden Fleece, in taking revenge on his uncle Pelias on his return to Iolcus, and then in establishing himself on the Corinthian throne. So, when the king of Thebes offered Jason his daughter's hand in marriage, he plucked up courage to tell Medea he planned to divorce her. She pretended to accept, but in fact lost little time in taking revenge

◁ Statue of Jason and the Golden Fleece (Pietro Francavilla, 1589)

by giving his intended a wedding robe that burst into flames when she put it on, killing her and the guests. Only Jason survived but, abandoned by the gods for his broken marriage oath, he eked out a miserable existence. However, Medea prospered and was offered sanctuary in Athens, where she married the city-state's king. (Euripides tells a different version of this story: see p.181.)

Procrustes' Bed

Born to be king of Athens but raised in Troezen across the Isthmus of Corinth, Theseus set out as a young man to claim his rightful inheritance. But on the way he faced a series of daunting challenges. He laid low a ruffian nicknamed Club-clouter, taking away his weapon; overcame a murderous wrestler at his own game; and subjected a brigand who hurled victims to their death in the sea to that same fate. His final trial came in the house of a villain known as Procrustes, "the stretcher," who offered travelers accommodation only to kill them as they slept. His method was to fit his victims to the size of the bed in which they slept; if they were longer than the bed, he cut off their feet with an ax, if shorter, he stretched them, as on a rack. Theseus dispatched Procrustes by using the same method he had inflicted on others, before proceeding on his way to be duly recognized as Athens' heir apparent.

Theseus and the Minotaur

Having established his rightful claim to be king of Athens against fearful odds (see above),

△ Roman fresco of Theseus after having killed the Minotaur (House of Gavius Rufus, Pompeii, 1st century CE)

Theseus set out to prove himself by confronting the Minotaur. This fearsome monster, half-man and half-bull, was confined in the specially prepared Labyrinth on the island of Crete. Following a military victory over Athens, Crete's King Minos imposed a terrible condition: seven young Athenian men and seven young women should be sacrificed to the Minotaur annually. Intent on killing the beast, Theseus volunteered as one of the youths and sailed with them to Crete. There, he won the love of Minos's daughter, Ariadne who gave him a sword to kill the Minotaur and a ball of twine that he could unspool to guide himself out of the Labyrinth. She also obtained keys to the prison where his companions were held. After slaying the Minotaur, Theseus and the rest of the group escaped to their ship and made a triumphant return to Athens.

Ariadne on Naxos

Ariadne had sacrificed her home and family to help Theseus secure his claim to the throne of Athens (see p.367). So, understandably, she expected to become his wife on their return to the capital. However, quite inexplicably, the hero abandoned Ariadne on the island of Naxos, sailing away with his companions as she lay sleeping. But the gods were on her side: Dionysus descended on the island with a train of satyrs to rescue her and take her up to Mount Olympus. The couple fell in love, and over subsequent years, she and Dionysus had many children together. In later times, Ariadne was worshipped on the island of Naxos as a goddess in her own right.

▽ Painting depicting Atalanta's running race (Noël Hallé, c. 1762–1765)

Daedalus and Icarus

Daedalus was a famous inventor employed by King Minos of Crete, for whom he built the Labyrinth in which the Minotaur was confined (see p.367). Wanting to leave the island after having been imprisoned by the king, Daedalus created wings for himself and his son, made from feathers and wax. But, ignoring his father's orders, Icarus flew too close to the sun and the wax melted (see p.354.) He fell to his death in the sea and was buried on the island later called Icaria.

The Calydonian Boar

When Calydon's ruler failed to make sacrifices to Artemis, the goddess sent a huge boar to ravage the land. Under the leadership of the king's son Meleager, heroes from all over Greece assembled to dispatch it. From the start, the hunt—jinxed by Artemis—went badly. Some hunters were killed by the boar, others died accidentally. When two centaurs tried to rape the hunter Atalanta, she shot them. It was Atalanta who first wounded the beast, but Meleager killed it. Even then, trouble ensued: when Meleager awarded Atalanta its hide, two of his uncles disputed the decision, and in a rage he killed them. His own mother then orchestrated his death; she cast a log the Oracle of Delphi had proclaimed essential to his survival into a fire to burn up. When his sisters shrieked in mourning, Artemis turned them into guinea fowl.

Atalanta's Race

On her return from the Calydonian Boar Hunt, Atalanta's father insisted that his daughter should take a husband, despite the Delphic Oracle having warned her against marriage. To delay the event, Atalanta set a condition: that any suitor must beat her in a foot race, at the risk of being killed if he failed. Since she was the fastest runner in Greece, many princes died before one, Melanion, sought the help of Aphrodite. The goddess gave him three golden apples, telling him to throw them in Atalanta's path to distract her as she ran. The tactic worked, and the couple were wed—although Zeus subsequently prevented them from having children.

The Labors of Heracles

Half-human, half-god, Heracles was the strongest being on Earth. The son of Zeus and a mortal woman, he suffered the animosity of Zeus's wife Hera,

who was tricked by her husband into suckling the infant hero on the milk of immortality. She waited until Heracles was in Thebes, happily married to the king's daughter and with three sons, before taking revenge. Then she struck, causing insanity in Heracles that caused him to kill his wife and children. Devastated, he consulted the Delphic Oracle, which told him that he must perform any tasks King Eurystheus of Mycenae chose. Fearing a rival for the throne, the ruler devised daunting challenges: the Twelve Labors, whose successful completion would win Heracles fame and respect for eternity.

The hero's first labor was to kill the fearsome Nemean lion. Next came his slaying of the monstrous nine-headed Hydra. The third and fourth tasks saw the capture of the elusive hind of Arcadia and then the boar of Mount Erymanthus. In the fifth

labor, Heracles cleared dung from the stables of King Augeas of Elis. For the sixth labor, he shot the human-eating birds of the Stymphalian marshes. Capture of the mad bull that tormented the island of Crete was the seventh labor, while the eighth involved stealing the human-eating mares of King Diomedes of the Bistones. For his ninth labor, Heracles seized the girdle of Hippolyte, queen of the fierce female warriors known as the Amazons. Task ten involved capturing cattle belonging to the three-bodied Giant Geryon, and in the eleventh task, the hero took golden apples from the tree guarded by the Hesperides, nymphs of the evening. Heracles' twelfth and final task was the most challenging: to descend to the Underworld and bring back its guardian, the three-headed dog Cerberus. After completing his 12 labors, Heracles secured his fame and renown.

The Judgment of Paris

At a marriage feast attended by the Olympian gods, the goddess of discord, Eris, threw down a golden apple marked "For the fairest." Three goddesses soon claimed it: Zeus's wife, Hera; his daughter, Athena; and Aphrodite, divinity of love and beauty. The trio appealed to Zeus to judge the dispute, but he delegated this task to a mortal, Paris (born to Priam, king of Troy), who, owing to a damning prophecy, was then earning his living as a herdsman. Each of the goddesses tried to win Paris's favor: Hera offered him wealth and power; Athena wisdom and military might. But, it was Aphrodite's promise that swayed him—she said if he

△ Roman fresco of the sacrifice of Iphigenia (1st century CE, Pompeii)

chose her, he would secure the love of the most beautiful of all mortal women. But his choice was fateful—the most beautiful mortal woman was Helen, wife of Menelaus, king of Sparta, and Paris's abduction of her would provoke the 10-year Trojan War.

The Sacrifice of Iphigenia

Seeking revenge for Helen's abduction (see above), a huge fleet assembled on the Greek side of the Aegean Sea. But when no favorable wind sprang up to carry them to Troy, the prophet Calchas claimed that the army's leader, Agamemnon, had angered the gods, who would only be propitiated by the sacrifice of something dear to him—namely, his own daughter, Iphigenia. At first Agamemnon refused, but the horde grew restless so the girl was summoned from her

home in Mycenae on the pretext that she was to be married to the hero Achilles—but on her arrival the sacrifice was carried out.

Achilles' Heel

Homer's *Iliad* recounts how Agamemnon, leader of the Greek forces besieging Troy, angered Achilles, the greatest warrior of his day, by taking his concubine Chryseis (see p.352). Achilles retired to his tent in anger, and the Trojan forces gained the upper hand. But when Troy's hero, Hector, killed Patroclus (according to some accounts, Achilles' lover), Achilles slayed Hector, turning the tide of battle in the Greeks' favor. Yet he too died in combat, by an arrow in his heel, the one part of his body not rendered invulnerable when his mother had dipped him at birth in the Styx, the river of immortality.

△ Painting showing Oedipus being guided by his daughter Antigone after having blinded himself (Charles Jalabert, 1842)

The Trojan Horse

After 10 years' conflict in which Troy had not fallen, the Greek hero Odysseus persuaded his comrades to adopt a strategy to gain access to the city. At his urging, they built a huge, hollow, wooden horse with room for armed warriors to hide inside. Then they made a show of giving up the siege and heading back to Greece, leaving the horse on the beach, with an inscription on its side dedicating it to the goddess Athena. When they found it, the Trojans decided—despite warnings from the priestess Cassandra—to drag it into the city for their own temple to Athena. But the Greek ships were waiting over the horizon, and at midnight the soldiers hidden inside the horse broke free to slaughter the sentries guarding the city gates; a fiery signal soon brought the sailors back to rape and slaughter the Trojans.

Wandering Odysseus

Having engineered the Greek victory at Troy, Odysseus set off with his followers to return to his home on the island of Ithaca and to his beloved wife Penelope. But the journey, as described in Homer's *Odyssey*, turned out to be full of perils. The hero survived storms, shipwrecks, encounters with human-eating giants, and the fatal attractions of the Sirens, whose songs lured sailors to their death if they failed to block their ears. The sorceress Circe (see p.258) bewitched Odysseus's men for 12 months, and he lost even more time to the beautiful sea-nymph Calypso, who held him prisoner for seven years. When eventually he reached Ithaca, 10 years after leaving Troy, it was to find that 100 princely suitors, assuming him dead, were vying for the hand of Penelope. Only by massacring them all was he finally able to win her back and reclaim the Ithacan throne.

Scylla and Charybdis

One of the most terrifying incidents in Odysseus's journey (see left) was when the fleet had to pass between two facing cliffs, each one inhabited by a voracious monster. One of them, Scylla, had six heads that she would crane out on long necks to snatch up sailors from the sea to gulp down; the other monster, Charybdis, sucked in huge volumes of water, creating whirlpools that could swallow entire ships. Evading her grasp, Odysseus sailed too close to the other shore and, as a result, lost six of his best men to Scylla.

Tiresias the Prophet

Seeing two snakes coupling, Tiresias struck them with a staff, killing the female. Instantly, he was transformed into a woman. When the same thing happened years later, he killed the male and turned back into a man. When Zeus and Hera were later arguing about whether men or women derive most pleasure from sex, they turned to Tiresias, who had experienced sex as both these genders. He said he preferred sex as a woman. Enraged by this, Hera struck him blind. To make amends, Zeus gave him the power of prophecy and also long life, so he eventually saw out seven normal lifespans.

Oedipus, King of Thebes

The Delphic Oracle warned King Laius of Thebes that he would be killed by his own son, so the ruler left his infant boy to die on a nearby mountainside. But the baby was rescued by a herdsman and then adopted by the childless ruler of nearby Corinth. When Oedipus reached adulthood, he happened to meet Laius by chance on a road. Ordered to give way, he fulfilled the Oracle's prediction by killing the stranger, unaware he was his father. Carrying on to Thebes, Oedipus inherited the now-vacant throne by ridding the city of the Sphinx, a monster that had been terrorizing the area. As ruler, he married Laius's widow, Queen Jocasta—in fact, his own mother. He learned the enormity of what he had done when plague later hit the city and the Oracle proclaimed that it would end only when Laius's killer was driven out. It was the blind prophet Tiresias (see left) who revealed that the guilty man was Oedipus himself. Horrified by what he had done, Oedipus blinded himself and fled the city to wander the world aimlessly in a desperate search for atonement. However, his daughter Antigone cared for and was loyal to him.

Bellerophon Slays the Chimera

Falsely accused of seducing King Proetus's wife, Anteia, Bellerophon came as an unwelcome supplicant to the king of Lycia. Seeking to be rid of him, the king gave Bellerophon a seemingly impossible task: to slay the Chimera, a fearsome monster (see p.71). After having tamed the winged horse Pegasus, the hero was able to ride on its back and shoot arrows on his prey from above. He failed to kill it at first, but finally succeeded by thrusting a lead-tipped spear into the creature's mouth. Its fiery breath melted the metal, choking it with its molten heat.

The Winged Horse Pegasus

Pegasus was the offspring of the Gorgon Medusa. He had magical powers that included the ability to raise springs of fresh water by stamping a hoof on the ground. Bellerophon was able to tame Pegasus with the help of the goddess Athena, who gave him a golden bridle to cast over the horse's head. Thereafter, rider and mount were inseparable, until Bellerophon tried to ride to the gods' home on Mount Olympus. For his audacity, he was cast to Earth, where he was left disabled and blind. Pegasus, however, reached the summit, where Zeus took him in hand, using him to carry thunderbolts.

The Sculptor Pygmalion

As recounted in *Metamorphoses* by the Roman poet Ovid, the Greek sculptor Pygmalion fell in love with an ivory figure he had made. After having prayed to Aphrodite for a living bride replicating his creation, he kissed the statue and found its lips were warm. The couple were married and their daughter, Paphos, gave her name to the Cypriot city.

The Danaids: Husband-killers

The twin brothers Danaus and Aegyptus were rivals for power. When Aegyptus insisted his 50 sons should marry Danaus's 50 daughters (known as the Danaids), Danaus provided the intended brides with pins and instructions on how to kill their husbands on their wedding night. All did so, except one girl, Hypermnestra, who spared her bridegroom, Lynceus, because he did not attempt to force himself on her. Later, this surviving son would kill Danaus and rule the city of Argos in his stead.

△ Painting of Pygmalion adoring the statue he created (Jean Raoux, 1717)

Sites

Mainland Greece

Visitors still flock to Greece to marvel at the numerous sites that dot the ancient heartland, especially in the Peloponnese and nearby areas and in the northern lands that once formed the kingdom of Macedonia. Temples and shrines compete for attention with theaters, fortifications, and agoras.

Pella Archaeological Site

First mentioned during the 5th century BCE, Pella replaced neighboring Aigai as the capital of the kingdom of Macedonia in northern Greece. Alexander the Great was born in the city, as his father Philip II had been, and the playwright Euripides (see p.323) spent his last years there. The site is now land-locked, but in ancient times it was a port, connected to the sea by an inlet that has long since dried up. Archaeologists have excavated the remains of the palace complex, located on a hill north of the city, to which it was connected by a bridge over marshland. The urban area itself was built according to a grid pattern around a central agora. The Pella Archaeological Museum contains spectacular floor mosaics and findings from the sanctuaries and houses excavated in the area.

Aigai Burial Complex

Replaced by Pella as Macedonia's capital, Aigai retained a special place in the kingdom's heritage

◁ The Palace of Aigai (4th century BCE), after a 16-year restoration project

as the burial place of its rulers. Today, visitors to the modern town of Vergina, which in recent centuries has risen over Aigai's ruins, can explore the extraordinary underground complex that housed the remains of the Macedonian ruler Philip II and later kings, where spectacular finds in gold, silver, and ivory are preserved in a subterranean museum. The remains of the palace in which Alexander the Great was proclaimed king in 336 BCE are also open to the public.

Sanctuary of Dion

Located at the foot of Mount Olympus, Dion was a sacred site for Macedonians, housing the kingdom's most important sanctuary of Zeus; Alexander the Great performed a number of sacrifices there before launching his invasion of Asia in 334 BCE. In Hellenistic times, a city grew up around the sanctuary, its importance boosted by a nine-day festival dedicated to Zeus and to the Muses. Around the 5th century BCE, the site was abandoned following a series of devastating earthquakes and floods. It was rediscovered only at the beginning of the 19th century. Since that time, archaeologists have traced the

foundations of the ancient city, turning up statues and mosaic floors that are now on display in an archaeological park and a museum.

Oracle Shrine of Dodona

Located near modern Ioannina, ancient Dodona was home to an oracle that was second in prestige only to Delphi in Greece (see pp.154–155). Referred to in the Iliad, it may have been active in Mycenaean times; it thrived in the Classical era, by which time it was dedicated to Zeus, the king of the gods (see p.346), and to the Muses. Priests and priestesses would carefully observe the rustlings of the leaves of a sacred oak tree and then inscribe their interpretations on tablets, of which more than 4,000 have

now been found. Visitors to the site today can see the remains of a bouleuterion (senate house) and theater that date back to the 4th and 3rd centuries BCE.

Sanctuary of Apollo, Delphi

The ancient Greeks considered this sanctuary to be the religious center of the world and it was marked by a navel-shaped stone known as the omphalos. Supplicants came from all over Greece and beyond to consult the Delphic Oracle, voiced by a priestess, the Pythia, on a spectacular site beneath Mount Parnassus. Today, visitors to the steeply sloping precinct can view an upper sanctuary whose dominant features are the ruins of a 4th-century bce temple dedicated to Apollo and the remains of a theater whose steps cascade down the hillside, giving outstanding views of the valley below. The temple path is dotted with the remains of buildings, termed treasuries, erected over the centuries by city-states to give thanks for the Oracle's help. The remains of a stadium, for 6,500 spectators, lie further up the hill. Votive offerings and statues from the site, including the famous bronze Charioteer of Delphi, are on display in an on-site museum. (See main entry pp.154–155.)

Lefkandi Archaeological Site

The archaeological site at Lefkandi, a village facing Attica from the coast of the island of Euboea, owes its importance to the evidence it has provided of continuous occupation from c. 2100 BCE to c. 700 BCE. Excavations at the site are ongoing, and exhibits from the dig are on show at the Archaeological Museum of Eretria, some 8 miles (12 km) away along the coast. The most significant discovery so far at Lefkandi has been the remains of a presumed heroon—a hero's burial place—containing the graves of a man and a woman and four horses, seemingly sacrificial victims. Precious goods found on the site have also indicated ongoing trade links with Cyprus and the Levant at a time when trade was thought to have virtually collapsed. (See main entry pp.48–49.)

Sanctuary of Eleusis

Now an industrial suburb of Athens, 12 miles (20 km) from the center of the Greek capital, Eleusis was in ancient times the birthplace of the playwright Aeschylus (see p.321) and home of the Eleusinian Mysteries: a cult whose sacred rites offered initiates the promise of life after death. It owed its significance to its role as the seat of worship of Demeter and her daughter Persephone, whom the goddess sought to rescue from the Underworld after her abduction by its ruler, Hades (see p.359). The rite's secret ceremonies (votaries were bound by a vow of silence) were conducted in the Telesterion, a temple able to house as many as 3,000 people. The vestiges of the temple, destroyed by Persian invaders after the Battle of Thermopylae (480 BCE) and rebuilt under the aegis of the Athenian statesman Pericles (see pp.168–169) can be viewed, along with those of surrounding buildings, in an archaeological site in the center of the modern suburb of Eleusis.

Ancient Agora, Athens

As the working heart of ancient Athens, the Agora was lined with stoas (covered walkways), some of which housed shops, and also provided a setting for temples dedicated to Ares, Apollo, and other gods. The best preserved is the Temple of Hephaestus (see p.172), which survives almost intact today. The Stoa of Attalos, originally built in Hellenistic times, was rebuilt in the 1950s, and now houses the Museum of the Ancient Agora. (See main entry pp.120–121.)

Acropolis of Athens

No group of buildings conjures up the spirit of ancient Greece more vividly than those of the Acropolis in Athens, which occupy a hilltop site in the center of the Greek capital. Of these buildings, none is more iconic than the Parthenon (see pp.176–177), built as a temple to Athena, the deity who is said to have given the city its name (see p.360). The complex dates back to the city's golden age in the 5th century BCE, and owes its inspiration to the statesman Pericles (see pp.168–169). Of the other structures, the Propylaea functioned as a monumental gateway to the citadel, while

△ Remains of the ancient Agora, Athens, with a view of the Acropolis in the background

△ Aerial view of the Acropolis of Athens (5th century BCE)

the Erechtheion and the Temple of Athena Nike both served to honor the city's patron goddess. In Athens' heyday, Athena was also exalted by a huge bronze statue, cast by the renowned master sculptor Phidias, that stood 30 ft (9 m) high; Athena held a shield in one hand and a lance in the other—its tip could be seen from ships some 40 miles (60 km) away. Today, the Acropolis is Greece's most celebrated ancient site, attracting around three million visitors a year. (See main entry pp.174–175.)

Panathenaic Stadium, Athens

Starting life as a racecourse in the 6th century BCE, the stadium in Athens was dramatically remodeled two centuries later by the Athenian statesman Lycurgus to serve as a fitting venue for the quadrennial Panathenaic Games. After the Roman conquest, the concourse was again rebuilt, but this time entirely in marble, making it the only such stadium in the world. Subsequently allowed to fall into ruin, the stadium was rebuilt, again in marble, in time to host the first modern Olympic Games in 1896.

Sanctuary of Artemis, Brauron

Twenty miles (30 kilometers) from the heart of Athens on Attica's east coast, Brauron was in ancient times famed as a cult center of the hunter goddess Artemis, who was honored every four years by a ceremonial procession from the Athenian Acropolis (see opposite). Little now remains of Artemis's temple, which was destroyed by Persian invaders in 480 BCE and rebuilt half a century later. Instead, a dozen columns of a Doric stoa (colonnaded walkway) dominate the site, which also features a sacred spring and a stone bridge, still clearly showing the marks of wheel ruts from centuries ago. Reliefs and sculptures from recent excavations are preserved in the Brauron Archaeological Museum nearby.

△ View of the well-preserved remains of the impressive ancient theater of Epidaurus, with its rows of stepped seating

Temple of Poseidon, Sounion

Perched on top of Cape Sounion, on the tip of the Attica peninsula, 43 miles (70 km) south of Athens, the ruins of the Temple of Poseidon are one of the most picturesquely sited of Greece's Classical remains. Erected in the 440s BCE as part of the Periclean construction program (see pp.172–173), the shrine paid tribute to the sea god from a clifftop aerie 200 ft (60 m) above the shoreline. Its romantic setting later attracted English poet Lord Byron, whose name is graffitied on the base of one of the temple's columns. Remains of a smaller sanctuary dedicated to Athena and of a fortress dating to the Peloponnesian War stand nearby.

Sanctuary and Theater at Epidaurus

Claimed in ancient times to be the birthplace of Asclepius, god of healing (see p.362), the small city-state of Epidaurus, located in the Peloponnese's Argolis peninsula, was home to the god's sanctuary, which now lies about 5 miles (8 km) from the modern town. Patients once traveled there from all over the Greek world, seeking divine help to cure their ailments. Built in the early 4th century BCE, the complex remained in use until the closure of all pagan sites later in the century. Only fragments have survived, with sculptures from the temple pediments now housed in their own room at the National Archaeological Museum in Athens. Today, the principal attraction of this site is its theater, the best preserved of any theater in the Greek world. Built shortly after the sanctuary, it would once have housed more than 13,000 spectators. The theater is still in use for an annual festival of classical drama, as well as for occasional concerts and opera performances.

Citadel of Tiryns

"Mighty-walled Tiryns," as Homer described it, was one of the main strongholds of Mycenaean Greece, and also the spot from which Heracles set off on his legendary Twelve Labors (see p.369). The walls, in places still 23 ft (7 m) high, were once said to have been built by the one-eyed Cyclopes, because humans could not have lifted the huge stones used in their construction. They were built to protect the royal palace, whose central feature was a megaron (great hall) that had at its heart a circular fireplace surrounded by four wooden columns. Relics of the excavations that have been conducted at the site, which shares UNESCO World Heritage status with Mycenae, just 12 miles (20 km) to the north, are preserved in the archaeological museum of Nafplio, on the Aegean coast nearby.

Agora of Argos

With a claim to be Europe's oldest inhabited urban area (see p.64), Argos lent its name both to the Argive forces—Homer's name for the Greek troops that besieged Troy—and to the Argead dynasty that ruled Macedonia under Philip II and Alexander the Great. In myth, it was the birthplace of the hero Perseus, Gorgon-slayer and rescuer of Andromeda. The monuments preserved today in its archaeological site include the terrace of a 3rd-century BCE theater that would have seated around 3,000 spectators, and the adjacent Agora with the foundations of a *palaestra* (wrestling school) and a *bouleuterion* (senate house). The remains of the Heraion, dedicated to the city's patron deity Hera (see p.345), lie 5 miles (8 km) away on a hillside dominating the Argive Plain.

Mycenae

The city that gave its name to an entire era of Greek history grew to greatness as a military stronghold in the middle of the 2nd millennium BCE, before facing catastrophic destruction in the 12th century BCE. Mycenae was the base from which King Agamemnon gathered supporters from across the Greek world for his legendary assault on Troy; it was here that he returned, only to be killed by his wife, Clytemnestra, and her lover and to be avenged by his son, Orestes, providing one of the central themes of subsequent Greek drama (see pp.180–181). Lost for many centuries, Mycenae was returned to prominence by German businessman and amateur archaeologist Heinrich Schliemann, who excavated the site in the 1870s, but discarded objects that did not endorse his theories. The most celebrated of

Mycenae's remains today are the Lion Gate—the principal entranceway through the Cyclopean wall surrounding the citadel—and the so-called Tomb of Clytemnestra, a circular burial chamber approached through a passageway built into the hillside outside the citadel wall.

Ancient Corinth

Corinth was always of pivotal importance from its position on the neck of land separating the Peloponnese peninsula from the rest of the Greek mainland. Growing wealthy from trade, it became a major urban center, with a population approaching 100,000 by 400 BCE. The city played a large part in myth too: it was here, for example, that the hero Jason abandoned his wife Medea (see p.366). Today, the archaeological site lies just

3 miles (5 km) southwest of the modern conurbation. Highlights include the Temple of Apollo and the Peirene Fountain, from which the spring that Pegasus purportedly drank from emerged into a stone-lined open-air pool.

Ancient Olympia

Held every four years from a traditional starting date of 776 BCE, the Olympic Games were the greatest of Panhellenic festivals, attracting competitors from all over the Greek world to Olympia. Rival city-states showered generosity on the site, which was dedicated principally to Zeus. His temple dominated the festival grounds, housing a massive statue, fashioned from gold and ivory by the master sculptor Phidias, that ranked as one of the Seven Wonders of the Ancient World. The stadium

itself—an open field with start and end markers and room for spectators along its sides—is relatively unadorned, but elsewhere, visitors can admire relics of many of the 760 separate buildings whose foundations have been uncovered, including the Pelopion, or tomb of the legendary King Pelops, who gave his name to the Peloponnese, and the Temple of Hera, dating back to around 600 BCE. Covered for centuries by flood deposits, the site was rediscovered in the 18th century, and excavated from 1829 onward. (See main entry pp.88–89.)

Temple of Apollo Epicurius, Bassae

The first Greek site to be placed on the World Heritage List, the Temple of Apollo Epicurius in Bassae occupies an isolated

△ Partial view of the remains of the palaestra (part of the gymnasium at ancient Olympia (c. 3rd century BCE)

site 3,700 ft (1,100 m) up in the mountains of the western Peloponnese. Praised by the Greek geographer Pausanias, the building has been compared to the Parthenon in Athens (see p.374), which was constructed at about the same time, with some authorities suggesting that it may have been built by the same architect. British antiquaries were drawn to the site in the early 19th century, and an inner frieze showing Athenians fighting Amazons and Lapiths battling with centaurs was taken and is now on display in the British Museum in London. The remoteness of the sanctuary helped preserve it from human defacement, but its exposed position has left it vulnerable to the elements, and

▷ **The heroon (1st century BCE) was part of the stadium at ancient Messene.**

since 1987 the structure has been covered by a gigantic white tent for protection.

Ancient Messene

For centuries in ancient times, the Peloponnesian region of Messenia in which Messene lay was subservient to neighboring Sparta, defeated in war and forced to provide many of Sparta's helots: enslaved people who supplied most of the labor for its soldier-citizens (see p.106). It was only after a Theban-led coalition defeated Sparta in 371 BCE that Messene was rebuilt and began to flourish. Today,

impressive remains of structures erected at that time include an Asclepieion (healing sanctuary), a stadium, a heroon, and a theater, as well as surviving elements of the 6-mile (9.5-km) wall, put up as a defensive shield, complete with towers and gates.

Sparta

Sparta's name is familiar to this day, kept alive in the English words "spartan" and "laconic" (derived from the region of Laconia in which the city-state was situated) to describe its puritanical mindset. Owing its uniquely militaristic constitution

to the legendary statesman Lycurgus (see p.75), Sparta emerged as the leading land power in mainland Greece from the mid-7th century BCE onward. Occupying a sheltered position in the south of the Peloponnese, protected on three sides by mountains and on the fourth by the sea, it followed its own course through the Classical era. During the 5th century BCE, the historian Thucydides (see p.328) noted that the city "has no splendid temples or other edifices"—consequently, it has left fewer monuments for posterity than many other less celebrated centers. In the modern day, visitors to the archaeological site are able to view the sparse remains of a theater and of a temple of Artemis; artifacts excavated from the ancient acropolis are housed in the Archaeological Museum.

Islands and Asia Minor

In its heyday, Greek culture spread from Greece's heartland across the waters of the Aegean—dotted then, as now, with hundreds of islands. From early on there was a presence on the sea's eastern shores, bringing citizens of the city-states established there into contact with their Asian neighbors.

Temple of Aphaea, Aegina

The remains of the Temple of Aphaea stand on a hilltop in the island of Aegina, just 18 miles (27 km) from Athens in the Saronic Gulf. Dedicated to the island's patron divinity, the surviving building dates back to c. 500 BCE, but remains of older structures suggest a continuous history of occupation stretching back more than 1,000 years. In 1811, the temple's magnificent pediment sculptures were reportedly purchased for a paltry sum by an English architect visiting the site; he promptly put them up for auction and they were bought by a German prince. They are now on display in the Munich Glyptothek museum.

Delos

Located off Mykonos in the central Cyclades, the tiny island of Delos, which today has only about 20 inhabitants, occupied a central position in ancient Greek history, giving its name to the Delian League that dominated much of the country under Athenian hegemony after the Greco-Persian wars (see pp.158–159). In myth, it was the birthplace of the gods Apollo and Artemis, and it was also sacred to their divine mother Leto, and to Dionysus. On instructions from the Oracle at Delphi, no one was allowed to give birth or be buried on the island to keep it sacrosanct. Its special status in ancient times has now made Delos one of Greece's richest archaeological sites. Highlights include a theater, the Terrace of the Lions, featuring a row of guardian beasts with their mouths agape, and the House of Dionysus, named for a 2nd-century BCE floor mosaic of the god riding on a panther's back. Delos has been registered on UNESCO's World Heritage List since 1990.

Temple of Apollo, Naxos

Famed in myth as the place where Theseus abandoned Ariadne (see p.368), Naxos lies in the central Cyclades 35 miles (50 km) south of Delos. The historian Herodotus (see pp.148–149) described it as the wealthiest of all the Greek islands. A failed Persian attempt to seize it in 499 BCE led to the Ionian Revolt. Today, the main surviving monument of that time is the portal of an unfinished Temple of Apollo, begun by the tyrant Lygdamis around 530 BCE but left incomplete at his death. The remains stand perched on a hilltop promontory, framing a view of Naxos's Old Town.

Skarkos Settlement, Ios

Archaeologists are excited by the discoveries they have made at Skarkos hill on the Aegean island of Ios for the light they throw on the Cycladic culture of the Early Bronze Age (c. 3200–2050 BCE). Excavations in the 1980s and 1990s turned up evidence of a terraced settlement of two-story houses built around inner courtyards, with the upper floors serving as living areas and the ground level for food preparation. Current estimates suggest that the site, dating back as far as 2800 BCE, was home to between 200 and 300 people.

△ Lion statues in the Terrace of the Lions, Delos (pre-600 BCE)

△ Remains of the 4th-century CE Doric temple dedicated to the goddess Athena at the Acropolis of Lindos

Settlement of Akrotiri, Santorini

Akrotiri, on the volcanic island of Santorini (ancient Thera), can in some ways claim to be ancient Greece's Pompeii. Much like the Roman town, it was destroyed by a volcanic eruption—in 1627 BCE in Akrotiri's case. In the wake of the disaster, its streets were covered by a thick layer of ash, which helped preserve them from decay. Since systematic archaeological exploration began in the 1960s, the excavations (protected now under a wood-and-glass roof) have revealed a settlement that boasted paved streets lined with two- and three-story houses and harbored a sophisticated drainage system.

They have also turned up crucial evidence of the influence of Minoan Crete, which lies around 130 miles (200 km) south across the Aegean Sea, in the form of startlingly well-preserved murals that reflect the strong influence of Minoan art, as well as a wealth of pottery vessels, some of which are decorated with paintings of animals and flowers.

Palace of Knossos, Crete

One of the great treasures of antiquity, the impressive remains of the capital of Minoan Crete were first revealed to the world by Cretan businessman and amateur archaeologist Minos Kalokairinos. He initiated a comprehensive excavation program that began in 1877. Work on the site was then taken up from 1900 on by British archaeologist Arthur Evans; research at Knossos continues to the present day. The finds have revealed not just an imposing royal residence but also a hive of industry: sprawling over a total area of almost 6 acres (2.5 hectares), the complex had space for workshops and counting houses as well as storerooms big enough to serve the entire surrounding district. The mazelike nature of the site was to feed through into later myths of the Cretan Labyrinth, where the hero Theseus went to kill the Minotaur (see p.367). Highlights for visitors today include the 3,500-year-old Throne Room and a number of playful frescoes, vividly retouched by Evans's team in an attempt to restore their original bright colors.

Palaikastro Archaeological Site, Crete

Located 1½ miles (2 km) east of the modern town of Palaikastro, Crete, the remains of an entire Minoan city dating to the Late Bronze Age in the mid-2nd millennium BCE have been uncovered by archaeologists working on the site since the early years of the 20th century. The surrounding area had significance in ancient times as one of the locales proposed as the birthplace of Zeus, king of the gods. Evidence of his cult has been found in the form of a 3,500-year-old statue of him, which is now on view in the Archaeological Museum of Sitia, 12 miles (17 km) away, and also in the vestigial remains of a temple in his honor.

Acropolis of Lindos, Rhodes

Dramatically situated on a headland above coastal Lindos on the island of Rhodes, the walled acropolis contains a medley of remains dating not just from ancient Greece, but also from Roman and Byzantine times. Passing a relief of a Rhodian trireme (warship) on the modern stairs leading to the site, visitors reach a Hellenistic staircase from the 2nd century BCE that provides access to the main archaeological area. There, a second, monumental stairway dating back some two centuries earlier leads up to the propylaea, or monumental gateway, entering into the sanctuary. Beyond this lie the remains of a temple dedicated to Athena, whose cult played a major part in the island's life. Alexander the Great is said to have made sacrificial offerings there, seeking the goddess's help in his military campaigns.

Camirus, Rhodes

Dorian invaders founded Camirus, northwestern Rhodes, in the 10th or 9th centuries BCE, on a site that was previously inhabited in Mycenaean times 300 or 400 years earlier. In the *Iliad*, Homer lists the city as capital of one of the three divisions of the island and

also makes mention of its "white escarpments." Today, the closely packed remains of houses line a central street descending down steps to the sea. Many of the foundations date to after 226 BCE, when an earthquake devastated the city. The ruins of the main sanctuary, a temple dedicated to Rhodes' patron goddess Athena, are thought to date from that time, replacing earlier structures stretching back as far as the 9th century BCE.

Asclepieion, Cos

The island of Cos was famed in antiquity as the birthplace of Hippocrates, physician and "father of medicine." One of

its principal monuments is an Asclepieion, or sanctuary of healing, whose remains lie about 2½ miles (4 km) from Cos Town. The ruins descend down three terraces on a hillside site overlooking the island's capital; beyond it is the modern Turkish mainland, just 6 miles (10 km) away. The oldest surviving parts of the structure lie on the second terrace, where the ruins of an altar dating from the 4th century BCE have been located.

Heraion of Samos

Home to Pythagoras, the renowned mathematician (see p.338), as well as to Epicurus, the philosopher (see

p.333), and the legendary fabulist Aesop, the island of Samos was a significant center of culture during ancient times. Today, its most famous monument is a sanctuary that is dedicated to the goddess Hera, wife of Zeus, which is now listed as a UNESCO World Heritage Site. Construction of the Heraion began in the 8th century BCE, and the site was expanded two centuries later to create a temple that the historian Herodotus described as bigger than any other he knew of. Now only foundations remain, but it is still possible to appreciate from their vast extent the significance the complex had in its day; the numerous votive offerings that have been dug up from its grounds reinforce the message.

△ Ancient foundations of the Temple of Hera, Samos (8th century BCE)

Temple of Apollo, Didyma

Just 10 miles (16 km) from Miletus, the sanctuary of Didyma was famed in late antiquity for its Oracle of Apollo, housed in a temple to the god that was one of the largest in ancient Greece. The imposing ruins visible today date from the 2nd century BCE, and lie at the end of a Sacred Way that linked the sacred precinct to Miletus. Alexander the Great visited the site in 334 BCE after taking Miletus from Persian control, and sponsored the rebuilding of the temple, a previous structure having been destroyed 160 years earlier. In the years that followed, Didyma benefited from the generosity of rulers eager to consult the Oracle, and came to host a festival, held every four years, that attracted celebrants from all over Greece. Despite earthquake damage in the 15th century, much still remains for visitors to admire.

Archaeological Site of Miletus

Miletus was one of the wealthiest and most powerful members of the Ionian League (see p.80). During the Archaic period in the 7th and 6th centuries BCE, it presided over the birth of Greek philosophy, in the work of the Milesian School led by Thales (p.338) and Anaximander (see p.330). Destroyed by its Persian overlords in 491 BCE, after the failure of the Ionian Revolt, it was rebuilt on a grid pattern following the Persian defeat on the Greek mainland 12 years later. The site has been excavated by German archaeologists since the late 19th century. In the early 20th century, fragments of Miletus's most stunning monument, the Market Gate, built under Roman rule in the 2nd century CE, were taken to Berlin's Pergamon Museum. Today, the outstanding structure at Miletus is the massive theater, which, in its present form, again dates from the Roman period, replacing an earlier, smaller Hellenistic odeon (theater).

Temple of Athena, Priene

What remains of ancient Priene was built from about 350 BCE on, because an earlier port location on the Aegean's eastern shore was abandoned after the harbor silted up. The new city's founder was Mausolus, the man whose funerary monument, the Mausoleum at Halicarnassus 75 miles (120 km) to the south, was to rank as one of the Seven Wonders of the Ancient World. When Alexander the Great took over the area after 334 BCE, he assumed responsibility for the rebuilding, offering to pay for the planned Temple of Athena on condition it was dedicated to him. Thought to have been designed by the Mausoleum's architect, the temple occupied a prime location, perched on a terrace overlooking the lower town. Five of its Ionic columns still stand, dramatically sited against a mountain backdrop.

Ephesus Ancient City

In its heyday, Ephesus was home to one of the Seven Wonders of the Ancient World: the Temple of Artemis, the goddess known to St. Paul in Roman times as "Diana of the Ephesians." Little survives of the temple now, although many other spectacular remains still exist, including a vast open-air theater that held 25,000 spectators, paved streets, and the celebrated Library of Celsus, whose columned, two-story facade dates from Roman times, having been commissioned around 110 CE. In ancient times, Ephesus was one of the major players in the Ionian League of Greek city-states along the Aegean Sea's east coast (see p.80). It continued to thrive in the Roman and Byzantine eras, reaching a peak of prosperity in the 5th and 6th centuries CE. Subsequently, the harbor silted up, and by the 15th century CE the site was abandoned, to be thoroughly explored by Western archaeologists four centuries later.

△ View of the spectacular ruins of the Temple of Apollo, Didyma (2nd century BCE)

△ Hierapolis's paved main street runs for nearly a mile (1.5 km); this view also shows its monumental entrance.

Hierapolis Archaeological Site

Directly topping the astounding white limestone terraces left by the hot mineral springs of modern Pamukkale, Hierapolis attracted visitors to its thermal spas from its foundation in the 2nd century BCE. The number of people who hoped to benefit from their healing properties is still attested by the vast ancient necropolis, containing some 1,200 tombs, that stretches for 1.2 miles (2 km) outside the city. Much of what remains dates to the Roman era, but the paved main street, running in parallel with the top of the terraces, dates to the Hellenistic period, as do the foundations of the Temple of Apollo, which, like many other structures, was rebuilt in later times after earthquake damage.

Pergamon Archaeological Site

Pergamon's ruins stand some 1,100 ft (335 m) high on a spur dominating the Caicus Plain that stretches west to the Aegean Sea. From this aerie, its rulers governed a kingdom that in Hellenistic times stretched from the Hellespont across much of what is now western Türkiye. German archaeologists unearthed the site in the 19th century, taking its key feature, the Great Altar, to form the centerpiece of Berlin's Pergamon Museum. But spectacular structures are still in place, including the steepest of all Greek theaters—plunging some 118 ft (36 m) through 73 rows of seats down a precipitous hillside—dating back to the 3rd century BCE. The oldest survivor is the 4th-century BCE Temple of Athena, whose foundations are visible at the back of the theater.

Troy

Rediscovered in the 19th century by German businessman and amateur archaeologist Heinrich Schliemann, who damaged much of the site, the remains of Troy have since been assigned by experts to nine separate time periods that stretch from the Neolithic period to the Roman era. Set on a hilltop dominating the plain on what is today the Turkish side of the Bosporus Strait's southern mouth, the site has a strategic position that helps explain its significance in ancient times as the target of the Trojan War. The most visible remains today date mainly from the latter two time periods, stretching from c. 950 BCE on, when Troy was recognizably a Greek town; earlier incarnations had been more noticeably Anatolian, and at one stage it was a Hittite vassal. Surviving structures include an odeon (theater) and the remains of a temple of Athena; earlier relics mostly take the form of wall segments or fortifications.

Magna Graecia and North Africa

The Greek diaspora started early. In the Archaic period, by the beginning of the 8th century BCE, there were already colonies across the Mediterranean in Italy, and subsequently settlements also flourished in North Africa and Pharaonic Egypt. Impressive vestiges of the sites remain today.

Temples of Paestum, Italy

Founded around 600 BCE by Greek settlers in southern Italy and originally named Poseidonia, Paestum fell to local peoples two centuries later and to Rome in 273 BCE. It then suffered economic decline as its harbor silted up, and was abandoned until the 18th century CE, when it attracted antiquarians and artists. Today, it draws visitors to its three exceptionally well-preserved temples, two of which were likely dedicated to Hera and one to Athena. An on-site museum preserves striking friezes and frescoes excavated locally, including a celebrated image of a diver in midair leaping into water (see pp.126–127).

Segesta, Sicily

The magnificent hilltop site of Segesta in northwestern Sicily contains one of the most picturesquely situated of all surviving Doric temples, as well as the remains of an impressive tiered theater that commands spectacular views over the adjoining valley. Unusually, the structures are thought not to have been built by Greeks but by local Elymians, a native Sicilian population who were in close contact with but nonetheless separate from the Greek city-states on the coasts of the island. The temple is thought to date from about 420 BCE, at a time when Segesta shared a close military alliance with Athens.

Selinunte, Sicily

Throughout ancient times, the neighboring communities of Selinunte and Segesta (see above left) were bitter rivals. Unlike Segesta, Selinunte, on Sicily's southwest coast, was a Greek foundation, established in the 7th century BCE. It occupied an extensive area and at its peak may have housed some 30,000 citizens as well as a substantial enslaved population. It survived until the 3rd century BCE, when it was destroyed by Carthaginian forces from North Africa in the course of Rome's First Punic War

△ Painting depicting the Temple of Segesta in Sicily (Thomas Cole, c.1842)

and was never rebuilt. On a hilltop site overlooking the sea, the present archaeological park stretches more than a square mile (270 hectares) in extent. The surviving structures include an acropolis and the ruins of at least seven temples.

Valley of the Temples, Agrigento, Sicily

Known to the ancient Greeks as Akragas, the city of Agrigento was founded around 580 BCE and flourished as one of the main Sicilian city-states of the Classical era. It remained important in Roman times, and fell into decline only from the 7th century CE on. The outstanding Greek remains are located in the misnamed Valley of the Temples, which is actually situated on a ridge more than a mile (a couple of kilometers) outside the modern city. Their size and extent recall the philosopher Plato's remark that Akragas's inhabitants "build like they intend to live forever"; they include the remains of five separate temples, one of which, the Temple of Concord, is described on UNESCO's World Heritage list as "the most impressive surviving Doric temple in the Greek world after the Parthenon in Athens." The site also includes remnants of the residential area, which was laid out on a grid pattern, with some houses retaining well-preserved mosaic pavements.

Ancient Syracuse, Sicily

Founded in the 8th century BCE on the southeast corner of Sicily, Syracuse became one of the great cities of the Classical world, rivaling Athens in size in the 5th century BCE. Among the remains now preserved in the ancient city, the Temple of Apollo dates back to the 7th century BCE, making it one of the most ancient of all Doric sanctuaries; and the Temple of Athena is also particularly well preserved. There is also an ancient theater that can claim to have been in continuous use from the 5th century BCE to the present day; it is still used for concerts and performances of classical drama. Near the theater, visitors can enter the spectacular Orecchio di Dionisio (Ear of Dionysius), a cave, 75 ft (23 m) high, carved out of old limestone quarries and used by Dionysius I, Greek ruler of the island, as a prison in the 4th century BCE.

Sanctuaries of Zeus & Demeter, Cyrene, Libya

Located approximately 10 miles (16 km) inland from Libya's Mediterranean coast, Cyrene was established by settlers from the Greek island of Thera (modern-day Santorini) around 631 BCE. By the Greek Classical period, it had become the chief settlement of the North African region of Cyrenaica and one of the artistic and intellectual centers of the Greek world. Today, its extensive remains stretch across a wide hillside site that is cluttered with the remnants of stoas (covered walkways) and private residences as well as places of worship. Of these structures, the Temple of Zeus is one of the largest Doric monuments ever built (see p.76), rivaling its namesake at Olympia and the Parthenon at Athens. Constructed outside the ancient city walls about a mile (1.5 km)

△ View of the limestone cave near Syracuse, known as the Ear of Dionysius

away, the sanctuary of Demeter originally sprawled over a large area; an active archaeological site, it includes the remains of another temple and a theater.

Serapeum of Alexandria, Egypt

Now a vast archaeological site in the middle of the bustling Egyptian port city of Alexandria, the Serapeum was built on the orders of the city's Hellenistic ruler Ptolemy III during the late 3rd century BCE. The temple was dedicated to the god Serapis (see p.239), who was promoted at the time as a figure whose cult could draw in both the ruling Greek and native Egyptian populations. The temple and surrounding buildings were destroyed in 391 CE as vestiges of paganism, leaving the modern visitor little to see, apart from a towering Victory Pillar that was erected by the Roman emperor Diocletian around 300 CE. Subterranean galleries have been excavated beneath the temple site.

Glossary

A

Achaemenid Empire The Persian empire founded by Cyrus II ("the Great") in 550 BCE, which extended from Anatolia and Egypt across Western Asia to northern India and Central Asia until it was finally conquered by Alexander the Great around 330 BCE.

acropolis Meaning "high city," the acropolis was the citadel of an ancient Greek city; it was usually sited on rocky, elevated ground, often a steep-sided hill, for the purposes of defense.

agora The marketplace and central gathering space in Greek cities, where the people would meet to fulfill their role in the political functions of the *polis*.

amphora A two-handled vessel with a neck considerably narrower than its body. Amphorae were typically used for storage of items such as wine and oil, but painted versions were also used as prizes in competitions.

Anatolia Also known as Asia Minor, Anatolia (meaning "place of the rising sun") was the name the Greeks gave to the southwestern part of Asia that comprises most of modern-day Türkiye.

andron A room in a Greek house reserved for use by the men of the household, where they could entertain guests at symposia.

Archaic period The age from around 750 BCE to 500 BCE characterized by changes in Greek society, architecture, art, language, and politics that were driven by population growth, trade, colonization, and the development of philosophy.

archon The chief magistrate in many Greek city-states.

ascetic Used to describe a person, practice, or philosophy characterized by strict discipline and abstention from all forms of indulgence.

Asia Minor
See entry for Anatolia.

B

basileus A Greek title understood to mean "king" or "monarch." It was used by the rulers of the Hellenistic kingdoms and the Byzantine Empire.

black-figure painting A technique in which figural and ornamental motifs were applied to pottery with a slip (liquefied clay) that turned black during firing; the background was left the color of the clay. Vase painters could add detail by incising the slip or by adding white and purple enhancements made with clay and pigment.

C

Cabiri A group of mysterious chthonic deities associated with certain mystery sanctuaries, including those at Thebes, Lemnos, and probably Samothrace. Their number and function varied according to local customs. At Thebes, for example, there were two: a father and son named Cabirus and Pais.

caryatid A carved female figure used instead of a column to support an architectural structure in ancient Greece. Originating in Western Asia, caryatids appeared in Greece around 550 BCE. However, the Roman writer Vitruvius claimed that caryatids represented the women of Caryae, doomed to hard labor after the town sided with the Persians in 480 BCE.

chlamys A short cloak worn only by men. It was draped around the upper shoulders and pinned at the right side, leaving the right arm free.

chthonic Inhabiting or relating to the Underworld. Among the chthonic figures in Greek mythology were Persephone, Hades, Demeter, the Furies, and Hecate.

cist grave A prehistoric grave that was either lined with stones and covered with slabs or enclosed on four sides by upright stone slabs and closed with a lid. Cists could house the remains of one person or several.

citizen The members of Greek society accorded full legal status and the right to vote, hold public office, and own property. Each *polis* determined the particular rights given to its citizens. Only free men could be citizens.

Classical period The age from around 500 BCE to the death of Alexander the Great in 323 BCE. It was marked by conflict, notably the Greco-Persian Wars, the Peloponnesian War (between Sparta and Athens), and Alexander's conquest of the Achaemenid Empire.

consul The highest elected office in the Roman Republic. Two consuls served at the same time, for a period of one year.

Corinthian One of the orders of architecture (along with Ionic and Doric). Corinthian columns were characterized by an ornate capital (the top part) carved with acanthus leaves.

cosmogony A theory or account of the origin and development of the cosmos or universe.

culture hero A legendary figure important to a particular group for their contribution to the group's culture or existence. A culture hero might be credited with the discovery of agriculture or fire, or with establishing traditions, religion, and laws, or they might be the group's legendary founder.

Cyclopes Literally meaning "round eyes," the Cyclopes were strong, one-eyed creatures in Greek mythology. Homer presented them as cannibals living in a distant land, while Hesiod asserted that they were sons of Uranus (sky) and Gaia (Earth).

D

"Dark Age" The modern-day term for the period from 1200 BCE to 800 BCE, a time marked by the collapse of Mycenaean civilization and a decline in the wealth, art, writing, and culture that defined the Bronze Age civilizations.

deme A district, village, or town in ancient Greece that was the basic political unit of a city-state.

demigod The offspring of a god and a mortal in Greek mythology. Among the best known are Achilles, Heracles, and Theseus.

dithyramb A wild choral song in honor of Dionysus, the god of wine.

Doric One of the three architectural orders, characterized by squat, tapered columns without a separate base and with a simple circular capital.

E

Eleusinian Mysteries Initiations into the cult of Demeter and Persephone held every year at the Panhellenic Sanctuary of Eleusis, west of Athens.

ephor Title given to five magistrates in Sparta who governed along with the *gerousia* (council of elders) and assembly and were responsible for the execution of their decrees.

epic poem In Greek literature, a lengthy narrative poem in hexameter verse and often about the deeds of gods and heroes. Examples include the works attributed to Homer, including the *Iliad* and *Odyssey*, and to Hesiod, including *Theogony* and *Works and Days*.

F

fresco The art of painting on plastered walls, fresco was one of ancient Greece's key art forms, often used to decorate tombs and palaces. Notable examples of frescoes remain from Knossos on Crete and Akrotiri on the island of Thera.

Furies Three chthonic goddesses of vengeance in ancient Greek religion and mythology; they are also known as the Erinyes and the Eumenides.

G

Geometric period A period of artistic development from c. 900 BCE to 700 BCE, named for the prevalence of geometric patterns on pottery. Toward the end of the period, scenes with animals and human figures began to be depicted, especially in funerary contexts.

Giants A mythical race of creatures born from Gaia after Uranus's blood dropped on the ground. The Giants were said to be aggressive and strong, but not necessarily particularly tall.

Gorgon One of three monstrous winged sisters, Medusa, Stheno, and Euryale, with snakes for hair.

griffin A mythological creature with the body of a lion and the head of a bird. As a decorative motif, the griffin had traveled from West Asia to Greece by the 14th century BCE.

H

harmost A governor appointed by Sparta to control the towns and people it had subjugated.

hegemon A leading or major power with influence or authority over others.

Hellenistic period The age between the death of Alexander the Great in 323 BCE and 31 BCE when Rome conquered Egypt.

Hellenization The process by which the non-Greek people of Alexander's empire, adopted, to a greater or lesser degree, Greek language, customs, and culture.

Hellespont The ancient name for the narrow passage between the Aegean Sea and the Sea of Marmara; today it is known as the Dardanelles.

helot A class of unfree men subjugated by Sparta who worked the state-owned land and had serf status.

heroes Figures from Greece's distant past who were revered and sometimes worshipped as representatives of *arete* (broadly "virtue," "excellence," and "courage," to which the ancient Greeks aspired), as founders of the community, and as doers of spectacular feats of strength and bravery.

hetaira A professional, well-educated female sex worker. *Hetairai* often attended symposia, where they would provide conversation and entertainment, including music.

Hittites An Indo-European people that created a powerful empire in Anatolia before 1700 BCE.

hoplite A foot soldier armed with spear and shield who fought in close formation as part of a phalanx. Hoplites were citizens with a duty to defend their *polis*.

I

intaglio The process of cutting a design into a surface; it is often seen on engraved gems, seals, and the dies (stamps) made to strike coins.

Ionic One of the three orders of architecture. Ionic columns are distinguished by the scrolls, or volutes, on the capital.

K

kore and *kouros* A type of freestanding sculpture from the Archaic period: *korai* (plural of *kore*) were figures of young women, always shown clothed; *kouroi* (plural of *kouros*) were figures of young men, always shown naked.

kottabos A popular game in symposia in which players would flick the dregs of their wine at a target.

krater A large, two-handled vessel used for mixing wine and water together.

kylix A wide-bowled drinking cup with horizontal handles and often decorated both inside and out.

L

lekythos An oil flask with a tapered base, a long cylindrical body, and a narrow neck for use at the baths or gymnasium, and often found in graves as a funerary offering.

M

Macedonia (or Macedon) An ancient kingdom in the north of the Greek peninsula founded in the 7th century BCE. For centuries, the Greeks and the people of Macedonia regarded each other with suspicion and contempt. In the 4th century BCE, Philip II and Alexander the Great brought the Greek world under Macedonian control.

maenads Female followers of Dionysus, who performed ecstatic dances. Under Dionysus's influence, maenads were believed to be imbued with great strength and capable of tearing animals or people apart.

metic A foreigner living in an ancient Greek city; metics were given more privileges than transient foreigners.

metopes The rectangular slabs that alternate with triglyphs (tablets with vertical grooves) in the frieze adorning Doric buildings in ancient Greece.

N

necropolis A significant burial place, often sited outside the city it serves; it literally means "city of the dead."

O

Olympians The most powerful Greek gods and goddesses, so called because their home was Mount Olympus (in northeastern Greece).

omphalos A rounded sacred stone in the Temple of Apollo at Delphi that was believed to mark the center, or "navel," of Earth, from which all life sprang.

oracle A person through whom a god is believed to speak, as well as the messages that they give and the shrine at which they operate.

orchestra A circular area at the bottom of the theatron (the seating stands) where the chorus performed.

ostracon (pl. ostraca) A potsherd used as a surface for drawing or writing. Many that survive from ancient Greece had been used as voting tokens, particularly in the context of ostracism, when Athens' citizens voted to exile a fellow citizen for ten years.

P

Panhellenic Of or relating to all of Greece. For example, the Panhellenic Games drew competitors from across the Greek city-states.

pediment The triangular gable at the front of a classical building (such as a Greek temple) that supported the roof. The pediment was often decorated with sculpture.

Peloponnese The large peninsula at the southwest tip of the Greek mainland. The Peloponnese was the location of Sparta, Corinth, Argos, and Mycenae.

phalanx A rectangular military formation in which infantry were formed up in deep ranks (rows) and files (columns), their shields interlocking to create an impenetrable wall.

phratry A group in Greek city-states, notably Athens and those in Ionia, with hereditary membership. Phratries had a role in deciding matters relating to legitimacy, including access to citizenship and inheritances.

phyle (pl. *phylai*) One of several clans or kinship groups of many Greek city-states among which the citizens were divided.

polis (pl. *poleis*) The Greek city-state which characterized Greek urban life from the end of the 8th century BCE and was marked by political autonomy, social homogeneity, a sense of community, and respect for the law.

proconsul A former consul who then became the governor of a province or a military commander.

R

red-figure painting A technique for decorating pottery in which the decorative motifs were left the color of the clay, while the background was filled with a slip that turned black on firing. Glaze lines or washes of glaze helped to add definition to the motifs.

relief A sculptural technique in which a block of material is carved so the figures stand out from the background.

repoussé A method for decorating metals in which designs are hammered through from the underside so they appear in relief on the top side.

S

sanctuary A place reserved for devotion to the gods, and a place of refuge. Sanctuaries could be natural features such as caves, simple structures, or complex areas including monumental temples and other buildings.

satrap A provincial governor in the Achaemenid Empire. After conquering the empire, Alexander the Great continued to use the satrapy system.

satyr A drunken, lecherous woodland god in Greek mythology. Satyrs were often depicted in art as men with horses' tails and ears.

serfdom A system in which agricultural laborers were tied to the land, but were not the property of the landowner.

shaft grave A grave consisting of a rectangular shaft leading to a stone-walled burial chamber.

stele A block of stone or wood bearing an inscription and/or carved images and created for political, funerary, or religious purposes.

strategos The title of the commander of a Greek army. From the 5th century BCE in Athens, *strategoi* had both political and military roles.

suzerainty The relationship between a dominant state (suzerain) and the states (vassal or subject states) over which it has dominion. Typically, a suzerain controls the foreign affairs of its subject states while leaving them to govern themselves.

symposium A social gathering in which male citizens would meet to eat, drink, converse, and enjoy music and entertainment.

synoikismos Literally a "gathering together," *synoikismos* was the process by which villages in ancient Greece joined together to form *poleis*.

T

Titan A child of Uranus and Gaia in Greek mythology. The Titans were consigned to an abyss called Tartarus after the Titanomachy, a ten-year conflict with the god Zeus and his allies.

tondo A term used to refer to the circular paintings found inside a drinking cup.

tribute A payment, often in the form of goods, materials, or services, made by the ruler of one state to another as a sign of submission to their authority.

trierarch The term given to the commander of a trireme and to an Athenian citizen who had to outfit a trireme for public service.

trireme A highly maneuverable, oar-powered warship employed by the navies of the Greek city-states and Persia. With as many as 170 oarsmen in three tiers, the trireme was known for its speed and played a vital role in both the Persian and the Peloponnesian wars.

tyrant A ruler who seized power unconstitutionally or inherited such power. Tyranny did not necessarily involve cruel or harsh government.

U

Underworld The sunless realm of the dead ruled over by Hades, brother of the Olympian gods Zeus and Poseidon, and his wife, Persephone.

V

volute A spiral scroll-like ornament found on Ionic columns and ancient Greek pottery.

W

West Asia The westernmost region of Asia that comprises the modern-day territories of Afghanistan, Armenia, Azerbaijan, Bahrain, Cyprus, Gaza Strip, Georgia, Iran, Iraq, Israel, Jordan, Kuwait, Lebanon, Oman, Qatar, Saudi Arabia, Syria, Türkiye, United Arab Emirates, West Bank, and Yemen.

Index

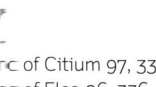

Acknowledgments

DK would like to thank the following for their help with this book:
Alice Hughes for editorial assistance; Lori Hand for editorial support; Steve Crozier, Butterfly Creative Services Ltd, for image retouching; Kirsty Seymour-Ure for proofreading; Vanessa Bird for indexing; and Mohd Rizwan and Nand Kishor for creative technical support. Senior Jacket Designer: Suhita Dharamjit.

The publisher would like to thank the following for their kind permission to reproduce their photographs:

(Key: a-above; b-below/bottom; c-centre; f-far; l-left; r-right; t-top)

British Museum. All rights reserved. 108-109 © The Trustees of the British Museum. All rights reserved. 109 The Metropolitan Museum of Art. 110 Alamy Stock Photo: Peter Eastland (r); Peter Horree (c). The Metropolitan Museum of Art. 111 Getty Images: DEA / G. Dagli Orti / De Agostini (l, c); DEA / G. Nimatallah (r). 112 Alamy Stock Photo: Album. Photo Scala, Florence: bpk, Bildagentur fuer Kunst, Kultur und Geschichte, Berlin (br). 113 © The Trustees of the British Museum. All rights reserved. Photo Scala, Florence: RMN-Grand Palais (br). 114 Alamy Stock Photo: SJArt. 115 Bridgeman Images: Giancarlo Costa (cr). Science Photo Library: Science Source (bl). 116 Alamy Stock Photo: Artefact (bl). © The Trustees of the British Museum. All rights reserved. 117 Getty Images: Hulton Fine Art Collection / Mondadori Portfolio (r). Photo Scala, Florence: Courtesy of the Ministero Beni e Att. Culturali e del Turismo (bl). 118 Alamy Stock Photo: Gina Rodgers (tl, tr). Bridgeman Images: British Library Archive (bl). 119 Getty Images: Heritage Images / Fine Art Images. 120 Science Photo Library: David Parker (tc). 122 © The Trustees of the British Museum. All rights reserved. Getty Images: DEA / G. Nimatallah (tr). The Metropolitan Museum of Art. 123 © The Trustees of the British Museum. All rights reserved. The Metropolitan Museum of Art. The Walters Art Museum, Baltimore: (tr). 124 Alamy Stock Photo: funkyfood London - Paul Williams (t). 125 Getty Images: DEA / G. Dagli Orti / De Agostini (br). The Metropolitan Museum of Art. 126-127 Alamy Stock Photo: Simone Crespiatico (t). 127 Alamy Stock Photo: Erin Babnik (br). 128 © The Trustees of the British Museum. All rights reserved. Getty Images: DEA / G. Dagli Orti / De Agostini (cr). 129 © The Trustees of the British Museum. All rights reserved. Dreamstime.com: Michele Ponzio (t). 130-131 The Metropolitan Museum of Art. 131 Bridgeman Images. © The Trustees of the British Museum. All rights reserved. 132 Wikimedia Commons: Oren Rozen / CC BY-SA 3.0 (tl). 132-133 Alamy Stock Photo: Album (b). 133 © The Trustees of the British Museum. All rights reserved. 134 Alamy Stock Photo: Peter Eastland (tr); Greg Balfour Evans (bc). The Metropolitan Museum of Art: (tl). 135 Bridgeman Images. 136 Archive, Art, Culture and Historical Heritage Head Office Department, Intesa Sanpaolo: (tl). © The Trustees of the British Museum. All rights reserved. The Metropolitan Museum of Art. 137 © The Trustees of the British Museum. All rights reserved. 138-139 akg-images: Manuel Cohen. 140 Bridgeman Images. 141 Alamy Stock Photo: eFesenko (tr); Turkey (tl); Oleg Znamenskiy (tc). 142 Bridgeman Images: National Museums Scotland (tl). Getty Images: Corbis News / Stephanie Rabemiafara / Art in All of Us (bc); DEA / J. E. Bulloz (tr). 143 Getty Images: DEA / G. Dagli Orti / De Agostini. 144 Alamy Stock Photo: DeAgostini Picture Library (bl); Gina Rodgers (ca). 145 Alamy Stock Photo: Christian Delbert. 146 Alamy Stock Photo: Peter Horree (l). Princeton Papyri Collections (c). Photo Scala, Florence: bpk, Bildagentur fuer Kunst, Kultur und Geschichte, Berlin (br). 147 Alamy Stock Photo: PjrStatues (c). Bridgeman Images: Luisa Ricciarini (br). 148 Alamy Stock Photo: Peter Horree. 149 akg-images: (br); Fototeca Gilardi (tr). 150 Getty Images: Heritage Images / Fine Art Images. 151 akg-images: Manuel Cohen (tr). Alamy Stock Photo: Zev Radovan (bl). © J. Paul Getty Trust / Open Content Program. 152 Bridgeman Images: Giancarlo Costa (b). 153 Alamy Stock Photo: Tibor Bognar (tl); Science History Images (bc). Getty Images: DEA / G. Dagli Orti / De Agostini (cr). 154 Alamy Stock Photo: Todd Strand (tl). Getty Images: Heritage Images / Vivienne Sharp (tr). Science Photo Library: David Parker (bl). 155 © The Trustees of the British Museum. All rights reserved. 156 Photo Scala, Florence: bpk, Bildagentur fuer Kunst, Kultur und Geschichte, Berlin. 157 © The Trustees of the British Museum. All rights reserved. Harold B. Lee Library, Brigham Young University: (tr). 158 Getty Images / iStock: zoroasto. 159 AWL Images: Hemis (bl). Wikimedia Commons: / CC BY-SA 3.0 (tl). 162 Bridgeman Images: © 2024 Museum of Fine Arts, Boston. All rights reserved. / Francis Bartlett Donation of 1912 (br). Getty Images: DEA / G. Dagli Orti / De Agostini (tl). The Metropolitan Museum of Art. 163 Getty Images: DEA / G. Dagli Orti / De Agostini. 164 © The Trustees of the British Museum. All rights reserved. © J. Paul Getty Trust / Open Content Program. 165 © J. Paul Getty Trust / Open Content Program. Minneapolis Institute of Art: (tr). 166 Getty Images: DEA / G. Nimatallah (br). 167 Photo Scala, Florence: Courtesy of the Ministero Beni e Att. Culturali e del Turismo (l); Courtesy of the Ministero Beni e Att. Culturali e del Turismo (r). 168 © The Trustees of the British Museum. All rights reserved. 169 Photo Scala, Florence: RMN-Grand Palais (br). Wikimedia Commons: Wally Gobetz / CC BY 2.0 (tr). 170-171 Getty Images / iStock: extravagantni. 172 Getty Images / iStock: Starcevic (b). 173 Getty Images / iStock: lucky-photographer (t). Wikimedia Commons: / CC BY-SA 3.0 (br). 174 Getty Images: DEA / G.

Nimatallah (cl). 176 Alamy Stock Photo: E. Westmacott (ftl, tl, tr, ftr); World History Archive (bl). 178 Alamy Stock Photo: North Wind Picture Archives (bl). Princeton University Art Museum: (ca). 179 Alamy Stock Photo: Album (br); Heritage Image Partnership Ltd (l). 180 Alamy Stock Photo: Album (r). Bridgeman Images. Getty Images: DEA / G. Dagli Orti / De Agostini (l). 181 Alamy Stock Photo: colaimages (l). Getty Images: De Agostini Editorial (c); DEA / Archivio J. Lange (r). Science Photo Library: David Parker (tr). 182 © The Trustees of the British Museum. All rights reserved. 183 Alamy Stock Photo: Lanmas (tl). Los Angeles County Museum of Art: (b). 184 BiblePlaces. com / Todd Bolen. Science Photo Library: David Parker (b). 185 Alamy Stock Photo: Shim Harno (t). Getty Images: De Agostini Editorial (br). 186 The Metropolitan Museum of Art. 187 Getty Images / iStock: photooiasson (cr). 188 Alamy Stock Photo: Prisma Archivo. 189 Alamy Stock Photo: De Luan (tr). 190-191 © The Trustees of the British Museum. All rights reserved. 192 © The Trustees of the British Museum. All rights reserved. 193 Alamy Stock Photo: Suzuki Kaku (tc); Martel art (tl); Wirestock, Inc. (tr). 194 Alamy Stock Photo: Interfoto (ca). 195 Photo Scala, Florence: Marie Mauzy. 196 Photo Scala, Florence: RMN-Grand Palais / Hervè Lewandowski / RMN-GP (ca). Tap Service Archaeological Receipts Fund, Hellenic Republic Ministry Of Culture: Acropolis Museum / Photo: Yiannis Koulelis, 2018 (bl). 197 Bridgeman Images: National Museums Scotland (l). Collection of the Nasher Museum of Art at Duke University, Durham, NC, USA: Gift of Barbara Newborg, M.D., from the collection of Walter (br). 198 © The Trustees of the British Museum. All rights reserved. 199 Wikimedia Commons: Jastrow (tr, br). 200 Bridgeman Images: Bradford Museums & Galleries. 201 Alamy Stock Photo: MET / BOT (tr). Bridgeman Images. 202 Alamy Stock Photo: World History Archive (r). Bridgeman Images: © 2024 Museum of Fine Arts, Boston / Henry Lillie Pierce Fund (c); Jonathan Cooper, Park Walk Gallery, London, UK (l). 203 Alamy Stock Photo: Adam Eastland (r). Bridgeman Images: Ashmolean Museum (tr). © The Trustees of the British Museum. All rights reserved. Museum of Fine Arts Budapest: Photo: László Mátyus (b). 204 Alamy Stock Photo: Hercules Milas (cr). The Cleveland Museum of Art. 205 Photo Scala, Florence: RMN-Grand Palais / BenoÔt Touchard / RMN-GP. 206 Tap Service Archaeological Receipts Fund, Hellenic Republic Ministry Of Culture: Acropolis Museum / Photo: Vangelis Tsiamis, 2011 (ca). 206-207 Wikimedia Commons: Egisto Sani / CC BY 2.0. 207 Wikimedia Commons: Bibi Saint-Pol (br). 208 © The Trustees of the British Museum. All rights reserved. 209 © The Trustees of the British Museum. All rights reserved. 210 Bibliothèque nationale de France, Paris: (br). © The Trustees of the British Museum. All rights reserved. © J. Paul Getty Trust / Open Content Program. 211 National Archaeological Museum of Naples: By permission of the Italian Ministry of Heritage and Culture and. 212 Bridgeman Images: Derek Bayes (bl). Photo Scala, Florence: Museum of Fine Arts, Boston. All rights reserved (ca). 213 Board of Trustees of the Science Museum: (bl). Getty Images: DEA / G. Dagli Orti / De Agostini (t). 214 Bridgeman Images: Ashmolean Museum, University of Oxford (cra); Ashmolean Museum, University of Oxford (fcla, ca). © The Trustees of the British Museum. All rights reserved. Getty Images: Heritage Images / Ashmolean Museum (fcra); Universal Images Group / Hoberman Collection (cc). The Metropolitan Museum of Art. Yale University Art Gallery: (bl). 215 Alamy Stock Photo: Penta Springs Limited (fbl). Bridgeman Images: Ashmolean Museum, University of Oxford (cra). © The Trustees of the British Museum. All rights reserved. Dumbarton Oaks Research Library And Collections, Washington, D.c.: (tr). Getty Images: DEA / G. Cigolini (bl); Sepia Times / Universal Images Group (fcrb); Heritage Images / Ashmolean Museum (fbr); Hulton Archive / Heritage Images (br). © J. Paul Getty Trust / Open Content Program. Yale University Art Gallery. 216 Photo Scala, Florence: RMN-Grand Palais / image BnF / RMN-GP. 217 KHM-Museumsverband: (c). Photo Scala, Florence: RMN-Grand Palais / Mathieu Rabeau / RMN-GP (br). 218 Getty Images: DEA / G. Dagli Orti / De Agostini (br). 219 Tap Service Archaeological Receipts Fund, Hellenic Republic Ministry Of Culture: Archaeological Museum of Thessaloniki: Getty Images / De Agostini Editorial (l); Dreamstime / Konstantinos Moraitis (br). 220 Bridgeman Images: © 2024 Museum of Fine Arts, Boston. All rights reserved. (cr). Getty Images: DEA / G. Dagli Orti / De Agostini (cl). Photo Scala, Florence: RMN-Grand Palais / Stèphane Marèchalle / RMN-GP (bc). 221 The Metropolitan Museum of Art. 222 Alamy Stock Photo: Hercules Milas (bl). Bridgeman Images: Tarker (ca). 223 Alamy Stock Photo: Ian Dagnall C (r). Bridgeman Images. 224 Getty Images: De Agostini Editorial (ca). 224-225 Getty Images: DEA / G. Dagli Orti / De Agostini. 226 © The Trustees of the British Museum. All rights reserved. Getty Images: DEA /

G. Dagli Orti / De Agostini (bl). **227 Alamy Stock Photo:** Design Pics Inc / Reynold Mainse / Destinations (b). **Bridgeman Images:** Ashmolean Museum (tr). **228 © The Trustees of the British Museum. All rights reserved. Getty Images:** Hulton Archive / Heritage Images (t). **229 AWL Images:** Nigel Pavitt (b). **Bridgeman Images:** British Library Archive (tr). **230-231 Getty Images:** De Agostini Editorial. **232 Alamy Stock Photo:** Alto Vintage Images (cl); World History Archive (bc). **233 Bridgeman Images:** Bibliotheque Mazarine / Archives Charmet. **234-235 Bridgeman Images:** Luisa Ricciarini. **236 © J. Paul Getty Trust / Open Content Program. 237 Alamy Stock Photo:** Nick Brundle (tl); Francesco Dazzi (tc). **Bridgeman Images:** G. Dagli Orti / NPL - DeA Picture Library (tr). **238 © The Trustees of the British Museum. All rights reserved. The Metropolitan Museum of Art. 239 Getty Images:** De Agostini Editorial (br). **© J. Paul Getty Trust / Open Content Program. © KHM-Museumsverband:** (tc). **240 © The Trustees of the British Museum. All rights reserved. 241 Getty Images:** AFP / Amir Makar (tr). **Photo Scala, Florence:** RMN-Grand Palais / image BnF / RMN-GP (br). **242-243 Getty Images / iStock:** Konstantin Aksenov (b). **243 Alamy Stock Photo:** Jon Bower (t). **Bridgeman Images:** Ancient Art and Architecture Collection Ltd. (br). **244 Alamy Stock Photo:** Zev Radovan (tl). **Stéphane Compoint:** (bc). **Getty Images:** Paris Match Archive / Manuel Litran (cr). **246 Getty Images:** Heritage Images / Fine Art Images (bl). **247 © The Trustees of the British Museum. All rights reserved. Getty Images:** DEA / G. Dagli Orti / De Agostini (bc). **248 Alamy Stock Photo:** Kumar Sriskandan (bl). **© The Trustees of the British Museum. All rights reserved. Photo Scala, Florence:** RMN-Grand Palais / Hervè Lewandowski / RMN-GP (cr). **249 Alamy Stock Photo:** Dmitriy Moroz. **250 Bridgeman Images. The Walters Art Museum, Baltimore. 251 akg-images:** Erich Lessing. **252 Alamy Stock Photo:** Pictorial Press Ltd (ca). **Getty Images:** Hulton Archive / Heritage Images (br). **Princeton University Library:** (bl). **253 Bridgeman Images:** Minneapolis Institute of Arts, MN, USA. **254 Alamy Stock Photo:** Stefano Ravera. **255 © The Trustees of the British Museum. All rights reserved. Photo Scala, Florence:** RMN-Grand Palais / Stéphane Maréchalle (cra). **256 Getty Images:** Sepia Times / Universal Images Group (bl). **Yale University Art Gallery. 257 Alamy Stock Photo:** Lanmas (l). **258 Dreamstime.com:** Fotogigi85 (r). **Photo Scala, Florence:** bpk, Bildagentur fuer Kunst, Kultur und Geschichte, Berlin (c); bpk, Bildagentur fuer Kunst, Kultur und Geschichte, Berlin (l). **259 Bridgeman Images:** British Library Archive (r); Christie's Images (l). **Getty Images:** De Agostini Editorial (c). **© J. Paul Getty Trust / Open Content Program. 260 akg-images:** Erich Lessing (bl). **Alamy Stock Photo:** The History Collection (t). **261 Getty Images / iStock:** Sinan Dogan (tr). **Carole Raddato:** (bl). **262-263 Alamy Stock Photo:** Adam Eastland. **264 Getty Images:** Gamma-Rapho / Eric Vandeville. **265 Alamy Stock Photo:** Peter Eastland (br). **National Museum of History Bulgaria:** (ca). **Science Photo Library:** David Parker (tr). **266 Alamy Stock Photo:** Lanmas (br). **267 Alamy Stock Photo:** Vito Arcomano (l); Hercules Milas (tr). **268 Bridgeman Images:** Photo Josse (br); Veneranda Biblioteca Ambrosiana / Mondadori Portfolio (tl); Veneranda Biblioteca Ambrosiana / Mondadori Portfolio (tc); Veneranda Biblioteca Ambrosiana / Mondadori Portfolio (tr). **269 Bridgeman Images:** Veneranda Biblioteca Ambrosiana / Mondadori Portfolio (tl); Veneranda Biblioteca Ambrosiana / Mondadori Portfolio (tc). **Getty Images:** DEA / Pinaider (br). **270 Getty Images:** Heritage Images / Fine Art Images. **271 Bridgeman Images:** Christie's Images (tr). **Getty Images:** Paris Matvch Archive / Hubert Fanthomme (ca). **272 Alamy Stock Photo:** epa european pressphoto agency b.v. (bl); robertharding / Karol Kozlowski (cra). **273 Getty Images:** DEA / ICAS94 / De Agostini Editorial (tr). **NOESIS Technological Museum of Thessaloniki. 274 Getty Images:** DEA / G. Dagli Orti / De Agostini (br). **The Metropolitan Museum of Art. National Museum Of Denmark Besøg Nationalmuseets hjemmeside:** (ca). **275 Getty Images:** Heritage Images / Fine Art Images. **276 Alamy Stock Photo:** Heritage Image Partnership Ltd (bl). **277 © The Trustees of the British Museum. All rights reserved. Getty Images:** DEA / G. Dagli Orti / De Agostini (br). **Photo Scala, Florence:** The Museum of Fine Arts Budapest (tl). **278 Bridgeman Images:** © 2024 Museum of Fine Arts, Boston. All rights reserved. / Francis Bartlett Donation of 1912 (cla); Museum of Fine Arts, Boston (br). **© The Trustees of the British Museum. All rights reserved. The Metropolitan Museum of Art. Photo Scala, Florence:** White Images (bl). **279 © The Trustees of the British Museum. All rights reserved. © J. Paul Getty Trust / Open Content Program. The Metropolitan Museum of Art. 280 Bridgeman Images:** Iberfoto (bl). **281 Alamy Stock Photo:** Artepics (t). **Getty Images:** Universal History Archive / PHAS (bc). **282 Photo Scala, Florence:** RMN-Grand Palais / Hervé Lewandowski. **283 © J. Paul Getty Trust / Open Content Program. Yale**

University Art Gallery. 284-285 Bridgeman Images: Veneranda Biblioteca Ambrosiana / Mondadori Portfolio. **286 The Metropolitan Museum of Art. 287 Alamy Stock Photo:** Illustration Art (tl); Stefano Politi Markovina (tc); imageBROKER.com GmbH & Co. KG (tr). **288 Bridgeman Images:** Ashmolean Museum, University of Oxford (cla). **Photo Scala, Florence:** Courtesy of the Ministero Beni e Att. Culturali e del Turismo (br). **289 Getty Images:** Moment / Ayhan Altun (t). **290 Alamy Stock Photo:** Chronicle (ca). **Science Photo Library:** CCI Archives (bl). **290-291 Getty Images:** Corbis Historical / Fine Art. **292-293 akg-images:** Erich Lessing. **294 Bridgeman Images:** Zev Radovan (bl). **Wikimedia Commons:** Sailko (ca). **295 Getty Images:** DEA / G. Dagli Orti / De Agostini. **296 Alamy Stock Photo:** incamerastock (bc). **297 Alamy Stock Photo:** Photo12 / Archives Snark (br). **Getty Images:** DEA / G. Dagli Orti / De Agostini (t). **298 Alamy Stock Photo:** The Picture Art Collection. **299 Alamy Stock Photo. Yale University Art Gallery. 300 Getty Images:** Universal Images Group / Werner Forman (bl). **Yale University Art Gallery. 301 Getty Images:** Universal Images Group / Bildagentur-online (b). **302 Getty Images:** DEA / G. Dagli Orti / De Agostini. **303 Alamy Stock Photo:** Karl Allen Lugmayer. **304 Alamy Stock Photo:** Greg Balfour Evans (bl). **Wikimedia Commons:** The Yorck Project (cra). **Steven Zucker:** (tl). **305 Getty Images:** Fine Art (t). **306-307 The Metropolitan Museum of Art:** Rogers Fund, 1962. **306 Getty Images:** Corbis Historical / Fine Art. **307 Alamy Stock Photo:** Penta Springs Limited. **310 Alamy Stock Photo:** Pavel Dudek (t). **311 Alamy Stock Photo:** Peter van Evert. **312 Alamy Stock Photo:** Azoor Photo. **313 Alamy Stock Photo:** Heritage Image Partnership Ltd. **315 Alamy Stock Photo:** Greg Balfour Evans. **316 Alamy Stock Photo:** Ozgur Tolga Ildun. **318 Alamy Stock Photo:** Ian Rutherford. **319 Getty Images:** DEA / G. Cappellani. **320 Alamy Stock Photo:** Carlo Bollo. **321 Alamy Stock Photo:** Universal Art Archive. **322 Alamy Stock Photo:** Anastasiya Piatrova. **323 Alamy Stock Photo:** Gokhan Dogan. **324 Alamy Stock Photo:** Granger - Historical Picture Archive. **325 Alamy Stock Photo:** Marko Rupena. **326-327 Alamy Stock Photo:** Peter Horree. **328 Alamy Stock Photo:** Marinos Karafyllidis. **329 Photo Scala, Florence:** bpk, Bildagentur fuer Kunst, Kultur und Geschichte, Berlin. **330 Alamy Stock Photo:** Album (t); funkyfood London - Paul Williams (b). **331 Alamy Stock Photo:** Roberto Morgenthaler. **332 Bridgeman Images:** Bonhams, London, UK. **333 Alamy Stock Photo:** Erin Babnik. **334 Alamy Stock Photo:** Visual Arts Resource. **335 Alamy Stock Photo:** Peter Horree. **336 Alamy Stock Photo:** Visual Arts Resource. **337 Alamy Stock Photo:** SJArt. **338 Alamy Stock Photo:** Vintage Archives. **339 Alamy Stock Photo:** imageBROKER.com GmbH & Co. KG. **340 Getty Images:** Hulton Archive / Heritage Images. **341 Alamy Stock Photo:** M.J. Daviduik. **342 Alamy Stock Photo:** Hemis. **343 Alamy Stock Photo:** Svintage Archive. **344 Alamy Stock Photo:** Universal Art Archive. **345 Alamy Stock Photo:** Prisma Archivo. **346 Alamy Stock Photo:** ILN. **347 Alamy Stock Photo:** Peter Horree. **348 Alamy Stock Photo:** funkyfood London - Paul Williams. **349 Alamy Stock Photo:** Heritage Image Partnership Ltd. **350 Alamy Stock Photo:** MehmetO. **351 Alamy Stock Photo:** Perseomedusa. **352 Alamy Stock Photo:** Album. **353 Alamy Stock Photo:** Recall Pictures. **354 Alamy Stock Photo:** Vintage Archives. **355 Alamy Stock Photo:** Prisma Archivo. **356 Alamy Stock Photo:** Universal Images Group North America LLC. **357 Alamy Stock Photo:** Art Collection 2. **358 Alamy Stock Photo:** Adam Eastland. **359 Alamy Stock Photo:** Azoor Travel Photo. **360 Photo Scala, Florence:** Liechtenstein. The Princely Collections - Vaduz-Vienna. **361 © J. Paul Getty Trust / Open Content Program. 362 © J. Paul Getty Trust / Open Content Program. 363 Alamy Stock Photo:** Universal Art Archive. **364 Alamy Stock Photo:** Prisma Archivo. **365 Alamy Stock Photo:** SuperStock. **366 Alamy Stock Photo:** Damian Byrne. **367 Alamy Stock Photo:** Azoor Photo. **368-369 Photo Scala, Florence:** RMN-Grand Palais / Hervè Lewandowski / RMN-GP. **369 Alamy Stock Photo:** Historic Images. **370 Bridgeman Images:** Jean Bernard. **371 Wikimedia Commons:** Musée Fabre. **372 Alamy Stock Photo:** Julia Dahlkvist. **374 Alamy Stock Photo:** Ivan Vdovin. **375 Getty Images:** George Pachantouris. **376 Alamy Stock Photo:** Anze Furlan. **377 Alamy Stock Photo:** Graham Mulrooney. **378 Alamy Stock Photo:** Giannis Katsaros. **379 Alamy Stock Photo:** Kartouchken. **380 Getty Images:** Vladimir Timofeev. **381 Alamy Stock Photo:** robertharding. **382 Alamy Stock Photo:** Vahit Özalp. **383 Alamy Stock Photo:** Image Professionals GmbH. **384 Alamy Stock Photo:** The Picture Art Collection. **385 Alamy Stock Photo:** Stefano Ravera

Cover images: *Front:* **Alamy Stock Photo:** Ivy Close Images l; *Back:* **Alamy Stock Photo:** Falkensteinfoto r